Applied Innovation and Technology Management

Technology is not just limited to technology companies. Managing innovation and technology is no longer a luxury and needs to be understood by all sectors around the world and by both technical and non-technical managers. This book series explores existing and emerging technologies that address current challenges within innovation and technology managements. Each title is developed to provide a set of frameworks, tools and methods that can be adopted by researchers, managers and student in engineering, innovation and technology fields. Research, policy and practice-based books in the series cover topics such as roadmapping, portfolio management, technology forecasting, R&D management, health technologies, bio technologies, transportation management, smart cities, and open innovation, among many others

More information about this series at https://link.springer.com/bookseries/16548

Leong Chan • Liliya Hogaboam
Renzhi Cao

Applied Artificial Intelligence in Business

Concepts and Cases

Springer

Leong Chan
School of Business
Pacific Lutheran University
Tacoma, WA, USA

Liliya Hogaboam
Engineering and Technology
Portland State University
Portland, OR, USA

Renzhi Cao
Department of Computer Science
Pacific Lutheran University
Tacoma, WA, USA

ISSN 2662-9402 ISSN 2662-9410 (electronic)
Applied Innovation and Technology Management
ISBN 978-3-031-05739-7 ISBN 978-3-031-05740-3 (eBook)
https://doi.org/10.1007/978-3-031-05740-3

This Springer imprint is published by the registered company Springer Nature Switzerland AG
The registered company address is: Gewerbestrasse 11, 6330 Cham, Switzerland

Preface

When we think about the future of artificial intelligence and machine learning, movies such as The Terminator or iRobot usually come to mind, in which robots grow smarter than humans and begin to take over the world. AI technologies, which are embedded in various business software applications, can make its own judgments based on real-world scenarios, interpret human language, and see, hear, and react to other senses. AI and machine learning are considered as one of the most important applications companies can implement within their business to advance their products and build their technological edge. Whether a startup company or a long-standing firm, many corporations have already started to implement AI into the operations of their business. The ones that have implemented this emerging technology are already starting to see the results and achieve an increase in the speed or efficiency of their operations.

This book explores the concepts and cases of artificial intelligence applications in three interconnected parts. Part I consists of Chaps. 1, 2, 3 and 4. These beginning chapters focus on the technical concepts and build up a foundation for the discussion in the following chapters. Part II ranges from Chap. 5 to Chap. 11. These few chapters address the AI applications in core business functions. Part III is from Chap. 12 to Chap. 23. The chapters will explore AI tools in various industrial sectors.

Part I introduces the concepts and theories of artificial intelligence specifically for business applications. We are going to explore the relationship between big data and artificial intelligence, and focus on how they will be used in the business. We will also introduce the business intelligence concept, and different kinds of AI technologies, especially on how they are used in the business world. One of the most important subfields of AI is machine learning, and we are going to introduce basic ideas for most commonly used machine learning techniques so that readers without technical background can understand.

Part II focuses on how AI applications can improve business processes in the key business departments. The most popular area for AI in business is definitely marketing and sales. We will explore related concepts in two sections, Chap. 5 in marketing and Chap. 6 in customer services. Another popular area for AI applications in business is finance. Artificial intelligence is a key element for fintech (financial technology). We will explore fintech applications in Chap. 7 and related accounting technologies in Chap. 8. Human resources management is a main business requirement in all companies, no matter their sizes. Chapter 9 introduces how AI can support companies to manage people internally. Manufacturing and supply chains are important business functions for many globalized businesses. We will examine related AI applications in Chaps. 10 and 11.

Part III explores AI applications in various industries. Industries such as energy, healthcare, manufacturing, education, finance, and many others are using artificial intelligence and machine learning nowadays.

Chapter 12 introduces the impact of big data and AI in the insurance industry. It discusses development of insurance technology (insurtech), uses of AI for health and automotive insurance, and enabling technologies of AI (chatbots, NLP, robotic process automation, and others). AI applications in the insurance industry are presented in this chapter as well. We present four case studies: Allstate, Liberty Mutual, State Farm, and Progressive.

Implementations of AI and big data in credit and mortgage are explored in Chap. 13: AI for credit and mortgage. AI plays a big role in credit and mortgage in areas of fraud detection, risk assessment, loan performance prediction, and customer/borrower experience. Along with discussions of AI technology and application development in this industry, three case studies—Upstart, Affirm, and Monedo—are covered in this chapter.

In Chap. 14, AI for tourism, we explore enabling technologies (chatbots, ANNs, belief networks, fuzzy logic systems, and others) as well as applications like smart tourism, demand forecasting, and customer data analytics. Four case studies (Henn Na Hotel, Hilton Hotel (Connie), AI at Airbnb, and Expedia) explore various uses of AI in the tourism industry, while Chap. 15, AI for transportation, describes three case studies of AI in Tesla Cars, Uber AI, and AI in WeRide. AI in transportation has been making headlines in autonomous vehicles, powered by neural networks and genetic algorithms.

Real estate has been utilizing AI in inventory management, new sales identification, placement and promotion of house listings, and customer management. Chapter 16, AI for real estate, discusses those AI application areas and AI-supported real estate platforms as well as explores case studies about Zillow, Redfin, and Compass Real Estate.

In Chap. 17, AI for education, we present the evolution of AI in education, as well as application of AI in learning platforms. Some highlights include adaptive learning technologies, learning personalization and case studies, Realizeit, Nuance, and Civitas.

AI advancements in healthcare is one of the fascinating and rapidly developing areas, which we discuss in Chap. 18, AI for healthcare. AI is evolving in diagnostics, research application, data collection and processing, wearables, and other applications for quality-of-life improvements. Case analysis of COTA Health and Babylon are presented in Chap. 18.

In Chap. 19, AI for energy, we explore different AI technologies and their applications in the energy industry. We discuss how smart grids use AI and how smart homes, particularly their tenants, employ and benefit from AI. Chapter 19 also presents the case study "E.ON: Building a New AI-Powered Energy Grid."

Chapter 20, AI for media services, examines AI for traditional media services (TV, radio, and cinema) as well as AI for new media streaming services. We also discuss AI for social media and Web analytics as well as the music industry and present two case studies: Spotify and Netflix. Fashion industry has been employing AI in various aspects: from textiles and garment manufacturing to supply chain management and consumer analysis.

Chapter 21, AI for fashion, explores history and research highlights of AI in fashion as well as current and emerging AI applications and the StitchFix case study.

Chapter 22, AI for gaming and esports, presents evolution of AI in gaming and esports, enabling technologies (virtual reality, GPUs and AI chips, cloud platforms etc.), AI applications, and two case studies—Google DeepMind: AlphaGo and AlphaStar, and Microsoft's HoloLens.

Chapter 23, AI for sports, presents AI for sports management and sports marketing, and AI applications for basketball, baseball, and golf.

This book presents innovative AI concepts and applications in the dynamic business world. It features real-world cases and examples to enrich the understanding of AI technology and principles. The chapters provide insights and strategies for business practitioners to enhance their managerial tasks using artificial intelligence. This book balances the emphasis on "business processes" and "AI applications" in various industries. The book is aimed at the general trade market of business books, but it is also appropriate for university classes on information technology and innovation management. The authors would like to thank Justin Hogaboam and Octavia Hogaboam for their contributions in editing the book.

Seattle, WA, USA — Leong Chan
Portland, OR, USA — Liliya Hogaboam
Tacoma, WA, USA — Renzhi Cao

Contents

Part I

Artificial Intelligence Concepts

1 Artificial Intelligence for Business

Abstract

This chapter provides an overview of artificial intelligence for business. It introduces the basics of AI and how AI can be applied to the fast-paced business world. The first chapter covers the following important topics: AI origin and development; Big Data supporting AI; technology landscape of AI in business; different business perspectives on AI; and a case on CB Insights.

Keywords

Artificial intelligence · AI · Data · Business · Algorithms · Machine learning · Big data · Neural networks · Business processes

1.1 Introduction

Artificial intelligence (AI) is a field of science dedicated to solving problems commonly associated with human intelligence, such as learning, problem-solving, and pattern recognition. AI technologies are being developed to make machines intelligent, and the intelligence enables an entity to function appropriately and with foresight in its environment (Ertel, 2018). These features of AI perfectly match our needs in business.

Since the emergence of AI, there has been no unified concept of its potential impact on business. AI is a comprehensive subject developed by the interpenetration of computer science, information theory, cybernetics, linguistics, neurophysiology, psychology, mathematics, philosophy, and other disciplines (Boullart, 1992). AI has gone through ups and downs since it appeared, but it has finally been recognized by the business world as a new frontier discipline and has increasingly aroused people's interest and attention.

L. Chan et al., *Applied Artificial Intelligence in Business*, Applied Innovation and Technology Management, https://doi.org/10.1007/978-3-031-05740-3_1

Over the past decade, society has seen technology evolve from handheld smart devices to self-driving cars, all the way to face recognition technology. This is all possible because of artificial intelligence that has established a foundation for technological advancement in the business world. Artificial intelligence has significantly promoted various business sectors because of its ability to help forecast market trends and satisfy customer needs using data and machine learning.

In this beginning chapter, we will start with AI's origin and its commercialization process in the industry. Then we introduce how big data has been fueling the fast development of AI. We will look at the current technology landscape of AI, machine learning, and big data. Business applications will be further explored to highlight the interconnections between AI and business. There are two mini cases to demonstrate these concepts. Different perspectives on AI are introduced and will be examined in the following chapters.

1.2 AI Origin and Commercialization

The origin of artificial intelligence began in scientific research, without much relevance with business practice. Alan Turing is widely given credit for his work with artificial intelligence and the creation of his AI test. In 1950, he came up with the Turing test, which is still used today as a benchmark for intelligent machines. As Turing envisioned it, if a machine could communicate with a human interrogator without being identified as a machine, it would be considered intelligent. In the same year, Turing boldly predicted the feasibility of truly intelligent machines. The 1950s was also the time in which "artificial intelligence" truly started becoming common terminology. In 1956, John McCarthy, a mathematics professor, coined the term "artificial intelligence" at a conference hosted by Dartmouth College. The initial research on applications of AI to the business field began in the late 1950s with the development of artificial neural networks. The first influential journal article was written by Frank Rosenblatt on the principles of neurodynamics and artificial neural networks. In the 1960s, the Naive Bayesian classifier was developed. Around the same time, support vector machines (1963) and deep learning (1965) were developed (both are areas of machine learning). The early 1970s was a low point in the development of artificial intelligence, but some algorithms such as the decision tree algorithm were developed in the late 1970s (1979). In some AI research projects, the lack of researchers' estimation directly led to the failure of the cooperation program of the Defense Advanced Research Projects Agency (DARPA). Meanwhile, society's expectations on artificial intelligence have been lowered, and a lot of artificial intelligence research funding was cut off. These events cast a shadow on the development prospect of artificial intelligence in business.

More efforts on commercialization of AI started in the 1980s. In 1980, Carnegie Mellon University designed a set of "expert systems" with complete professional knowledge and experience for a digital equipment company and used the artificial intelligence program named XCON. This computer system can only be understood as the combination of "knowledge base + reasoning machine." Based on this system, Symbolics, Lisp Machines, IntelliCorp, Aion, and other hardware and software companies were derived. Artificial intelligence ushered in a peak in development history again. Anomaly detection was introduced in 1986, which helped detect the outliers in datasets. About a decade after anomaly detection, genetic algorithms were introduced in 1995, based on Darwin's theory of natural selection. All of these artificial intelligence techniques have been applied to different areas in business.

The rapid growth of computer hardware and software as well as the extensive adoption of network and telecommunication technologies were boosters for the development of artificial intelligence during the 1990s. In 1997, IBM's Deep Blue became the first computer that defeated the world chess champion. All of a sudden, AI and machine learning became one of the hottest fields in science and technology.

It was not until the beginning of the twenty-first century that artificial intelligence really took off and rapidly applied in the world of business. More sophisticated algorithms such as reinforcement learning (also an area of machine learning) were introduced (2004). There have been large strides taken in the scientific community in research and development in order to apply the technology to as many areas as possible. In recent years, there are numerous AI applications developed to streamline productivity and efficiency in the business workplace and daily life. The overall technology around artificial intelligence has changed the world of business for the better. "AI is changing the way we do business. A Japanese venture capital firm recently became the first company in history to nominate an AI board member for its ability to predict market trends faster than humans" (Shani, 2015).

1.3 Big Data Fueling Artificial Intelligence

Big data refers to how the amount of data that is collected and analyzed has grown tremendously over the recent years. As the ability to collect data has grown exponentially over the last few decades and the number of people and items generating data has also grown massively, companies are increasingly turning toward using the massive amounts of data generated to improve efficiency, tailor marketing strategies, and improve overall performance. Big data analytics can be applied to nearly any topic that lies within the business realm, which makes it much more important when looking at every single factor that goes into running a successful business.

Big data, cloud computing, and the internet of things set the momentum for artificial intelligence to grow at high speed. It is much easier now for businesses to acquire and store huge amounts of data to train machine learning systems. Internet of things and handheld electronic devices create numerous data points to be collected, while cloud computing provides huge storage capacity for companies at relatively low cost. Artificial intelligence applications utilize big data most commonly within their algorithms to better analyze their clientele. Digital transformation of business processes made it possible for companies to accumulate more data and make better decisions. Machine learning-powered algorithms are used for business to adapt to unstructured data, including natural language processing, pattern recognition, computer vision, etc. Artificial intelligence sets new guidelines to optimize the achievement of business tasks, while machine learning always changes its actions to improve the current tasks.

Big data has become increasingly important in the business world. AI applications supported by big data have drastically improved an organization's ability to make better decisions. Big data has provided the business world the opportunity to utilize "data and rigor" to make predictions that were traditionally dominated by "gut and intuition," thus providing organizations with the opportunity to revolutionize their management teams. The vast amount of data has also improved the effectiveness of the machine learning algorithms used to make decisions, as more accurate conclusions can be drawn from the larger data pools. Big data is already one of the most fundamental aspects of a successful business model in the twenty-first century. From Hollywood to social media, to retail, data collection has become a staple requirement of organizations in all industries in order to improve the efficiency of operations. Big data helps businesses improve their efficiency in improving decision-making, personalizing promotions, improving timeliness, and more.

1.4 Technology Landscape of AI in Business

The AI and data science research community has seen rapid growth of technologies in the last few years. Technology landscape analysis on big data and AI has been published and updated annually since 2012. So far there are eight versions landscape infographics available for public access through website.[1] In the latest version of the 2021 Machine Learning, AI and Data Landscape, a total of 1969 AI-related companies are included and sorted in nine main categories. Among these AI categories, there are 632 companies categorized as AI Applications for Industries and Enterprises. It can be clearly observed that artificial intelligence has revolutionized multiple industries and has been applied to improve the many different functions of varying areas of business.

The AI and big data landscape for business are very vibrant and dynamic. This matches the primary focus of AI, which is to create technology that allows machines and computers to function in an intelligent manner to solve problems. The rapid development of AI technology provides ample opportunities for high-tech startups. Among the companies listed in the 2021 AI landscape, most are small- to medium-sized tech startups, but there are also large established companies such as Microsoft, Google, IBM, Amazon, Oracle, etc. These giant AI players are also very active in acquiring some emerging high-tech startups. For example, Microsoft has acquired Citus Data, Avere Systems, Bonsai, Nuance, Revolution Analytics, CyberX, and SwiftKey, etc. Another giant player Google has acquired Apigee, Cask, Alooma, Deepmind, Looker, Kaggle, etc. This book will explore many business cases of AI in different chapters, including both established corporations and emerging high-tech startups. In this first chapter, let us first look at a case of a famous long-established player in this field, IBM.

[1] mattturck.com

When it comes to business, being profitable is one of the highlights of being successful. Being up to date on technological advances gives businesses that competitive advantage over their competitors. What AI provides is invaluable in the sense that money can be made, while being as cost and time efficient as a company could possibly be. Throughout this book, we will outline the breadth and depth of artificial intelligence in various business sectors to show how streamline processes have become to be and why different departments in companies strive to use this new-era technology.

AI technologies used in intelligent systems totally depend on various machine learning algorithms. The companies use algorithms to help improve their business processes and seek solutions faster than it would be to do without AI assistance. For example, if a bank is using Al technologies, they are most likely going to be using the AI algorithms to predict the outcome on how to move forward in making investment decisions. Credit and mortgage companies use big data to evaluate who they are going to lend their money to and how credible they are to repay that loan amount. Machine learning algorithms examine large amounts of data, such as purchase history and spending records, to detect any activity that may cause harm to the company. AI products have already diffused into our daily lives. Examples such as Apple Siri, Amazon's echo dot, and Google's translation system are all based on AI technologies. Using advanced algorithms would also include places like a hospital; it helps the doctor be able to make the right diagnosis faster than they could have with the help of AI. In manufacturing, it helps with eliminating time inputs while also limiting the amount of trial and error. Depending on what type of algorithm the company chooses, the algorithms could either provide a solution or provide an answer with how it has come to that conclusion. If companies do not advance with using artificial intelligence, they would most likely be left behind in the competitive business environment.

1.5 Business Perspectives on Artificial Intelligence

In this book, we will be covering the business applications of AI from five different perspectives: users, managers, investors, developers, and legislators.

From the user perspective, we benefit from AI as users every day, in fact more than half of us are using it without even knowing it. Siri uses machine learning to learn and become smarter, and Gmail uses machine learning as well to sort your email for you. Users can free up their time with AI products so you can possibly live more efficiently, just depends how you spend that free time. An example is owning a Roomba, it uses AI to scan the room size, identify obstacles, and remember the most efficient routes for cleaning. This saves us time from unplugging and plugging into different outlets to get to each room. Third benefit is that users do not have to spend so long picking a movie or shopping since websites will use cookies to recommend products that are similar to what you have viewed or purchased before.

From a manager's perspective, they can manage business processes better with AI since their time is utilized more efficiently. According to Harvard Business

Review, 54% of their time is taken up by administrative work so with AI, they will have answers quicker from large sets of data and can formulate a decision in a more timely manner. With that being said, managers will be able to focus on more important parts of a business. 72% of employees said that their work performance would improve if they got more feedback, but before or without AI, managers did not have the time to provide timely fact-based feedback. Finally, AI helps teams to set up better targets and will outline how to achieve them with improved accuracy using goal setting software (HBR, 2016).

From the investor perspective, it is good to know the valuable parts of AI to invest in. The AI chip market is expected to reach $91.2 mil just 6 years from now. AI chips are specialized silicon chips, which incorporate AI technology and are used for machine learning and that is now being widely used so key players in the IT industry are focused on developing the chips. Next, we have the self-driving cars, and Waymo has self-driving vans which are now in use on the Lyft app in Phoenix Arizona. General Motors is committed to this market as well, since by 2040, about 16% of all new cars sold annually will be autonomous. Lastly, the cloud computing market will be worth $278 billion by 2021 so whichever company has the lead with its AI services will hold a clear advantage. Amazon currently holds the largest share of this market at 32%, which uses machine learning and AI systems in a host of its cloud products (Neiger, 2019).

From the developer's perspective, this would be looking at how they can improve AI applications. Deep learning produces promising but very slow results and uses networks of simulated neurons. If a developer found a way to speed this method up significantly by building simulated neural networks 100 times larger, that could process thousands of times more data (Raygun, 2017). This means that developers can now code more quickly and with accuracy than before with these larger networks. From any improvement, it comes from user feedback. Some bugs slip by testing and analysis to affect the end users' experience, so in order for developers to fix these, they rely on users to provide feedback. Otherwise, they have software intelligence and error tracking tools that will tell the business what is wrong with the AI application.

From the legislator's perspective, this is how the government can support AI. There seems to be a lack of standardization among all companies with the use of AI; they are left to determine what is ethical. A case in the Department of Defense left Google to not renew their deal to work on a project that was analyzing drone footage using AI techniques. More than 3000 Google employees signed a letter that expressed how this technology could help target people for death. Therefore, Google announced they are drafting ethical principles for AI. Next, under Trump's "American AI initiative" executive order, he worked to remove regulatory barriers for companies to have flexibility to grow and be as innovative as they can. With the government sharing data, this is to trail AI algorithms to be as smart as humans or even smarter. But these collaborations bring up concerns about data and privacy since companies are already known for leaking consumer data. Government data would pose a huge risk that may not be worth it just for AI to advance.

Ultimately, consolidating all the findings from the various perspectives, we will provide authors' insights and recommendations. From our research, we came across many cases from various areas in business. Along with the technological issues of AI, users might not be aware of some implicit information or perspectives when using, managing, or developing AI products. We will explore and explain our findings throughout this book in different chapters.

Case 1.1: CBInsights

AI and usage of big data are ever present in society and growing and revolutionizing the business today. AI is being used in every business sector from market insights, customer and financial modeling in analytics, and risk management and fraud prevention. Venture capital and investment firms are able to assess company data through brand new ways that were not available to them before such as sales projections and market potentials to better evaluate their risks and discover business opportunities. Here we provide the first case showing how AI is powering business and investment.

CBinsights is one of the major technology and innovation consulting companies that develop AI applications in marketing research. Businesses in different industries can pay CBinsights in return for one of their products or services that they provide. A few of these services include industry analytics, patent analytics, market sizing, market map makers, etc. CBinsights uses machine learning, data mining, and algorithms to make strategic decisions about the market. They collect data concerning market size and related markets to give other businesses an idea of which markets are growing, which ones are going down, and in which markets people are spending their money. This helps businesses get a better understanding of the potential opportunities for market expansion. This also lets them know in which markets they should be investing more of their time and money. They collect data about investments, which helps them understand which markets look promising. Finally, they collect data about emerging markets, financial trends, and emerging AI startups so they can see which businesses could potentially start partnerships.

The way CBinsights processes this data is innovative. They receive 70% of their data from algorithms and the other 30% comes directly from investors. All of this data that they receive is unstructured data, meaning that there is a bunch of different data, and it is not organized. CBinsights then takes this data and uses machine learning, data mining, and algorithms to transform this data into structured data. The structured data is the output, and it includes company names, investor names, dates, amounts of funding, patents, etc. (Company Mosaic). CBinsights uses many different AI technologies to process their data. Some of these technologies include machine learning, data mining, algorithms, market analytics, predictive analytics, and data visualization. All of these AI technologies are used to process and structure data that fits the customers' needs. CBinsights claims that its secret weapon has been Mosaic, which is a series of proprietary machine learning algorithms developed with initial support from the National Science Foundation (NSF). NSF grants totaled about one million from 2011 to 2013. The Mosaic algorithms would aggregate and synthesize information from disparate sources and programmatically assess the health and likelihood of future success of emerging high-tech startups. The Mosaic algorithms evaluate the companies using the 4 Ms:

1. Momentum – how much traction does the company have?
2. Market – how healthy is the industry the company is in?
3. Money – what is the financial health of the company?
4. Management – who are the leaders of the company?

The outputs of Mosaic algorithms include both positive and negative criteria in a specific timeline (CBinsights, 2020).

Positive outputs include:

- Successful IPO
- Acquisition with valuation that is greater than last private valuation
- A $1B+ private market valuation (unicorn status)

Negative outcomes include:

- Bankruptcy/death
- Asset sale
- Acquisition (talent)

By examining the outputs of the Mosaic model and algorithms, CBinsights is able to assess if a high-tech startup is on the right track rising to unicorn glory or descending into the pit of startup failure.

CBinsights provides many different services to its customers and so the output that customers receive varies depending on the service that they purchase. One of the outputs that customers might receive from CBinsights is information on the visualization of the moves that industry leaders are making and where the market is heading. They also might receive information on what industries are growing, where investors are placing their bets, and what businesses or markets show promising health and momentum based on their Mosaic scores. There are many popular businesses that have used CBinsights to benefit their organization. A few of these businesses are BuzzFeed, CitiBank, New York Times, IBM, Fortune, and GE. All of these businesses have used a multitude of services from CBinsights that have helped their marketing teams make strategic decisions.

References

Boullart, L. (1992). A gentle introduction to artificial intelligence. *Application of Artificial Intelligence in Process Control*, 5–40.

Cbinsights. (2020). *Understanding tech company health and predicting future success*. Retrieved: www.cbinsights.com

Ertel, W. (2018). *Introduction to artificial intelligence*. Springer.

HBR. (2016, November). V. Kolbjørnsrud, R. Amico, and R. J. Thomas. How artificial intelligence will redefine management. *Harvard Business Review.*

Neiger, C. (2019). *5 reasons why investors should believe the artificial intelligence hype*. Retrieved from https://www.fool.com/investing/2019/04/13/reasons-investors-believe-artificial-intelligence.aspx

Raygun. (2017). *Developers are building better software, faster, using AI*. Retrieved from https://thenextweb.com/dd/2017/09/19/developers-are-building-better-software-faster-using-ai/

Shani, A. (2015). *From science fiction to reality: The evolution of artificial intelligence*. Wired. www.wired.com/insights/2015/01/theevolution-of-artificial-intelligence/

Big Data Powering Business Intelligence

2

Abstract

This chapter introduces big data and how it is used for business intelligence. It covers the following important topics: business processes and operations; business data sources and types; big data characteristics and analytics; types of business analytics; business intelligence methods; big data storage; and cloud computing technologies. Two cases are provided on Facebook and Amazon.

Keywords

Artificial intelligence · Big data · Business analytics · Business intelligence · Structured data · Semi-structured data · Unstructured data · Relational database management systems · Descriptive analytics · Diagnostic analytics · Predictive analytics · Prescriptive analytics · Cloud computing · Data mining · Data warehousing · Infrastructure-as-a-Service · Software-as-a-Service · Platform-as-a-Service · Online analytical processing

2.1 Introduction

Artificial intelligence is changing how companies execute business. But what does it do internally? This chapter will discuss the interconnection of artificial intelligence, Big Data, and business analytics. It is obvious that Big Data is quickly spilling over the business world. Big data is present in almost every aspect of people's lives; it is involved with the way we socialize, travel, eat, watch television, etc. even if we do not realize it. Corporations use our day-to-day information that they gather to help with their marketing, operations, and many other general business decisions. Throughout the past decade, businesses have been able to thrive and evolve rapidly because of Big Data. As more business activity is being digitized, more data is coming from smartphones, social media, electronic communication, GPS on cell phones,

L. Chan et al., *Applied Artificial Intelligence in Business*, Applied Innovation and Technology Management, https://doi.org/10.1007/978-3-031-05740-3_2

readings from sensors, online shopping, and many other sources. Since the vast majority of people own one or more electronic devices, consumers are walking data generators for businesses.

The internet of things (IoT) is creating a huge amount of data for business. IoT devices could range from individual wearable gadgets, robot sensors, and home security systems. Among others are smart watches, phones, computers, tablets, and any other Wi-Fi accessible items, and there are a plethora of available sources to generate data. Each device offers speed in communication, space-saving, and provides broad reach remotely. According to IDC, there are 127 new devices connected to the internet for each single second. These electronic devices produce 5 quintillion bytes of data daily, which could amount to 79.4 Zettabytes of data by 2025 (Petrov, 2021). Different IoT systems, in the future, will communicate and learn from each other. AI from different organizations will gather and translate such data for their own purposes. An increasing number of businesses are going digital and creating mobile apps, marketing through social media, and reaching out customers electronically. All kinds of business processes are generating data, collecting data, and using data in different ways.

The revolution of digital transformation is upon us and all businesses. One trend that is prevalent for all industries is the rate by which it is growing. It is no question that in the last 20 years, there have been impressive increases in electronic devices able to connect to the internet. According to IBM, in 2020, there was about 2.5 quintillion bytes of data generated on the internet every day. Data created and collected will be more than 180 zettabytes by 2025 (Petrov, 2021). These numbers will only continue to rise. There is no question that this amount of data could be overwhelming for businesses attempting to gather useful information.

2.2 Business Process and Big Data

Artificial intelligence is reinventing business processes and benchmarks for so many industries. What managers need to understand is the benefit and the type of analytics they need to implement in order to maximize the outcomes. The more prevalent issue that concerns managers today is the extent of involvement in AI. Data is vastly immense in business operations. Information is collected and stored through different business processes and various business models. Companies in each industrial sector may generate different data sources that are more relevant to their operations (Daim et al., 2018). The data to collect relies on which one the companies decide to pursue and incorporate in their AI applications. Here we introduce two key sources of how data is generated for business. The first type is data from business operations. The second type is from social media sites.

2.2.1 Data from Business Operations

AI has allowed companies to maximize sales by analyzing a range of factors about customers to offer products at the right time, right place, and through the right channel. Customer data including demographic information and input from surveys and online responses are used by companies to improve their products to fit customer wants and needs. Demographic data as well as seasonal events provide valuable information to businesses about the buying habits of customers to optimize the amount of product needed at a given time (Leonard, 2014). Product data is made up of the various attributes of products, such as size, color, shape, and price, and is collected to see what features of products customers respond to most. Inventory can be optimized by keeping a constant supply of products in stock by utilizing real-time information to and tracking what time customers typically shop. AI can help businesses see patterns in customer's buying behaviors and predict the level of inventory necessary to meet demand. Locational data is also gathered and used to place products in certain spots to increase the amount that customers purchase. Also, market channel data refers to where consumers get information about products. Consumers today research from many different websites and go to many different stores before making a purchase. By harnessing data from various channels customers get more information, retailers can better target those areas to lead customers to buy their products and increase their sales as a result (Bradlow et al., 2017). Customized promotions, product recommendations, and coupons are possible due to the vast amounts of data gathered about customers, enhancing their shopping experience. These personalized services bring in more business from customers for business because the customers are receiving benefits or discounts on the items that they typically buy (Aloysius et al., 2016).

2.2.2 Social Media Data

The most impressive sources of data nowadays come from social media sites like Facebook, Twitter, and Instagram. These sources of information provide businesses with a plethora of information from their consumers offering more than just what food they like to eat. Businesses can use cookies to find out a surprisingly large amount of information about various people. For every five posts that a social media user scrolls through, they see an ad. With people spending an average of hours on social media per day, the number of ads they see is beginning to skyrocket. Instagram can offer different businesses insights into their ads and even give their advertising customers options for what kinds of demographics they want to target. They can sort people based on their followers, who they follow, their likes, posts, and saved posts to wrap up their interests into different categories. These sources of data help their AI algorithms to suggest new people and businesses to follow in their "discover" page, similarly to how Amazon and Netflix use algorithms to suggest new movies and products. Data obtained from social media is beneficial to companies to utilize in order to track how customers are responding to their products so they can improve their business. By analyzing posts on social media about products, companies can learn what consumers like and dislike about their products and potentially change certain aspects in order to improve their products and services (He et al., 2015).

Another useful source of business data would be the information derived directly from rewards cards for grocery stores. Consumers buy food and other various products and then swipe their rewards card to receive various discounts. What they are unaware of when they are swiping their card is that they are actually being given lower prices in exchange for user data, not necessarily loyalty. Every time a customer types in a phone number or swipes a loyalty card, they are providing companies with useful data about themselves that can help companies like Safeway and Walgreens to better target the market.

2.2.3 Types of Business Data

Business data is growing at an exponential rate, and it is a constant race among competitors to be able to keep up with the increases in information available. The primary challenge for businesses is attempting to collect and convert the data into useful information. Machine learning is growing and capturing the attention of many businesses across industries. The different variations of machine learning algorithms depend on the type of data or information the machine is programmed to examine and what is most valuable to a business. There are issues of interpretability or accuracy of data (Jothimani, 2016). Here we need to distinguish different types of data in business: structured data, unstructured data, and semi-structured data.

Structured data is the foundation of relational database systems. Traditionally, the data collected follows certain formats such as numbers, texts, dates, etc. These data obey the tabular structure models and are thus categorized as structured data. This type of data usually includes many columns and rows of records. The datasets are organized with tables and relationships. Companies would use relational database management systems (RDBMS) and structured query language (SQL) in order to store and retrieve the data gathered.

Semi-structured data contains more elements than structured data. The data format does not strictly obey the tabular structure of traditional data models. These data formats are usually not supported by relational database management systems. It may contain tags or markers to separate semantic elements or to enforce hierarchies of the data. Some examples of semi-structured data include html, xml, emails, electronic data interchange (EDI), etc.

Unstructured data indicates that the data is not stored in a structured database format. Although we can think of it as a free format structure, unstructured data does have a certain type of internal storage structure, but it is totally different to traditional data models such as relational database systems. Some examples of unstructured data include voice, images, videos, sensor data, geospatial data, etc. These unstructured data are generated from a wide variety of sources in different formats. It could be human generated or machine generated stream data such as textual or non-textual formats.

2.2.4 Big Data in Business

All types of data combined, including structured, semi-structured, and unstructured, we have BIG DATA in the real business world. When describing such big data, there are multiple characteristics which are high volume, high velocity, and high variety. These features have been extended further to include veracity, visibility, and value. Volume relates to the amount of data generated and all of the files that are saved in the company's records and is measured in bytes. Velocity relates to the speed at which data is obtained and stored within the management system. The speed at which the data is stored is extremely valuable to all parties involved as it can improve the consumer's overall experience while providing the company with more insightful information. Variety steps determine if the data is structured, semi-structured, or not structured at all. This is all about collecting and organizing data into different categories with data such as photos, videos, digital music files, and other scanned content. Data veracity describes how accurate or truthful a data set may be. It refers to the quality of data that is to be analyzed. Data visibility describes the state of being able to see or be seen. It refers to the degree of ease through which an enterprise can monitor, display, and analyze data from disparate sources. Lastly, the value of data is straightforward from a business perspective. It refers to the benefits that data could bring to companies. Businesses that can capture the value of data hold the upper advantage compared to competitors in the market.

Currently, it is estimated that about 80–90% of the big data collected is unstructured (CIO, 2019). Today more than ever, large amounts of unstructured data are generated daily, at scales of petabytes, exabytes, and zettabytes levels. This high volume of data plays an important role in contributing to the improvement of business decisions and performance. The information collected is through various sources, from GPS, temperature, messages, and images to social media. The big data attributes (volume, velocity, variety, etc.) also perfectly describe business data. In business, the velocity and variety of real-time data can give an edge over the competitors. Analyzing big data using AI can be a business strategy to win in the global market. Studies show that data-driven competitors perform better in the market resulting in higher financial and operational efficiency gains. Artificial intelligence is implementable in many business procedures, relying on big data to train and enhance its functions. Automation is a trend in many processes of the business to gain an edge over the competition.

2.3 Big Data Analytics

You may see a joke from the internet saying that a data scientist is a person who is better at statistics than any software engineer and better at software engineering than any statistician. In fact, data science is the combination of math, advanced statistics, predictive modeling, machine learning, programming, etc. In general, data science is a field that deals with all kinds of data, including structured and unstructured data (Dhar, 2013; Leek, 2013). Figure 2.1 demonstrates the important

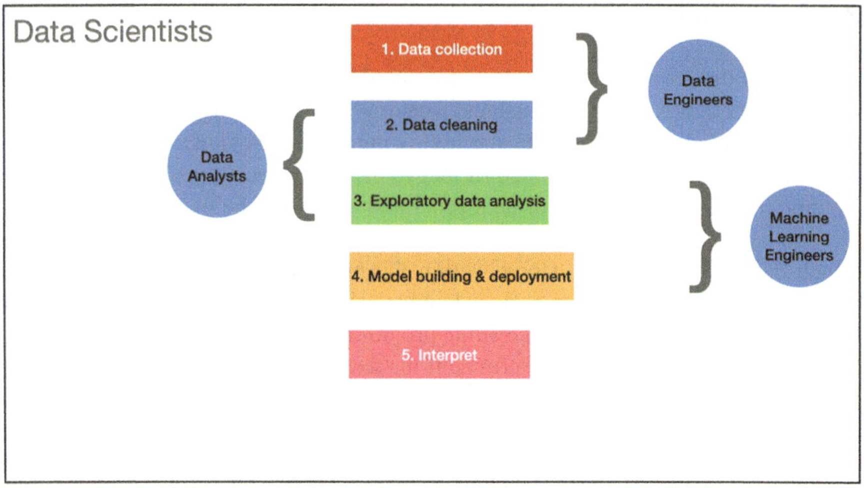

Fig. 2.1 Overall data science process and different roles

data processing steps in data science. Usually, the work of data engineers will be mainly on the first two steps, and the work of data analysts will be mainly on the second and third steps, and machine learning engineers will mainly work on model building and deployment and may also need to do some data analysis in step 3. Now we are going to explore each step in more detail.

First of all, *step 1 – data collection* is straightforward; you need to first collect the data you need for solving the specific problem. There are different ways to collect the data. You can query relational databases using MYSQL, or even non-relational databases (NoSQL) like MongoDB. You can also obtain the data by scraping the websites using scraping tools. In addition, you can use the most popular programming languages Python or R in data science to read data from different sources. Moreover, you may gather data by Web APIs, such as Twitter, which provides Web APIs for anyone to get the tweets from the world. Finally, you can also use traditional ways to download data from existing databases or manually collect them like surveys in paper format. Overall, this step is the first step for any data science-related project, and you need to understand the objectives and requirements of your project to decide what type of data to collect. Some technical skills may be needed, such as database management, or know how to use MySQL, PostgreSQL, or MongoDB, or programming skills like Python and R.

Second, *step 2 – data cleaning* will format the raw dataset into an understandable format. This step is fundamental to future data analysis and may directly affect the outcomes of the next few steps. Sometimes we call the data collected in the previous step raw data. The raw data can be any format, it can be stored in Excel, or as text format, or in a database. Depending on the problem you want to solve, you may want to transform the data from the raw format to a standard format like Excel. But this step may not be that easy, since there could be missing data in your raw dataset.

In that case, you may need to clean your data. There are several standard ways. You can remove the record with missing data in your raw dataset; you can also use the mean, median, or mode to replace the missing data. Let's take a look at one example; you want to know customers' preference of a new product from your company, so you decide to do some surveys. The raw data would be the surveys you collected from the customers, and that is the data gathering. Once you get those surveys, you need to do the data cleaning and preprocessing. If the survey you did is in paper format, you may want to first store it in a computer in Excel format or any other format that you are familiar with.

Table 2.1 shows an example of the survey data. First of all, the answer for the second survey question is a categorical variable ("Yes" or "No"), and it may be difficult for computers to understand the text and process them, rather than numbers. So you can use 1 to represent "Yes" and use 0 to represent "No." Second, as you may notice that customer 2 has an unrelated answer to your question, customers 3 and 5 did not answer all questions. You could decide to remove all data records with missing value or dirty data (refers to data that contains erroneous information, just like data from customer 2), so you will remove data records for customers 2, 3, and 5. However, you will only have two data records left if you do that. You can also use the mean to replace the missing data. Since you have used 0 to represent "No," and 1 to represent "Yes" for the second survey question, overall, the data you have collected for the second question in this survey is [1, 0, 0, 0], and the mean of that will be 0.25, so you will use 0.25 to replace the missing data of customer 3.

Third, *step 3 – exploratory data analysis* will inspect the data and its properties. Some descriptive statistics may be needed in this step. In the previous step, you have got a clean dataset, and you need to do different kinds of analysis based on the types of the data (e.g., numerical data, categorical data, ordinal and nominal data, etc.). Some descriptive statistics knowledge is needed to extract the features. The term "features" is used a lot in the next step for machine learning or modeling to help us to identify the characteristics that represent the data. Just like the business example of surveys on customers' interests of buying a product, whether the price is cheap or expensive could be an important feature. In this step, you may also need to visualize the data to better understand the trend. Some technical skills may be needed, such as using the packages of Numpy, Matplotlib, Pandas, Scipy, and ggplot2 in Python or R.

Fourth, *step 4 – model building and deployment* will perform modeling and deploy the models. Usually machine learning techniques are needed in this step. We

Table 2.1 Example of surveys for data collection

Customer ID	1. Do you think the price is expensive or cheap?	2. Are you interested in buying the product
1	Expensive	Yes
2	Yes	No
3	Expensive	
4	Cheap	No
5		No

will train machine learning models to perform classification or regression. More details will be provided in the next chapter. In summary, to forecast future values, we can use regression models, and to identify classes, we can use classification models. The technical skills needed for this step will include Python programming, and machine learning framework like Scikit learn or tensor flow or Pytorch.

Finally, *step 5 – interpret* will be the final step to interpret your model and data. We also need to do forecasting and make predictions on unseen data and explain the result. Your audience can be nontechnical people, so it is important to provide your findings with visualizations and technical skills that are not required in this step. Communication skill is very important in this step, and you may also need strong business domain knowledge to present your findings and answer business questions.

Similar to the steps we have described, there are several famous frameworks in the data science field and business. Just to name a few, the Cross Industry Standard Process for Data Mining (CRISP-DM) was introduced in 1996 (Chapman, 2000) to serve as a standard and reliable workflow that can be adopted and applied in various industries, and it has six major steps (Business understanding, Data understanding, Data preparation, Modelling, Evaluation, Deployment). The OSEMN framework was introduced by Davenport and Patil in 2012 (Davenport & Patil, 2012) and has five major steps (Obtain Data, Scrub Data, Explore Data, Model Data, Interpret Results).

2.4 Business Analytics

Business analytics refers to applying data analytic methods for the purpose of business decision-making. There are four types of data analytics within the spectrum of business. There are various AI applications and approaches that companies can choose to conduct data analytics, predict market trends, and research customer purchasing behavior. Machine learning algorithms can implement all types of analytics in business.

The first type of data analytics is descriptive data. This type of data describes the current state of a business through historical data. It uses previous trends to forecast things like sales rates, seasonal impacts, and more. In AI, the use of far-reaching market data and customer insights help maintain internal metrics and increase the intelligence of a business's position among its competitors. Descriptive analytics are good for calculating rates such as total stock in inventory, average dollars spent per customer, and year over year change in sales. Descriptive analytics helps produce historical reports that contain the company's production, financials, operations, sales, finance, inventory, and customers (Halo, 2017). This enables retailers to avoid past mistakes and understand how they might influence future outcomes of the business.

The next type of data analytics within AI is diagnostics. The main reason for diagnostic data is to explain why a problem is happening. AI allows analytics to take a deep dive into things like customer information, marketing metrics, and key performance indicators to explain why certain actions did not produce the expected results. Projects are undertaken with an expectation of certain results based on certain estimations of markets, customers, and other similar criteria. Diagnostic analytics digs into which assumed contributors did not meet their projected metrics.

Thirdly, we have predictive data analytics, and this type of analysis projects future results based on historical data. By highlighting patterns and evaluating trajectories of relevant metrics, predictive analytics estimates future efforts. Predictive analytics plays a big role in business. It helps to create more competitive advantages among companies as well as helps create a better shopping experience for consumers. For example, retailers use predictive analytics to analyze past data patterns to predict future purchases and business trends. With this method, retailers can understand how a customer shopping at a specific location chooses from an assortment of products. This enables companies to increase their sales and their margins by placing the right products at the right time and place across all channels (Halo, 2017).

The last type of data analytics within the spectrum AI is a prescriptive approach. Prescriptive analytics can analyze data in real time and provide insights on how to approach the future. This takes predictive analytics a step further by projecting the best future efforts. By tweaking inputs and changing actions, prescriptive analytics allows businesses to decide how to put their best foot forward. Different actions will yield different results, and prescriptive analytics helps decision-makers select the best way to proceed.

2.5 Business Intelligence

Business intelligence (BI) can be defined as the integration of business analytics and artificial intelligence. BI methods are powerful tools that have been used in popularity among businesses of all kinds due to its perceived usefulness and benefits across every single industry. The foundations of business intelligence are databases, statistics, data sciences, and artificial intelligence. Business intelligence makes it possible for managers to measure and therefore know a lot more about their businesses. They can directly translate data into information, further into knowledge, and ultimately into improved decision-making for business. BI turns the massive, daunting amount of data into something that will give us a business advantage. Data-driven decisions are better decisions—it is as simple as that. Using big data enables managers to decide on the basis of evidence rather than intuition. "The more companies characterized themselves as data-driven, the better they performed on objective measures of financial and operational results" (HBR, 2012).

In recent years, the exponential growth of big data is becoming the front-runner for the future success of businesses. Business intelligence has enabled companies to measure their business in a more efficient manner and take the knowledge they have learned to help make insightful business decisions and improve performance. Here we introduce two important concepts in business intelligence: data mining and data warehousing.

2.5.1 Data Mining

Data mining and analytics is an important category of business intelligence because it differentiates from the other approaches where big data is being organized and analyzed to provide insights for a company or person, so they can better adjust and improve on their decision. It includes classical, modern, and advanced aspects of AI algorithms. Data mining helps to explore different and varying patterns or trends in data over several periods of time. Companies can obtain incredible information and knowledge that they could not know without data mining.

The mining aspect of this method is the process of how the raw data is collected and analyzed to generate new data information and insights. Data analytics is the aspect of collecting the information obtained from data mining, analyzing it, and using it to answer specific questions about a business. To deeply understand the mined data, visualization tools such as Python and R languages need to be used. Data mining is very close to machine learning, but rather than answering questions during the process they wait until after the data is collected overtime to make any solid and robust conclusions. Managers use data mining to develop standard reports, identify exceptions that could be causes of problems and/or advantages, identify the causes of these problems/advantages, develop models for possible alternatives, and track the business's efficiency and effectiveness. Typically, businesses will have several questions that they can answer through data mining and analysis such as "Is this marketing tactic working better or worse than the other?" or "What gender is buying more of our product at Target?" These questions will be converted into mathematical query expressions that computers can understand. Different companies will customize their questions and use their algorithms and data to find answers to such questions. They can track effectiveness through three solid components: intelligence, application framework, and enterprise scale.

2.5.2 Data Warehousing

Data warehousing is closely tied with data mining. While data mining focuses on retrieving and analyzing data, data warehousing focuses more on storage and securing data. Although big data can be helpful in organization properly, many companies find themselves overwhelmed with the truly large amounts of data they must hold and sort through. For this mass amount of data to be properly handled, machines must adapt and improve their coding abilities to continue utilizing big data. Firms are collecting and storing big data in data warehouses from different sources such as their sales records, customers spending habits, and shopping behaviors. The data stored in data warehouses could also be gathered from corporate databases, summarized information systems, and acquired from other companies or external sources. These data are then used in several types of business functions, one of the most popular being customer relationship management (CRM). A common application is online analytical processing (OLAP) cube, which requires powerful database manipulations and computational capabilities and is a fast analysis of shared multidimensional information. This could be described as a predictive AI algorithm.

There are multiple emerging technologies that have unlocked the potential within the data warehouses. Traditionally, companies have to store huge data files safely and securely in data warehouses onsite in their company. Therein lies the problem of managing hardware and software on database servers. This significantly increased the cost of maintenance and technical support. As the companies grow, so does their data. Whether it is customer and client, companies must find a way to manage the database which may contain sensitive information, for example, payment information, address, emails, etc. Therefore, only large established companies were capable of using data warehousing and data mining. However, new technologies have changed the rules of the game. With improved bandwidth of internet and communication, as well as increased computing hardware and software, smaller companies can also take the advantage of data mining today. There have been three technology breakthroughs over the last 10 years. The first is cloud-based computing and services. By managing data warehouses with cloud computing, it makes processing big data affordable for most companies. It allows smaller companies to prepare for larger amounts of data at a relatively low cost. The second technology is the massively parallel processing (MPP) architecture, which could spread user queries across hundreds or even thousands of machines. This method can bring huge performance improvements for data mining. For example, Google's BigQuery can perform a full regular expression match on 314 million rows of data with no indices and return a result within 10 s. The third technological breakthrough was the development and spread of columnar data warehouses. Compared with the traditional row-based relational databases, the new columnar database has a shift in structure which allows for higher efficiency in reading, sorting, and indexing of datasets. It also compresses data better and saves more storage space. Big tech companies are always developing new methods to manage big data. Here let's explore a case on Facebook's innovation.

Case 2.1: Facebook's Big Data Storage

Facebook uses many database management systems to sort and store big data. These database management systems include Hive, Hadoop, and Operational Data Store (ODS). These systems are a nontraditional relational database and process data for analysis, like who to advertise to, not to actually serve users. Hadoop is the base for Facebook's Database Management Systems, but Facebook is constantly looking and trying to create new database management systems to become more efficient. There is so much data that Facebook receives every day and every minute. On average Facebook's system "processes 2.5 billion pieces of content and 500+ terabytes of data per day. It is pulling in 2.7 billion like actions and 300 million photos per day, and it scans roughly 105 terabytes of data each half hour" (Constine, 2012). The database management systems they have traditionally used are not as efficient as data has grown. In order to gain an advantage, Facebook is working to create better database management systems.

Facebook's data warehouses, also known as the Hive, are capable of storing more than 300 petabytes of data in more than 800,000 tables. It runs more than 600,000 queries and 1 million map-reduce jobs per day. The common query engines over Hive include Presto, HiveQL, Hadoop, and Giraph. The data is used for a variety of applications, from traditional database processing to image analytics, machine learning, and real-time interactive analytics (Wiener and Bronson, 2014). Facebook uses operational data store to support data mining of operational data or base data that is summarized for a data warehouse. ODS stores about 2 billion time series records. The data is loaded into an enterprise data architecture after being extracted from operational databases. The process includes standardization, cleansing, consolidation, and transformation. It is used most commonly in alerts and dashboards and for troubleshooting system metrics with 1–5 min of time lag. There are about 40,000 queries per second (Wiener and Bronson, 2014).

Two database management systems that Facebook specifically created to sort data faster for advertising are Scuba and Cubrick. These database management systems work fast to find the data they can use to purposefully advertise on Facebook. This helps with knowing what users want in that instance. The time it takes to process this data has shortened dramatically. Facebook receives millions of data every second, but Facebook's drive to create new database management systems is to significantly advance the speed of information analysis, and they are always working toward this goal.

Scuba is just "one of many 'Big Data' software platforms Facebook has produced to control the information generated by its online operation – platforms that push the boundaries of distributed computing, the art of training hundreds or even thousands of computers on a single task" (Metz, 2017). Scuba is mainly used at Facebook for performance monitoring, trend spotting, and pattern mining. It grabs the data and sorts it faster and deletes data by itself. They have to delete certain data sometimes because it is either old, or there is limited space in the table. It deletes the oldest data in that table and provides the most relevant data. Scuba keeps all data in "high-speed memory systems running across hundreds of computer servers – not the hard disks, the memory systems – and this means you can query the data in near real-time" (Metz, 2017). By sorting current data and finding what users are doing now, Facebook can choose which advertisements users will respond to the best. Facebook can gain a lot more money when an advertisement is liked, clicked on, commented, or shared. Advertising strategically makes more money for Facebook. Data scientists can use database management systems to analyze how effective Facebook is running and the behavior of its users. This means Facebook can feed data directly to users (Metz, 2017).

Cubrick is used more for sorting generic data. They input a table of information into the database management system, and Cubrick takes all the attributes and connects the similar ones. The attributes are connected in relation with the colored dots as the user and the attributes are connected by the bricks, which form one cube. It is like graphing but with multiple graphs connected by the same range and dimension. This enables an improved and lean database mechanism only able to function over primitive data types. They sort the data and are able to rapidly group people together based on similar characteristics like gender or region. That is how they can group certain people to advertise.

Facebook uses these database management systems because they are faster and get them just the data they want. This helps them advertise to what the consumer wants now, not what they wanted in the past. They group people together using the data, and this can be based on simple things like demographics, people's gender, age, income, housing type, and education level. All this information is able to be filled out on a person's profile and can be public, like we mentioned before. They can also market based on the geographic market, marketing only in certain countries, states, or regions because of the impacts from having different weather in areas and certain distinct cultures and values in an area. Again, they gain this information when you fill out a profile, specifying where you live and if you have your location on, they can track where you go. Price segmentation can be used as well but can be harder to track. They can decide what products to market to users such as cheap products, medium-priced, or expensive products. In order to do this, they target users based on what they put on their profile as their occupation, their degree level, and posts. After they get the data, they put it into their prediction algorithm.

Facebook uses the machine learning algorithm to rank what they think you would like to see in your feed. The algorithm does not just predict whether you will actually "hit the like button on a post based on your past behavior. It also predicts whether you'll click, comment, share, or hide it, or even mark it as spam. It will predict each of these outcomes, and others, with a certain degree of confidence, then combine them all to produce a single relevancy score that's specific to both you and that post" (Oremus, 2016). This is how they can choose which advertisements they should advertise to people. The higher chance that a consumer will respond to the advertisement in any positive way will, in turn, make the advertisement a success. If the user shares it, likes it, or tags someone recommending the product, it allows other people to see the ad and make a purchase as well. There is a high chance that many friends of someone who likes the product will also like the product, making this system very effective.

2.6 Cloud Technology and Big Data Analytics

Traditional large database systems are becoming incapable of processing big data that is generated with the current speed and volume. This is the reason many are looking to new developments for cloud-based big data analytics. Beneficial to developing AI, advancements in cloud technology can store more data and are accessible via the internet.

Cloud computing is based on remote servers on the internet that provides services to the users in different ways. AI technology in cloud computing is usually programmed to think just like a human would mimic his reactions and actions in certain circumstances. "By using the internet and central remote services it maintains the data, applications, etc. which offers much more efficient computing by centralizing storage, memory, processing, bandwidth and so on" (Mollah et al.

2012). Infrastructure as a service (IaaS) provides renting storage, network, operating system, servers, and virtual machines. It allows you to pay based on the usage of the services provided. Platform as a service (PaaS) designed mobile apps and web creation more easily. It eliminates the need to constantly update them or manage them. Software as a service (SaaS) is a cloud service that allows the user to gain access to an application on the phone, tablet, or other electronic devices. Cloud computing has unique features that enable open access to wide resources, and it can be accessed easily from your phone, laptops, and computers. It opens up applications that can provide rapid elasticity to resources used by clients and is automatically monitored. The fusion of cloud computing and AI technology will bring a significant change in the technology industry.

Cloud computing, where computing services can be delivered to virtually anywhere there is an internet connection, has also seen significant growth in recent years, as many companies are moving toward using the cloud to deliver services. Together, big data and cloud computing are setting the trend of ever greater connectivity and improved data collection and analytics.

Although the cloud is not necessarily new to the world, since it has been around since the later 1990s, it is still something of great interest because of its vast amount of use. Almost every aspect of technology in our lives is affiliated with the cloud, such as video game storage, iTunes storage, business information, etc. With technology advancing at a very rapid pace, the use of the cloud will still be as important, if not more important by the year 2020, which is when 5G is expected to launch globally. Even though 5G would increase the speed and vastness of technology, there will still need to be a place for easy and large amounts of storage. An outlook into the cloud is the increasing security in the cloud. Since many people are capable of hacking today, that causes a huge problem for not only individuals but the majority for businesses.

Case 2.2: Amazon Cloud Services

Amazon Web Services (AWS) is using many different technologies to streamline and improve their cloud computing services for customers. They are taking advantage of current advancements in machine learning. Thousands of customers are turning to Amazon Web Services for their machine learning. AWS is using their machine learning to improve the quality of health care, provide better customer service, optimize their business, create new customer experiences, and many more things.

Many financial companies are taking advantage of the machine learning offered to customers through Amazon Web Services. NerdWallet uses AWS to build a recommendations platform based on machine learning that provides more value to customers and allows data scientists to move projects from design to production swiftly. Another company using machine learning through AWS is OakNorth. The company is based in the United Kingdom and is a financial services provider focused on small- and medium-sized enterprise (SME) lending. They use machine learning to gather and analyze large amounts of data needed to make decisions and meet security and regulatory requirements. These companies are using machine learning to reduce their cost of operations and provide customers with the most accurate data to make decisions about their personal finances.

Another reason Amazon Web Services is dominating the cloud computing market is through their artificial intelligence. "AWS pre-trained AI Services provide ready-made intelligence for your applications and workflows." The services that AWS offers are easy to integrate and provide many useful services. Amazon also ensures high-quality AI by using the same deep learning technology that powers Amazon.com and the machine learning services. AWS offers many different AI services including chatbots, advanced text analytics, demand forecasting, document analysis, fraud prevention, image and video analysis, and personalized recommendations. GE Appliances takes advantage of the many AI services that Amazon Web Services offers. Using Amazon Connect, Amazon Lex, and Amazon Polly, they are able to automate simple tasks such as looking up product information, taking down customer details, and answering common questions before an agent answers. GE also added Amazon Transcribe to create call transcripts for automated analysis to improve the process. AI is growing everyday, and Amazon Web Services is using their AI services to continue to grow their business.

Amazon is not only a leader in ecommerce and cloud computing but also a frontrunner in the area of artificial intelligence. AI has monumentally impacted the business world and the entire economy by increasing the efficiency of companies, as well as the rate of demand by consumers. It has transformed the business processes of all industries and will reshape the economy.

References

Aloysius, J. A., Hoehle, H., & Venkatesh, V. (2016). Exploiting Big Data for customer and retailer benefits. *International Journal of Operations & Production Management, 36*(4), 467–486.

Benefiting from Big Data. (2013). Retrieved 2020, from https://www.strategyand.pwc.com/media/file/Strategyand_Benefiting-from-Big-Data_A-New-Approach-for-the-Telecom-Industry.pdf

Bradlow, E. T., Gangwar, M., Kopalle, P., & Voleti, S. (2017). The role of big data and predictive-analytics in retailing. *Journal of Retailing, 93*(1), 79–95.

Chapman, P. (2000). *CRISP-DM 1.0: Step-by-step data mining guide.*

CIO. (2019). *AI unleashes the power of unstructured data.* Retrieved 2021, from https://www.cio.com/article/3406806/ai-unleashes-the-power-of-unstructured-data.html

Constine, J. (2012, August 22). *How big is Facebook's data? 2.5 billion pieces of content and 500 terabytes ingested every day.* Retrieved November 27, 2017, from https://techcrunch.com/2012/08/22/how-big-is-facebooks-data-2-5-billion-pieces-of-content-and-500-terabytes-ingested-every-day/

Daim, T., Chan, L., & Estep, J. (2018). *Infrastructure and technology management.* Springer. ISBN-13:978-3319689869, ISBN-10:331968986X.

Davenport, T. and Patil, D. (2012). Data Scientist: The Sexiest Job of the 21st Century. *Harvard Business Review.* Retrieved from https://hbr.org/2012/10/data-scientist-the-sexiest-job-of-the-21st-century

Dhar, V. (2013). Data science and prediction. *Communications of the ACM, 56*(12), 64–73.

Halo Business Intelligence. (2017). *Descriptive, predictive, and prescriptive analytics explained.* Retrieved from https://halobi.com/blog/descriptive-predictive-and-prescriptive-analytics-explained/

HBR. (2012) A. McAfee and E. Brynjolfsson, Big Data: The Management Revolution. *Harvard Business Review*.

He, W., Shen, J., Tian, X., Li, Y., Akula, V., Yan, G., & Tao, R. (2015). Gaining competitive intelligence from social media data. *Industrial Management & Data Systems, 115*(9), 1622–1636.

Jothimani, D. (2016). *Big Data: Challenges, opportunities and realities*. Retrieved 2020, from https://arxiv.org/pdf/1705.04928.pdf

Leek, J. (2013). The key word in "data science"is not data, it is science. *Simply Statistics, 12*.

Leonard, P. (2014). Customer data analytics: Privacy settings for 'Big Data' business. *International Data Privacy Law, 4*(1), 53–68. https://doi.org/10.1093/idpl/ipt032

Metz, C. (2017, June 4). *Meet the data brains behind the rise of Facebook*. Retrieved 2020, from https://www.wired.com/2013/02/facebook-data-team/

Mollah, M. B., Islam, K. R., & Islam, S. S. (2012). Next generation of computing through cloud computing technology. In *2012 25th IEEE Canadian conference on electrical and computer engineering (CCECE)* (pp. 1–6).

Oremus, W. (2016, January 3). *Who really controls what you see in your Facebook feed – And why they keep changing it*. Retrieved 2021, from http://www.slate.com/articles/technology/cover_story/2016/01/how_facebook_s_news_feed_algorithm_works.html

Petrov, C. (2021). *25+ impressive Big Data statistics for 2021*. Retrieved https://techjury.net/blog/big-data-statistics/

Sato, K. (2012). *An inside look at Google BigQuery*. Retrieved 2021, https://cloud.google.com/files/BigQueryTechnicalWP.pdf

Wall, M. (2014, March 4). *Big Data: Are you ready for blast-off?* Retrieved 2020, from http://www.bbc.com/news/business-26383058

Wiener, J., & Bronson, N. (2014). *Facebook's top open data problems*. Retrieved 2021, https://research.fb.com/blog/2014/10/facebook-s-top-open-data-problems/

Artificial Intelligence Technologies for Business Applications

3

Abstract

This chapter introduces key artificial intelligence technologies and related business applications. The following important topics are covered: business expert systems, robotic process automation, fuzzy logic, interactive decision support systems, case-based reasoning, procedural content generation, voice chatbots, genetic algorithms, and hybrid AI systems. These AI technologies will also be referred to in different following chapters. Two cases are provided in this chapter, including IBM and Hyperscience.

Keywords

Artificial intelligence · Expert systems · Robotic process automation · Fuzzy logic · Interactive decision support systems · Case-based reasoning · Procedural content generation · Voice chatbots · Genetic algorithm-radial basis function · Hybrid AI systems

3.1 Introduction

Artificial intelligence (AI) is an emerging field that studies how the computer can simulate human intelligence, think like humans, and act like humans. Dating back to the time of ancient Greece, inventor Daedalus created Talos—a giant automaton made of bronze to protect Europa in Crete from pirates and invaders, and inventor Hephaestus created Pandora—the first human female, so artificial intelligence has been a dream of humans for a long time. A lot of tasks are easy for humans, but those problems are still challenging for artificial intelligence, such as recognizing human faces. Nowadays, AI is a thriving field with many practical applications from speech recognition, image classification, drug discovery, product recommendation, etc.

L. Chan et al., *Applied Artificial Intelligence in Business*, Applied Innovation and Technology Management, https://doi.org/10.1007/978-3-031-05740-3_3

This chapter will focus on some widely adopted AI technologies in business settings. These AI technologies are more successful and popular for business applications, including Expert Systems, Robotic Process Automation, Fuzzy Logic, Decision Support Systems, Time-series Forecasting, Case-Based Reasoning, Procedural Content Generation, Chatbots, Genetic Algorithm, and Hybrid AI systems. Machine learning techniques are very important categories of AI, which will be further discussed in the next chapter.

3.2 Expert Systems

Expert systems are designed for specific types of applications that store extracted knowledge from experts in order to assist in problem-solving in the decision-making process. Starting in the 1970s (Leondes, 2002), expert systems were very successful as a special type of AI software. The expert system uses AI to emulate human experts to make decisions (Jackson, 1986). It is developed to solve complex problems using AI technology, such as the decision tree technique. Figure 3.1a illustrates the configuration of an expert system.

Figure 3.1b shows the flowchart of an expert system. The knowledge engineer can extract the knowledge from the human expert and make the expert system so that users (usually nonexpert) can use the knowledge. Here, the knowledge can be the useful information that we can get from the data. For example, the user can be a patient, and the expert system can be a system with the knowledge of a doctor and

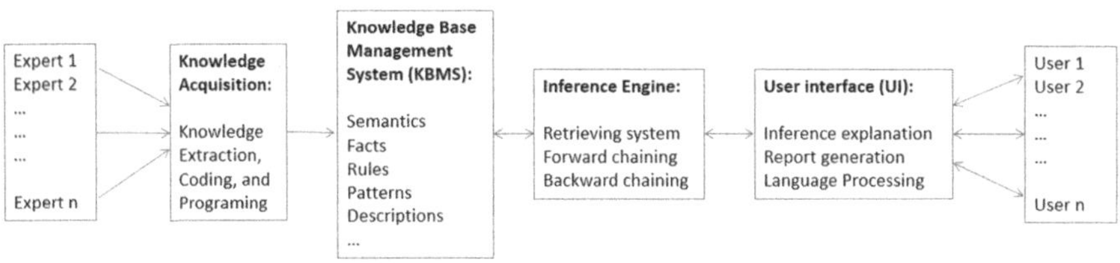

Fig. 3.1a Configuration of an expert system
Experts: The system starts with having human experts to provide their knowledge and expertise in certain fields
Knowledge acquisition is the process where software engineers extract and acquire the know-how or knowledge from human experts. The human expertise and knowledge were then coded and programmed to represent facts and rules that computer software could use
Knowledge base management system (KBMS) is similar and comparable to a traditional database management system (DBMS). KBMS is used to store the knowledge database, which includes extracted facts, logical rules, and patterns. Knowledge could be represented in multiple formats and types, including factual data, heuristic rules, and meta-knowledge
Inference engine is used to retrieve the KBMS component. It uses different techniques such as forward chaining (if-then-else mechanism) or backward chaining (goal seek solver) in retrieving the data and matching the rules
User interface (UI) provides human-machine interfaces or web portals for the general access of expert systems. The systems may convert between text and voice
Users will typically be using queries to interact with the system UI and access the expert systems

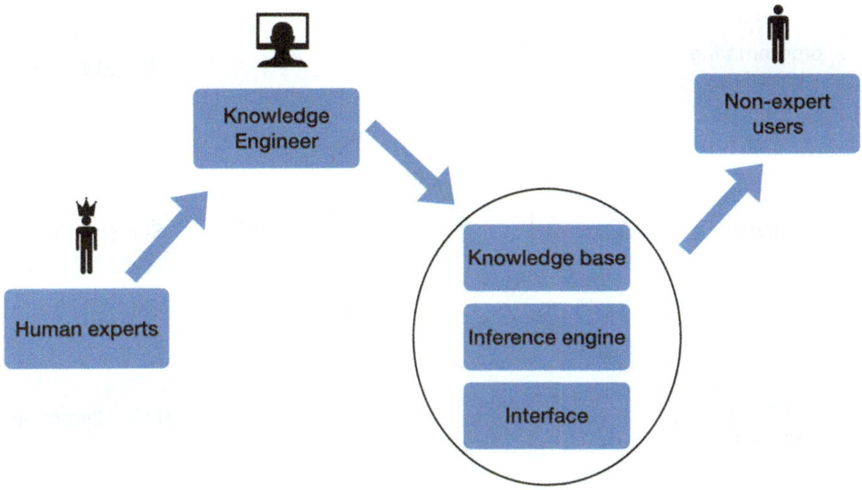

Fig. 3.1b Knowledge flow through an expert system

help to diagnose the disease from the patient, even though the patient doesn't have any knowledge of the specific field.

Expert systems still have a lot of uses and applications today. It could be built together with the decision support system (DSS) that provides expertise in certain business fields, such as marketing or investment. It could also be used in different industries. For example, the research project LEXMED is an expert system for the diagnosis of appendicitis (Schramm & Ertel, 2000). It uses the database of patient data to generate a decision tree and make predictions on the new patient data.

3.3 Robotic Process Automation

Robotic process automation (RPA), also called software robotics, is a form of business process automation technology based on robotics and AI. Robots are machines that can automatically carry out tasks with or without human intervention, and usually, the computer program is used to manage the robots. The general idea of RPA is that the robots will watch the user perform a task in the application's graphical user interface (GUI), and the AI technique may be used to develop the action list and tackle the same task automatically. By doing that, we don't need a software developer to write scripts in the backend system to produce the list of actions, so that it will lower the barrier to using the automation in a product. Companies usually use AI technology and robotics to automate their business processes, for example, transaction processing, data manipulation, record maintenance, communication, etc.

There are several features of RPA making it very important in business (see Fig. 3.2). First of all, user friendly means that the system is easy to use and we don't need a lot of technical knowledge to use it. Second, no programming knowledge

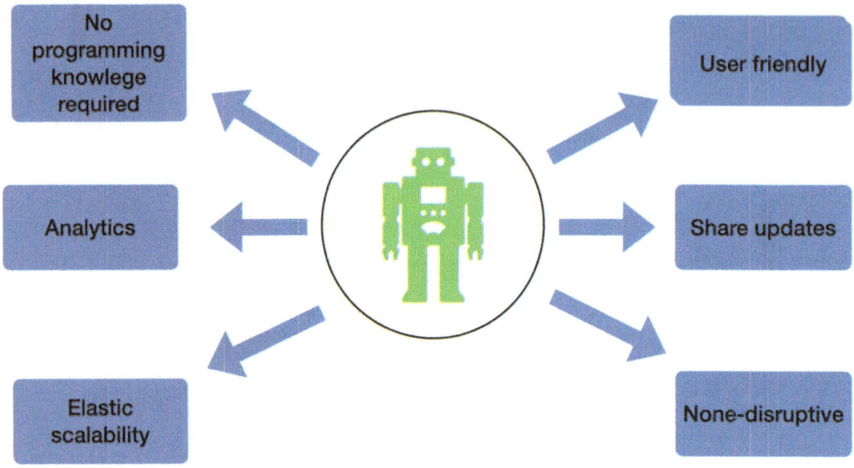

Fig. 3.2 Important features of RPA

required means that the users don't need to have any programming background, which is always good as most of the users don't need to have training on using the system. Third, nondisruptive means that RPA can usually seamlessly fit into the organization without big changes. Fourth, sharing updates for the system means that all software robots can share the information and update the system easily because the system stores the data on the cloud. Fifth, analytics means that the system has the ability to collect, process, and analyze the data for the company. Sixth, elastic scalability means the system can scale up and down depending on the usage, so users can control the number of robots that they want anytime.

3.4 Fuzzy Logic

The term fuzzy logic is introduced in the fuzzy set theory and is based on the observation that people make decisions based on imprecise and nonnumerical information (Zadeh, 1996). The value of a variable in the fuzzy logic can be any value between 0 and 1, which is used to describe imprecise information. In the fuzzy logic system, the membership is fuzzy and unclear. For example, when we describe the weather (like "cloudy") in the fuzzy logic system, you can use any number between 0 and 1 to describe how cloudy it is. It is different from other systems where the boundaries are very clear between different categories (e.g., when you try to detect the type of object in a picture, it can be an apple or orange, where these two types are representing the full membership of each category). The fuzzy logic can be integrated with many AI techniques like decision-making and machine learning.

Fuzzy logic and expert systems are both modeling techniques used for prediction modeling where fuzzy modeling represents a more flexible approach to mimic real-world scenarios. Fuzzy logic uses Fuzzy set theory to simulate the uncertain nature to be studied. Various rules are used to define the fuzzy membership functions. The choices of functional expressions are inherently problem-dependent. Triangular,

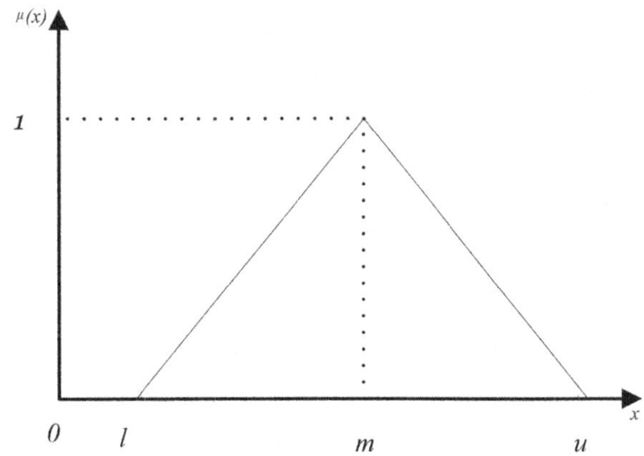

Fig. 3.3 Triangular fuzzy vector

trapezoidal, Gaussian, and bell-shaped functions are the most commonly used in modeling. Adopting a triangular fuzzy expression with three real numbers (l,m,u) are used for its definition where l, m, and u represent the lower limits, mean value, and upper limits of the triangular fuzzy vector. Figure 3.3 indicates the graphical expression of a triangular fuzzy vector.

In any business setting, there are usually multiple fuzzy vectors. There are different methods to construct a fuzzy model to represent a business problem, such as heuristic selection, clustering, adaptive approach, and self-organizing map. Hybrid fuzzy models could be used together with many AI technologies such as evolutionary algorithms and artificial neural networks. Fuzzy models simulate the complex reasoning processes that assist humans to make rational decisions in an environment that they are not too certain of. Fuzzy logic systems could enable business users to perform advanced analytics on products or services based on their needs.

3.5 Interactive Decision Support Systems

A **decision support system (DSS)** is an information system that supports business decision-making activities, and an interactive decision support system is going to provide interactive assistance in selecting the most appropriate methods for decision-making, especially on complicated problems, like rapidly changing and not easily specified in advance problems. Sprague (1980) defines a properly termed DSS as follows: DSS tends to be aimed at the less well-structured, underspecified problem that upper-level managers typically face; DSS attempts to combine the use of models or analytic techniques with traditional data access and retrieval functions; DSS specifically focuses on features which make them easy to use by non-computer-proficient people in an interactive mode; DSS emphasizes flexibility and adaptability to accommodate changes in the environment and the decision-making approach of the user. Sometimes, the DSSs can be fully computer-based with the help of AI technology, and we also call it an **intelligent decision support system (IDSS)** (Holsapple & Whinston, 1987). For example, the flexible manufacturing systems (FMS) (Chan et al., 2000), intelligent marketing decision support systems (Matsatsinis & Siskos, 2012), and

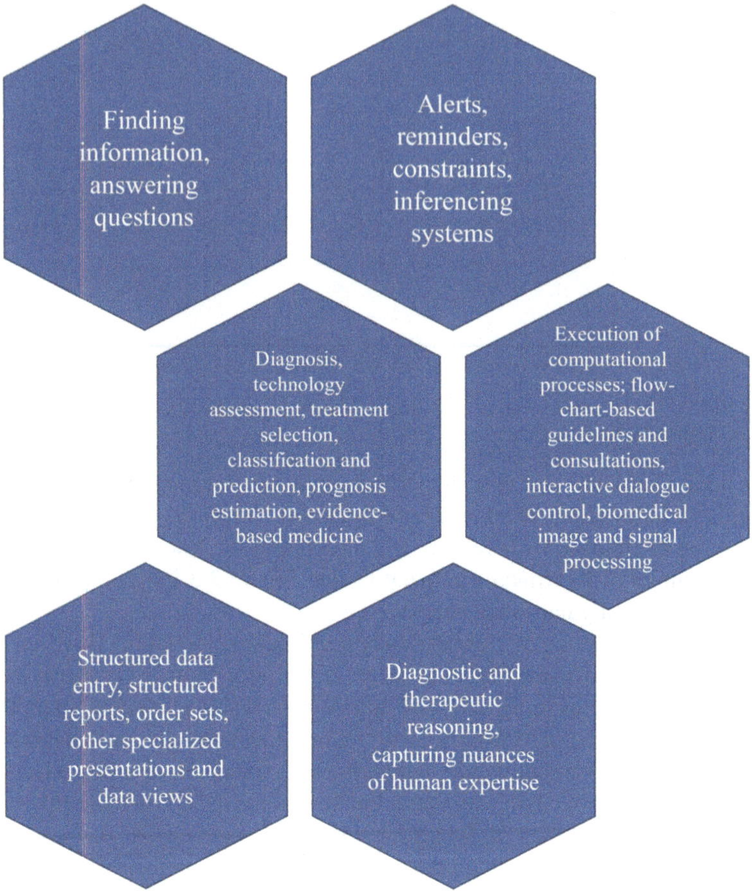

Fig. 3.4 Major uses of decision support system in clinical support and healthcare quality improvement. (Daim et al., 2016; Hogaboam, 2018; Hogaboam & Daim, 2018)

medical diagnosis systems (Walker, 2007) are one type of IDSS. The IDSS usually behaves like a human consultant by analyzing and processing the input data, identifying or diagnosing the problems, and proposing solutions. It is very often that the IDSS is based on expert systems, and it can even achieve better performance than human experts in some circumstances (Baron, 2000; Turban & Volonino, 2010). Figure 3.4 illustrates the major uses of DSS in clinical support and healthcare quality improvement.

3.6 Time Series Forecasting

Time series forecasting is one important field in machine learning with a time component. It is very important because a lot of applications in machine learning have a time component involved. Here, the time series is a series of data points indexed (or listed or graphed) in time order. For example, the heights of ocean tides are time

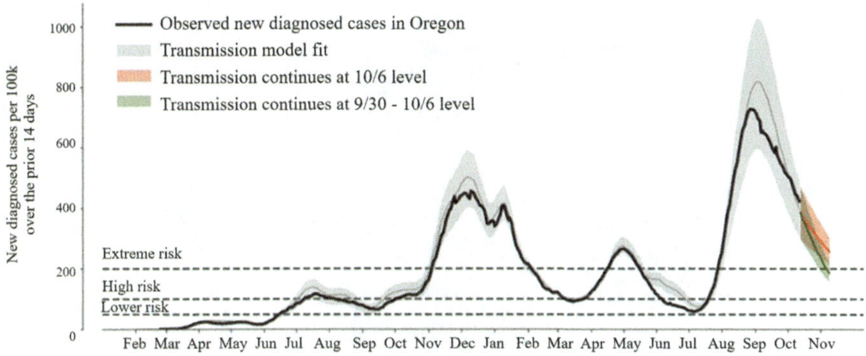

Fig. 3.5 Example of time-series forecasting. ("Rapid Status," 2021)

series and also the daily closing value of the Dow Jones Industrial Average. Time series forecasting is the use of a model (usually one or several AI techniques) to predict future values based on previously observed values. Figure 3.5 shows one example of time series forecasting on the number of newly diagnosed cases in Oregon.

3.7 Case-Based Reasoning

Case-based reasoning (CBR) is an approach that is based on experience. It will solve new problems by adapting the successful experience of solving similar problems (Weir et al., 1988). It has wide applications in machine learning, medicine, etc. There are usually four steps for the CBR (Aamodt & Plaza, 1994):

Step 1: Retrieve – Retrieving from memory cases and finding out the case closest to the current problem. A case consists of a problem, its solution, and, typically, annotations about how the solution was derived.

Step 2: Reuse – Based on the experience and the case found in the previous step, suggest a solution, and adapt it to meet the demands of the new situation.

Step 3: Revise – Test and evaluate the new solution in the real world (or a simulation), and revise it if necessary.

Step 4: Retain – Store this new problem-solving method as a new case in the memory system.

A query engine could be used in the CBR, which is a piece of software that executes queries against data in the database or server to provide answers for users or applications. Figure 3.6 shows the overall flowchart of CBR.

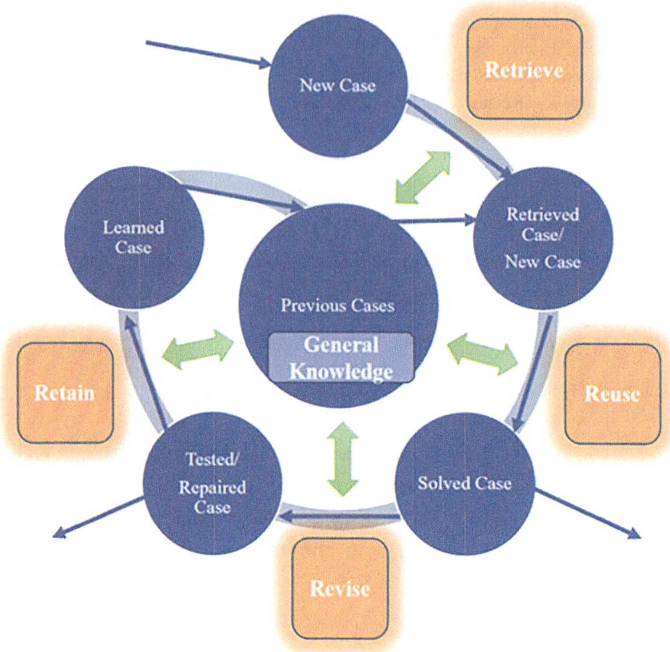

Fig. 3.6 The flowchart of CBR

3.8 Procedural Content Generation

In the computing field, procedural content generation is the method of generating data using computer algorithms, which is different from manually generated data. The term procedural refers to the process that computes a particular function. The procedural content generation method is widely used in computer vision, computer games, etc. For example, AI technology can be used to generate fake pictures (Westerlund, 2019), and the game Advanced Dungeons & Dragons provided ways for the "dungeon master" to generate dungeons and terrain using random die rolls. Figure 3.7 illustrates several images with human faces. They all look real, but you may be surprised to know that all of those are generated by AI techniques (Karras et al., 2020), and it is one example of procedural content generation.

3.9 Voice Chatbots

In business, **voice chatbots** are usually AI-based software that could take voice commands as input from the customers and reply by voice. Compared to text-based bots, voice chatbots are usually much faster, and sometimes more convenient. For example, it is very difficult for a driver to use text-based bots for navigation. There

Fig. 3.7 The fake image generated by AI technique

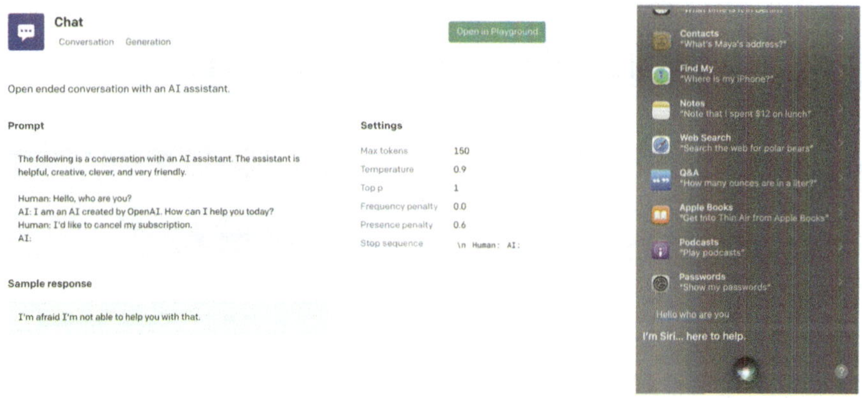

Fig. 3.8a Example of text-based bots from OpenAI and voice-based bots from Apple's Siri

are a lot of other examples using voice chatbots in business, like Siri from Apple, Alexa from Amazon, and Google assistant from Google. Figure 3.8a shows the text-based bots from OpenAI and voice-based bots from Apple's Siri. To use the bots from OpenAI, users have to type their questions and read the answers generated by the AI technique. However, Apple's Siri will take the voice input, and it can also reply with voice, which is much more convenient for someone who is not familiar with computers and is also much faster than text-based bots. Figure 3.8b illustrates the flowchart of a voice chatbot using the AI and natural language processing technique, and there are more discussions in the next few chapters about the chatbot.

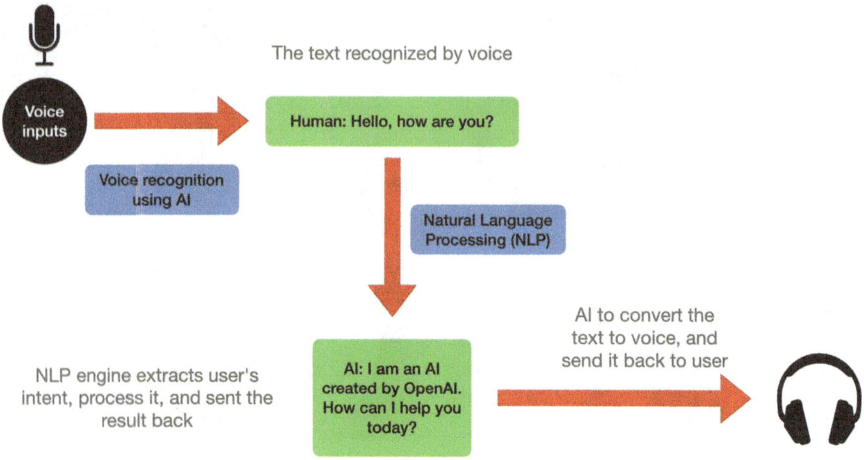

Fig. 3.8b Flowchart of chatbot using AI

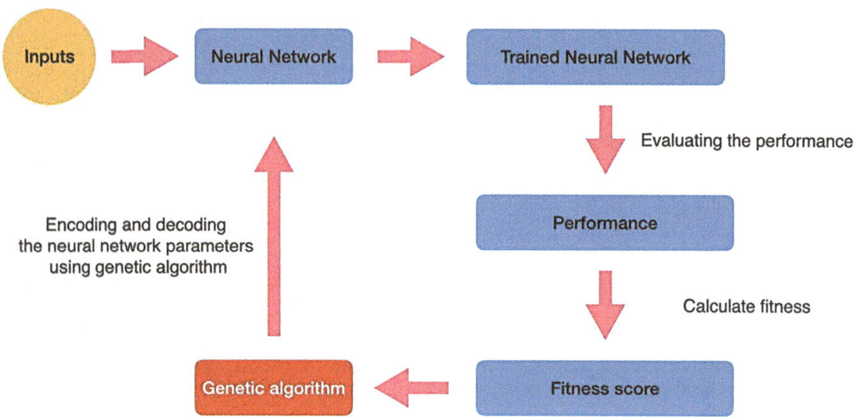

Fig. 3.9 The flowchart of GA-RBF

3.10 Genetic Algorithm-Radial Basis Function (GA-RBF)

The radial basis function (RBF) neural network is a three-layer feedforward network with a single hidden layer, and it has the advantages of adaptive and self-learning ability for complex problems, but it is difficult to determine the parameters, like the number of hidden neurons in the hidden layer. To overcome this, the GA-RBF technique is proposed by using the genetic algorithm to optimize the parameters in the RBF neural network, and it achieves good generalization capability and learning speed (Jia et al., 2014). The GA-RBF technique has wide applications in the business field. For example, researchers used GA-RBF for stock forecasting (Du et al., 2010). Figure 3.9 shows the flowchart of GA_RBF, while the

RBF neural network is trained based on the input data, and the genetic algorithm will be used to evaluate the fitness score and update the parameters in RBF neural network to find the best neural network model for the input.

3.11 Hybrid AI Systems

Hybrid AI systems are software systems that employ different types of AI technologies. For example, the integration of fuzzy logic and the expert system (fuzzy expert system); the integration of neural networks and genetic algorithms (evolutionary neural network); reinforcement learning with fuzzy, neural, or evolutionary methods as well as symbolic reasoning methods; etc. We have a lot of simple and specific AI systems (e.g., human face recognition in computer vision (Guo et al., n.d.), language translation (Deng & Liu, 2018), protein function/structure prediction (Hippe et al., 2020, 2021), etc.), and now it is the time to integrate those AI technologies to create hybrid AI systems. One example is the **hierarchical control system**, which is a form of control system organized hierarchically, and the higher layers are capable of performing planning and lower layers are less abstract to perform specific tasks. Figure 3.10 illustrates an example of hybrid AI systems. Given the inputs for a specific business problem, such as the history stock price, several AI techniques will be used to process those inputs and generate their output. And we will have a decision system to use all of those outputs from different AI technology and make the final decision. For example, if we are interested in a space technology company ASTRA's stock price, we can collect all historical stock prices for this company as inputs, and then we will use different AI techniques to predict the price for the future. The simple decision system may just take the average of all predictions from those AI techniques and use that as the final stock price prediction to the customer.

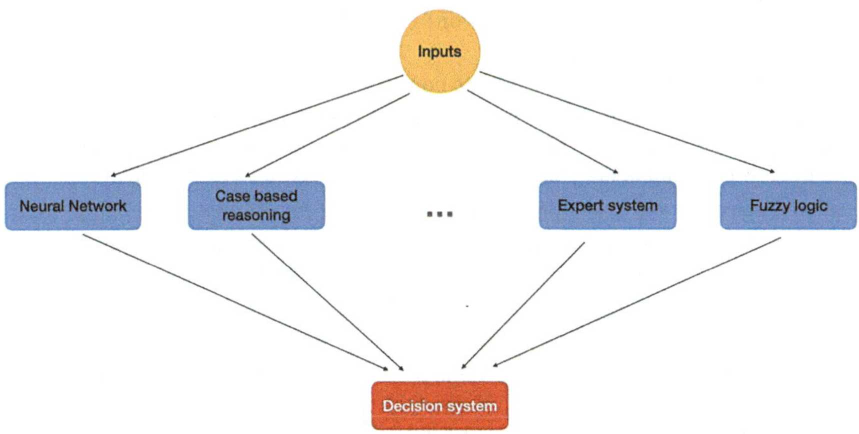

Fig. 3.10 Flowchart of hybrid AI systems

Artificial intelligence is a process and procedure by which knowledge is gained through experience. In other words, computers could potentially learn without being explicitly programmed. AI consists of related technologies that try to stimulate and reproduce human thought behavior, including thinking, speaking, feeling, and reasoning. The AI technologies have been applied to areas that require knowledge, perception, reasoning, understanding, and cognitive abilities. Here, we introduce how IBM moves into this exciting area and its initiatives in AI technology.

Case 3.1: IBM Watson

International Business Machines Corporation, better known as IBM, is a leading technology company that produces and sells hardware, software, IT services, cloud solutions, and everything in between. IBM provides hosting and consulting services in areas ranging from mainframe computers to nanotechnology. One of their most popular AI products is IBM Watson, which was named in memory of the company's leader Thomas J. Watson. The project started in 2007, led by David Ferrucci with an initial goal to create a system that can understand human language and extract knowledge faster than any other computer or human. IBM Watson is built as a supercomputer system that utilizes many AI technologies. The system uses natural language processing (NLP) and machine learning algorithms to reveal useful information and patterns from huge amounts of unstructured data. The cognitive and analytical processing of IBM Watson makes it one of the world's leading AI technology platforms.

Watson can respond to human speech, store lots of data, and generate answers that companies could not come up with before if just using human minds. In the mid-2000s, there was an idea floating around of playing Jeopardy! with an IBM system. After initial struggles such as only getting some answers correct and long response time, by 2010, IBM Watson played with real people in the live television show Jeopardy! and outwit humans. In 55 real-time sparring against former Tournament of Champion Players Ken Jennings and Brad Rutter, Watson put on a very competitive performance, winning 71%. In the final Exhibition Match against the two former champions, Watson won! From there, the possibilities of applications of this system were endless.

AI systems such as Watson can help companies further their knowledge of market trends based on variables that have never been used before as part of the decision-making process. One of the biggest goals of Watson, during the conception period, was to be able to understand human natural language across a multitude of scenarios and to understand the questions humans have and provide answers to those questions that humans can rationalize. Currently, Watson works as an artificial intelligence for business and other information-intensive fields such as health care, supply chain, media, finance, etc. Watson is available to help companies to predict future possibilities, automate complex processes, and enhance employees' time. Watson offers many benefits to organizations that are looking for an edge or just to enhance their overall working experience. Watson is designed to analyze big data from diverse sources and is designed to understand the language of business to make sense of unstructured data. Watson is also there to enhance the business process via automation.

IBM is one of the first companies applying AI technologies in customer service operations. IBM Watson is very suitable in customer service units as it decreases the amount of downtime, errors, and human involvement. When interacting with customers, it is important to respond fast and accurately while also showing an understanding of what is going on. IBM Watson offers both text-to-speech and speech-to-text interactions making it very flexible. This flexibility allows companies such as IBM to offer better services when dealing with customers. IBM Watson utilizes data and past experiences to generate the right response for the right customer since each customer has different requirements for their situation. IBM Watson does not utilize emotion and can accurately come up with responses very quickly reducing the amount of waiting time. This enables IBM to deal with more customers much more quickly, resolving their problems and making the customer's experience with the company much more memorable.

IBM Watson has been making improvements in various industries. One example is the healthcare industry. Watson is available to provide solutions for image diagnosing and can gain insights into provider performance with data analytics, consulting, and data management solutions. There are many more solutions Watson can offer just in health care, but the goal for Watson Health is to combine technology, data, and expertise to transform the healthcare communities. Providers will have more time with their patients and become more efficient in the long run. Watson also provides solutions for media analytics, livestreaming events, content management, etc. Watson Media can reduce manual effort by automating livestream captioning, working on video analytics, and powering video searches. Watson Media is built for hosting livestream events while optimizing video quality, running automated captioning, and reaching a virtually unlimited audience.

Watson AI has come very far from being just a question answering machine on Jeopardy. Seeing the potential for a multitude of applications allowed for Watson to expand into the AI we know today, penetrating various industries and optimizing the working environment to become a reliable and near fundamental resource for those industries. Watson is one of many working AI platforms that allow other companies to thrive in this technology-driven world.

Case 3.2: Hyperscience AI Platform

Artificial intelligence technologies have been increasing the efficiency and optimization of businesses which, in turn, have also improved the overall employee and customer experience. Here, we will look at an AI platform company known as Hyperscience. The company was established in 2014, which offers platforms and products to other companies in varying industries to increase their business's efficiency and overall competitiveness. Their platforms are AI-based and evolve to become much more effective than others.

The Hyperscience AI platform promotes six aspects: Document Processing, Flow Studio, Code Blocks, Connectivity, Reporting, and Supervision (https://hyperscience.com/). For Document Processing, the Hyperscience Platform can decrypt and pull important data out of complex documents. The input can be any unstructured text, and the company will use AI technology to convert the input into actionable data that is easy to process. For the Flow Studio and Code Blocks, the company will increase the data analyzing efficiency, which includes data visualization and a clear user interface. End-to-end solutions will be generated based on the background of their company customer. For connectivity, companies can use the Hyperscience Platform alongside other technological systems. The Hyperscience platform will confirm the accuracy of the extracted data by verifying it on different platforms. For reporting, the platform will gather much more data outside of the input documents, like how exactly the company's automation is improving customer experience and satisfaction, pinpoints and locates bottlenecks within the processing, and also employee performance. For supervision, the platform will incorporate their "human-in-the-loop technology" in combination with their AI technology.

The classification-based AI technology is used for Intelligent Document Processing (IDP) solutions in Hyperscience. The AI will automatically process the big data and extract the knowledge that is needed without any human intervention. The data is converted to a useful form using Hyperscience IDP software, such as the well-known languages JSON format (Javascript Object Notation). After the confirmation from a firm, the data extraction for documentation is begun by scanning and/or uploading documents to the platform. Once uploaded, the AI technology can be used to process the data (structured, unstructured, or semi-structured) automatically, such as recognizing handwritten texts. The process is usually fast, which will lead to a better customer service experience. In addition, the user will get notifications to supervise the low-confidence fields of data that AI may have trouble processing.

Based on the user's initial requirements, Hyperscience provides well-formatted data using AI and machine learning techniques. This data is presented in the form of organized Code Blocks, which are the core of the Hyperscience platform. The blocks can be independently developed and deployed by business users. Hyperscience offers competitive advantages over legacy technologies (old-school tech) and greatly reduces the manpower that would be required to cover large quantities of big data.

The final output for Hyperscience can be a website that neatly displays the relevant data for the firm as Code Blocks. With the help of AI technology, it is relatively easy to use the final output, and it is not limited to the specific type of data provided by the user. Hyperscience technology can assist a firm in reducing the volume of manual work and clerical errors, improving the work performance of employees, and delivering better customer experiences. These benefits will help reduce the overall costs for a firm and increase customer satisfaction. IDP (as the primary component of the Hyperscience platform) provides a strong competitive advantage with data extraction via AI technology and enterprise-wide automation.

References

Aamodt, A., & Plaza, E. (1994). Case-based reasoning: Foundational issues, methodological variations, and system approaches. *AI Communications, 7*(1), 39–59. https://doi.org/10.3233/aic-1994-7104

Baron, J. (2000). *Thinking and deciding*. Cambridge University Press.

Chan, F. T. S., Jiang, B., & Tang, N. K. H. (2000). The development of intelligent decision support tools to aid the design of flexible manufacturing systems. *International Journal of Production Economics, 65*(1), 73–84.

Daim, T. U., Behkami, N., Basoglu, N., Kök, O. M., & Hogaboam, L. (2016). Healthcare technology innovation adoption. In *Innovation, technology, and knowledge management*. Springer.

Deng, L., & Liu, Y. (2018). *Deep learning in natural language processing*. Springer.

Du, P., Luo, X., He, Z., & Xie, L. (2010). *The application of genetic algorithm-radial basis function (GA-RBF) neural network in stock forecasting* (pp. 1745–1748). 2010 Chinese Control and Decision Conference.

Guo, G., Li, S. Z., & Chan, K. (n.d.). Face recognition by support vector machines. In *Proceedings Fourth IEEE International Conference on Automatic Face and Gesture Recognition (Cat. No. PR00580)*. https://doi.org/10.1109/afgr.2000.840634

Hippe, K., Gbenro, S., & Cao, R. (2020). ProLanGO2. In *Proceedings of the 11th ACM International Conference on Bioinformatics, Computational Biology and Health Informatics*. https://doi.org/10.1145/3388440.3414701

Hippe, K., Lilley, C., William Berkenpas, J., Chandana Pocha, C., Kishaba, K., Ding, H., Hou, J., Si, D., & Cao, R. (2021). ZoomQA: Residue-level protein model accuracy estimation with machine learning on sequential and 3D structural features. *Briefings in Bioinformatics*. https://doi.org/10.1093/bib/bbab384

Hogaboam, L. S. (2018). *Assessment of technology adoption potential of medical devices: Case of wearable sensor products for pervasive care in neurosurgery and orthopedics*. Doctoral dissertation, Portland State University.

Hogaboam, L., & Daim, T. (2018). Technology adoption potential of medical devices: The case of wearable sensor products for pervasive care in neurosurgery and orthopedics. *Health Policy and Technology, 7*(4), 409–419.

Holsapple, C. W., & Whinston, A. B. (1987). *Business Expert Systems*. Richard d Irwin.

Jackson, P. (1986). *Introduction to expert systems*. https://www.osti.gov/biblio/5675197

Jia, W., Zhao, D., Shen, T., Su, C., Hu, C., & Zhao, Y. (2014). A new optimized GA-RBF neural network algorithm. *Computational Intelligence and Neuroscience, 2014*, 982045.

Karras, T., Laine, S., Aittala, M., Hellsten, J., Lehtinen, J., & Aila, T. (2020). Analyzing and Improving the Image Quality of StyleGAN. In *2020 IEEE/CVF Conference on Computer Vision and Pattern Recognition (CVPR)*. https://doi.org/10.1109/cvpr42600.2020.00813

Leondes, C. T. (2002). *Expert systems: The technology of knowledge management for the 21st century*. Academic Press.

Matsatsinis, N. F., & Siskos, Y. (2012). *Intelligent support systems for marketing decisions*. Springer Science & Business Media.

Rapid Status Update: Covid-19 Epidemic Trends And Scenario Projections In Oregon Results (October, 20, 2021). Retrieved from https://www.oregon.gov/oha/covid19/Documents/DataReports/Epidemic-Trends-and-Projections.pdf

Schramm, M., & Ertel, W. (2000). *Reasoning with probabilities and maximum entropy: The system PIT and its application in LEXMED* (pp. 274–280). Operations Research Proceedings 1999.

Sprague, R. H. (1980). A framework for the development of decision support systems. *The Mississippi Quarterly, 4*(4), 1–26.

Turban, E., & Volonino, L. (2010). *Information technology for management*. John Wiley & Sons Asia.

Walker, D. (2007). *Similarity determination and case retrieval in an intelligent decision support system for diabetes management*. Ohio University. https://rave.ohiolink.edu/etdc/view?acc_num=ohiou1194562654

Weir, B. S., Eisen, E. J., Goodman, M. M., & Namkoong, G. (1988). *Proceedings of the Second International Conference on Quantitative Genetics*. Sinauer Associates, Incorporated.

Westerlund, M. (2019). The emergence of deepfake technology: A review. *Technology Innovation Management Review, 9*(11), 39–52. https://doi.org/10.22215/timreview/1282

Zadeh, L. A. (1996). Fuzzy sets. *Fuzzy Sets, Fuzzy Logic, and Fuzzy Systems, 6*, 394–432. World Scientific.

Machine Learning for Business Applications

4

Abstract

This chapter introduces machine learning techniques and its applications in business. It covers three basic types of machine learning and various algorithms, including linear and multiple regression, polynomial and logistic regression, decision tree, neural networks, deep learning, recurrent neural network, genetic algorithms, support vector machine, Naive Bayes algorithm, and the Bayesian network. A case study on Microsoft is provided to illustrate AI research.

Keywords

Machine learning · Supervised learning · Unsupervised learning · Reinforcement learning · Classification algorithm · Regression algorithm · Polynomial regression · Logistic regression · Decision tree · Neural networks · Deep learning · Convolutional neural network · Recurrent neural network · Genetic algorithms · Support vector machine · Naive bayes algorithm · Bayesian network

4.1 Introduction

Machine learning is a very important tool in today's business world. Many companies are taking advantage of its power to streamline complex processes and achieve higher revenues and market share. Artificial intelligence (AI) is a broader term to describe how a machine can simulate human thinking and behaviors (Goodfellow et al., 2016). Machine learning is the most popular approach in the AI field. There can be different approaches for AI. For example, anyone can design a lot of rules and then hard-code the knowledge as a computer program to describe if there is an apple or orange in an image. This is referred to as the knowledge base approach. The background color of an image could be very different for the same apple, and there are different types of apples, so you can imagine how difficult it is to design all the

L. Chan et al., *Applied Artificial Intelligence in Business*, Applied Innovation and Technology Management, https://doi.org/10.1007/978-3-031-05740-3_4

rules to consider different scenarios. Instead of writing programs with all different rules, another approach is to have a computer program that will acquire knowledge from raw data automatically, which is the machine learning (ML) approach. The formal definition of ML is provided by Arthur Samuel in 1959: "ML is a field of study that gives computers the ability to learn without being explicitly programmed." There are a lot of ML techniques, such as neural networks, linear regression, naive Bayes, decision tree, etc. In the next few sections, we will first describe the three types of machine learning and then describe a few commonly used machine learning techniques with applications in business.

4.2 Three Types of Machine Learning

As a subset of AI, there are generally three types in machine learning: supervised learning, unsupervised learning, and reinforcement learning. For all three types of machine learning techniques, the data to train the model is very important. Let's first talk about the data before we talk about the details of those three types. In general, there are two types of data: labeled and unlabeled data. The labeled data contains both the input and the labeled output, and the unlabeled data only contains input without any labeled output. Let's take the self-driving car in business as an example; one of the important parts is to recognize the object from an image. The car should slow down when it recognizes humans in the camera. In this example, the input data can be millions of images, and the data is labeled if there is object type information (e.g., is that a human or a tree) for this image and unlabeled if we don't have the object type information. Obviously, the labeled data will be more helpful for training machine learning models, but labeling the data needs a huge amount of human labor. Now, let's learn each type of machine learning technique.

4.2.1 Supervised Learning

Supervised learning is trained on labeled data. The data used for the machine learning technique to learn the pattern is called training data, which is usually one portion of the whole dataset. It learns the relationship between the input data and output and saves that as a machine learning model. Now the machine learning model knows the pattern between input and output data, and it can be deployed to predict the output based on any new input data just like the training dataset. It's worth mentioning that this type of machine learning technique can be improved even after the deployment, and once you have more training data, it can train new models to discover new patterns and relationships. In the self-driving car example, you can train a machine learning model based on the training data with two types of images—human and trees—and later on you can use this model to predict either human or tree for any new image. After a while, let's assume you have collected images with birds, and then you can train a new machine learning model on the new training dataset to predict birds in any new image. In this example, the output label is a discrete class label like human, tree, or bird, and we call this **a classification algorithm**. However, the output label can be a real number, such as how likely there is a human in the image, and we call this **a regression algorithm**. In real-world applications, there may be overlaps between these two problems. For example, your classification algorithm may predict the probability for a class label.

4.2.2 Unsupervised Learning

Unsupervised learning is trained on unlabeled data. Over the last few decades, unsupervised learning is actually ignored by the machine learning community, largely because it is hard to define the goal of unsupervised learning, and there are very limited types of techniques for unsupervised learning (e.g., many researchers thought that clustering is the only unsupervised learning). The advantage of unsupervised learning is that we don't require human labor to label the data. However, it is also difficult to learn patterns from data without any labels. Usually, unsupervised learning tries to find hidden patterns and insights from the unlabeled training data. Let's still take the self-driving car as an example; since we don't have the label information for input data of all images, the unsupervised learning algorithm like clustering algorithm tries to find out the relationship between those images, so we know some images are similar to each other, and we will put them into one class. For any new image, the unsupervised learning algorithm can still classify it even though it doesn't have any label information.

4.2.3 Reinforcement Learning

Reinforcement learning is different from supervised learning or unsupervised learning. The output is usually an action or sequence of actions, and the only supervisory signal is an occasional scalar reward. The goal of reinforcement learning is to find out the actions in an environment in order to maximize the notion of cumulative reward. In the self-driving car example, the action can be turned left, kept straight, and turned right, while the reinforcement learning algorithm explores a sequence of actions, and you can define the rewards that it will get at the end depending on the final status (e.g., reward 1 if it doesn't crash at the end, 1 if it crashes). So the training of reinforcement learning algorithms is to find out the optimal behavior or action, which is reinforced by a positive reward. Reinforcement learning is similar to how the babies learn to walk, he/she will get rewards based on the outcomes of the actions (e.g., will the previous step make he/she fall?) and adjust the actions.

4.3 Machine Learning Algorithms

As we learned in the previous section, there are three types of machine learning. In this section, we are going to learn the concept of a few selected machine learning algorithms and their applications in business. There are a lot of machine learning algorithms, and each of them has pros and cons and can be used in different scenarios. To better understand the concept, let's still think about the example of the self-driving car. Suppose you are going to design a computer algorithm to decide if the self-driving car should slow down or not. The first thing you want to do is to collect the training data, and your driving experience may be useful here. There will be a lot of factors to make the final decision, such as the distance between your car and the car in front of you, the weather conditions (raining, strong wind, etc.), and the environment (e.g., do you identify a human walking in front of your car?). All of those will be input data, which could be a number or multiple numbers as vectors, which can refer to like **features** (we can use x to represent it, x can be a vector with multiple values). In our example, the **output** is whether the self-driving car should slow down or not (we can use y to represent it, y can be a vector with multiple values as well, but here y can be either 0 or 1 to represent slow down or not). The training data we will collect is a good number of (x_i, y_i) pairs. You can think about each machine learning model as a function that captures the relationship between input and output. So you can train different machine learning models using different machine learning techniques. Table 4.1 shows example training data that can be used to train machine learning models, and we are going to learn concepts of several machine learning techniques in the following section.

4.3.1 Linear and Multiple Regression

Linear regression is one type of machine learning technique that is used to find the linear relationships between input and output data. Let's start with the simple situation when there is only one feature x; the linear regression will calculate the output y using the following equation: $y = a * x + b$, where a is the gradient (or slope) and b is a correction term. The slope can be calculated once you have two pairs of points (x_1, y_1) and (x_2, y_2): $a = (y_2 - y_1) / (x_2 - x_1)$. Of course, you may have many pairs of

Table 4.1 Training data example for self-driving car

Output y (1 means slow down, 0 means not slow down)	Feature 1: distance (1 means it is very close to car in the front)	Feature 2: human (1 means there is human in the front)	Feature 3: windy (1 means windy)	Feature 4: raining (1 means raining)
1	1	1	1	1
1	0	0	1	0
0	0	1	0	0
1	1	0	1	1
1	0	1	0	1
0	0	0	0	0
1	0	0	0	1
0	0	0	1	0
1	**0**	**0**	**1**	**1**
0	**0**	**0**	**1**	**1**

points, so the slope might be different when you choose different points pairs. The linear regression technique is trying to find the slope and correction term that best captures the relationship between input and output.

Now let's consider a more complicated case, where you have multiple features as input, as shown in Table 4.1. We want to find out the relationship between the input with multiple independent variables/features and the output, and this type of regression is called multiple regression with the following formula: $y = w_1 x_1 + w_2 x_2 + \ldots + w_i x_i + \ldots w_n x_n + b$, where n is the total number of independent variables/features. Obviously, you may ask how we learn these weights on w_i. It is relatively easy for our brain but not that easy for the machine to learn the relationship. Usually we will use a loss function to guide the selection of weights by minimizing the loss, such as $(y_i' - y_i) * (y_i' - y_i) / 2$, where y_i' is the predicted output and y_i is the true output. Our final goal is to minimize the loss on all of the training data when we train the machine learning model, and that is the overall training process.

4.3.2 Polynomial and Logistic Regression

The relationship between input and output might not be linear in the real-world application, so we may need to have other machine learning techniques to capture more complicated nonlinear relationships as a variant of linear regression. One of the techniques is called **polynomial regression**, which uses the following equation: $y = w_1 x + w_2 x^2 + \ldots + w_i x^i + \ldots + w_n x^n + b$. The polynomial regression can capture both the linear relationship and nonlinear relationship. Similar to linear regression, the x can be a vector when you have multiple features. Another technique is called **logistic regression**, which uses the logistic function: $y = 1 / (1 + e^z)$, while $z = w_1 x + w_2 x^2 + \ldots + w_i x^i + \ldots + w_n x^n + b$.

4.3.3 Decision Tree

A decision tree is one of the machine learning techniques that is widely used in business. It is a diagram or chart to describe the decisions, while each internal node will be used to test one feature x_i, each branch represents one value of x_i, and each leaf is a prediction for the output y. Each decision tree is a hypothesis to map input x to output y. Let's still learn this by the example in Table 3. The decision tree is intuitive as it is similar to how people make decisions. To build the decision tree, we can start with feature 1, which can be 0 or 1. As we can see from the table when the value of feature 1 is 1, the output is always 1, so we have the internal node f1 to test the value of feature 1, and the right branch represents the value of feature 1 is 1, and the value 1 in the box is the leaf as the final decision. Now when feature 1 is 0, the output varies as we can see in the table, so we will test feature 2 now. We notice when feature 1 is 0, and feature 2 is 1, the output is always 1 in the table, so we will set up the leaf as 1 in Fig. 4.1. We will do that same thing when feature 2 is 0, feature 3 will be tested, and then we will generate the rest of the decision tree. It's worth

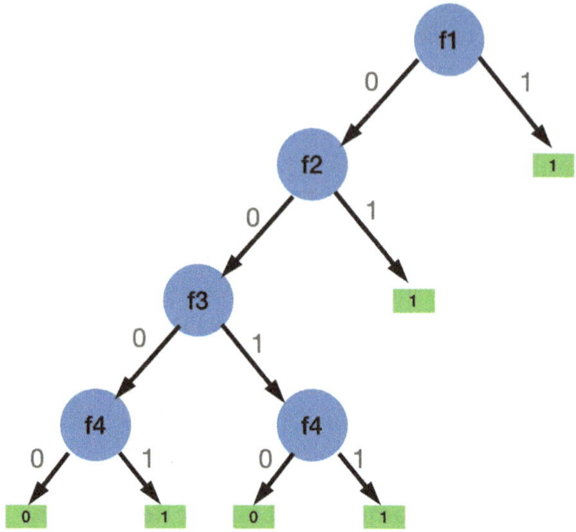

Fig. 4.1 Decision tree example

mentioning that there will be different trees as hypotheses for the same input data. For example, some of you may ask why we test feature 1 first and then test feature 2? Indeed, the order matters to the final decision tree you build, so some trees are much more complicated than other trees for the same training data. In addition, there might be errors in the decision tree, such as the last two records in Table 3 actually conflict with each other since they have the same input but different output. So the decision tree in Fig. 4.2 is not perfect, and you may still need to decide the leaf to minimize the total number of errors in your training data. In order to build a good decision tree, you may need to consider **information gains** or other methods, but this book only focuses on the concept of those machine learning techniques, so you may need to refer to other books to understand all the details if you are interested.

4.3.4 Neural Networks

The neural network is a machine learning technique that is inspired by neural science to mimic how the human brain works (McCulloch & Pitts, 1990; Nielsen, 2015). Our brain can process very complex information easily based on millions of neurons that are connected to each other. Each biological neuron could receive and process information and pass it to the next neuron. All of those neurons connected to each other and helped us to process all kinds of information every day. Each neuron may not be that powerful, but it is very powerful when all neurons are connected to each other and process information in parallel. The first mathematical model to mimic the biological neuron was created by Warren McCulloch and Walter Pitts in 1943 (McCulloch & Pitts, 1990). It takes the binary value input and outputs a binary value based on a threshold value. The output is 1 if the summation of all input x_i is

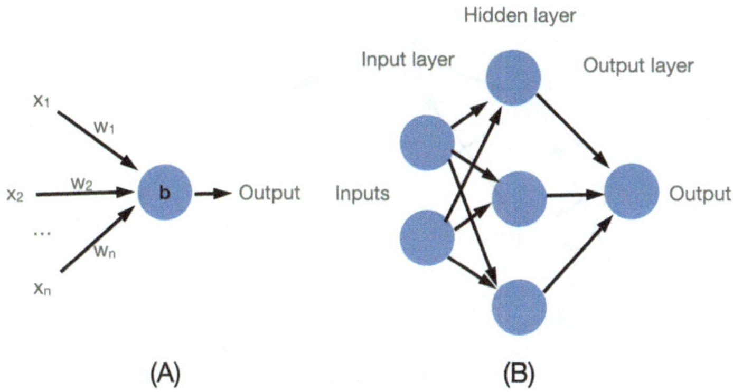

Fig. 4.2 Perceptron and neural network architecture

larger or equal to the threshold b; otherwise, the output is 0. Later on, Frank Rosenblatt proposed an improved version called the perceptron model in 1958 (Rosenblatt, 1958). The weight is introduced for each input, and instead of summation of inputs, the perceptron model uses the sum of the weighted inputs and threshold to decide the output (see Fig. 4.2a as an example of one neural in the perceptron). The output y is 1 if $x_1\ w_1 + x_2\ w_2 + \ldots + x_i\ w_i + \ldots + x_n\ w_n > = b$ (otherwise y is 0), where b is the threshold, and w_i is the weight for input x_i. One neuron in the perceptron model is similar to linear regression that can separate the linear input data, and a larger weight of w_i means there is a bigger impact for the input x_i. Even though you can add more neurons in the perceptron model, multiple linear models connected to each other are still linear models, so they cannot process nonlinear data. The modern-day perceptrons introduce the nonlinear activation function to solve this problem. One of the commonly used activation functions is sigmoid function: 1 / $(1 + e^z)$, where z is the input for the sigmoid function. To put things together, now each perceptron neuron's output y is 1 if 1 / $(1 + e^{x1\ w1\ +\ x2\ w2\ +\ \ldots\ +\ xi\ wi\ +\ \ldots\ +\ xn\ wn\ +\ b}) > =$ 0. Now those neurons can be connected layer by layer as a network, while the output of the previous layer will be used as input for the next layer. This is the simplest version of the neural network, and training the neural network is to find out the best weights for all neurons to minimize the difference between the predicted output (can be calculated based on the input features and the neural network) and real output (see Fig. 4.2b as an example of neural network with one input layer, one hidden layer, and one output layer). For any new data, you can also use the trained neural network to make predictions. This is the basic concept of neural networks with some details missed because that is not the focus of this book. For example, how can you adjust the weight (e.g., the back-propagation algorithm), other activation functions like softmax, rectified linear unit, parameter settings like the number of neurons, layers, etc.

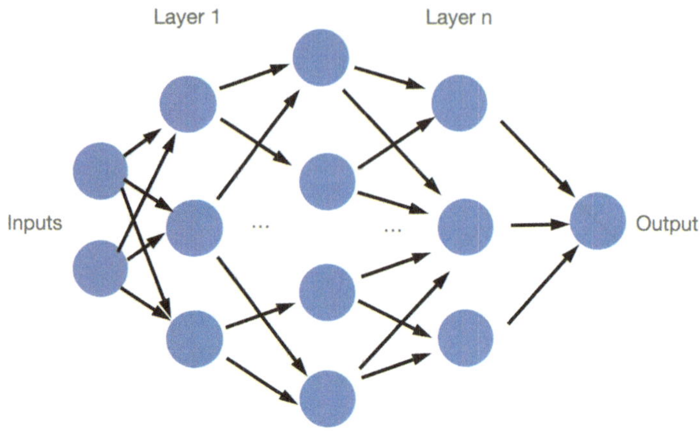

Fig. 4.3 A deep network architecture.

4.3.5 Deep Learning

Generally speaking, adding more neurons and more layers in Fig. 4.2 will make your neural network more powerful to handle more complicated tasks. As you can see in Fig. 4.3, we have more than one hidden layer, and the architecture of the neural network looks more complicated than the one in Fig. 4.2. You could imagine different hidden layers can handle different subtasks, just like recognizing a dog picture, the first hidden layer can focus on the overall shape, and the second hidden layer can focus on the color, etc. Normally, when the number of hidden layers is more than two, we call it the deep neural network and the technique to train this deep network is the **deep learning** technique. It turns out to be super difficult to train the deep network by adjusting the weight. The modern deep learning techniques would include **convolutional neural networks** (CNN)s, **deep belief networks**, **deep Boltzmann machines**, etc. (LeCun & Bengio, n.d.; Hinton, 2009; Salakhutdinov & Hinton, 2009; Goodfellow et al., 2016).

4.3.5.1 Convolutional Neural Networks

The convolutional neural network (CNN) is commonly applied in the image processing and also called shift invariant or space invariant artificial neural networks (SIANN), because of the based on the shared-weight architecture of the convolution kernels. Figure 4.4 illustrates the general architecture for CNNs (it can be much deeper in reality; the picture is created to show the basic concept). There are three basic ideas in CNNs: **local receptive fields**, **shared weights**, and **pooling**. Overall, the CNNs were inspired by biological processes, while each individual cortical neuron responds to stimuli only in a restricted region of the visual field. As we can see in Fig. 4.4, the 3 × 3 red input nodes on the left figure represent **the local receptive field** (corresponding to the restricted region of the visual field in biological process), and it is connected to the red node in the middle figure as the hidden node. Similarly,

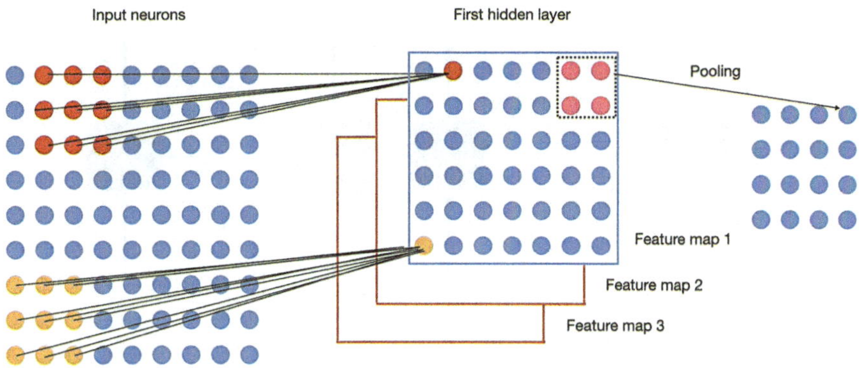

Fig. 4.4 Convolutional neural network

you can find a lot of local receptive fields in the input layers as you can move the 3 × 3 box, such as the yellow 3 × 3 local receptive fields. All of those local receptive fields are connected to the hidden node in the next layer, which is similar to the neural network, and we call them the **convolutional layer**, but they share the same weights (**shared weights**). All of those hidden nodes will be together as a feature map to describe one important feature of your input, and you can generate several feature maps. For example, when you try to use CNNs to detect the object in the figure, you can have one feature map to learn the overall shape of this object, and another feature map to learn the color, etc. The last idea is the **pooling layer**, as we can see in Fig. 4.4. It is usually used immediately after convolutional layers, and the pooling layer is used to simplify the information in the output. We can continue to add more convolutional layers and pooling layers to make the CNNs deeper.

4.3.5.2 Recurrent Neural Network

The recurrent neural network (RNN) is another type of machine learning technique that is directed from neural networks. The RNN has the memory as an internal state to store the input information and can handle various lengths of input, instead of fixed length of input in the neural network. Because of that, the RNN has wide applications in handwriting recognition, speech recognition, bioinformatics, etc. (Conover et al., 2019; Graves et al., 2009; Sak et al., 2014). Figure 4.5 shows the general idea of RNN (the left figure is the rolled RNN with loops, and the right figure is the unrolled RNN), where the output can be used as input, so ultimately it can be very deep and can process arbitrary length of input.

Let's take a look at one specific example; we can use RNN to process the English word "HELLO" by characters. The I_0 can be "H," and the output O_0 will be the output based on the current internal state of the RNN. Similar to the normal neural network, after it is trained, the output O_0 can be the letter "E," but the internal state of the RNN will be updated after that. So when you have "E" as input I_1, the output O_1 will be "L," and the internal state of RNN will be updated again. Later, when you have "L" as input I_2, we will have the output O_2 as "L," and finally we will have O_3

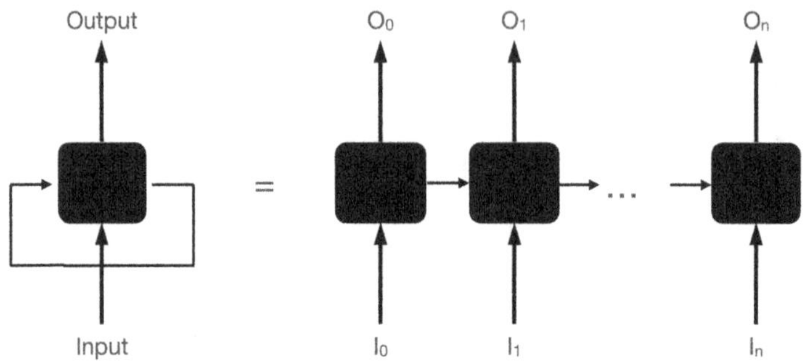

Fig. 4.5 Recurrent neural network architecture

as "O." The RNN is designed to remember the history statement for a sequence of input, and the commonly used techniques are LSTM (long short-term memory) (Hochreiter & Schmidhuber, 1997) and GRU (gated recurrent unit) (Heck & Salem, 2017). Although there are a lot of variants for RNN, the general idea is very similar. All of them have an internal state to remember and forget some information when it is processing a sequence of input.

There are a lot of applications for deep learning in business from finance to drug discovery. For example, DeepMind from Google proposes the AlphaFold 2 using deep learning to tackle the protein folding problem, which has been a grand challenge in biology for the past 50 years (Jumper et al., 2021). The work shows that AI can have a big impact on scientific discovery and also in the business world since the AlphaFold 2 can potentially accelerate drug discovery (e.g., the protein for drug discovery of COVID-19).

4.3.6 Genetic Algorithms

The genetic algorithm (GA) is usually used in machine learning as a search-based method for optimization problems, and it is inspired by Charles Darwin's theory of natural evolution. This type of computation simulation of evolution started in 1954 (Barricelli, 1957) and became more common in the early 1960s, while those methods were described in books by Fraser and Burnell (1970) (Fraser & Burnell, 1970) and Crosby (1973) (Crosby, 1973). In addition, the method became a widely recognized optimization method in the 1960s and early 1970s, as it demonstrates the ability to solve complex engineering problems (Schwefel, 1981). It is worth mentioning the world's first commercial GA product for desktop computers Evolver was released by Axcelis, Inc. in 1989.

The general idea of this genetic algorithm is to use computers to simulate the natural selection process, and the fittest individuals will be selected to produce offspring in the next generation. The characteristics of parents will be added to the offspring in order to improve the fitness score of the offspring, and we will iterate the process of generating offspring to find the fittest individuals in the population.

Here, we have mentioned several concepts, so let's take a look at several important concepts in the GA to understand those concepts.

Concept 1, **initialize the population**. We call **individuals** for the solution of the problem that you want to solve. It can be a string, but usually the binary values (0 s and 1 s) are used since they are easier to be processed in computers. For example, one individual A can be [0,0,0,1,1,1], and another individual B can be [1,1,1,0,0,0]. It is worth mentioning that the length for each individual could be very long (instead of 6 in the example), so you may find millions of unique individuals, and we call the set of individuals a **population**. Now, we need to understand which individual is a better solution, which would be Concept 2.

Concept 2, define **fitness function**. We will need to define a function (called **fitness function**) to describe the fitness of each individual. This function will be different depending on your problem, and it will generate the **fitness scores** for each individual. This score will be used to determine if an individual will be selected for reproduction in the next generation.

Concept 3, **selection**. The selection is to select the individual with high fitness scores to generate the offspring. Normally, we will select two individuals (**parents**) using the fitness scores, and individuals with higher fitness scores will have higher probabilities to be selected, so they are more likely to generate offspring. To explain the process of generating offspring, we need to understand the next concept.

Concept 4, **crossover**. The **crossover** is very important for GA as it will be used to generate offspring from parents. A point will be generated randomly as **crossover point** for the crossover. For example, the random crossover point at position 3 is applied to the two individuals A [0,1,0,1,1,1] and B [1,1,1,0,0,1], so we will exchange the part before the crossover point in A and B, and the **offspring** A' from A would be [1,1,1,1,1,1], and B′ from B would be [0,1,0,0,0,1]. Of course, you may have the question that if we continue to do the crossover between A' and B′ at the same crossover point, we would get the same A and B, which is not very interesting and helpful (we may want to find some better solutions, so we would like to explore more different individuals). To explore more different individuals, we will need to understand the next concept.

Concept 5, **mutation**. A mutation is going to flip a value in the individual, and usually, we have a random probability (usually quite small) to do the mutation. For example, the individual A [0,1,0,1,1,1] may be mutated to a new individual A1 [1,1,0,1,1,1] if it is randomly mutated at the first position. The mutation is very important to maintain the diversity in the population, and very helpful for us to explore all possible results to find the fittest individual as a solution to our problem.

Concept 6, **termination**. The GA algorithm needs to terminate at a certain point while there are no significant changes between the current population and their offspring.

In summary, the GA algorithm would usually start with an initial population and predefined fitness function. In the iterative process, we will do the selection to select parents to generate the next offspring with crossover and mutation. Some individuals will be kept, and others will be dropped based on the fitness score to keep the fixed size of the population. This process will be repeated until the termination of GA, and you will find the individuals with the best fitness score as the solution to your problem.

4.3.7 Support Vector Machine

Support vector machines (SVMs) belong to the supervised learning category in machine learning, and it is one of the most robust and accurate supervised learning algorithms with wide applications in different fields (e.g., business (Ma & Guo, 2014; Decoste & Schölkopf, 2002; Warner et al., 2020), bioinformatics (Hippe et al., 2021; Hunt et al., 2021), etc.). The SVM was developed at AT&T Bell Laboratories in the 1990s (Boser et al., 1992; Drucker et al., 1997), which is based on the statistical learning frameworks or VC theory proposed by Vapnik (2013).

Let's learn the basic concept of SVM by the example of classifying two sets of points in 2D (the example can be expanded to 3D space or higher dimension space, then we will need to draw a hyperplane) as shown in Fig. 4.6a. It is not very difficult to draw a line between the two sets of points, but there is an unlimited number of lines that can separate the two sets of points. For example, in Fig. 4.6b, we can find three different lines h1, h2, and h3, and all of them can successfully separate the two sets of points (blue class in the left and red class in the right), but which one is the best? One reasonable choice is to choose the line that is farthest from both classes or maximize the distance from the line to the nearest data point on each side. As Fig. 4.6c shows, we can find the points (those points are described as vectors and are called **support vector**) on each class that is closest to h2, we can draw two lines h2Left and h2Right on those points (they are in parallel with h2), and the distance between h2Left and h2Right is the **margin**. The basic idea of SVM is to find a line to separate the two classes by maximizing the margin, which will minimize the risk of mislabeling any data point.

Of course, in reality, the data points might be much more complicated than the example we showed in Fig. 4.6. For example, in Figure 4.7a, we have the two data points, which we might not be able to find a line to separate them. However, we can create a hyperplane $z = x^2 + y^2$ to separate those two data points, as is shown in Figure 4.7b. Now, we can use a similar idea to maximize the margin between those two data points in the higher dimensional space z. Figure 4.7c shows what happens when you transform the hyperplane back to the original 2D dimensional space. So here the function ($x^2 + y^2$) that we have used to map the 2D dimensional space to higher-dimensional space is called the **kernel function**. It is worth noting that the kernel function can be much more complicated than we have shown here, and the SVM algorithm can map your data points to a very high dimensional space and find out the best way to separate the two classes. In addition, the SVM doesn't need any

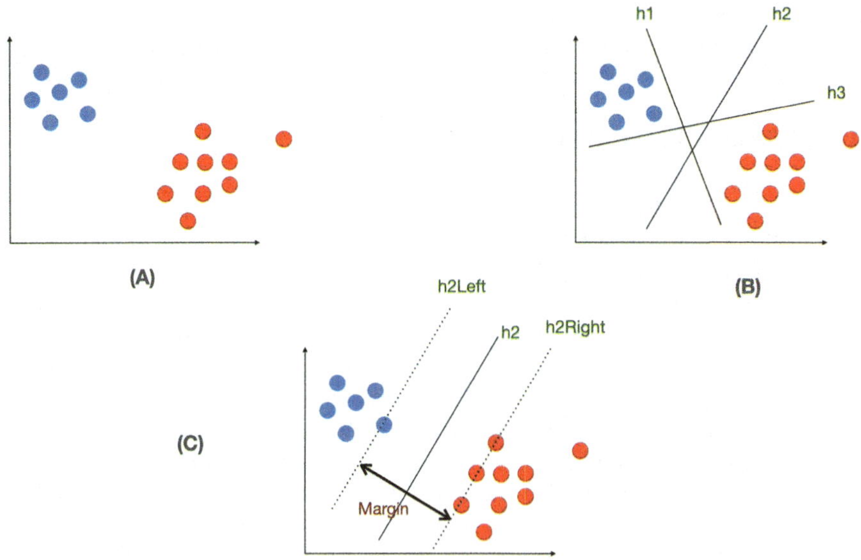

Fig. 4.6 Support vector machine with linear separation

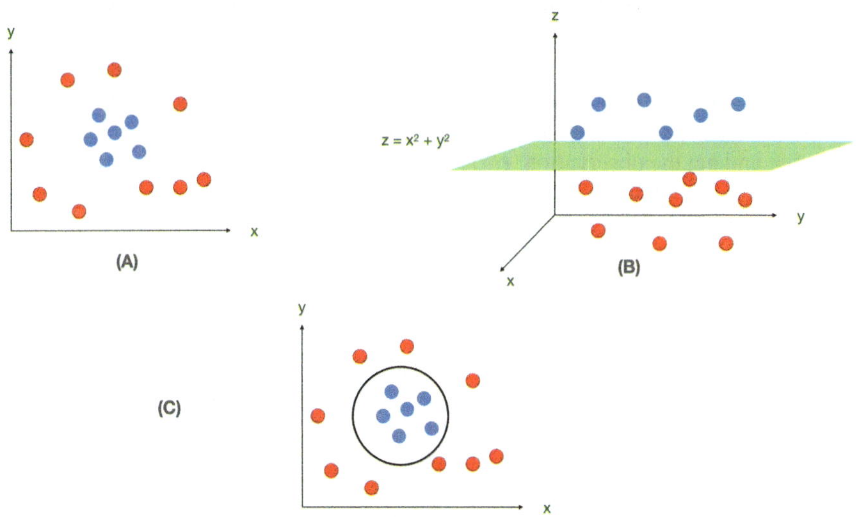

Fig. 4.7 Support vector machine with nonlinear separation

prior knowledge of your data points, and it can use kernel functions to solve nonlinear problems which cannot be separated using linear functions like a line. Some commonly used kernel functions are linear kernel, polynomial, RBF, etc.

We have introduced the basic ideas of SVM through a few examples, but there are a lot more details like parameter settings that are not covered in this book. For example, there might be noisy data, and SVM uses regularization parameters to adjust the model to tolerate the misclassification (e.g., it can use a larger-margin separating line in our example, even if it will misclassify a few data points.).

4.3.8 Naive Bayes Algorithm

Naive Bayes is one type of supervised learning technique in machine learning based on statistics and probability theories. To understand it, we first need to know some probability theories and Naive Bayes.

Let's assume you want to do some gambling by guessing the head or tail by tossing a coin. We could use $P(A)$ to describe the probability, while A is the event that the coin is heads-up. The probability can be any number between 0 and 1, 0 means the event is impossible to happen, and 1 means the event will happen. In our case, we could assume $P(A)$ is 0.5, which means it will have 50% probability to be heads-up. So if you do the gambling in the long term, you will have the same number of wins and losses. To make it more interesting, let's have another coin and use $P(B)$ to describe the probability of heads-up for the other coin. When I toss the other coin and tell you the result (let's say it is heads-up), the probability of A is still 0.5 because these two events A and B didn't influence each other. Here, we can use the **conditional probability** $P(A|B)$ to describe the probability of A given B, and we can say A and B are **independent** when $P(A) = P(A|B)$. What happens if someone is cheating and makes a fake coin, such as $P(B) = 0.9$? You may want to guess heads-up if you know they used the fake coin, since you will have a 90% chance to win. It is relatively easy to guess when you already know the coin type, but not that easy to guess the coin type from the observations. For example, you observe someone play the game and get the observation: $H, T, T, T, H, H, H, H, H, H$. Can you guess if they are cheating or not? Naive Bayes theory can be used here to solve the problem:

$$P(C_k | x) = P(C_k) P(x | C_k) / P(x)$$

In the formula, $P(C_k \mid x)$ is the posterior probability to describe the output C_k given the input x. In our example, the output C could be the coin is normal or fake. It's worth the mention that the input x can be a vector with a list of numbers, and each number in the list can be a feature. The $P(C_k)$ is the prior probability to describe the overall probability of output C_k. The $P(x \mid C_k)$ is the likelihood, which is the conditional probability of input x given output C_k. $P(x)$ is the evidence to describe the overall probability of input x.

The Naive Bayes algorithm in machine learning is based on the Naive Bayes theory with the assumption that each input feature x_i is independent of each other given the output C. It uses **the maximum a posteriori or MAP** decision rule, which means you will guess the one that provides the maximum posterior probability. For example, you will calculate $P(C = \text{normal} \mid x)$ and $P(\text{C} = \text{fake} \mid x)$ and compare those probabilities. If $P(C = \text{normal} \mid x)$ is larger, you would guess it is a normal coin. To calculate $P(C \mid x)$, the Naive Bayes algorithm uses the following formula:

$$P(C|x) \approx P(C)^{*} P(x_1|C)^{*} P(x_2|C)....^{*} P(x_n|C)$$

The x_1, x_2, …, and x_n are the n number of features as input, and in our example, we will have ten features to describe our ten observations [$H, T, T, T, H, H, H, H, H, H$]. The $P(C)$ and $P(x_k \mid C)$ can be trained from the existing dataset using the program, and that is the training step for the Naive Bayes algorithm, and for any new input x, the Naive Bayes algorithm can make predictions based on the MAP rule.

4.3.9 Bayesian Network

The Bayesian network (BN) is a machine learning technique that is based on a probabilistic graphical model with two important components. The first is the directed acyclic graph (DAG), and the second is the conditional probability table for each node. In the previous section, we learned that the Naive Bayes technique is making the predictions based on the conditional probability table, and actually, it is one special case of the Naive Bayesian technique. Let's take a look at one specific example; we know both Flu and COVID-19 can cause the symptom of cough, so we can draw the directed acyclic graph in Fig. 4.8 with our prior knowledge. The directed edge tells the conditional dependencies between the nodes. For example, there is an edge from node Flu to node Cough, which means the Cough is conditional depending on the Flu, and also on the COVID-19. However, there is no route to connect node Flu with node COVID-19, which means the two nodes are independent. Each node has the conditional probability table that is given its parent node. For example, the node Cough has parent node Flu and COVID-19, and the conditional probability table will contain the probability of Cough given different possible values of the parent nodes as is shown in Fig. 4.8. *P*(Cough = 0 | COVID-19 = 0, Flu = 0) means the probability of someone didn't have Cough, given he/she didn't have COVID-19 and also didn't have Flu. All of those conditional probabilities can

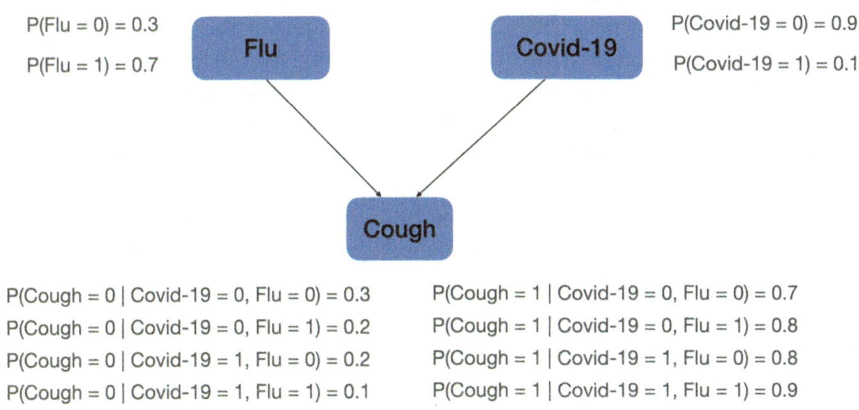

Fig. 4.8 Example of Bayesian network

be learned from the data, similar to the Naive Bayes algorithm. The general idea of BN will first construct the graph based on prior knowledge or learn it from the data and also construct those conditional probabilities tables for each node given its parent nodes. After that, we can make predictions on the new input. For example, if you want to calculate the probability of someone with Cough, COVID-19 but not Flu, you can use $P(\text{Cough} = 1, \text{COVID-19} = 1, \text{Flu} = 1) = P(\text{COVID-19} = 1) * P(\text{Flu} = 1) * P(\text{Cough} = 1 \mid \text{COVID-19} = 1, \text{Flu} = 1)$, and those conditional probabilities can be found from the conditional probability tables in BN.

Case 4.1: AI Initiatives in Microsoft

Microsoft is one of the corporations that has invested greatly in artificial intelligence in recent years. Recently, Microsoft invested $1 billion in OpenAI, which is an independent research organization that conducts research in the field of artificial intelligence with the stated aim to promote and develop AI to benefit humanity as a whole. Microsoft has also hired long-time Apple employee and head Siri Developer Bill Stasior to help the company with its AI development. OpenAI and Microsoft have been jointly building "new Microsoft Azure AI supercomputing technologies." On July 22 of 2019, OpenAI stated that Microsoft will become their preferred partner for commercializing AI technologies.

One of the AI-based software developed by Microsoft is called BrainMaker, which is used to maximize the return on its direct mailing campaigns (Brodzinski & Crable, 1992). Every year, the company sends approximately 40 million pieces of direct mail to almost 9 million customers. First, they sent mail to everyone in the database, but it didn't work out well. And then, they only sent to those that were most likely to respond. But how do we find those customers? Microsoft used BrainMaker, and with the help of machine learning, it determined which variables were most significant. For example, the significant variables could be (1) date of last purchase, (2) date of first purchase, (3) number of products bought and registered, (4) value of the products bought and registered, (5) number of days from the time the product came out and when the customer purchased the product, and (6) the information gathered from the registration card included yes/no answers to certain questions, areas of interest, personal finances, age, and whether a person is retired or has children. The neural networks were used to train the model from the existing data. The BrainMaker eliminated most variables and found that approximately nine were significant. The output was a quantitative score (between 0 and 1) that indicated if an individual should receive a second mailing. Company spokesman Jim Minervino found that customers with a score higher than 0.45 on the given scale, were more responsive. The results of the BrainMaker using neural networks were very significant to the company, where their response rate from an average mailing almost doubled; before BrainMaker, the response was 4.9%, but after BrainMaker, the response was 8.2%. It was also explained that with BrainMaker, Microsoft is able to bring in the same amount of revenue with 35% less cost.

So, what does Microsoft's BrainMaker using neural network do for us as the customer? The first positive as shoppers relate to all direct email marketing, they provide us with detailed information like new hard and software coming out or on sale. Microsoft states, "Our mission is to empower every person and every organization on the planet to achieve more." In addition, with the help of BrainMaker, the number of emails for us as the customer is significantly reduced. But at the same time, we also want to mention the privacy issues that personalized marketing brings up since Microsoft will use your previous purchase history to improve their AI technology and serve the customers better. In addition, there are also concerns about AI taking jobs of customers and developers, as OpenAI Codex can write code using AI. Microsoft warned stockholders, "AI algorithms may be flawed. Datasets may be insufficient or contain biased information. Inappropriate or controversial data practices by Microsoft or others could impair the acceptance of AI solutions. These deficiencies could undermine the decisions, predictions, or analysis AI applications produce, subjecting us to competitive harm, legal liability, and brand or reputational harm. Some AI scenarios present ethical issues. If we enable or offer AI solutions that are controversial because of their impact on human rights, privacy, employment, or other social issues, we may experience brand or reputational harm."

Of course, besides those concerns, there is also a huge benefit that AI brings to us. For example, BrainMaker helped Microsoft maximize its returns on personalized marketing by increasing the response rate from 4.9% to 8.2% on average mailing. It is worth mentioning that we don't need to give up privacy and human rights to use AI technology. The 2018 General Data Protection Regulation (GDPR) recently approved in the EU could be the most important change in data privacy for the last decade. This new regulation will reshape the way how important data will be handled in every service or product like health care or banking. The main goal of the GDPR is to give control to the customer over their personal data like the use of their data, protection over that data, and how it can be shared. Even though this bill has only been passed in the European Union, it will affect most corporations like Microsoft since they have consumers or employees within the EU.

References

Barricelli, N. A. (1957). Symbiogenetic evolution processes realized by artificial methods. *Methodos, 9*, 143–182.

Boser, B. E., Guyon, I. M., Vapnik, V. N. (1992). A training algorithm for optimal margin classifiers. *Proceedings of the Fifth Annual Workshop on Computational Learning Theory – COLT '92*. https://doi.org/10.1145/130385.130401

Brodzinski, J. D., & Crable, E. A. (1992). BrainMaker v2. 3. *Journal of International Information Management, 1*(1), 10.

Conover, M., Staples, M., Si, D., Sun, M., & Cao, R. (2019). AngularQA: Protein model quality assessment with LSTM networks. *Computational and Mathematical Biophysics, 7*(1), 1–9.

Crosby, J. L. (1973). *Computer Simulation in Genetics*. Wiley.

Decoste, D., & Schölkopf, B. (2002). Training invariant support vector machines. *Machine Learning, 46*(1), 161–190.

Drucker, H., Burges, C. J. C., Kaufman, L., Smola, A., Vapnik, V., et al. (1997). Support vector regression machines. *Advances in Neural Information Processing Systems, 9*, 155–161.

Fraser, A., & Burnell, D. G. (1970). *Computer models in genetics*. McGraw-Hill.

Goodfellow, I., Bengio, Y., & Courville, A. (2016). *Deep learning*. MIT Press.

Graves, A., Liwicki, M., Fernández, S., Bertolami, R., Bunke, H., & Schmidhuber, J. (2009). A novel connectionist system for unconstrained handwriting recognition. *IEEE Transactions on Pattern Analysis and Machine Intelligence, 31*(5), 855–868.

Heck, J. C., & Salem, F. M. (2017). Simplified minimal gated unit variations for recurrent neural networks. In *2017 IEEE 60th International Midwest Symposium on Circuits and Systems (MWSCAS)* (pp. 1593–1596) https://ieeexplore.ieee.org

Hinton, G. E. (2009). Deep belief networks. *Scholarpedia Journal, 4*(5), 5947.

Hippe, K., Lilley, C., Berkenpas, J. W., Pocha, C. C., Kishaba, K., Ding, H., Hou, J., Si, D., & Cao, R. (2021). ZoomQA: Residue-level protein model accuracy estimation with machine learning on sequential and 3D structural features. *Briefings in Bioinformatics, September.* https://doi.org/10.1093/bib/bbab384

Hochreiter, S., & Schmidhuber, J. (1997). Long short-term memory. *Neural Computation, 9*(8), 1735–1780.

Hunt, C., Montgomery, S., Berkenpas, J. W., Sigafoos, N., Oakley, J. C., Espinosa, J., Justice, N., et al. (2021). Recent progress of machine learning in gene therapy. *Current Gene Therapy, June.* https://doi.org/10.2174/1566523221666210622164133

Jumper, J., Evans, R., Pritzel, A., Green, T., Figurnov, M., Ronneberger, O., Tunyasuvunakool, K., et al. (2021). Highly accurate protein structure prediction with AlphaFold. *Nature, 596*(7873), 583–589.

LeCun, Y., Bengio, Y. (n.d.). Convolutional networks for images, speech, and time series. *Iro.umontreal.ca.* http://www.iro.umontreal.ca/~lisa/pointeurs/handbook-convo.pdf

Ma, Y., & Guo, G. (2014). *Support vector machines applications.* Springer Science & Business Media.

McCulloch, W. S., & Pitts, W. (1990). A logical calculus of the ideas immanent in nervous activity. 1943. *Bulletin of Mathematical Biology, 52*(1-2), 99–115. discussion 73–97.

Nielsen, M. A. (2015). *Neural networks and deep learning* (Vol. 25). Determination Press.

Rosenblatt, F. (1958). The perceptron: A probabilistic model for information storage and organization in the brain. *Psychological Review, 65*(6), 386–408.

Sak, H., Senior, A., & Beaufays, F. (2014). *Long short-term memory recurrent neural network architectures for large scale acoustic modeling.* Interspeech 2014. https://doi.org/10.21437/interspeech.2014-80

Salakhutdinov, R., & Hinton, G. (2009). Deep Boltzmann machines. In D. van Dyk & M. Welling (Eds.), *Proceedings of the Twelth International Conference on Artificial Intelligence and Statistics* (Vol. 5, pp. 448–455). Proceedings of Machine Learning Research. Hilton Clearwater Beach Resort, Clearwater Beach, PMLR.

Schwefel, H.-P. (1981). *Numerical optimization of computer models.* John Wiley & Sons.

Vapnik, V. (2013). *The nature of statistical learning theory.* Springer Science & Business Media.

Warner, B., Crook, A., & Cao, R. (2020). Predicting the DJIA with news headlines and historic data using hybrid genetic algorithm/support vector regression and BERT. In *Big Data – BigData 2020* (pp. 23–37). Springer International Publishing.

Part II

Artificial Intelligence for Core Business Functions

Artificial Intelligence in Marketing and Sales

5

Abstract

Marketing is a core business function that has the most artificial intelligence applications nowadays. This chapter starts by introducing the evolution of AI in marketing, and then explores various AI technologies and features for marketing. These AI technologies include deep learning, neural networks, Naïve Bayes classifier, decision tree, anomaly detection, and genetic algorithms. The marketing applications and features are segmentation, targeting, forecasting, advertising, product pricing, sales management, and brand positioning. Two cases are provided on how Starbucks and App Annie are using AI in marketing.

Keywords

Deep learning · Neural networks · Naïve Bayes classifier · Decision tree · Anomaly detection · Rule-based system · Genetic algorithms · Segmentation · Targeting · Forecasting · Advertising · Product pricing · Sales management · Brand positioning · Marketing · Digital marketing · Personalized marketing

5.1 Introduction

Artificial intelligence has been introduced to the marketing and sales industry over the last decade. The difference it has made in the industry has increased and will continue to grow as time goes on. It has made our lives easier in ways we may not even think it would. Marketing and sales are important parts of a business because it is the way companies can attract customers to buy their products. AI can help businesses increase the visibility of a product which, in turn, increases sales for the company.

L. Chan et al., *Applied Artificial Intelligence in Business*, Applied Innovation and Technology Management, https://doi.org/10.1007/978-3-031-05740-3_5

AI has particular strengths in supporting decision-based situations that corporations face, especially when strategic intelligence is necessary. Although the concept is still relatively new, we know that AI can be applied to marketing because most of the marketing is based on collecting, processing, analyzing, and disseminating data, which can generally be quantified with mathematical formulas. We will introduce some artificial intelligence technologies and methods that have been recently applied to different areas of marketing. The processes and functions of businesses can run more efficiently and effectively due to the development of the different AI techniques (artificial neural networks, naive Bayesian classifiers, support vector machines, deep learning, decision tree, anomaly detection, genetic detection, genetic algorithms, reinforcement learning, etc.) and the applications of these techniques in different areas of marketing.

Marketing managers are responsible for making business decisions about products, prices, brands, advertising, etc. aiming to generate high sales for their company. As computational power has increased, we have seen a rise in the utilization of artificial intelligence. This technology has become more prominent in such marketing fields as sales and product pricing, market segmentation, customer profiling, and much more. The reasoning behind this increasing role of the use of AI algorithms is in savings of time and money for the businesses through upgrade of time-consuming or ineffective processes. Businesses are also able to make better decisions that are more catered toward their target audience based on data collection.

The advancements in machine learning combined with lower computing costs drive increased use of AI in the field of marketing. AI applied in marketing plays a substantial role in the execution of marketing decisions and actions. It is used in both traditional and digital marketing. Strategic marketing planning process incorporates marketing strategy, marketing research, and marketing action (Huang & Rust, 2021). AI benefits in these strategic marketing planning stages could be divided into mechanical, thinking, and feeling. Thus, in the process of strategic marketing decisions, mechanical, thinking, and feeling benefits of AI for market research stage, for example, are the following:

- Mechanical AI is used to collect data about the environment, customers, and the firm through multiple sources, such as video surveillance, in-car sensors, and surveys.
- Thinking AI can be used for market analysis, to predict market trends and identify competitors through the usage of machine learning algorithms.
- Feeling AI is used to better understand the customers on an emotional level—to understand customer needs, wants, feelings, and attitudes (Huang & Rust, 2021).

The marketing strategy sections of segmentation, targeting, and positioning correspond to mechanical, thinking, and feeling AI benefits accordingly. The components of marketing action: standardization, personalization, and relationalization could relate accordingly to benefits of mechanical AI, thinking AI, and feeling AI, respectively (Huang & Rust, 2021).

5.2 The Development of AI Technologies in Marketing

Artificial intelligence has already become an essential element in the marketing and sales area. Although AI was invented in the 1950s, the computational technology was not mature enough to be useful in business immediately and required future advancements in order to be used in business analytics decades later. Now the concept of big data is well known, as its popularity has been increasing since 2005. Artificial intelligence in marketing has advanced to a greater extent by using big data and algorithms. In 1984, one of the first products in business strategy software, The Sales Edge, developed in the area of the decision-making and interpersonal skills by Human Edge Software Corporation of Palo Alto and combined technologies of simple human factor assessment, expert systems, codification of research-based finding, and expert opinions and decision theory (Collins, 1984). The program would base its evaluations and recommendations on three main steps: self-assessment, customer assessment, and sales strategy report.

In the 2000s, a large number of artificial intelligence systems were developed. The GA-RBF algorithm is one of them (Doganis et al., 2006). This unique conversational program is one of the few microcomputer programs. The system is a combination of two artificial intelligence technologies, which are the radial basis function (RBF) neutral network architecture and a specifically designed genetic algorithm (GA). These methodologies have been used to improve sales forecasting. Accurate sales forecasting is important to meet sales goals and reduce the waste. Especially for the food industry, a successful sales forecasting system can be very beneficial because of the short shelf-life of many food products, the uncertainty in consumer demand, and the maintenance of the product quality which is related to human health. The methodology is applied well to deal with the short shelf-life of food products, especially fresh milk provided by a major manufacturing company of dairy products. The main goals of this system are to illustrate a new technology and use of microcomputers and to solve day-to-day selling problems faced by sales representatives.

Since the 2010s, the development of artificial intelligence in marketing grew in areas of brand management and customer experience personalization, connecting with customers and tracking the marketing efforts. Marketing teams must find the best AI technologies and methodologies to use if they want to have a positive impact in brand recognition, market penetration, and revenues for the company. Implementation of custom artificial intelligence algorithms can help give that brand an edge in the marketplace. Currently, the demand for professionals in AI (professional mathematicians, data scientists, and software engineers) outweighs the supply of qualified professionals and continues to grow.

The current state of AI in market research is difficult to pinpoint due to the technological changes in trends that are happening in our world today. Over the past few years, we have seen a significant shift from traditional in-store shopping to online shopping. This has caused marketers to make changes to their own marketing techniques in order to reach their consumers. Some of these changes include the applications of intelligent agent technologies (IATs) into marketing research. An example of such an IAT application is GloBuddy2 which learns contextually relevant concepts through phrase extraction based on user data and ConceptNet (a large-scale semantic network created with natural language processing) commonsense approach (Kumar et al., 2016; Lieberman et al., 2004). This allows market researchers to further understand what their consumers are searching, and they can then narrow their research to better connect with those consumers.

Apart from traditional marketing, AI is also used in the customer relationship and promotional aspect to reach out and communicate with consumers through all the noise present in social media marketing. It is also used in advertising to optimize ad spending, improve ad placement and relevance, enhance ad quality, tailor customer messages, and effectively communicate with potential customers. Employed by marketing and trained on data from the internet and advertisements, AI-enabled systems can determine what kind of ads is best suited for their specific audience (Schmelzer, 2020). These systems track performances of ad campaigns and changes in the market, aiding in development of advertisement expenditure plans with estimated optimal costs, means, and timing of promotions. Ad content could be tailored by AI-enabled tools to reach global consumers quickly and efficiently, designed to adhere to their particular cultural aspects, beliefs, and languages. Automatic AI ad monitoring helps reduce ads that violate various community and platform rules and fraudulent ads (Schmelzer, 2020). Ad monitoring and moderation with AI has become important especially for social media firms, since they are constantly challenged by foreign bots, political campaigns, and other ethically challenging advertising (Schmelzer, 2020).

5.3 AI Technologies for Marketing

Various kinds of AI technologies are used in the marketing world, providing numerous advantages for their users. Machine learning has allowed marketers to gain insights and propose solutions to the interactions between businesses and consumers. Various machine learning methods like support-vector machine, topic models, ensemble trees, deep neural networks, and network embedding have been used in marketing research, forecasting, and decision-making (Ma & Sun, 2020).

5.3.1 Deep Learning

Deep learning is an area of machine learning that can be applied to many different subfields of marketing. Deep learning is machine learning that focuses on algorithms that are inspired by the structure and function of the human brain. Deep learning methods use multiple representation levels, implemented with multilevel neural networks, using big data and large amounts of computing power (Ma & Sun, 2020). Specific data problems that require deep learning include semantic indexing, data tagging, fast information retrieval, and discriminative modeling (Najafabadi et al. 2015). Siau and Yang (2017) summarized that AI, robotics, and machine learning are revolutionizing the field of marketing and sales. AI algorithms could be helpful for the world of business and marketing in eliminating some company performance errors that arise from worker fatigue or accidental errors. Deep learning can be applied to different areas of marketing with extensive amounts of data including areas like consumer data, consumer behavior, and forecasting. The recommender systems for content platforms and e-commerce sites like Netflix and Amazon are powered by complex machine learning algorithms, while Facebook uses deep learning to analyze and categorize billion social media images (Ma & Sun, 2020). Deep learning in big data analytics can also be applied to market segmentation through classification (to classify and group current and future customers based on different factors) and prediction.

5.3.2 Artificial Neural Networks (ANNs)

Artificial neural networks have been applied to different categories of marketing that can greatly contribute to corporations gaining a competitive advantage. Artificial neural networks are intelligent systems that were inspired by neural networks in brains (Ma & Sun, 2020). Neural networks are composed of artificial neurons—interconnected processing units—and trained by the adjustment of the values of the connections of those neurons. They have many different capabilities including self-learning capabilities, fault tolerance, and noise immunity. Some applications of artificial neural networks include system identification, pattern recognition, classification, speech recognition, and image processing. Artificial neural networks can be applied to the marketing industry by measuring the effectiveness of advertisements and studying the factors that influence the effectiveness. Ramalingam et al. (2006) used ANN to measure advertisement effectiveness. Weights adjustments in the ANN were done using the backpropagation algorithm for this application. In an experiment conducted in 2005, the results showed (using the S3 model) that the backpropagation algorithm was effective (99%), as it was able to use the 13 input factors (affective, attention, attraction, changes, desire, economics, emotions, exposure, influence, persuasion, psychological, senses, and social) and outputs and capture the nonlinear relationships between them (Ramalingam et al., 2006). ANN captured nonlinear relationships of 13 factors and output. One of the three models used showed 99% accuracy for measuring advertising effectiveness, based on criteria of engaging customers, delivering relevant messages, and achieving advertiser's objectives (Ramalingam et al., 2006). Overall, artificial intelligence in the form of artificial neural networks has revolutionized many different industries, especially the marketing sector.

5.3.3 Naïve Bayes Classifier

The Naïve Bayes classifier is an artificial intelligence technique that has contributed greatly to the marketing field. Batrinca and Treleaven (2015) explain the naive

Bayesian classifier to be a probabilistic classifier that is based on Bayes' theorem that assumes features or attributes within each class are independent of one another. Zhang and Su (2004) explain Naïve Bayes to be a high-performance classification as well as ranking algorithm even when compared to state-of-the-art decision tree algorithms. Classification learning problems start with learners trying to construct classifiers from training examples containing class labels. There are many areas of marketing where classifiers may be applied, including marketing segmentation, direct marketing, forecasting, analyzing data, classifying data, and ranking. One area that naïve Bayes performs extremely well in is ranking, even though it does not perform too well for regression problems or probability estimates. Zhang and Su (2004) prove theorems that Naive Bayes is globally optimal in ranking on conjunctive concepts (having multiple attributes) as well as on m-of-n concepts (function that is true if m or more out of n attributes are true). It does well in ranking and classification because it tolerates the estimation error of class probabilities (Zhang & Su, 2004).

Zhang and Su conducted an experiment to compare the effectiveness of the naïve Bayesian classifier and the decision tree algorithm in ranking. They compared the two algorithms, one being naïve Bayes and the other C4.4 (decision tree), with a T-test of a confidence level of 95%. They concluded that with AUC (area under the receiver operating characteristics curve) being the criteria, Naive Bayes scored at 90.36% on average, while the C4.4 scored 85.25% on average. Considering that C4.4 decision tree algorithm was specifically designed for high AUC, this shows how well Naive Bayesian performs at ranking. The outstanding performance of naïve Bayes on ranking can be applied by marketers in the business world to the ranking of customers on the likelihood of them buying certain products. Using ranking in this scenario is very important and useful in direct marketing, and the method may be used in forecasting. Naïve Bayes classifier can also be employed in social media analytics since it calculates the probability of a text belonging to different categories it is tested against (Batrinca & Treleaven, 2015). Xia and Jin (2008) also explain that classifiers (like decision trees and naïve Bayesian) are able to predict customer churn effectively as well.

5.3.4 Decision Tree

Another artificial intelligence technique that can be applied to the marketing field is the decision tree algorithm. The decision tree algorithm is a classification algorithm that can classify large amounts of data. The most common and popular algorithm that is used is the C4.5 algorithm. C4.5 is an efficient decision tree algorithm that creates a tree model by using values of one attribute at a time (Karim & Rahman, 2013). The first application that is suggested from the decision tree algorithm for businesses is for profit maximization. Profit optimal decision trees are constructed when algorithms split data sets and make decision trees from them. These decision trees are able to help corporations maximize profit. Karim and Rahman (2013) also explain that the rules of the decision tree induction algorithm, specifically the k-action rules, can be applied to maximize profit when moving from one decision to another. The algorithm utilizes decision trees for the maximization of profit by taking the decision tree as input and finding the best actions to take. Another application of decision trees in the marketing field is for advertising. Other research articles state that decision trees may be applied to predict customer churn (Kim et al., 2001). Although research shows that traditional decision tree algorithms do not produce good probability estimates or probability-based rankings, there has been substantial work put into improving the ranking quality of decision tree algorithms.

5.3.5 Anomaly Detection

Another artificial intelligence technique that can greatly benefit the marketing field is anomaly detection. Anomaly detection is the detection, prediction, and identification of data, items, or values that do not match the expected results of a group or a set of values. Multiple areas of marketing can apply anomaly detection including market forecasting, social media analytics, and advertising. Advertising is a very important field of marketing with the goal of customer communication, influencing, and buying persuasion. The objectives of advertising are attracting customers to potentially buy the products, defining the target market, and reaching out to the customers with an effective and persuasive ad campaign. Advertising was revolutionized by the Internet with personalization, customization, and direct marketing. Advertising can essentially enable marketers to engage with their audiences and potential customers in real time (Zhou & Shariat, 2016). The third-party data, module, or incoming traffic in online advertising and in real-time bidding (buying and selling of advertising in real time) can result in an unexpected behavior of systems, which in turn can negatively affect multiple advertisers. The advertisers can screen the health of the system with the monitoring systems that use anomaly detection algorithms. Some of the important key performance indicators in advertising are campaign spending, conversion rate, number of submitted ad impressions, and click-through rate. Zhou and Shariat (2016) propose anomaly detection algorithms as a robust and reliable monitoring system on the outputs of campaign spending and performance. The authors' anomaly detection system was deployed in their production cluster and successfully detected several significant system issues. Although anomaly detection is a fairly new development, it has a high potential to benefit marketers and advertising firms.

5.3.6 Genetic Algorithms

Genetic algorithms have greatly benefited many industries, including the marketing industry. Genetic algorithms are methods for solving problems (usually optimization) based on Darwin's theory of natural selection. Genetic algorithms (GAs) are found to provide near-optimal solutions for optimization problems. GAs are able to group data based on similar attributes (Gruca and Klemz, 2003). Some areas of marketing that can benefit from genetic algorithms are market segmentation, brand management, pricing strategies, advertising, and product positioning. The experiment conducted by Gruca and Klemz in 2011 explained how genetic algorithm procedure (GA SEARCH) was combined with a neural network to solve an optimal product positioning problem and outperformed the best available algorithm at that time (PRODSRCH). Considering GA is very effective at clustering, it shows that it would be really effective in market segmentation. It was also found that genetic algorithms are very effective in optimization. One example is optimal pricing in competitive markets. Sohn et al. (2009) explain how genetic algorithms can be applied to pricing strategies. The researchers perform scenario analysis to find the optimal pricing policy that will maximize revenue under different price elasticities. Because the process is so complex, artificial intelligence needs to be applied in the form of genetic algorithms. The results of the scenario showed that the dynamic pricing model produced higher profit outcomes than previously achieved and, as a result, shows the effectiveness of genetic algorithms for optimal pricing of products with profit maximization.

5.3.7 Rule-Based System

Another, but less popular type of AI that is used in marketing is rule-based system AI (also known as expert systems or production systems). Although not as effective, compared to machine learning AI, it can still provide marketers with a faster solution or workarounds that some machine learning methods cannot. The benefit that rule-based AI has brought to marketers is the ability to store and sort data while producing predefined outcomes (which are usually based on specific rules created by a human expert in a specific field). These benefits have then helped marketers interpret information in a way that is helpful for them to run operations more efficiently and effectively. Rule-based AI can be useful during decision-making situations that are known in advance, while machine learning algorithms, while learning, can adjust those rules (Pradeep et al., 2018). The term usually applies to systems with man-made rules, mostly requiring the knowledge of human experts and containing a series of IF-THEN statements that could be useful for marketing approval programs and recommendation systems (Pradeep et al., 2018).

The introduction of machine learning and other AI-based methods has helped the marketing field significantly. With these emerging technologies, marketing teams become more operationally efficient and can reach out to the customers much more effectively.

5.4 Application Areas of AI in Marketing

There are different subfields of marketing that use artificial intelligence, including market segmentation, market targeting, sales and product pricing, customer churn analysis, market forecasting, advertising, and social media analytics. These

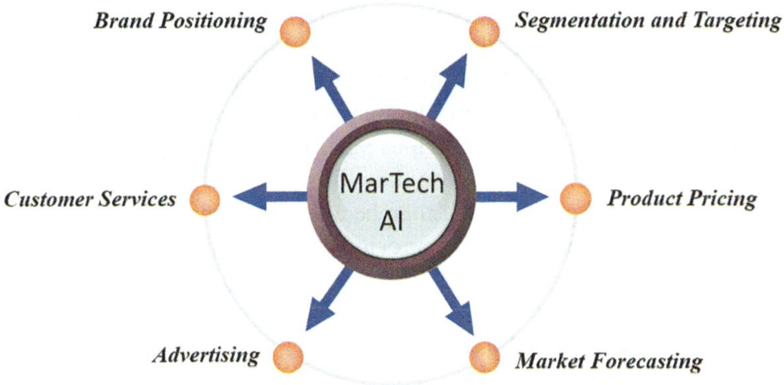

Fig. 5.1 AI application areas in marketing

subsections of marketing and sales all have been affected by AI and machine learning. The following sections will describe how the subsections of marketing have utilized artificial intelligence to be more effective and efficient to their advantage in the business world. AI applications for customer services are an important category, and we will explore more details about it in the next chapter (Fig. 5.1).

5.4.1 Market Segmentation and Targeting

Artificial intelligence can be directly applied to market segmentation by segmenting customers very adequately. Research shows that personalized marketing outreaches are up to 14% more effective than mass marketing methods. This being said, consumer demand for personalized outreach creates the need for accurate and unbiased customer segmentation. By segmenting consumers into groups of similar interests and needs, businesses can tailor marketing campaigns to suit the groups' needs and make ads more relevant to individuals within the group. Some ways that AI can help in marketing segmentation include:

- Removing human bias when placing consumers in groups.
- Finding hidden patterns within data that a human marketer may miss.
- Automatically updating segments in a rapidly changing environment.
- Having a nearly infinite level of scalability.

AI has also been applied to market targeting in recent years. Large corporations such as Amazon have applied AI to market targeting through the combination of market segmentation and a prediction method based on previous consumer input, search history, and buying habits. A complex AI recommendation algorithm then generates purchasing recommendations for the consumer based on the data that was collected. Since Amazon has implemented this system, they have noticed a 29% increase in sales. Amazon is a great example for a highly scalable AI market targeting system because of the large amount of data that Amazon has collected in the past years, ascribed to the high amount of website traffic it receives. Systems such as these are able to give high-quality recommendations within seconds based on the amount of data that the algorithm has on a consumer. When such corporations get a new user, they have no previous purchase or search history and therefore have no data for a recommendation to draw from. But, as soon as that user starts purchasing items, the algorithm will then be able to accumulate different items to recommend to the customer, based on previous buying habits.

5.4.2 Sales and Product Pricing

Sales and product pricing is a marketing subfield that has seen recent applications of artificial intelligence. For many years, corporations have based their pricing from supply and demand. This is a basic law of economics, and a successful business is well aware of this law and how to use it to its advantage through the concept of dynamic pricing. Although this has been the common technique for pricing for a long time, with the help of AI, it can be improved based on algorithms that compare historical and current demand, supply, competition, and sales. AI can thus use this method to automatically read through data and determine a product's equilibrium price.

Examples of this application are travel companies such as Uber and American Airlines, using this process to determine their prices at any given time. Uber uses this method by adjusting their prices based on driver supply and demand conditions. When there are a limited number of drivers, Uber will notify both the consumer and potential drivers of higher fare charges, so that they may limit the demand and increase the supply by attempting to get more Uber drivers on the road. On the pricing side of the marketing dynamic, society is seeing the growth of AI in forecasting systems that implement AI technologies to research, analyze, and develop effective pricing information based on consumer data from the community or area.

Product pricing is a complex process. A price tag too low can hinder a business' ability to generate revenue, while a price too high can drive away potential consumers. Marketers started to utilize AI systems in price forecasting and are continuously developing and updating the technologies to provide even more accurate predictions. For example, in the Australian electricity market, marketers have begun using artificial neural network (ANN) methods, automatically mapping the relationship between input and output vectors, learning about it and saving their weights and biases, and fuzzy logic models (FLMs) that transfer structured human knowledge into feasible mathematics (Aggarwal et al., 2008).

While there are a multitude of artificial intelligence software programs currently serving various functions in applications across a wide spectrum of market segments, there are particular technologies that stir up more excitement and immediate technological, if not financial, windfalls. For example, Pace is an artificial intelligence program that utilizes machine learning to enable hotel management professionals to explore pricing that matches supply and demand. This could allow hotels to maximize their profits by offering the price that customers are willing to pay based on their demographics and the time of year among other factors. These hotels would have the ability to forecast increases or decreases in booking frequency based on customer demographics and adjust prices accordingly. Then, after taking Pace's pricing suggestion into account, management could more easily make a final decision and post the price to websites such Booking.com or Trivago.

5.4.3 Market Research and Forecasting

There have been many AI techniques that have been applied to market forecasting in recent years. AI-powered sales forecasting software is beginning to outperform and outpredict human representatives. Dave Stone, the founder of Red Sky Solutions, says that AI-powered sales forecasting software vendor Clari can get within 5–7% of forecast accuracy, while most people may only get within 25–30% (Kaneshige, 2018). AI forecasting software vendors like Clari promise to double forecast accuracy and, as a result, fix the long-standing "business blind spot." Clari CEO Andy Byrne mentioned that their AI-powered forecasting software collects data on past deals; gathers related data signals like emails, phone calls, and meetings; and analyzes their relationship with sales outcomes (Kaneshige, 2018). AI sales forecasting is increasingly integrated with CRM (customer relationship management) systems, maximizing corporation's profits.

Forecasting programs from only several years ago have been adapted to include AI technology to track patterns and come up with more accurate sales forecasts. These advanced systems are now being implemented to correct older systems and provide businesses with better data analysis so that they may see a better business flow as well as increase productivity and profit. New technologies move forward toward intelligent automation through partnerships, such as IBM's Watson (combining systems that analyze raw data) and Salesforce's Einstein, that emphasizes on business analytics and forecasting data, to create accurate personalized and localized customer recommendations (Needle, 2017).

The market research department uses a multitude of AI technologies to help better understand their consumers' needs. One of those technologies is the use of multi-agent software systems. This software system communicates between multiple different intelligent agents in the system in order to receive information provided by the customer (type of purchase, quantity, time of purchase, etc.). Researchers Daskou and Mangina (2003) discussed the use of new intelligent software frameworks that can integrate databases of loyalty programs, customer surveys and qualitative studies to establish information-based relationships with end users and retailers. This helps market researchers interpret the data that they are receiving so they can adapt their marketing techniques to better suit the needs of their customers.

5.4.4 Advertising

Advertising is an area of marketing that has seen many applications of AI in the past few years. The current available AI techniques for advertising are primarily based on collaborative filtering, preference scoring, or rule-based techniques. Collaborative filtering selects advertisements for customers based on the opinions of other customers with similar past preferences. The preference-scoring approach to personalized recommendation uses a preference-score concept to select personalized advertisements based on initial customer profile, purchase history, and behavior in internet stores. In the rule-based approach, marketing rules from marketing experts are a core component in providing personalized advertisements. This rule-based technique greatly depends on the quality of the knowledge in the rule base. Machine learning through AI derives insightful knowledge from data, observations, and past solutions that could help strengthen the rule-based technique.

Since artificial intelligence has been introduced into the advertising world, it has changed the means of advertising in order to reach the right consumers. For example, advertisers are changing from newspaper advertisements, popular in the past, to online advertisements that pop up on websites displaying web users' recent browsing products or purchases. AI has changed the way advertisers spend their time on their advertisements. Caroline Klatt, the CEO of a chatbot technology company called Headliner Labs, said "AI capabilities are making ad-spend decisions simpler, more efficient and cost-effective" (Liffreing, 2018). AI is helping put advertisements out easier than ever before so the advertisers can focus more on customer experience and strategy.

One of the most often used AI technologies in advertising is image recognition. Image recognition helps advertisers identify consumer products in pictures and interpret their depiction. The advertisers then can analyze the types of consumers that like particular types of products and look at ways to market the product to more consumers like that or strategize how to reach certain market segments. Advertisers also use machine learning to help them advertise the right products to consumers. Using machine learning, advertisers can gather information from customers' online search activity and display searched items in ads that pop up on user browsers, so the person will keep looking at the same thing, making them more convinced to buy it. For example, if a person is looking at Nike shoes on a certain website, AI can embed the picture of the product this person just looked at in the online ad at another site so the picture of the product that was searched keeps popping up.

5.4.5 Brand Positioning

Brand positioning is another subfield of marketing that has seen recent applications of artificial intelligence. Kevin Keohane in his recent article "Brand Management in the age of AI" describes three emerging principles of brand management in the current age of AI: "purpose is king," "limber up," and "radical, real-time collaboration" (Keohane, 2021). The first principle, "purpose is king," describes the importance of corporate strategy for competitive advantage. In the new AI era, corporations know more about their consumer base than ever before, and vice versa as well. To stay competitive, it is important for them to display a clear goal, mission statement, vision, and values and to use these to guide the decisions they make. The second principle—"limber up"—describes the importance of brand management consistency and redefining brand guidelines. Having brand guidelines is important, but it is equally important to remain fluid and open to change to reflect changes in society. The third principle—"radical, real-time collaboration"—stresses the importance of balance in organizations. Corporations need to let the data findings (and other inputs) about their customers impact the edges of their band ecosystem in real time. It is important for corporations to balance maintaining long-term purpose, health, and equity of the brand while also evolving and managing the brand on an ongoing, iterative basis (Keohane, 2021).

AI technologies like expert systems, machine learning, and image recognition are used in brand positioning. Brand positioning requires successful decision-making strategies. Therefore, decision-making AI technologies will impact the future of this field. Expert systems (ES) and interactive decision support systems (IDSS) are the technologies that assist in marketing decision-making efforts. An article on marketing expert systems discusses the emergence of those systems through interactive logic and the importance of ES and IDSS for analysis, diagnosis, and decision assistance (Orzan et al., 2011). New decision-making environment emerged based on the learning capabilities of those systems, their situational and solution-based memorization (Orzan et al., 2011). Assistance, analysis, and intelligent diagnosis of market expert systems lead to development of intelligent marketing decision-making.

There are more related topics on AI for marketing and sales. We will discuss it in another chapter on AI for retail and customer services. In the following section, we introduce two cases to illustrate how marketing applications can use AI algorithms to provide better business solutions.

Case 5.1: Starbucks: Personalized Marketing

Personalized marketing has completely changed the online marketing industry through the use of big data and artificial intelligence. Data collection and use are growing in our information technology era. The global Coronavirus pandemic has shifted everything online within the past year with millions of people worldwide spending more time browsing the internet. Personalized marketing is a form of a direct marketing strategy, where a marketer directly promotes an advertisement to a specific individual or group. This strategy is different in comparison to traditional marketing approaches, wherein customer groups were targeted via billboards, print advertisements, cold calls, TV, radio, and other tactics. New marketing strategies can take advantage of both online marketing and traditional marketing.

Starbucks and its marketing team are no exception when it comes to using these technologies to gain a competitive advantage. A few examples of the Starbucks marketing team's use of AI to gain a competitive advantage are:

- Predictive analytics (allowing marketers to bring personalized messages).
- Deep Brew (AI that allows deeper insights into consumer preferences and marketers to have a deeper understanding of consumers).
- Chatbots ("My Starbucks Barista"—an AI-based conversational ordering system, which can keep track of customer orders and be helpful to marketers).

The use of predictive analytics has allowed Starbucks to create and bring personalized marketing messages to their consumers. By using collected data, algorithms, and machine learning techniques, Starbucks can better understand consumer needs and deliver personalized marketing messages to their consumers. These business practices enable Starbucks to bring returning customers back to their stores and increase public awareness about their products and services.

Deep Brew, one of Starbucks' major technological initiatives, uses AI tools to drive the brand's personalization engine, optimize store labor allocations, and more. But most importantly, it allows the company and their marketing team to gain a deeper insight and better understanding of their consumers, which leads to creation of better marketing strategies. Deep Brew is applied to the company's rewards program (Future Stores), collecting large amounts of data from consumers, and providing marketers with analytics on the consumer needs.

Starbucks chatbot, My Starbucks Barista, can keep track of customer orders and provide valuable data to the company's market team. My Starbucks Barista serves as a virtual assistant that can take customer orders and payment information for customers' drinks or food without the need to stay in line at the physical store, streamlining the ordering process.

Predictive and prescriptive analytics are implemented in various business areas, providing valued suggestions for marketing professionals' strategies and tactics, while processing collected big data. Historically marketers have been utilizing past sales, inventory, customer count, and hundreds of other variables to predict future outcomes. The growth in AI implementation in marketing services focuses on customer retention flowed into the area of predictive intelligence. In a situation of a predictive analysis AI, initially, the system collects information from different aspects of the business, such as customer interactions or an expected project timeline, based on similar previous projects. Then, the data is formulated into a report for marketers that show previous trends and the likelihood of events based on certain scenarios (e.g., predictions of an increased need in customer service between Thanksgiving and Christmas due to increases in gift orders). Machine learning and pattern recognition are used to predict certain outcomes and outline several scenarios based on the learned information. Some companies outsource predictive and prescriptive analytics platform design work to companies specializing in those services. An example of such a company would be the small start-up in Seattle, Amperity, which provides their AI program "Fridays" for their customers, small businesses. Their AI program is able to collect data from the customer purchases of the client and online interactions with the client's website and provide a structured report and detailed recommendations for those businesses based on the data received.

Combining all these uses of AI and ML put Starbucks' marketing at a competitive advantage compared to companies that have not integrated AI in their marketing strategies.

Case 5.2: App Annie: Digital Marketing Optimization
In recent years, businesses are rapidly transforming to digital marketing. We are aware how consumers are bombarded with advertising constantly on digital media every day. Businesses know how strategically placed ads are crucial to catching consumer attention. If a company has amazing advertisements that do not reach the target market, it is the same as if the marketing does not exist. AI has been rapidly adopted into this area of marketing in order to streamline the process and make things easier for marketers. This application pinpoints how marketers are using the new technologies to successfully get the message of their product or service out to the public in the most efficient way possible.

App Annie is a software company specialized in enabling client businesses to gain a competitive advantage through intelligent software application analysis. They currently offer a tiered pricing system for companies to strategize with free or premium options. The free option contains basic functionality for smaller businesses, while the premium option contains a suite of additional capabilities for companies looking to maximize their sales and pricing potential. This is accomplished by optimizing data search and usage by client companies emphasizing five core principles: discover, strategize, acquire, engage, and monetize. App Annie company currently has two main software products, App Annie Intelligence platform and App Annie Connect. The platform is the focus of this case.

The App Annie Intelligence platform aggregates raw sales, growth, and revenue data on an annual basis from the client company and industry competitors to produce a graphical interface product, comparing various aspects of growth, loss, and efficiency. It also aggregates downloads, usage, and engagement metrics, streamlining the raw data into an easily accessible end product in order for clients to recognize industry opportunities and threats. The software also uses keyword search technology to drive users to client company app store websites while monitoring competitors' app store data and helping to optimize advertising budgets by averaging cost-per-install conversion rate across countries and categories.

The App Annie platform automatically creates algorithms based on keywords, phrases, and technological clues in order to search for and collect data based on previously selected parameters. The software also learns as it collects, becoming smarter and more efficient at repeated tasks and program priorities, increasing the processing accuracy of the data collection and analysis each time the function is performed. The App Annie software's graphical interface is dynamic and displays information on any number of metrics, including keyword searches, industry competitor brand positioning, and marketing budget optimization. This enables companies to build and maintain relevant sales and pricing applications.

In order to assist marketers in getting their advertisements sufficient online viewership, the AI technologies collect data from consumers through tracking things such as cookies or the number of times a certain advertisement was clicked on for a certain period of time. This data is then compiled for the marketers who are given a report detailing the amount of attention their content is receiving, which allows them to make a decision, for example, whether to keep investing in an online click-on advertisement that is only getting ten views/interactions a day. The AI uses algorithms such as deep learning to adapt to and recognize patterns in the data, allowing the system to provide suggestions or business strategies.

The most prominent aspect of this application is the ability for most businesses with an online presence to utilize this technology in some way or another. Established corporations may have a section within their marketing department to fund their own research and create customized programs to collect and analyze data. Businesses in this scenario will need to invest more resources in related market research, in order to fully utilize the AI technologies.

5.5 Key Takeaways

Overall, marketing sectors can benefit tremendously from AI technology, especially when a number of companies are turning to e-commerce branding and e-marketing. AI technology helps marketers develop their content and perform their research. Businesses and marketers with the help of AI technologies can increase their customer's engagement with content, product promotion, and "product push," by publishing games and contests on their sites. For example, companies may implement a reward program that is also a game that consumers can play and win a promo code to their sites or other benefits. This not only creates more engagements but also increases customer interest and brand loyalty. A company that has successfully implemented gamification is Samsung. Samsung has created a section on their site that allows customers to watch videos and discuss their issues. Such customer activities gain them badges and points as well as campaigns that fit their taste.

Other advantages of AI technology to marketers are quicker and convenient consumer data processing, allowing quicker customer response; timely data analytics reports and better ability to react to changes in the marketplace.

5.6 Conclusion

Marketing is already a field that is constantly growing and being redeveloped at its core and outlying spheres, and with the addition of AI to the ranks, the field is revolutionizing with continuous improvements. Any marketer knows the three key strategic decisions: segmentation, targeting, and positioning (Huang & Rust, 2021). By using AI technology, companies can curate a personalized experience and content for their consumers. This means that it allows companies and consumers to have a deeper relationship through using AI technology mixed with the marketing strategic decision method. This outcome is something that marketers dream of, finding ways to promote a loyal customer base that will consistently buy the given product or service. We also have to consider the 4Ps and 4Cs of marketing that can be satisfied through AI. By using joint analysis, the marketing department has a much easier time deciding how the product will be received by the general public and the customers. This area is very important when it comes to marketing, because how much you push and market a product and service can impact how well the product sells and grabs people's attention.

Due to the recent development of AI technology within the marketing field, it has grown to new depths. The slow acceptance of technology mixed with marketing strategies enabled a more mainstream form of marketing to become a powerhouse for consumer interaction with businesses. Third-party software and applications that help curate big data and aid marketing departments' content reach new levels have become possible because of AI. Engagement of AI technologies allows marketers to personalize and analyze consumer interests, positioning platforms, engagement strategies, and their duration. AI technology gives marketers a greater power in predicting consumers' wants without having to exhaust as many previously required pre-AI resources. Even though the use of AI technology is still new and needs to be studied further, the marketing sector has been successfully utilizing AI-based technologies in various aspects of their work.

References

Aggarwal, S. K., Saini, L. M., & Kumar, A. (2008). Price forecasting using wavelet transform and LSE based mixed model in Australian electricity market. *International Journal of Energy Sector Management, 2*(4), 521–546.

Batrinca, B., & Treleaven, P. C. (2015). Social media analytics: A survey of techniques, tools and platforms. *AI & SOCIETY, 30*(1), 89–116.

Collins, R. H. (1984). Artificial intelligence in personal selling. *Journal of Personal Selling & Sales Management, 4*(1), 58–66.

Daskou, S., & Mangina, E. E. (2003). Artificial intelligence in managing market relationships: The use of intelligence agents. *Journal of Relationship Marketing, 2*(1-2), 85–102.

Doganis, P., Alexandridis, A., Patrinos, P., & Sarimveis, H. (2006). Time series sales forecasting for short shelf-life food products based on artificial neural networks and evolutionary computing. *Journal of Food Engineering, 75*(2), 196–204.

Gruca, T. S., & Klemz, B. R. (2003). Optimal new product positioning: A genetic algorithm approach. *European Journal of Operational Research, 146*(3), 621–633.

Huang, M. H., & Rust, R. T. (2021). A strategic framework for artificial intelligence in marketing. *Journal of the Academy of Marketing Science, 49*, 30–50. https://link.springer.com/article/10.1007/s11747-020-00749-9

Kaneshige, T. (February 20, 2018). *Zero One: AI transforms sales forecasting*. https://www.channelfutures.com/strategy/zero-one-ai-transforms-sales-forecasting

Karim, M., & Rahman, R. M. (2013). Decision tree and naive bayes algorithm for classification and generation of actionable knowledge for direct marketing. *Journal of Software Engineering and Applications, 6*(4), 196–206. https://doi.org/10.4236/jsea.2013.64025

Keohane, K. (2021). *Brand management in the age of AI*. https://marketingedge.com.ng/brand-management-in-the-age-of-ai/

Kim, J. W., Lee, B. H., Shaw, M. J., Chang, H. L., & Nelson, M. (2001). Application of decision-tree induction techniques to personalized advertisements on internet storefronts. *International Journal of Electronic Commerce, 5*(3), 45–62.

Kumar, V., Dixit, A., Javalgi, R. R. G., & Dass, M. (2016). Research framework, strategies, and applications of intelligent agent technologies (IATs) in marketing. *Journal of the Academy of Marketing Science, 44*(1), 24–45.

Lieberman, H., Faaborg, A., Espinosa, J., & Stocky, T. (2004). Commonsense on the go. *BT Technology Journal, 22*(4), 241–252. https://doi.org/10.1023/B:BTTJ.0000047602.54693.3d

Liffreing, I. (January 19, 2018). *The state of AI in marketing in 5 charts*. https://digiday.com/marketing/state-ai-marketing-5-charts/

Ma, L., & Sun, B. (2020). Machine learning and AI in marketing – Connecting computing power to human insights. *International Journal of Research in Marketing, 37*(3), 481–504.

Najafabadi, M. M., Villanustre, F., Khoshgoftaar, T. M., Seliya, N., Wald, R., & Muharemagic, E. (2015). Deep learning applications and challenges in big data analytics. *Journal of big data, 2*(1), 1–21.

Needle, D. (March 7, 2017). IBM Watson, Salesforce Einstein Team Up in AI App Partnership. https://www.eweek.com/storage/ibm-watson-salesforce-einstein-team-up-in-ai-app-partnership/

Orzan, G., Orzan, M., & Stoica, I. (2011). Marketing expert systems. *International Journal of Arts & Sciences, 4*(22), 233.

Pradeep, A. K., Appel, A., & Sthanunathan, S. (2018). *AI for marketing and product innovation: Powerful new tools for predicting trends, connecting with customers, and closing sales*. John Wiley & Sons.

Ramalingam, V., Palaniappan, B., Panchanatham, N., & Palanivel, S. (2006). Measuring advertisement effectiveness—A neural network approach. *Expert Systems with Applications, 31*(1), 159–163.

Schmelzer, R. (2020). AI makes a splash in advertising. *Forbes*, June 18, 2020. https://www.forbes.com/sites/cognitiveworld/2020/06/18/ai-makes-a-splash-in-advertising/?sh=55ddc7ad7682

Siau, K., & Yang, Y. (2017). *Impact of artificial intelligence, robotics, and machine learning on sales and marketing* (pp. 18–19). Twelve Annual Midwest Association for Information Systems Conference (MWAIS 2017).

Sohn, S. Y., Moon, T. H., & Seok, K. J. (2009). Optimal pricing for mobile manufacturers in competitive market using genetic algorithm. *Expert Systems with Applications, 36*(2), 3448–3453.

Xia, G. E., & Jin, W. D. (2008). Model of customer churn prediction on support vector machine. *Systems Engineering - Theory & Practice, 28*(1), 71–77.

Zhang, H., & Su, J. (2004). Naive bayesian classifiers for ranking. In *European conference on machine learning* (pp. 501–512). Springer.

Zhou, B., & Shariat, S. (2016). *Finding needle in a million metrics: Anomaly detection in a large-scale computational advertising platform*. TargetAd 2016: 2nd International Workshop on Ad Targeting at Scale, WSDM, February 22–25, 2016, San Francisco, CA, USA.

Artificial Intelligence for Customer Service

6

Abstract

Customer services are closely related to marketing and sales. In this chapter, we focus on how AI can be used for improving customer services. Some key AI technologies for customer services include deep learning, support vector machines, natural language processing, and hybrid AI systems. The main features and applications include collaborative filtering, recommendation engines, customer profiling, and customer churn analysis. This chapter provides three case studies on Nordstrom, HashMe AI, and Massively Chatbots.

Keywords

Support vector machines · Natural language processing · Naive Bayesian classification · Chatbots · Hybrid AI systems · Collaborative filtering · Recommendation engines · Social media analytics · Customer service · Customer profiling · Customer loyalty · Customer churn analysis

6.1 Introduction

The ability to communicate and develop relationships with customers is instrumental to the success of a company. Customer service gives businesses an opportunity to market themselves to their customers through great customer service even after a product or service is provided, so it would be ideal if every customer interaction was consistent, fast, and effective. Therefore, many businesses turn to AI technology to increase their customer service bandwidth. Artificial intelligence can collect and utilize large amounts of data, making it ideal for customer service improvement. Many customer service interactions are highly dependent on parsing past data and experiences to assist current consumers, which plays to the strengths of artificial intelligence technology.

L. Chan et al., *Applied Artificial Intelligence in Business*, Applied Innovation and Technology Management, https://doi.org/10.1007/978-3-031-05740-3_6

Artificial intelligence is paving the path for a new and improved customer service experience, ranging from automated voices answering your questions when you call customer service, to live "chatbot" robots who will reply to your message directly on the company's website. This relatively new technology will be increasingly encountered by customers all around the world, as companies are encouraged to implement it. This compounding forward progression of artificial intelligence might get deeply intertwined in our daily lives and might make us more comfortable with the idea of automated customer services. The automated interactions should leave the customer satisfied, with correct procedures to address the issues quickly and acceptably. Some customers still prefer to interact with a real person from the company for particular issues, but most of the customer service in a modern company may be done with AI-enabled customer-interaction platform. The AI platform would understand what a customer is doing or asking and will prompt them to take action on specific issues. This implies that with new AI technology, companies will be able to track purchases and consumers in order to suggest or make it easier for them to navigate the website and find what they are looking for. This, of course, is just one of many ways that artificial intelligence is being implemented to improve the customer experience.

Customer service works hand in hand with marketing because it increases customer loyalty. Usually when we think of customer service, we think of talking to an actual person to help solve our issues. However, with the use of AI, our perception of traditional customer service is changing. In this chapter, we are going to delve into the development of AI technologies in customer service, AI applications, possible future implementations of AI, and, more specifically, the advantages of AI and how it improves the overall customer experience and operations within the business as well.

6.2 The Development of AI in Customer Service

The need to apply AI for the improvement of customer experience originated from the marketing and sales department of businesses. In the beginning days of using AI for services, the system was not as smooth and efficient as nowadays. Customers had to deal with faulty interactive voice response systems and chatbots, programmed with responses to a limited number of certain questions instead of the voice or hologram-enabled conversational smart systems (Ismail, 2018). Those interactions made customers increasingly frustrated with companies as well as created more problems for businesses that could not effectively communicate with their customers. Even though things have changed considerably since those early days, businesses continually worry that memories of those days will stop some customers from adopting the new AI today. It is important that the customer experience is effortless and seamless for the long-term viability of AI.

Artificial intelligence has changed the customer service businesses department for the better. AI added significant advantages for customer call centers, for example. Businesses can use this technology to improve their overall customer experience by increasing the functionality of the contact center agents, by allowing AI to complete tasks that would normally be time-consuming for employees. AI can recognize call patterns of customers, which enables the agents to have the right information at the right time, so a problem can be resolved easily and without the need for a manager or supervisor to step in. Using this AI technology can create a competitive advantage for businesses due to the efficiency of the technology in their customer service departments.

In today's business world, AI-based chatbots are smarter than ever. They are able to answer very simple questions about a customer's order, as well as book an entire vacation for customers. AI is trained to refer a customer to a human agent if it isn't able to resolve a certain issue. Today, customer service teams use AI to help create a truly personalized experience by collecting and analyzing user habits and data. Agents are able to upsell items and offer discounts to customers due to the customer data analysis. Famous virtual assistants Amazon Alexa and Apple Siri allow us to get more things done faster with minimal effort. Businesses around the world have seen the positive impact that AI has had for other companies, but more importantly the positive impact that it has had for the consumers. AI is like a sidekick to the agents of the companies. AI technologies may deliver a higher level of personalized service given the information on customers' history with the brand, preferences, while sharing suggestions and offers tailored to specific customers (Ismail, 2018). These improvements and advantages of AI can only lead to a stronger relationship between companies and their customers. Looking ahead, the future for AI in the customer experience sector looks bright. One of the most exciting things about AI is its fast maturity rate and high penetration rate into the customer service realm.

6.3 AI Technologies for Customer Service

AI is always changing, and new technologies are always being developed. In order for these areas of customer service to be maintained, companies must keep up with the different AI technologies being produced. The customer service uses many different AI technologies, but some of the main ones are machine learning, chatbots, and natural language processing. Machine learning is a key aspect of customer service because applications with machine learning can analyze the calls the customer service center receives and keep track of what questions are asked. When enough data is collected, a machine learning application can give customer service agents the most appropriate response to the question they are asked.

6.3.1 Deep Learning

Deep learning is a subset of machine learning and is capable of learning from either supervised or unsupervised data. Marketers will use this AI to target their customers by recommending products and services. An example of this usage is Netflix since the company's algorithm uses deep learning to create personalized recommendations. The collected customer data showed that subscribers only take an average of 90 s to look for a movie or show before giving up. Therefore Netflix recommendations based on previously watched shows saved an estimated $1 billion in lost revenue if people started to cancel their subscriptions (Wang et al., 2015). This was a necessary and profitable move for Netflix since it essentially saved their business, if not gave them more. Customers will now be drawn to this new use of AI technology since it reduces the time to find a movie or show that is related to one's interests. Even though this technology may cost more to implement, it is well worth it since it makes Netflix better. This gives Netflix a competitive advantage over its competitors if they are not using deep learning or any AI technology. Deep learning finds patterns in the data that the AI system can reason through and offers the best option for the consumers' needs. Deep learning gains its knowledge off of past memories that are stored in the system. This information can also be used toward problem-solving experiences. As discussed in previous chapters, unstructured data is not easily organized and is hard to interpret. However, machine learning can be more fine-tuned with the use of unstructured data. It is able to break down the data and make it more condensed so that it can provide a more insightful result for advertisers. An example of this is North face gathers data from searches on jackets and combines this information with actual transactions made by customers. The AI system is able to learn more accurately to predict recommendations that will fulfill the needs of the customer. It is able to refine the results and prioritize the options given (Kietzmann et al., 2018). Machine learning can predict a customer's lifetime value and conversion likelihood. The AI system can examine data from the past behavior of consumers when they first try out a product.

6.3.2 Support Vector Machines

Support vector machines (SVM) is an area of machine learning that is greatly beneficial to marketers for their many capabilities. Support vector machines are supervised learning models that have learning algorithms that are able to analyze data and recognize patterns. Being one of the earliest methods introduced to marketing, it generally predicts better than the other machine learning methods and outperforms traditional marketing methods such as being capable of learning algorithms as many as 100 attribute levels (Ma & Sun, 2020). This level of collecting and analyzing huge amounts of data far outpaces traditional marketing methods. The SVM method can also assist marketers in classification or regression problems (Batrinca & Treleaven, 2014). SVM is very important to corporations and especially marketers as they are proven to be a very effective measurement for customer churn prediction. It is a widely used machine learning method with the basis of structural risk minimization. Therefore, for multiclass classification, multiple binary classifiers are combined, and to measure customer churn, the kernel space theory (finding relationships in large datasets) is applied.

In order to collect a sufficient amount of customer information, it starts with data mining to obtain and recognize simple attributes such as age, gender, location, etc.

The information obtained helps businesses to recognize any opportunities to channel their resources effectively. With the use of a recent machine learning technique, the support vector machine, this process is streamlined to be more cost and time efficient. SVM is an algorithm that learns by example to assign labels to objects (Jansen, 2007). Based on the combination of the personal information (the customer profile), the segment can be estimated, and the usage behavior of the customer profile can be determined. A simple example is if you look off a graph and have different colored dots that represent different segments. As humans, we are able to recognize these patterns quickly, but it would be easier and quicker to go through a lot of data if we use support vector machines.

6.3.3 Naive Bayesian Classification

The Naive Bayesian, or Naives Bayes for short, is a simple yet effective and commonly used machine learning classification. It is a family of algorithms that all share a common principle; every pair of features being classified is independent of each other. It has been a traditional solution for problems such as spam detection. As businesses and people become more tech-savvy, there are an increasing number of new communication mediums. One medium that is known to have a problem with spam is electronic mail. As more and more unsolicited emails get generated, the need for a reliable anti-spam filter grows. Marketers will use electronic mail to reach a large population even though their content may not be specific toward that customer's interests. In order to deflect spam, keyword filters can be used to block or flag any messages that contain that specific word or phrase. But keyword filters that are constructed by hand can only detect so many unwanted emails, and therefore performance is low and not as superior without the use of machine learning. These unsolicited emails make their way into a large number of recipients' inboxes from data that is pulled off of web pages and newsgroup archives.

Another machine learning algorithm that achieves accurate and spam filtering is the memory-based classification. This method belongs to a family of memory-based methods by storing all training instances in a memory structure and then using them directly for classification. A memory-based approach is useful as it attempts to classify messages based on previously received ones. Usually, spam emails will have some type of spelling errors such as a number where vowels should be. This may be done to purposely avoid keyword filters that are done by hand and therefore make their way to the intended customer's inbox. However, that is not the case with a memory-based classification since it can compare the previously received emails and recognize the pattern in order to mark it as spam.

6.3.4 Natural Language Processing

One of the AI technologies used in the customer service sector is natural language processing (NLP). Natural language processing is a supportive AI technology that is built in chatbots for customer service. This technology can help with the analysis of calls as well because it can take the human language and translate it to machine language for the AI to analyze and produce an output. Natural language processing helps the computer understand and interpret human language. Based on OCR (optical character recognition), NLP can extract meaning from blog posts, product reviews, and even posts on social media. For example, Swedbank, which is a Swedish bank, uses a virtual assistant with NLP to answer customer questions on the homepage of the website. This allows customer service employees to focus more on revenue-generating sales without having to devalue service (Kietzmann et al., 2018). Chatbots can help with customer service on websites as well. They can pop up on the screen and ask if the customer needs help finding something on the website. These chatbots can assist customers without the need for human interaction. Chatbots essentially mimic interactions with a human. Some chatbots are even made to act like a normal social media user. Chatbots are able to provide useful information, create recommendations, and also make purchases with ease. Chatbots have changed the way consumers can interact through social media. Natural language generation (NLG) can convert data into plain English. An example of NLG is Wordsmith; it can turn your data into a narrative that is used to build advertising content. For example, Saatchi LA trained IBM Watson to write thousands of advertisement copies for Toyota. AI was used to tailor those copies to more than a hundred different customer segments (Kietzmann et al., 2018).

6.3.5 Hybrid AI Systems

Marketers of all industries alike have begun using AI technologies for customer services on their various websites, collecting data from previous searches and consumer browsing history to place their products or services into the minds of consumers and get them thinking about the products. Most cases utilize a form of weak AI instituted by simple algorithms that connect various tags on different items to those with similar descriptions or tags. Another method marketers use is by using "adaptive human-computer interfaces (HCIs)" to develop adaptive websites and decision support systems. These intelligent systems track consumer eye fixation on certain parts of a computer screen and design an outlay that draws attention to different products on display on the website (Yin et al., 2016). With rapid technology development, researchers are also continuing along the thread of improving HCI by creating AI systems that interact with customers the same as if customers were speaking directly with real business representatives, as opposed to a chatbot. This kind of research is also beginning to encompass "enculturing" AI systems as well, designing the technologies to be able to recognize certain cultural cues and behave in a way that is proper for the culture of the user interacting with the system (Rehm et al., 2009).

AI technologies could be built together in a web service system for customer service. An example of such a hybrid web service system can include case-based reasoning (CBR) and artificial neural networks (ANN). Traditional help centers assist customers through long calls which can be inefficient and costly. With the use of a web service system, not only does the company save time but it also saves money because they can eliminate the need for a physical person. Instead of using traditional CBR for matching, this hybrid system uses ANN alongside CBR to extract knowledge from the customer service database (Hui et al., 2001). It then uses that information to match it with the correct service record during the retrieval stage. The most preliminary form of online customer service is through bulletin board systems (BBS). Bulletin board systems are not user-friendly and require some training before using. The web service system has now taken over bulletin board systems due to how much more cost-effective they are.

6.4 Features of AI Applications in Customer Service

There are many uses of AI in customer experience and service. Utilizing AI has many benefits that can improve communications/interactions between the customer and the company. AI is always improving, and new technologies are always being developed. Areas that make for great customer service and experience include service level, contact time, response time, customer retention, and customer churn (Fig. 6.1). The related success factors are reliability, availability, simplicity, adaptation, anticipation, and accountability. Although there are other aspects involved, these are the main areas of customer service. AI plays a very large role in improving these areas of customer service within a business.

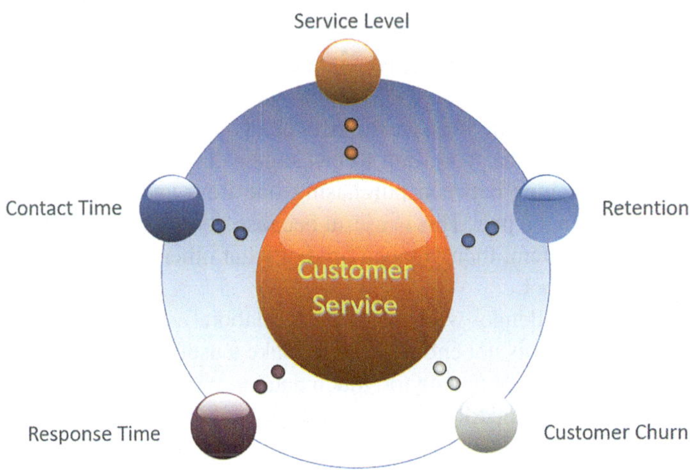

Fig. 6.1 Customer service areas

6.4.1 Collaborative Filtering

The most widely adopted AI applications for online business are recommendation engines. E-commerce has been steadily taking over brick-and-mortar stores. What used to be sales associates recommending a product or service has now become an algorithm that can do the same behind the screen. This AI-based technology is called collaborative filtering. An example of this is specific to Amazon, hence the name Amazon Personalize. Typical collaborative filtering algorithms use data about a customer's interest and ratings to come up with a list of possible recommendations. Amazon Personalize uses more than that; it aims to personalize the online site for each customer based on the data they have. Their algorithm will look at recently viewed items, purchased items, favorite artists, etc. In addition, their algorithm makes recommendations in real time, scales to massive data sets, and generates high-quality recommendations (Linden et al., 2003). Collaborative filtering may tend to focus on finding similar items to recommend based on a previous purchase or viewed item rather than look for similar customers in order to recommend a product. For every product that a customer has purchased or clicked on items that have a rating, the algorithm will look for similar items and recommend them as a section of the website or immediately after a purchase. A setback of collaborative filtering is that if the algorithm used only focuses on rated items, new items will not be able to make it on the recommended lists since there's no data available yet.

Collaborative filtering was first used by Amazon in 1998. This method is currently also utilized by Amazon, Netflix, and Spotify, as well as many other companies. This method has two branches, which are user based and item based. For user based, the focus is on the individual person, looking at all the information we know about the individual we want to recommend a product for. This method first looks for other users that have given similar ratings on products or have bought the same products as the target individual previously. It then uses these similar users to make a prediction for what to recommend to the target individual. This method makes the assumption that a given person A that has similar tastes as a given person B will agree on things not in the data provided with person B more than a randomly chosen other individual. The other method is item based. This does not involve individual users; instead, it looks at the relationship between pairs of items. The first step is to make a matrix of items that you want to investigate. Then from the purchase data, look at the relationships between purchasing one item and if customers usually purchase the other in the pair. This is useful because if you know the target user has purchased a specific item, then you can predict what other products they are more likely to purchase or not.

There are a few challenges with using AI in collaborative filtering. First, there are some cases where there is not enough data to make a useful prediction. Conversely, there is also the problem of having too much data, in which case if you use all of it, it will take a very long time to process and get a meaningful result. There is also the issue of shilling attacks; people know that reviews of products influence if they are recommended to users and if the user purchases them; because of this, some people write false reviews, giving their own products excellent reviews while giving negative reviews to their competitors. These false reviews will make any machine learning based on them incorrect. Sometimes this algorithm will give users the same recommendations repeatedly and not have diversity for the products they are recommending, rendering them less effective.

6.4.2 Customer Churn Analysis

Customer profiling is very useful in helping businesses know which customers to reach out to and how to do so in an effective manner. The goal is for a business to anticipate what a customer is going to need or want and then be readily prepared to provide that service or product. It is vital for a business to know their customer's needs and wants in order to be successful and compete with other businesses. By categorizing customers off of certain attributes from information collected, marketers can build a customer profile that will give them a better chance at retaining that customer within their business. However, profiling is not just for current customers; it is also used to search for prospective customers or finding previous customers that are not as active through external data to make an educated suggestion on how to better tailor communication to have them back as an active customer. The process of customer profiling actually starts after customer segmentation. Customer segmentation works hand in hand with customer profiling since it starts by segmenting or grouping customers based on similar characteristics or attributes. After that, marketers can have a more specific pool to tailor their communication.

Customer churn analysis is a very important field for business to be able to accurately predict customer churn to not suffer the costs it is associated with. Not accurately predicting customer churn results in opportunity cost from the lost sales and the cost of acquiring new customers. There are multiple areas of artificial intelligence that could help organizations predict customer churn, including artificial neural networks, decision tree algorithms, support vector machines, and the naive Bayesian classifier. These AI techniques are able to classify and analyze data to find the trends and attributes in customers that are associated with customer churn. They are then able to predict customer turnover from the applications of the data collected.

Customer churn (customer turnover) predictions are important to corporations so that corporations could predict when they will experience high rates of customer churn. Predicting such would equip them better to (in the case of customer churn) not produce as many products (so there would not be a lot of unsold inventory) and to potentially keep it from happening (if they could find the cause they could potentially eliminate the problem). There is also much cost associated with customer churn. Losing customers results in opportunity costs from reduction of sales, and also attracting new customers is very costly from organizations as well. Xia and Jin (2008) conducted an experiment on two different sets of data showing that among the different classifiers (decision tree, artificial neural networks, and naive Bayesian), the support vector machines performed the best in both datasets in identifying and predicting customer churn. The support vector machines were also able to identify which traits were evident in such customers. With the high performance of SVMs in customer churn predictions, the organizations that utilize SVMs in their organizations will have a competitive edge and will be able to reduce the costs that are associated with customer church including opportunity cost of sales and cost of acquiring new customers. Support vector machines can also be applied to many different areas of marketing including social media analytics by analyzing the data and recognizing patterns and market forecasting by finding the patterns in the data and applying that to forecasting.

6.4.3 Social Media Analytics

The use of social media has revolutionized marketing. Social media has made interacting with consumers easier and more effective. Double communication is used through social media which allows the company to respond to their customers while getting quick replies back. Social media also provides a lot of data which is what fuels marketing. The more data a company can acquire about their consumers, the better, and social media makes locating that data much easier. Marketers are able to extract more data through the use of artificial intelligence systems. One of the technologies that has helped grow the social media sector is image recognition. Image recognition helps marketers understand pictures and videos that are uploaded onto social media. Image recognition helps detect true consumer behavior. An example of this is when someone posts a selfie on social media; it can reveal brands pictured even when it is not explicitly mentioned in the user's post as well as the user's personal attributes (Kietzmann et al., 2018). Image recognition is also used in physical retail stores. For example, Cloverleaf which is based in San Diego has revolutionized shelf displays by using image recognition. The displays are made with optical sensors which collect data on customer demographics like age and gender. This AI system can even detect how the consumer feels about the product. The closer the customer stands to the display, the more personalized the data is. Another AI system that is used in social media is chatbots. Chatbots are AI computer software programs that simulate intelligent conversation by written text or voice through chat interface (Tuten & Solomon, 2014).

Several inputs that go into the content creation and advertising category would be social media sites, customer relationship management (CRM) data, and sample generated content. With social media sites as an input, the AI technology can suggest hashtags to use to bring more attention to your pages or it can find similar ways to help design your website. Using CRM data, AI tech can provide better ideas of content that will be more relatable to your customers. When companies use samples of previously generated content, AI technologies can test out how well they would work for the company and make suggested changes.

6.4.4 Customer Loyalty Programs

One useful source of data would be the information derived from rewards cards for grocery stores. Consumers buy food and other various products and then swipe their rewards card to receive various discounts. What they are unaware of when they are swiping their card is that they are actually being given lower prices in exchange for user data, not necessarily loyalty. Every time a customer types in a phone number or swipes a loyalty card, they are providing companies with useful data about themselves that can help companies like Safeway and Walgreens to better target the market. The newest, and arguably most helpful, sources of data come from social media sites like Facebook and Instagram. These sources of information provide businesses with a plethora of information from their consumers offering more than just what food they like to eat. Businesses can use cookies to find out a surprisingly large amount of information about various people. For every five posts that a social media user scrolls through, they see an ad. With people spending an average of hours on social media per day, the number of ads they see are beginning to skyrocket. Instagram can offer different businesses insights into their ads and even give their advertising customers options for what kinds of demographics they want to target. They can sort people based on their followers, who they follow, their likes, posts, and saved posts to wrap up their interests into different categories. These sources of data help their AI also to suggest new people and businesses to follow in their "discover" page, similar to how Amazon and Netflix use algorithms to suggest new movies and products.

In the following section, we explore several cases to illustrate how AI can improve traditional customer services in different industries.

Case 6.1: Nordstrom and AI

Nordstrom is a famous retail giant that provides premium quality products and services to customers. It is located in most high-end malls around the United States. As Nordstrom customers, many people have seen the importance that Nordstrom places on customer service and being the best in the industry when it comes to customer experience. One reason is because of their integration of big data and AI into their business to improve customer experience. With such a specific goal in mind, Nordstrom has been able to spend selectively on the programs and initiatives that align most accurately with their business model (delight the customer with unique features and continuously improve its financial performance). Here we introduce some details about how Nordstrom is using AI and machine learning to improve their customer experience as well as their financial performance year to year.

One concept that Nordstrom takes very seriously is getting to know the customer and understanding them better. Nordstrom uses AI to create a more personalized shopping experience for their customers. Nordstrom uses a tool called "its personal book software." This software system is able to build a detailed profile of each of their customers where it can tell their favorite brands/preferences to employee notes which include personal information and shopping styles. This is a big upside to Nordstrom employees for several reasons. They can contact any customer when their favorite brands are back in stock, or they can invite them to exclusive events that only a limited number of customers know about. By having all of this information at the fingertips of the employees, they can analyze which customers spend the most, and they can use that information to contact them with exclusive deals and other promotions. This ultimately benefits the customer as well as the company. The company gets more sales, and the customer has a greater experience as well as the opportunity at deals that are only available for certain customers.

Another aspect of Nordstrom's business that is using AI to benefit them is through social media. Nordstrom uses social media as a way to communicate effectively with their consumers. Nordstrom is able to engage with apps like Pinterest to see what is trending online. With this, Nordstrom is able to have a deeper understanding of consumer preferences. Nordstrom is able to link the in-store and online world together by tagging items with red markers which indicate that it is a popular Pinterest item. In fact, a few years ago an engagement lab study ranked Nordstrom at the top of retailers that are able to effectively communicate with their customers. Nordstrom understands the importance of online retail in today's world. The company has had a big focus on the "omnichannel" retailing, which is incorporating all of its capabilities to provide a seamless experience whether it's in store or online for the consumers. Both the Nordstrom app and Nordstrom.com have integrated the inventory management system. This allows customers to be able to easily find what they are looking for and have it be ordered to their exact location.

Nordstrom is using AI and machine learning to help build a greater relationship between them and their customers. By doing this, Nordstrom is able to build a more trusting bond with its consumers, and in turn, the consumers will keep coming back to Nordstrom to buy most of their clothes. This is ultimately a win-win scenario for Nordstrom because they will get more sales and the customers feel like the company cares about their needs. This just shows how helpful AI is to businesses in today's economy, and it is only relatively the beginning of AI being incorporated into businesses around the globe.

Case 6.2: Massively Chatbots

The ability to communicate and develop relationships with customers is instrumental to the success of a company. Customer service allows businesses to market themselves to their customers even after a product or service is provided, so it would be ideal if every customer interaction was consistent, fast, and effective. Therefore, many businesses have begun to turn to AI and technology to increase their customer service bandwidth. Artificial intelligence can collect and utilize large amounts of data, making it ideal for the customer service industry. Many customer service interactions are highly dependent on dissecting past data and experiences to assist current consumers, which play to the strengths of artificial intelligence technology. Customer service and chatbots can naturally work together because customer service is directly involved with a business's sales cycle and public image. Also, considering that artificial intelligence technology is already becoming deeply integrated into the customer service industry, especially with chatbots, there will most likely be major developments in business-to-customer communication.

Massively is a conversational marketing platform that utilizes artificial intelligence and machine learning in order to allow users to customize their own customer engagement bots and analyze consumer and product data. Customers of this app have the ability to create chatbots of various data processing levels and insert them into any application or website where messages can be exchanged. Massively's more advanced learning bots utilize natural language understanding, machine learning algorithms, company database information, and other general data to emulate different human interactions. The engineers of the app can also create basic scripted bots if that is the wish of the customer.

As a tech start-up, Massively works closely with their clients, mainly because most companies lack an in-house software engineer with AI or chatbot programming knowledge. In order for the business to earn revenue, Massively maintains and develops chatbots for their client, the client collects data from their own consumers by using the software/chatbots, and the consumer data can be analyzed by using Massively's conversational marketing platform (Massively provides subscriptions of their AI software and analytics to clients). This business model is relatively like other chatbot/customer service platform creators like Botsify and SnatchBot, though competitors are starting to move toward "plug and play" ChatBot bundles that clients can buy and use without consultation. As e-commerce continues to grow, the need for fast and easy customer communication will become a necessity creating a market where companies like Massively will thrive.

The utilization of artificial intelligence in the customer service industry allows companies to critique and create their own model for proactive customer interactions. For example, Massively's chatbots can be programmed and customized for different purposes, from following a preprogrammed script to utilizing NLP to create a unique interaction for each customer. Data inputs involved in developing AI customer services may include company data, consumer data, linguistic data inputs like NLP, machine learning algorithms, and even something as specific as regional language data. These inputs allow chatbots or other customer service aids to emulate human interactive experiences while also maintaining the ability to quickly access company information and communicate it to the customer. Massively provides customizable chatbot services using AI. The company explains the straightforward process of customizing a chatbot on their website. Not every company is going to want the same kind of bot to interact with their customers; this means that different bots will need different data inputs and designs. Massively addresses this customization need by allowing their chatbots architects to decide what datasets, layer integrations, and conversational designs a company needs to meet their customer service goal. They also find ways to optimize developed chat pots by monitoring and training the artificial intelligence systems.

Currently, there are multiple different companies that specialize in creating customer service software or chatbots that utilize artificial intelligence systems. Most of these businesses either sell prepackaged "plug and play" software or consist of a workforce that tailors AI systems to a company's specific wants or needs. This type of business has a wide customer base, since most companies both small and large implement some sort of customer service, especially online. In the future, as software engineers become more adept to artificial intelligence, the prepackaged software option may be more popular, since there will be more in-house programmers that could adjust the system to the company's specific needs.

Case 6.3: HashMe AI Analytics

An important marketing field that can greatly benefit from artificial intelligence is social media analytics. Social media analytics is concerned with developing and evaluating informatics tools and frameworks to collect, monitor, analyze, summarize, and visualize social media data, usually driven by specific requirements from a target application. Social media analytics can use AI through the use of natural language processing and machine learning to identify patterns within an unstructured text such as customer reviews. This method enables a machine to read through billions of reviews and get an accurate feel for customer sentiment toward the product or company. Another method that could be used in this subfield is image analytics, which allows a machine to identify not only logos and brands, but to judge emotions based on facial expressions.

HashMe is an application that generates hashtags for marketers or businesses to use on their social media platforms. These are hashtags that help direct traffic to the user's post, tapping into more online optimization. The data input into the app is words, phrases, or pictures of something related to a chosen post. This is then taken and processed with many AI techniques, such as machine learning and pattern recognition, to provide online optimization and increase consumer views to the posts. The output created from the search is hashtags that are most commonly associated with the word, phrase, or picture that was searched (e.g., a picture advertising a new blend of coffee would include a hashtag such as "#newblend"). The AI then organizes these hashtags in order of popularity that each suggestion will bring to the post and those that will drive more traffic toward the post. There is an easy copy and paste option once all the hashtags are provided, but there is a maximum of 30 hashtags that HashMe will provide for the user. Some sample outputs that are generated in these AI technologies are things such as websites, hashtags, and digital ads. These are created through processes such as pattern recognition and A/B testing. With processes like these, it is easy to find out what will be successful which is a lot of what the business itself struggles with.

A typical business model for companies that make content generation or advertising AI technology includes potential customers, investors, and competitors. Most likely potential customers would be established companies who are already successful but looking for a way to get an edge on other companies, since a lot of the AI technologies are probably expensive and not necessary for a company just starting out. Investors in advertising AI technology would probably be people with a bit of money and have much faith in the growth of AI in these areas. This could be someone who was previously successful in advertising and knows how hard it is to generate content on your own. Someone like this would see the major benefits that AI technologies could have on advertising in businesses.

In assessing the business model of HashMe, it can be seen that their customers are mostly small start-ups trying to draw more attention to themselves and HashMe lacks a large budget as the application is free to users. Some alliances that the company might have would be with Instagram or Twitter, as these are a few of the sites that use hashtags. The company could partner with these social media corporations to share the data of traffic drawn in by hashtags. Main competitors could also be businesses such as All-hashtag and Seek Metrics; these are both companies that provide the same kind of services. Lastly, competitors might be companies that generate content for businesses simply using a team of employees, without AI. It could be hard for an AI technology to surpass the creativity of an actual human being, but AI technology would also be faster and possibly cheaper than hiring a whole team in the long run.

6.5 Key Takeaways

AI proposes many potential advantages for the sector of customer service and experience. New technologies within AI have the ability to improve the overall customer experience. No matter what industry, customers are always wanting the best service and experience to be given to them and rating how they believe their experience was. This means that companies must work to enhance the overall customer experience and AI technologies prove to be a promising way of doing so. AI has the capacity to enhance customer experience by providing faster service, automated service, and personalized service.

In order for customer service/experience to be effective, it must be reliable. AI technologies utilize data and can access it much faster than any human could. The data does not incorporate any emotion, and mistakes are not frequently made. Customers can rely on the data, building up trust between the company and their customers. Trust and reliability are aspects that customers look for when looking for a service or product. AI is always available, allowing customers to interact with the system from anywhere at any time. A good example of this is chatbots which are used to relay information and responses to customers faster, accurately, and without the assistance of a human. This availability improves the customer's experience because they can get assistance at any time decreasing the amount of time they have to wait.

In order for customer service to be effective, communication must be simple and easy to understand. AI can improve this area of customer service because of its enhanced audio and facial recognition. Emotional analytics is an AI technology recently developed that can identify whether a customer is happy or not and decides where to transfer them. Simplicity is something that can really help a customer who may already be confused about a product or service. AI simplifies responses and solutions in order to improve the customer's experience with the company. AI is always changing and is a system that can adapt to any scenario. This adaptability is crucial in providing good customer service. AI is always learning and adapting allowing it to be up to date with what is going on with the customer. This adaptability allows AI to respond with correct solutions enhancing the experience of the customer. AI is very effective at anticipating questions asked by customers. This anticipation/prediction allows for a faster and more personalized service for each customer. This personalization makes customers feel more comfortable with the service being provided. Faster service is something that most customers look for. Customers do not want to wait in line in order to buy a product or service. These areas of customer service can be improved greatly with the use of AI. A company's ability to become more reliable, available, simple, adapted, and accountable improves the customer's experience with that company.

A major advantage of AI to customer experience is that it has the ability to provide customers with faster and more efficient service. Customers are always seeking the quickest service and most likely rate their experience as poor when they have to wait for a lengthy time. However, AI can improve service times by being able to serve many customers at the same time (Ameen et al., 2020). This means that customers would no longer have to be served one by one, in which case it causes extensive lines to form. Along with serving multiple customers at one, AI is also able to serve customers in a timelier manner by advising decisions in real time. This means that based on the most recent customer data, AI is able to advise customers with decisions as time demands. Another advantage that AI can bring to customer experience is by automating actions. Repetitive activities or tasks that customers have to perform are able to be automated by AI technologies. With automation, customers will no longer have to perform repetitive tasks such as vacuuming, improving the outcome, and saving time for customers. An example of automation is the Roomba; it is a vacuum powered by AI that vacuums your house for you (Hoyer et al., 2020). Through this technology and many more automated AI technologies, customers' experience could be improved by no longer having to perform repetitive tasks and saving time to do other things. Lastly, an advantage AI offers customers is providing a hyper-personalized experience to each customer. AI is able to collect data about previous purchases and search history in order to recommend content and products to each customer. This capability enhances the customers' experience by not having to search for what they want, as well as making them feel as though the company knows who they are and understands their wants and needs. Along with feeling heard, personability improves a customer's experience by not having to search hard for what they are wanting. AI technology is able to match customers to what they believe they want, creating an experience unique for each customer. As human beings, we are always wanting to be understood and connected with, and this technology makes us feel just that.

6.6 Conclusion

Overall, AI is and will be used in numerous ways to improve customer service and in turn customer experience. AI presents many advantages in customer service and experience, including, but not limited to, faster service, automated service, and personalized service. Advantage to the customers also means advantages to businesses, as they will be able to better retain their current customers as well as serve and attract more customers.

As we have seen and discussed in this chapter, artificial intelligence is something that we as consumers are going to have to get comfortable with. The rapid forward progression and implementation of artificial intelligence in regard to customer service are paving the way for a quicker, easier, and more efficient customer service experience. With artificial intelligence having a tremendous upside for the business as well as the consumer, it is going to be more and more likely that we will not be taking steps backward to an all in-person customer service experience. As well, the implications of COVID-19 pandemic have changed the consumer experience forever. We can all now see how easy and quick it is to shop online, so the trend of online interactions will continue to rise. This however plays into the favor of AI, and customers will be able to see what it is really capable of in the years to come. The world is forever changing, and so is the customer service experience, artificial intelligence is steering the ship, and we should all be excited for what the future holds in regards to a much-improved customer service experience in the years to come.

References

Ameen, N., Tarhini, A., Reppel, A., & Anand, A. (2020). Customer experience in the age of Artificial intelligence. *Computers in Human Behavior*. https://doi.org/10.1016/j.chb.2020.106548

Batrinca, B., & Treleaven, P. C. (2014, July 26). *Social media analytics: A survey of techniques, tools and platforms*. Retrieved from https://link.springer.com/content/pdf/10.1007/s00146-014-0549-4.pdf

Hoyer, W., Kroschke, M., Schmitt, B., et al. (2020). Transforming the customer experience through new technologies. *Journal of Interactive Marketing*. https://doi.org/10.1016/j.intmar.2020.04.001

Hui, S. C., Fong, A. C. M., & Jha, G. (2001). A web-based intelligent fault diagnosis system for customer service support. *Engineering Applications of Artificial Intelligence*. https://doi.org/10.1016/s0952-1976(01)00018-5

Ismail, N. (2018). *The evolution of Artificial intelligence in customer experience*. Retrieved https://www.information-age.com/evolution-artificial-intelligence-customer-exer-123471409/

Jansen, S. M. H. (2007). *Customer segmentation and customer profiling for a mobile telecommunications company based on usage behavior. A Vodafone Case Study*. Retrieved from https://dke.maastrichtuniversity.nl/westra/PhDMaBa-teaching/GraduationStudents/StephanJansen2007/Stephan_Jansen2007.pdf

Kietzmann, J., Paschen, J., & Treen, E. (2018, September 1). Artificial Intelligence in advertising. *Journal of Advertising Research, 58*(3), 263–267.

Linden, G., Smith, B., & York, J. (2003). Amazon. com recommendations: Item-to-item collaborative filtering. *IEEE Internet Computing, 1*, 76–80.

Ma, L., & Sun, B. (2020). Machine learning and AI in marketing – Connecting computing power to human insights. *International Journal of Research in Marketing, 37*(3), 481–504.

Mehr, H. (2017, August). *Artificial intelligence for citizens services and government*. Retrieved 2021, from https://ash.harvard.edu/files/ash/files/artificial_intelligence_for_citizen_services.pdf

Rehm, M., Nakano, Y., André, E., & Nishida, T. (2009). Enculturating human–computer interaction. *AI & Society, 24*(3), 209–211.

Tuten, T. L., & Solomon, M. R. (2014). *Social Media Marketing*. Sage.

Wang, H., Wang, N., & Yeung, D. Y. (2015, August). Collaborative deep learning for recommender systems. In *Proceedings of the 21th ACM SIGKDD international conference on knowledge discovery and data mining* (pp. 1235–1244).

Xia, G., & Jin, W. (2008). Model of customer churn prediction on support vector machine. *Systems Engineering – Theory & Practice, 28*(1), 71–77.

Yin, P., Day, R., & Wang, Y. (2016). Tabu search-based classification for eye-movement behavioral decisions. *Neural Computing and Applications, 29*(5), 1433–1443.

Artificial Intelligence in Finance

7

Abstract

Artificial intelligence is one of the most influential emerging technologies in the financial sector. This chapter will explore the evolution of AI in finance and introduce how AI technology can be used in various financial services. These technologies include machine learning, artificial neural network, decision analytic network, robo-advisors, and others. Some key features of AI applications will be explained, including investment banking, personalized finance, credit management, loans and lending, asset management, fraud detection, and regulation compliance. Two case studies are provided to explore AI in JPMorgan Chase and Goldman Sachs.

Keywords

Fintech · Financial expert system · Machine learning · Artificial neural network · Bayesian network · Decision analytics network · Robo-advisors · Investment banking · Personalized finance · Credit management · Asset management · High frequency trading · Fraud Detection, Regulation Compliance

7.1 Introduction

In the 1800s, British scientist Charles Darwin famously stated, "It is not the most intellectual of the species that survives, but the species that survives is the one that can adapt to and adjust best to the changing environment in which it finds itself" (Darwin, 2019). A similar sentiment can be made to the ever-changing global business environment, and more specifically, the financial services sector. As new technologies have emerged in recent years, well-known businesses alike have once again adapted rather than died, implementing new resources to improve the value

L. Chan et al., *Applied Artificial Intelligence in Business*, Applied Innovation and Technology Management, https://doi.org/10.1007/978-3-031-05740-3_7

creation process and increase their overall competitive advantage. The key driver that has aided this advancement is artificial intelligence.

The financial services industry has observed a transition to the digitization of data throughout recent years. Many large financial companies have been able to take advantage of big data, benefiting from the improved efficiency of their investment decision cycle. For financial companies to stay competitive, it has become more and more clear that they must adapt and implement financial technology (FinTech) with the help of AI, using it to enhance their business strategies. In addition, this has sped up the previously slow manual processes that companies have used which have given them a lot more time to shift their focus, freeing up their IT department to work on other important business operations. By implementing these emerging technologies, companies now have a much more reliable, user-friendly system in place for themselves and their customers.

With the digitization of many things about the stock market and other finance areas, emerging IT has sought out ways to make it easier to see how nontraditional data sources can predict insights into future market performance. This is one of the many things that come with the improvement of technology and the addition of big data. AI and machine learning play a huge role in the development of FinTech. Without AI, the financial service companies would not have the ability to put all of this information together, make insights on how the data can have predictive relevance to an aspect of the market, or use this new information to enhance profits and improve efficiency. The newfound ability to gather large and unheard-of datasets through AI enhances firms' and investors' ability to make more economically sound investment decisions, forever changing the financial services and investment management landscape for the better. This chapter will explore how financial services companies have been able to use AI technologies to create value for themselves and their clients as well as increase their overall competitive advantage.

7.2 Development of AI in Finance

The Evolution of Artificial Intelligence in Finance and Banking goes back even further than the 1950s. Those in the financial services field realized they could save a lot of time with the assistance of AI to help them in their calculations and analysis in their day-to-day tasks. This sparked the desire to research and develop artificial intelligence.

There are a lot of definitions that incorporate the meaning of artificial intelligence which cover a multitude of differing views. Most of which generalize the ability to reason, solve problems, and some sort of learning from experiences. Even before the 1950s, there were generations of scientists, mathematicians, and philosophers who had the concept and vision of what AI could deliver in their minds. "Gottfredson insinuated that the history of AI began in the periods of human classical civilization with myths and rumors of artificial beings endowed with intelligence or consciousness by master craftsmen. The attempt by the classical philosophers to describe the process of human thinking as the mechanical manipulation of symbols gave more meaning to the concept of AI" (Mhlanga, 2020). Mechanical usage with the insertion of human thought was what led to the invention of programmable computers. These computers could reason, and this was the start of AI.

In the 1960s and 1970s, AI's usefulness in finance was under research and development. The big step for financial analysis came in the 1970s and 1980s with the worldwide development in expert systems. These expert systems were used to determine the best strategy for investing, monitor stock premiums in the market, and most prevalently for financial planning. Financial planning was one of the biggest forces for the development of expert systems in the financial sector. These expert systems were used to help real people in making financial planning decisions. The expert systems provided the technical know-how, while a human element was required to apply both common sense and creativity to the problem. By the 1980s, there were some developments in its technology that enabled AI to be used as a predictive tool. It was realized that artificial intelligence could be used as a model to predict the stock market. It was successful in its implications in that it was able to accurately predict market gains and losses once appropriate perimeters and relevant data were imputed. The 1980s also served as a time to not only use AI in modeling but also financial planning. It had begun to be implemented in assisting financial planners in market research and could give specific individually tailored investment plans to their customers. Throughout the 1980s, the use of AI was expanded greatly in the planning aspects of the financial realm.

In the 1990s, expert systems were also applied by governments to catch instances of fraud and money laundering. FinCEN Artificial Intelligence System was sponsored by the US Treasury Department and was used by the government to observe and determine instances of money laundering. The biggest advantage to this over a human trying to determine fraud is that computers can analyze massive amounts of data faster than any human ever will be able to. FAIS began its use in 1993 and could process 200,000 transactions a week. Between 1993 and 1995, this program was able to detect over one billion dollars in possible laundered money. There was a great need for assistance in the criminal side of finance to help with fraud detection and deterrence. AI technologies were developed and implemented in this area in the mid-1990s. It was used to root through and analyze vast amounts of data to quickly spot discrepancies and catch money launderers and other so-called white-collar crimes. "AI is a vital tool in fraud/anomaly detection. Pattern recognition assists in the identification of behavior that differs from standard patterns. For example, it can be essential in the identification of fraudulent insurance claims, fraudulent use of cash cards and credit cards, illegal financial schemes and transactions, security threats, money laundering, transfer scams, and illicit transactions" (Tadapaneni, 2020). Without the use of AI, most of the crimes would have gone unnoticed and unprosecuted. These activities of finding, reporting, and tracking were just too labor-intensive and costly to be worthwhile.

More recently, moved on to the 2000s and the current day. The uses of AI in the finance and banking industries have greatly improved and are extremely complex today. The use of AI in finance now can handle every portion of your financial life from portfolio management to credit management and risk, to even giving you advice on whether those shoes you saw on Nike are a good buy or not considering it would use two-thirds of the funds in your checking account. This is enormous moving forward, and it will be very interesting to see how AI takes shape going forward into the future given its vast usages now. The advancements in AI that have further developed were predictions from the stock market of future values and risk assessments of every company largest to smallest to an individual's risk assessment of how likely they are to pay on a loan and what interest rate they should receive based on that prediction has been extremely fine-tuned through the uses of artificial intelligence. AI has been used to assist almost every aspect of the banking and finance industry and will likely get even better in the future and provide more efficient ways to conduct businesses in the future.

7.3 AI Technologies in Finance and Banking

AI in finance is focused on utilizing math and statistics to predict what individual stocks as well as what the market as a whole will do. Modern-day statistics, things like averages, variance, and standard deviations, are the backbones of trying to accurately predict financial movement, risk, and reward.

7.3.1 Financial Expert Systems

Expert systems are currently being used for loan evaluation. The combination of financial projections with qualitative information allows for loans to be properly evaluated. Expert systems are used to emulate the decision-making ability of a human expert. These systems can solve complex problems by reasoning through knowledge presented as rules rather than through conventional code. We can use expert systems to manage risk by using AI to get an expert opinion on possible allocations of a loan to make the best decision. To do this, these expert systems use traditional methods of regression analysis, polytomous probit analysis, and recursive partitioning. Regression analysis is a statistical method that allows us to examine the relationship between two or more variables of interest. Essentially, we can analyze the influence of one or more independent variables on a dependent variable. In the case of a loan, we would be analyzing the ability of a loanee to pay off their loan. Polytomous probit analysis is a method of analyzing the relationship between a stimulant and the quantal (all or nothing) response. This probit analysis is polytomous making it multinomial or consisting of several terms, meaning that we can analyze numerous stimuli and quantal responses rather than the traditional single stimulant and response. This analysis allows us to evaluate the credit risk that is associated with lending money to a prospective loanee. Recursive partitioning is a form of multivariable analysis; by creating a decision tree, this model can classify different members of the population by creating sub-populations based on several independent variables. This is used to assign credit to loanees through the evaluation of multiple variables such as the equity/asset ratio, return on assets, and current ratio.

Traditionally expert systems are used to solve complex problems. However, expert systems have not had as many applications as people might think, and there are a couple of reasons for this: The expectations did not meet the reality of their application they were more often than not too complicated for people to effectively utilize them, or the outcome of these systems did not meet a client's needs. Another major problem was that people were fascinated with the idea of AI solving every problem that presented itself without AI necessarily being the best course of action for the problem. Going forward into a new age with an increased interest in AI, the financial sector should focus more on what AI can do to help things like efficiency or accuracy, not necessarily replace human elements or have all of the answers.

7.3.2 Machine Learning

Machine learning (ML) is the most important subset of artificial intelligence technologies that are widely used in financial applications. It can analyze historical market behavior using large datasets and determine optimal inputs (predictors) to a strategy and also make trade predictions. The basic machine learning process is always started with specifying the problem statement. Then identify which type of machine learning problem represents, like supervised learning, unsupervised learning (e.g., clustering), or reinforcement learning. For instance, we can use one of these techniques to predict the price of a stock in 3 months from now, based on the company's past quarterly results, or we can also project whether a company will hike its benchmark interest rate, and so on. After figuring out the problems and techniques matched, it should encode historical data (stock price/forex data) with indicators to build a model. And the data will be divided into training data, which is the data that makes the machine learning learn the pattern and test data that is used to see how well the training algorithm performs. When the training data is used to teach the algorithm, while the trained algorithm is applied to test data for accuracy, the results then can be displayed and reviewed.

7.3.3 Artificial Neural Network in Finance

Artificial neural network (ANN) is an AI technique that uses machine learning to model data and provides meaningful output from several input channels. In finance, neural networks have a large potential to supplement traditional techniques like the statistical model and regression analyses to improve the returns on assets. It supports new ways of forecasting bonds, managing assets, and assisting in portfolio selection.

ANN is a digital display of the human neural network. It tries to copy some of its characteristics and structure. One of its early applications in finance was in the 1990s used to forecast potential bankruptcies using financial ratios as input data.

The area in which ANN is mostly used is on the asset management side. This could be because financial analysts use more time to manage assets rather than controlling liabilities. To find actual applications of neural networks in finance can be difficult because functioning software using AI can be a strategic advantage for companies; therefore, they choose to keep the intelligence within the company. But in the later years, analytical software and applications have been commercialized and are easier for the public to obtain. An example of software using ANN is Neuroshell. It can do forecasting from historical data and provide you with strategies for how you can trade in the secondary market. However, it still needs inputs from human intelligence to select what information it should extract its output from. Another weakness in software like these is the lack of understanding of qualitative data such as good/bad news and weak quarters. Because it can only rely on history as the data is provided, it does not predict the future, as well as human intelligence can do, but it could supplement traders with fast information from historical data. ANN in these types of software is useful in short-run trading, but in the long run, it still needs human interaction. One of the biggest growth potentials for AI in finance is to implement qualitative analysis for political, societal, and business news around the world.

When compared to traditional AI techniques such as expert systems, neural networks learn extremely fast, and a neural network can solve a problem even if some of its neurons make a mistake. A neural network can do this because, like the human brain, it has multiple neurons that can receive inputs, process those inputs, and determine which information should be stored and which information should be discarded as well as pass that information along to multiple different neurons. Even if one or multiple neurons fail to be functional, other neurons can process that information, which explains why a neural network can learn so much faster than an expert system.

7.3.4 Decision Analytics Network

Bayesian network (BN) is an AI technique used in a decision-analytic network. A Bayesian network is a probabilistic graphical model that uses Bayesian inference for probability computations. Bayesian inference is a method of statistical inference in which the probability for a hypothesis is updated as more evidence becomes available. These networks are a type of machine learning, which is the application of artificial intelligence that provides systems the ability to automatically learn and improve from experience without being explicitly programmed. Bayesian networks hold an advantage over other types of machine learning as it can model a domain in a way that is visually transparent and aims to capture causal relationships. These networks work well with assumptions which mean we can work with data sets that are missing a lot of data, such as forecasting models, and still achieve an accurate result. Bayesian networks are not perfect as when they are large, they tend to be slower and can be ineffective when compared to other, simpler models. However, when they are discrete, these networks are extremely fast and reliable.

These networks utilize multiple types of modeling such as influence diagram (ID), dependency modeling, and probabilistic logic sampling. The influence diagram is an intuitive visual display of a decision problem. It depicts the key elements of a decision problem such as the possible decisions you can make, uncertainties regarding a decision, and the objectives each decision holds. The diagram then shows how each possible decision influences the others. Dependency modeling is done to ensure that a firm can establish a uniform definition of risk across the operation. The model defines what relationships are allowed between different areas within the organization. Probabilistic logic sampling makes inferences in large, multiply (which means there are several paths between two variables within the network) connected networks, with a random degree of precision-controlled by the sample size. These techniques help to reduce risk by establishing a baseline of risk that the company can withstand as well as calculating the approximate optimal risk level that the company should maintain. By using a decision-analytic network, a firm can simulate the effects of a decision before they make it to make the best decisions possible.

7.3.5 AI Robo-Advisors

Wealth management companies came up with robo-advising as a way to offer automated, algorithm-driven financial advice or portfolio managing services with little to no human interaction and for a significantly lower price than their traditional counterparts. The AI technologies include natural language processing, machine learning, and voice pattern recognition to make reverse DNA queries, set up meetings, and connect customers with representatives to be able to have the best customer experience. Some services that robo-advisors offer are tax-loss harvesting and even threshold-based rebalancing of portfolios. Rebalancing is when the advisor reassesses an investor's portfolio and buys or sells certain assets to realign the portfolio with how risk averse the investor desired their portfolio to be. Tax-loss harvesting is the activity of selling off securities which have losses in order to realize capital losses to offset other incurred income in order to reduce taxes to be paid. According to Ji, most robo-advisors are similar in their fees and what they offer but vary slightly in human support and/or investment strategies (Ji, 2017).

The AI applications for robo-advisors are chatbots and other communicating devices to talk to customers and troubleshoot problems. A couple of examples of companies that use AI to engage with customers are Olivia, Zoe.AI, and Kasisto. These companies are using advanced artificial intelligence algorithms, conversation intelligence, bot analytics, and sentiment analysis to ultimately decode customers' requests and understand their needs in any situation. Another piece of AI technology similar to robo-advisors is something called a robo-trust. Like any other trust, a robo-trust is where a trustor transfers assets to a trustee. The trustor also has a full say on how and to whom the assets will be distributed. The difference being that robo-trusts are managed by an artificial computer program. This essentially allows the creator of the trust to influence the trustees long after their passing.

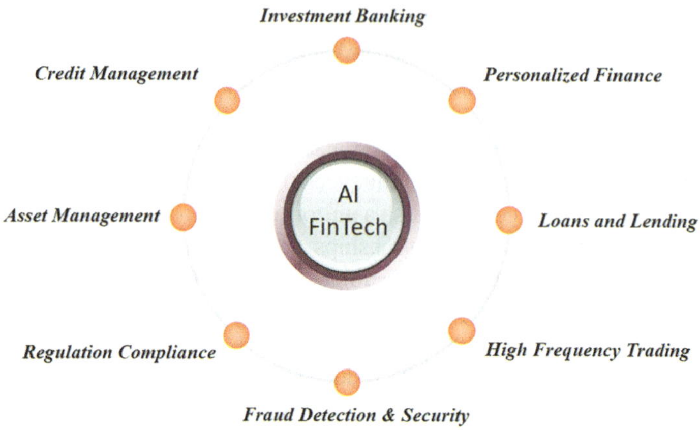

Fig. 7.1 AI application areas in finance

7.4 Features of AI Applications in Financial Services

As we witness many forms of artificial intelligence evolve, many industries around the world, especially in the financial sector, have already started to implement it in their traditional business model. We see these emerge in many different aspects of financial services transforming their efficiency and effectiveness to a degree that was unimaginable years ago. Investment banking, personalized finance, fraud detection, and credit management are some major areas of the financial industry that have been transformed with the move to digitization (Fig. 7.1). AI has allowed companies to use prescriptive analysis technologies with much larger datasets, helping them with much more accurate and profitable investment decisions.

7.4.1 Investment Banking

Artificial intelligence has become an integral part of the banking industry in recent years. The increase in the pace of the financial industry is impossible to keep up without taking advantage of technological improvements. What we can see is that inside investment banking at larger banks such as JP Morgan and Goldman Sachs, where more and more engineers and IT personnel are getting hired. This is because the banking industry is merging with the technology industry. Today applications of AI within investment banking are used for collecting and analyzing big datasets and scripts of individual companies such as 10K and 10Q reports. These datasets would take the human brain and body multiple minutes or even hours to analyze.

For investment banking specifically, the application of AI in data analytics will make it easier to run a discount cash flow and other financial models which are based on historical data such as a 10-K filing. What might take a professional analyst 30 min will take the computer only seconds. This progress might make the demand for accountants decrease over time as more and more of their jobs will be automated. The machine can at some point analyze a company's financials and how they might violate federal or state laws. That would lead to a decrease in demand for lawyers for financial institutions. The process for merging or acquiring a business usually takes 9–10 months on average. Improvement in data collection and analysis might decrease the length of these processes.

There are multiple applications for AI in investment banking. Most of these discoveries are not marketed for the stakeholders to be informed about. One of the topics within AI that have been discussed in banking is how AI can be applied to cybersecurity and money transactions. In the early stages of 2019, JP Morgan announced that their investment bank sector focusing on AI and financial technology (FinTech) will create their cryptocurrency named JPM Coin.

7.4.2 Personalized Finance

With the help of AI, individual investors who are trying to make the most of their money do not have to go to an institution to do so. The AI-embedded apps can advise through the form of messaging with customers and linking accounts to help spend money most efficiently. AI applications filter through financial filings, earnings reports, historical market data, and real-time market data. They process this data using sentiment analysis with artificial intelligence and running projections based on the inputs they receive. Outputs given to consumers consist of up-to-the-second market conditions, unbiased artificial intelligence reporting, and forecasting valuations and outlook on the market going forward. Companies like Bloomberg use devices like the Bloomberg Terminal to provide companies with up-to-date financial information of everything on the market.

Within personalized finance, AI has helped many financial institutions adjust their means of business to adapt to their growing demographic of tech-savvy customers. One of the many examples is Capital One's AI application, known as Eno. Created in 2017, Capital One launched the first US bank natural language SMS text-based assistant that customers can talk to 24/7 via text message, the Capital One mobile app, or online banking. Eno, through its 12 capabilities, can answer customers' questions by providing further detail and insight, as well as predict customers' future needs based on trends and gathered data. As Capital One explains several capabilities of Eno on the application's website, "When Eno spots unusual and suspicious activity, such as fraud, duplicate charges, and generous tips, Eno gives you a heads up through automated alerts and helps you resolve the issues on the spot," furthermore, "Eno helps you shop online safely by instantly creating unique virtual card numbers for each merchant site right from your browser." Eno is one of the many examples of AI technologies used by financial institutions in their personalized finance and banking—allowing them to supply the growing demand of tech-savvy customers. AI in commercial banking could change business processes and interactions with customers, which could create research opportunities for behavioral finance. Eno and its similar technologies provide exactly that.

7.4.3 Credit Management

Credit management is the process of granting credit, setting the terms it is granted on, recovering this credit when it is due, and ensuring compliance with company credit policy, among other credit-related functions. The goal within a bank or company controlling credit is to improve revenues and profit by facilitating sales and reducing financial risks. Cignifi is one artificial intelligence app being used in this field. The big data platform of Cignifi is the first to develop credit risk and marketing scores using mobile phone data. By applying machine learning techniques to the individualized customer data combined with insights from more traditional broad institutional data, not only for banks to analyze credit risk but it is also used to help consumers access services they might not know that they were eligible for and give financial services providers the ability to reach ideal and prequalified customers.

7.4.4 Loans and Lending

AI in business affects lending decisions by helping to access the creditworthiness of applicants across a range of services. "Banks use AI to collect information about customers, including financial transactions, spending habits, geolocations, account details, and social media data. The collection and input of customer data into an AI system creates a curated or targeted ecosystem that financial institutions could use algorithmically to increase customer loyalty. AI can also make predictions about customer behavior and help banks arrive at decisions about creditworthiness or even the interest rate offered to a specific loan applicant" (Truby et al., 2020). Companies collect data from an individual such as credit score, spending and saving habits, education, annual income, employment, financial history, and other personal information. They can process this data by using computer software that analyzes the input data that was collected. Once the data is done being processed, it delivers the output of the annual interest rate for borrowing. The artificial intelligence technique used in this process is machine learning which sorts, analyzes, and then determines the output which is the rate. SoftWorks AI is an example that creates software designs to determine accurate rates automatically by extracting key data information.

7.4.5 Asset Management

Asset management is an area that uses a wide range of machine learning and communication technology. Most models for these applications aggregate all the financial information in one place and compare portfolio data with the market data sources for normalization and reconciliation to see the best way for customers to invest their money. Clarity Money is one example of an app in asset management. The company combines machine learning with AI to create a product that can help with money management, by delivering insights into customers' accounts and spending patterns. As for high-security level protection, Clarity Money multi-level safeguards, including TLS 1.2 encryption, protect customers' information.

AI can hugely affect trading and investment advice that is given to investors/customers. "AI software is being used in research, for example, by mining data to gain sectoral insights that can derive actionable data points" (Truby et al., 2020); through this examination of data, AI can create significant value in trade and investments through the examination of masses of information and the derivation of seemingly unrelated correlations. Algorithmic trading is used to log market history, track current movements, and compile all of these to figure out when the best times are to execute trades to maximize profits. Artificial intelligence uses machine learning to constantly adapt and improve as it acts and takes in more information to be able to buy and sell stock at prime opportunities.

7.4.6 High-Frequency Trading

Another important application of AI in the financial field is high-frequency trading. The high-frequency trading algorithms make decisions using big data analytics. The algorithms allow the trading programs to read millions of articles, reports, statements, and related documents on the internet and form an aggregate statistic. The algorithm can then use this information to make the decision to buy or sell a certain security immediately. These high-frequency trading programs also use predictive algorithms, which give them a step up on low-frequency traders. The algorithms are able to use numerous methods to achieve their predictions; for example, one of the methods is to use a relationship correlation. When one stock goes up, it instantly calculates the probability of how a related stock will react depending on if it is positively or negatively correlated (O'Hara, 2014).

High-frequency trading has improved the overall market by helping increase and improve liquidity. When a buy order and a sell order do not show up to the exchange at exactly the same time, it causes the order to sit there, creating an "air bubble," and slowing down liquidity. High-frequency trading acts as a middleman, similar to a used car salesman, and buys orders to hold until another buyer is ready. This is called market making. The end goal is not to keep the inventory but to move it as fast as possible to turn a profit. Because the high-frequency trading algorithms can act in microseconds, this helps improve the liquidity of the market (O'Hara, 2014). In addition to market making, high-frequency trading also performs intermarket arbitrage. Arbitrage is very similar to market making, but arbitrage is buying on one market and selling on another. This is beneficial to the overall market as well because it is basically moving liquidity from one market to another.

7.4.7 Fraud Detection and Security

In the aspect of consumer finance and cybersecurity, Darktrace is a great example of a company with various AI technologies geared to fraud detection and security. As covered by Alyssa Schroer in Built In's article, *AI and the bottom line: 15 examples of artificial intelligence in finance*, "The company's machine learning platform analyzes network data and creates probability-based calculations, detecting suspicious activity before it can cause damage for some of the world's largest financial firms." Examples of different technologies Darktrace uses and provides to their clients are known as the Enterprise Immune System, Cyber AI Analyst, and the Darktrace Antigena. The company uses all three of these in combination with each other to provide the best form of cybersecurity that succeeds in the span of seconds. As promoted on their main company site, "While the Enterprise Immune System detects emerging threats in real-time, Cyber AI Analyst immediately launches automatic investigation into security incidents, and Darktrace Antigena generates an autonomous response to contain the threat in seconds – all without relying on any rules or signatures." It is here that we can see the substantial impact AI has had on not only allowing financial institutions to better serve their customers but also protecting them to a greater degree.

7.4.8 The "FinTech and RegTech" Paradigm

"The role of financial regulation is therefore far from over, especially in this new era as the financial sector transitions its products, services, processes, and systems to embrace new technologies" (Truby et al., 2020). AI is rapidly influencing the financial sector with innumerable potential benefits, such as enhancing financial services and improving regulatory compliance. The use of AI in the financial sector has developed greatly in five main areas. These five areas are compliance, fraud, and anti-money laundering detection, lending and credit assessments, cybersecurity, trading, and investment decisions. AI can take the human arrow out of financial crimes, error, and/or investment decisions by tracking trends and unusual spending in financial statements to be able to incriminate people that are taking advantage of the system to make themselves rich in an unlawful way.

There are many regulations on where AI can be used in the financial sector of business which is causing uncertainty for the future of AI in finance and banking, although it is much more preferred rather than human labor. "RegTech is the use of technology, including AI, for all manner of legal compliance, including financial regulatory compliance, reporting, and monitoring" (Truby et al., 2020). Therefore, Regtech will affect the foundations of financial services regulation because of a need for a more dynamic rather than a reactive regulatory system.

With the current technological revolution the business (specifically within finance) world is undertaking, the usage of big data and artificial intelligence is becoming increasingly popular to gather and analyze the vast amounts of data undertaken each day by various firms. At this point in this technological revolution, big data and AI are a necessity to run a successful business. Below, the applications of AI within the world of finance and investment banking will be demonstrated through two industry leaders, JPMorgan Chase and Goldman Sachs, and how their utilization of AI helps them to maintain their position at the forefront of the investment banking industry.

Case 7.1: JPMorgan Chase

J.P. Morgan has an annual technology budget of over 12 billion dollars, and more than 4 billion dollars of that budget are spent on artificial intelligence, robotic process automation, and blockchain (jpmorgan.com, 2021). JPMorgan Chase is currently looking to expand their approach to the application of AI and blockchain from its current uses within the organization. The focus with their AI has been on four main things. First, data and cryptology will allow new ways to integrate and generate data needed to train machine learning algorithms. Second, explore the boundaries of machine learning through the use of deep learning and reinforcement learning techniques. Third, create techniques and algorithms that are understandable to regulators and clients. Fourth, develop unbiased and ethical models to build and maintain trust. By building upon its current AI technology, JPMorgan Chase hopes to maintain their competitive advantage within the investment banking industry and use these processes to streamline its customer experience and overall operations.

In an attempt to better understand customer spending habits, in 2015, JPMorgan Chase attempted to analyze their customers' year-round spending data. This utilization of big data can be used to possibly signal the general direction in which the US economy is headed by analyzing increases or decreases in spending or income across various spreads of income. In addition to analyzing customer spending habits, JPMorgan Chase is additionally using big data to protect against fraud and to enhance customer experience. By having access to a bank member's transaction history, this data can help determine if a member's current purchases are in line with this history and developed artificial intelligence (AI) software can flag potential data points straying from this pattern. Such a method can help to reduce identity theft numbers throughout the United States by catching and stopping the problem early when minimal damage has occurred to a member's finances. Regarding enriching customer experience, analysis of various touchpoints in both the physical and web-based customer journey can be done with the help of big data to streamline efficiency and customer satisfaction within the firm.

JPMorgan Chase, while currently utilizing AI software, is looking for different approaches to utilizing this technology to stay ahead of other firms within the industry. One of these futures which they are pursuing is in the field of cryptography to help secure client and customer information more effectively. J.P. Morgan has been working closely with Feismith on several blockchain projects that explore concepts beyond cryptocurrency. One of these projects was Quorum, an ethereum-based enterprise-focused platform built from open-source code. J.P. will be using Quorum to process private transactions within a group of known participants. So you have to use Quorum through J.P., but that offers more privacy and security for you than other open-source codes would. It is completely free to use and even provides alternative consensus mechanisms meaning that you don't need Proof of Work/Proof of Stake in a permissioned network. Quorum is a vastly improved platform to the traditional ethereum-based platform. With increased information security, clients and customers will feel safer supplying their information to JPMorgan Chase which they can then utilize in various marketing areas.

J.P. has been able to further AI development by giving awards to researchers in AI to “empower and advance cutting-edge AI research to solve real-world problems.” The corporation has also hired Apoorv Saxena, a former Google executive who was in charge of cloud-based AI products; he is currently the head of artificial intelligence and machine learning services at J.P. Morgan. Saxena has been placed in charge of asset and wealth management AI technology, and he is the company’s second high-profile AI hire in the last year. Some of the current ways JPMorgan Chase is applying their artificial intelligence software is through anomaly detection, virtual assistants, and smart documents. They are utilizing AI, with the help of big data, to detect anomalies in their customers’ finances involving issues such as fraud as well as being able to identify potential anomalies within the market predicting a potential increase or decrease in its success rate. Additionally, their AI is being applied in the form of virtual assistants to allow for customer complaints or questions to be addressed by this software without having to take an employee’s time away from other work which could be undertaken. These virtual assistants have “the goal of improving client service and operational efficiency” in order to provide the best possible customer experience for JPMorgan Chase’s customers. Another example of JPMorgan Chase’s application of AI is smart documents. AI technology “identifies meaningful information and insights from lengthy text sources to reduce manual operations and improve workflow.”

Case 7.2: Goldman Sachs

Goldman Sachs is one of the largest investment banks globally. The investment banking division is at the forefront of Goldman Sachs’ client franchise. The company is using machine learning to analyze different data sets to come up with recommendations to make richer and more informed decisions.

Machine learning in the investment banking sector is more complex than in the IT world. Artificial intelligence has been heavily advertised in large companies such as Google’s AI computer program that is leading the board; it is well established and has a set of norms and regulations it is programmed to follow. However, in the financial world, analytics are constantly changing. “ML models provide statistical tools that help identify patterns of relevance from the data, and in doing so, can guide practitioners to a place that would have otherwise taken them much longer to get to” Goldman Sachs uses ML in their Fixed Income Clearing Corporation (FICC) business for business intelligence to aid them in understanding how their business is going to help their clients.

Through the usage of big data analytics, Goldman Sachs can track their performance in addition to being able to identify different outcomes of their client’s preferences. In equities, ML models at Goldman Sachs are being used in areas such as business intelligence and flow analysis to inventory management and derivative pricing. The investment company is also looking to add natural language processing to its list of AI processes. Language processing is “an AI technique that translates human language into structured data sets - to automate all sorts of tasks that are used to require human intervention like chat-based quote requests." With more and more data being publicly available from other private investment bankers, there is more data out there to analyze and turn into larger data sets to aid in their successes.

Goldman Sachs is heavily involved in investing in machine learning which can be proven by doing background research on all of their new hires. It is not to say that Goldman Sachs has it all 100% figured out, while they can use ML to create different results with given data, the quality of their results depends on the quality of the data they are using. The models they create through AI, and the outcome can be distorted or not accurate, and that is one of the unfortunate downfalls of predictive analytics. Although consumers can trust that Goldman Sachs is a reputable company that is consistently delivering great results and is backed by the numbers. If they continue to keep investing in their machine learning systems, the company will continue to deliver quality work.

The report shows how AI and big data are helping Goldman Sachs to create, acquire, and process large amounts of data, in turn enabling them to use insightful outside of the box analytics to generate value and enhance their overall competitive advantage. A Goldman professional states, "With the growth and availability of non-traditional data sources such as internet web traffic, patent filings, and satellite imagery, we have been using more nuanced and sometimes unconventional data to help us gain an informational advantage and make more informed investment decisions" (Goldman Sachs, 2016). Data like internet web traffic, patent filings, and satellite imagery are very vast and nontraditional sources of data to be used when it comes to making investment decisions. Though with the help of AI technology, an institution like Goldman Sachs is for the first time being able to acquire and process these unusual and large amounts of data that through provided analytics can tell a story about a company, industry, or any other type of security they may or may not want to invest in. Goldman Sachs is rapidly adopting AI technology within its investment space. "Research success for us is not finding a new stock to invest in, but rather finding a new investment factor that can help improve the way we select stocks. Investment factors should be fundamentally-based and economically-motivated, and the data enables us to empirically test our investment hypotheses" (Goldman Sachs, 2016). Goldman Sachs can apply these emerging technology tools to not only acquire large amounts of information but also to test their findings empirically to come to an investment decision. Though the role of AI is completely shifting how Goldman Sachs interacts and uncovers data to eventually come to an investment decision, it is important to note, "We do not have a computer in the corner simply shooting out trades with no human interaction" (Goldman Sachs, 2016). Overall, the commentary provided by decision-makers from Goldman Sachs in the financial management space goes to show how AI is enabling top financial services firms to acquire and process large amounts of data that has never before been considered to aid investment decisions. This new access is enhancing efficiency across the board, creating larger returns, and aiding advantage against the competition.

7.5 Key Takeaways

The main advantage of applying AI in finance and baking is that it is able to process data faster. Financial institutions are able to analyze a much higher volume of both structured and unstructured data much faster. This is the root of all of the advantages that AI has to offer. Because of this, financial institutions are able to do things that benefit their business and customers. The three main areas that AI allows its advantages are better services, operating more efficiently, and more protection.

The term better service is broad when it comes to financial institutions. With better services, AI offers a lot of benefits for financial institutions' customers. The first one is the ability to be more efficient. The use of chatbots in a financial institution allows more customers to be helped through automated responses. It is beneficial for banks that have a variety of users in different parts of the world because customer services are then available 24/7. The AI also allows personalized recommendations to its users. The AI is able to use its data to make recommendations that would benefit the customer. These are both an advantage to the business because customers are then more satisfied with the institution meaning that the loyalty for customers will be stronger.

The next advantage of AI is the ability for information to operate more efficiently. With AI, the financial institution is able to save on certain expenses. The main one is the reduced number of workers. Since AI is able to answer questions and do services that an actual human would be able to do, there is no need for workers to be doing it. With the amount that is saved, institutions are able to invest that into other areas of their business. They could even invest it into even bettering their AI technology.

A further advantage of AI is in the increased security. AI is able to analyze data to detect if there is fraud occurring based on patterns. AI is constantly growing and improving, but it also means that individuals are finding ways to beat this. By analyzing patterns, there is a better chance that it can catch the fraud occurring. Along with this, the increased amount of data processed means that it is also more accurate when it comes to catching fraud. This gives them an advantage over their competitors because their consumers feel more secure and safe.

Although many positive aspects come from the digitization of financial information, there are still some challenges that come with it. Regulatory requirements, data security, and quality are all challenges that these companies are facing (Talend, 2020). The Fundamental Review of the Trading Book (FRTB) is a regulatory requirement in which financial firms are required to report data information to regulatory agencies. Security is another area that must be taken very seriously by these companies due to the rise in hackers in the financial world. Data quality is another challenge that companies face. Because there is so much data out there, sometimes it does not always correlate. Companies must use their technologies to weed out the bad data and only take the reliable data into their systems. Without a filter on their data, their information and recommendations become less reliable.

7.6 Conclusions

The world of finance is like any other industry affected by technological innovations. Artificial intelligence can make a substantial impact within the financial service industry. While firms are already utilizing various forms of these technologies, further development would be revolutionary for this industry. With the development of AI technologies, firms can expect more reliable investing practices as businesses continue to gather information on the stock markets around the world and attempt to fit more reliable algorithms to the data provided. More reliable investing will result in the growth of wealth among consumers as the markets are able to stay healthy. An additional positive impact that further development of AI can have on organizations is improved efficiency. With the increased levels of technology within organizations, human judgment and error in decision-making are slowly phasing out, resulting in more accurate and in-real-time decision-making. AI also provides the opportunity for more advanced predictive analytics in other parts of the business, for example, the impact a potential merger between organizations would have on a firm and its financial position. With this advanced form of prescriptive analytics, businesses can make more informed decisions that will benefit the shareholders and other stakeholders in the company, which is the overall goal of any firm. One of the major issues which is present in every application of AI is the issue of privacy and the privacy of consumers' information. As demonstrated above, JPMorgan Chase is beginning to attack this problem with AI through new forms of data encryption and increased fraud monitoring. However, with big data continuing to grow exponentially, keeping each customer's information locked away will become increasingly difficult and is an issue which must be continually addressed by these firms wielding the power of AI. Another major issue with the usage of AI is human reliance on an algorithm. As is the case of AI in navigating the stock market, its predictions on where and when to invest are not always accurate because the stock market is virtually impossible to fit with an overarching algorithm. While there are various aspects which some algorithms can be applied to, it is difficult for AI to predict the success of companies, for example, Apple, and the potential impact these companies will have on their industries from a financial standpoint.

References

Darwin, C. (2019). *The origin of species*. London: Vintage.

Donepudi, P. K. (2017). Machine Learning and Artificial Intelligence in Banking. *Engineering International, 5*(2), 83–86. https://doi.org/10.18034/ei.v5i2.490

Fernández, Ana. (2019). Artificial intelligence in financial services. *Economic Bulletin*. https://doi.org/10.2139/ssrn.3366846

Goldman Sachs. (2016). *The role of big data in investing*. Retrieved 2021: https://www.gsam.com/content/gsam/us/en/institutions/market-insights/gsam-insights/gsam-perspectives/2016/big-data/gsam-roundtable.html

Ji, M. (2017). Are robots good fiduciaries? Regulating robo-advisors under the investment advisers act of 1940. *Columbia Law Review, 117*(6), 1543–1583.

Königstorfer, F., &, Thalmann, S. (2020). Applications of Artificial Intelligence in commercial banks – A research agenda for behavioral finance. *Journal of Behavioral and Experimental Finance*, *27*, 100352. https://doi.org/10.1016/j.jbef.2020.100352

Mhlanga, D. (2020). *Industry 4.0 in finance: The impact of Artificial Intelligence (AI) on digital financial inclusion*. https://www.mdpi.com/2227-7072/8/3/45/htm

O'Hara, M. (2014). High-frequency trading and its impact on markets. *Financial Analysts Journal*, *70*(3), 18–27.

Phaneuf, A. (2020, September 9). *Artificial intelligence in financial services: Applications and benefits of AI in finance*. Business Insider.

Schroer, A. (n.d.). *AI and the bottom line: 15 examples of artificial intelligence in finance*. Built In. https://builtin.com/artificial-intelligence/ai-finance-banking-applications-companies

Tadapaneni, N. R. (2020). *Artificial intelligence in finance and investments*. https://www.researchgate.net/profile/Narendra_Rao_Tadapaneni/publication/341526586_Artificial_Intelligence_in_Finance_and_Investments/links/5ec5bb41458515626cbbe68d/Artificial-Intelligence-in-Finance-and-Investments.pdf

Truby, J., Brown, R., & Dahdal, A. (2020). *Banking on AI: mandating a proactive approach to AI regulation in the financial sector*. Taylor & Francis. https://www.tandfonline.com/doi/full/10.1080/17521440.2020.1760454

Artificial Intelligence in Accounting and Auditing

8

Abstract

This chapter explores the development and applications of artificial intelligence in accounting services. Some key technologies are introduced for AI in accounting, including expert systems, robotic process automation, machine learning, and fuzzy neural networks. The featured application areas include general accounting, accounts payable, accounts receivable, purchasing, payment processing, billing, invoicing, debt collection, financial reporting, auditing, fraud detection, and financial risk management. Two case studies are provided on Deloitte and Intuit.

Keywords

Accounting · Expert systems · Robotic process automation · Machine learning · Fuzzy neural networks · General accounting · Accounts payable · Accounts receivable · Purchasing · Payment processing · Billing · Invoicing · Debt collection · Financial reporting · Auditing · Fraud detection · Financial risk management

8.1 Introduction

AI and machine learning have been increasingly applied in accounting practices in some large established corporations. It is important to explore how AI is playing such a critical role in this field today. Artificial intelligence is "the theory and development of information systems able to perform tasks that normally require human intelligence" (Rainer & Prince, 2020). Because accounting and auditing deal with mostly numbers, AI and big data both impact the department heavily. The data generated, sorted, and stored provide people with the information in each accounting decision and task. The strides made with AI make it possible for humans to focus on other important things rather than the busy work that technology could take care of.

L. Chan et al., *Applied Artificial Intelligence in Business*, Applied Innovation and Technology Management, https://doi.org/10.1007/978-3-031-05740-3_8

Not only does AI take big data and process it, but it learns from its work and provides better services as it does. Big data and AI make accounting and auditing easier.

With the advancement of technology, we are now in a time where real-time analysis can occur and essentially will aid you in selling services at a higher value to consumers (i.e., budget forecasting, cash flow management). Accountants have to constantly consider outside factors on a business's performance, watching for any inconsistencies that may be recorded. AI benefits a company by being able to have the capability to predict patterns and notice changes in the behaviors of consumers, also identifying any fraudulent behavior that raises a red flag which reflects positively on the company's performance. Intelligent accounting systems improve efficiency and accuracy within a company and lead it to potential success. Throughout this chapter, we will explore how AI has revolutionized over the decades, in what forms of technology it has been applied to, and the benefits of implementing these smart machines into businesses.

8.2 Development of AI in Accounting

Accounting and auditing have depended entirely on human control and judgment for longer than anyone alive could remember. These sectors in business involve P2P relationships that have been successful for much of human history without needing any artificial intermediary, especially with the discomfort many clients would likely experience if AI were to suddenly adopt a fairly large portion of the responsibilities of accountants to mediate much of both accounting and auditing transactions. AI has so far not grown faster than people are able to prepare for and so is consistently in functional phases where AI can outperform a general accountant in some areas and would be difficult to do the same in other areas of the profession.

In early years, expert systems were widely implemented into the AI component of auditing and tax planning. According to the British Computer Society Specialist Group, they defined an expert system as "the embodiment within a computer of a knowledge-based component, from an expert skill, in such a form that the system can offer intelligent advice or take an intelligent decision about a processing function. A desirable additional characteristic, which many would consider fundamental, is the capability of the system, on demand, to justify its own line of reasoning in a manner directly intelligible to the enquirer. The style adopted to attain these characteristics is rule-based programming" (Connell, 1987, 221). In 1993, Gillett created an audit expert system to help the auditor in adjusting audit programs. From 1989 to 2005, six volumes of book series were published by a variety of authors that discussed applications of these expert systems and the value these systems brought to accounting and auditing.

An efficient expert system allows automatic understanding of the audit task processes, increased knowledge, and transferability of that knowledge. Expert systems began to be apparent in accounting, tax services, and auditing in the early 1980s. The research of expert systems began as a test and then accountants began digging deeper into this field. This led to public accounting firms investing in the building of expert systems with larger knowledge bases to help with audit planning, testing, and decision-making. More case studies investigated real-world experiences and practitioners to develop more detailed expert systems. More research reflected knowledge acquisition from human experts, human interface, and implementation (Gray et al., 2014). Research in expert systems with accounting and auditing follows life cycle stages similar to those of the generic industry life cycle (Gray et al., 2014).

In the IRS, they have developed 13 expert systems with the focus on taxation. These systems are used for criminal tax investigations, finding problems with returns, and auditing in general. The allocation of income and expenses between different corporations is also incorporated into expert systems. These expert systems allow the IRS to prescreen and do routine work. Until 1977, expert systems were not available in accounting. Through McCarthy's development of TAXMAN, an expert system for taxes, more firms were influenced by this development (McCarthy, 1977). The importance of expert systems as a competitive tool becomes more crucial for these larger firms. The application of expert systems has been progressively growing the past 15 years in accounting services such as auditing, financial accounting, personal financial planning, and management accounting.

8.3 Enabling Technologies for AI in Accounting

The field of information technologies related to accounting and auditing can be broken down into several major categories: cloud computing, on-premises computing, desktop applications, and mobile applications. These four types of information technology can be further consolidated into two categories, computing and applications, for the purpose of comparison and analysis. Both cloud computing and on-premises computing share the fact that a third party is used to store, process, and manipulate data through some service that connects to the third party. In both scenarios, the general application of additional computing power comes from this outside source, but the major difference between these two computing styles is the actual location of the third party. On-premises computing means that the third party is onsite, but with cloud computing, the third party can be anywhere in the world and is connected through the internet via a web browser or application. Cloud models can take many shapes from a private cloud (single organization) or a public cloud (hosted by a cloud service provider and open to the public) to a hybrid model which combines different aspects of computing methods and locations (Peihani, 2017). Moreover, cloud services are classified in three ways: SaaS (software as a service), PaaS (platform as a service), and IaaS (infrastructure as a service). The first of these is the classification most people are familiar with as it makes up typical email services or web hosting services, while the last two are useful to programmers in creating customized software applications. For accounting software, there is a significant difference between computing styles and applications, where both types are long files of code that a computer reads and executes to create some function for the user. This can be done on a single device and does not require a third party to host a platform for the data stored and processed, platforms like on-premises or cloud services. When it comes to the distinction between desktop and mobile, the main difference is the devices they are loaded onto. For instance, desktop software packages are installed on computers (sometimes also small personal computers that are mobile), while mobile software is loaded onto mobile devices such as phones, tablets, or PDAs. Often when a product uses both desktop and mobile versions of a software, the desktop version is more complete with a wider array of functions to use when compared to a mobile application. However, mobile technology can clearly complement existing applications and infrastructure by adding an ad hoc element for data processing, information access, communication, and notification (Gebauer & Shaw, 2004).

Robotic process automation (RPA) is one of the major AI-embedded technologies applied in the accounting and auditing field. RPA implementation in accounting can be any software that uses an automated document-review platform, which utilizes cognitive technologies to read and automatically identify relevant information within a set of documents. Reviewing documents is a common, tedious task within the field of accounting and auditing. Auditors would often spend hundreds of hours reviewing relevant documents, contracts, and invoices for a company. In order to expedite this process, accounting agencies have constructed an automated document-review system. This system was developed using natural language processing to comb over documents and recognize any patterns and also applies machine learning to identify relevant terms or information that are needed from the document. Each input subsequently improves the accuracy of the system as more information and data is run through it. The AI is able to learn from that data, and also any previous inputs and outputs, and can adjust itself to become more precise. This automated document processing system is a very powerful tool that can improve accounting and auditing firm's service quality with their clients, help analyze large amounts of data and documents to bring valuable insights to the company, and also enables workers to spend more of their time on other important areas.

Another main type of artificial intelligence technology within the accounting and auditing field is machine learning. It has been widely used for business forecasting and decision-making. Machine learning algorithms have enhanced firms' ability to intelligently forecast certain financial decisions and their outcomes based on transactions. Through advanced data mining and analytics, businesses can improve investment decisions and increase profitability. AI has been utilized in organizations to forecast certain financial data and reports, such as short- and long-term revenue, gross margin, earnings, market demand, cash flow, or customers. This type of information can all be predicted by the AI system to provide insights in order to make better decisions within the company. Similar to the document review technology, the intelligent forecasting system continuously learns and gets better in order to enhance the prediction accuracy. Artificial intelligence is able to produce an unbiased opinion for businesses to analyze and apply to become better informed about any financial judgments, as an AI system cannot be influenced by any emotions that would normally occur through manual decision-making. Additionally, there are neural networks, a form of machine learning algorithm that attempts to mimic human brains. These technologies are useful for making predictions based on large amounts of data of past events and patterns.

A widely applied AI technique being used in the accounting industry is fuzzy neural network. These learning machine algorithms function as fraud detection systems and reduce failure of detecting fraudulent financial reporting cases. These "fuzzy" logic systems simulate human reasoning, but without the bias that accompanies human reasoning, especially when making decisions based on analyzed data sets. These neural networks are advantageous as far as problem-solving goes if problems presented have no existing mathematical models for the issue at hand. Predicting fraud via an auditor at their own devices can be difficult as fraudulent activity in firms is never initiated without the "evidence" being swept out of plain sight, so AI integration would inarguably be a must in auditing practices.

In auditing, judgments are made based on historical data and accounting records. Neural networks can be developed using that historical data for auditing and accounting companies to utilize. For example, a sample of some fraud and non-fraud engagements was analyzed and used to develop a logistic regression model that "predicts the possibility of fraudulent financial reporting for an audit client based on certain fraud risk factors such as weak internal control environment, rapid company growth, etc." (Omoteso, 2012). A study found that the model was more accurate than actual auditors at evaluating risk for the fraud engagements put into the system. By having the neural network's ability to assess trends and patterns, the system can help aid the audit decision-making process. For auditing, AI has also been implemented in "high-value information review" scenarios, where AI application is currently being used in detecting trends in large data sets for any relevant signs of fraudulent activity, or anomalies. Pacific Northwest National Laboratories of Washington State designed a system that works with high-value information in this same way, called "IN-SPIRE," and can be used in any application to show trends of large data sets that can be easy to miss. Applications such as IN-SPIRE work prominently as a preliminary audit function as trends that may be relevant to the auditor can be gathered, analyzed, and instated in the auditing process. IN-SPIRE should not be considered as "complete" AI, but still harbors the machine learning aspect of AI, and is very representative of how much more efficient AI can be for tasks that are difficult for human beings to manage.

AI has also been effectively used in internal accounting practices or managerial accounting as hybrid intelligent systems which have been used extensively in developing marketing strategies. ADAPT, a digital AI platform based on marketing research, provides competitive advantages in the market where information based on consumer data is processed through AI algorithms to provide the modern managerial accountant with valuable information to identify consumer needs and make decisions based on the data available.

Fig. 8.1 Accounting features

8.4 Features of AI Applications in Accounting

Since accounting has a very broad coverage, many subcategories of accounting technology exist. This section explores the different types of accounting AI applications, their features, and why they make accounting better. These areas include general accounting, accounts payable, accounts receivable, purchasing, payment processing, billing, invoicing, debt collection, financial reporting, auditing, fraud detection, and financial risk management (Fig. 8.1).

8.4.1 General Accounting

Intelligent accounting system is the main category of accounting software used to record and report a firm's financial transactions, store past financial data, and automate tedious processes associated with accounting using modules to sort between different core accounting practices like purchasing, accounts receivable, or billing. Additionally, some non-core modules are included in accounting software but vary by product (examples include expense, payroll, or timesheet modules). Firms operating in this field have used a combination of different AI technologies to provide a web-based cloud accounting solution with offline data entry capabilities to maximize flexibility of their solution.

Due to the general nature of this category of software, the AI technology that it utilizes is also more general with some product differentiation in non-core modules of accounting or in the combination of information technology to achieve offline data entry. For example, the accounting software firm ClearBooks utilizes a cloud-based service using Amazon Web Services (AWS) to provide web-based cloud accounting services. Even though ClearBooks requires internet access to use their service, they do have a method of offline data entry using a ClearBooks mobile application to input data offline, but it does require some manual synchronization to update the cloud version. ClearBooks product was designed to aid small to medium firms in organizing and structuring their accounting systems to be able to compete with larger firms and pave the way for large-scale expansion. With the usage of cloud accounting software like Clearbooks, small firms have the opportunity to increase their overall revenue while only having a small recurring operating expense rather than large investments in physical assets to store, process, and manipulate data.

8.4.2 Accounts Payable

It is critical that the accounts payable aspect of accounting for businesses is conducted in an accurate and timely fashion to ensure that both providers and consumers are generating and receiving their proper amounts of revenue. For example, OnPay Solutions automates the accounts payable process and eliminates manual paper-based incoming invoices and outgoing payments through AI technology. Their software solution is intended for mid-sized and large companies. The platform supports multiple banks and ERPs. OnPay's technology offers end-to-end AP automation, payables automation, and virtual cards for AP for a more error-free and streamlined experience. The accounts payable automation module uses AI technology such as optical character recognition (OCR) and machine learning. The combination of technology creates an electronic and low touch, even no-touch, process for handling both invoices and B2B payments. The invoice automation process converts paper invoices into electronic invoices (eInvoices) and uses OCR technology to enter them into a digital workflow and approval process. The software system matches the original invoice to supporting documents, such as purchase orders, in order to validate its authenticity and catch fraud. This follows a study done on the usage and impact of AI in accounting (Lee & Tajudeen, 2020) and includes five categories in which they are used: (1) storing images of invoices, (2) auto capturing of the invoice information, (3) risk management tool, (4) routing and monitoring of invoices' approval, and (5) tracking users' activities. Drawing a parallel between OnPay Solutions software, the use of OCR to capture invoice information is specifically highlighted, as the system is capable to train itself and help in extracting text from any image by using neural networks and the ability of machine learning (Garg et al., 2018).

8.4.3 Purchasing

Purchasing is the other necessary part of accounts payable for business of any type, as companies would not be able to acquire goods and services without it. Accounting software such as Bellwether PO and Inventory by Bellwether Software and Procurify are both cloud-based software that make accounting aspects of purchasing like spend management and tracking of inventory easier and more efficient. AI technologies are often embedded in the server end of the cloud platform. For example, Bellwether PO and Inventory is both an on-premise and cloud-based web application that offers better streamlining of key features of accounting such as requisition, purchase order management, and invoice matching. Bellwether software is hyper-flexible due to being completely web-based and provides further ease of use because it is designed to work on all devices including Mac, Windows, and Linux computers, as well as cellphones and tablets. This means that the software runs entirely through the user's web browser of choice, from Internet Explorer to Firefox to Google Chrome, and does not require any configuration or additional software. Because this software is so versatile, it is suitable for a wide range of businesses to utilize and can be used by companies of any size. Bellwether's model for their software follows the move for the majority of business functions to be cloud-based and through the web. Procurify is a cloud-based spend-management platform designed for use by mid-sized and enterprise-level companies. Being cloud-based allows for greater visibility and control for their purchase order processing system, and they also provide analytic reports for purchase tracking in real time. These services use machine learning algorithms through the cloud platforms. Like Bellwether, Procurify integrates directly into already existing accounting systems like NetSuite and QuickBooks, as well as giving an experience similar to online shopping when using it with Amazon Business PunchOut for purchasing.

8.4.4 Accounts Receivable

Accounts receivable is the amount owed to a company by its customers from the sale of goods or services. It is a crucial part of accounting due to the fact that it affects the future cash flow of the company. Accounts receivable make up a huge amount in total assets and result in higher sales revenue and profit (Mehar, 2005). AI-embedded software packages can be used in managing accounts receivable. For example, ReliaBills is a cloud-based platform that helps businesses navigate the subscription economy. It is also available on mobile devices such as Android and Apple iOS, for easy access on the go. The platform includes tools like check processing, collections management, receivables ledger, and more, helping businesses manage their billings more efficiently. Not only are there unlimited invoices and emails, ReliaBills free trial and subscription business model, which is ideal for small start-up businesses.

8.4.5 Payment Processing

Accountants utilize payment processing software to ensure the payment process goes smoothly in the context of avoiding errors and late payments as they oversee their client's business operations. AI software supports the automation of this process. This type of software is beneficial to any organization that accepts payment methods other than cash. It is especially beneficial to large companies with business-to-business transactions, as invoice processing is completed at a much faster rate than the traditional invoice processes. One important software in the payment processing field that is useful to organizations utilizing business-to-business payments is Balance. Co-founders Bar Geron and Yoni Shuster of the software company have created this payment platform to be utilized by business-to-business merchants. Although this is a relatively new company, founded in early 2020, it has raised $25 million in a Series A funding round led by Ribbit Capital. Balance offers a variety of payment approaches such as automatic payments, bank wires and checks, credit/debit cards, and other convenient payment methods for business-to-business transactions. Their overall goal is to make the online payments experience for businesses as seamless as it is for consumer payments. Balance has already become a successful startup IT company, as they have already partnered with e-commerce enterprises such as BigCommerce, Choco, Zilingo, and Magento.

8.4.6 Billing and Invoicing

Bills and invoices are documents that contain information on the purchase sales. The billing and receiving processes in accounting mainly focus on billing and invoicing customers about the sale transactions. Companies can use AI-based software to collect and analyze data to generate reports to send out to customers to be reviewed, confirmed, and paid. All processes are key to managing, organizing, and improving working capital in the business. Automation is essential to keeping track of sales transactions and customer payments, allowing both the business and customers to plan out their expenses to make sure their payments are in a timely manner. For example, the Square Point of Sale is a cloud-based, and mobile POS software system that tracks customer preferences and feedback for every transaction, allowing the companies to see sales and inventory reports on how their business is performing. It is best for small businesses but is also flexible to serve any type of business. They provide a free version and trial with no contract necessary, making it easy for any business to start using their system. Companies like ShakeShack, GreenKeys Locksmith, and Shopwave have used Square for their businesses' billing and invoicing needs. Another billing and invoicing platform is Recurly. Recurly is a cloud-based platform that simplifies billing and invoicing for mid-size to enterprise businesses. It protects the revenue with the different gateway support, routing, and intelligent retry. The features include ACH payment processing, billing and invoicing, data security, discount management, multicurrency, and more.

Billing and provisioning software can automate customer service, operational support, and accounting for the telecommunications industry. Some examples include: OpenBilling System, PortaBilling, Utilibill, and EZ BILL ASP. It is important to note, however, that billing and provisioning software also aids in other industries other than the telecommunications industry. For instance, Utilibill has combined its customer base of those within the utilities sector that provide the services of basic amenities such as gas, water, and electricity while also offering billing and provisioning solutions for telecommunication providers. The software offers a cloud-based utility billing and customer information platform which helps their clients manage the complete billing processes (Success & Insights, 2021). This is a cost-effective platform designed to help small- to mid-sized utility companies with their customers' billing solutions.

8.4.7 Debt Collection

Debt collection software is used by debt collection agencies to recover the amount owed on behalf of the original lenders. Collection agencies recover unpaid debt for accounting firms and for the accounting firm's clients. Software packages can represent the whole debt recovery program's data set and operative plans. It gathers all debtors' profiles in one place, consisting of their address, credit card information, current balance, and a thorough report about the subject of debt's delinquent payments: amount, age of debt, etc. (Mueller, 2021). Debt collection software is known to be "software-to-software," as there is a sense of collaboration between a creditor's software and through the collections agency's software to be able to obtain access to the creditor's file system in order to have the debtor's information accessible. Some AI-based intelligent debt recovery software packages even offer different strategies for debt recovery and suggest different collection methods depending on the debtor's personal issue. It can prescribe different payment plans to be offered to debtors, according to their monthly wage, credit history, etc. Large organizations deal with more unpaid debt from their customers and often need help from a debt collection agency to recover from the economic loss they face. It became widely known to these companies that implementing an AI-supported debt collection system would be more efficient in gathering and analyzing customer information. Employing smart credit collection software tools give the possibility to seamlessly interface with other enterprise systems to extract and exchange all relevant customer transactional and behavioral data (Mincu, 2012).

The AI technology can ensure the debt collection agencies have the most up-to-date methods, aiding in the process of coming up with the best strategies that will be most effective for repayment. By following a consistent credit and debt collection operations plan internally, the third parties need to set up their operations under the same philosophy of the outsourcer's operations with respect to customer focus, workforce, debt collection software, and technology. Some examples such as Simplicity by Katabat, Rocket Collector by GBS Corp, and YayPay by Quadient have helped in the process of getting lenders their money back. Simplicity allows an individual, group, or firm to enter and track all collection cases through the entire collection process. This software is powered by machine learning algorithms and is ideal for small- or medium-sized debt collection agencies. The platform helps clients synchronize customer offers, implement customer workflows, and build integrated content and treatments across all customer channels (Katabat, 2021).

8.4.8 Financial Reporting

Financial reporting allows businesses to accurately and efficiently produce errorless statements for themselves, their shareholders, and the public. Financial reporting software takes large amounts of data, compiles it, and produces easy-to-read financial statements for business use or for legal purposes if the business is public. Financial reporting and financial analysis are areas in accounting where AI has been successfully implemented and is showing more potential in the accounting area as progress is made in both AI research and accountants' increasing understanding of how AI systematically works, via different computer software programs, etc. Many accounting businesses find themselves replacing simple, repetitive tasks usually completed by humans with AI. Replacing these tasks with AI allows the human workers within the business predominantly focus their attention on relational and high-skilled tasks instead, making the business more effective overall.

An example of the financial reporting software is OneStream. OneStream looks to better streamline data as soon as it comes in to give business leaders better information to go from when making decisions, as well as verifying the accuracy of the reports they furnish to the Securities and Exchange Commission (SEC). OneStream supports data from various sources, including Excel. Since many accountants are familiar with and heavily use Excel, integrating it with their software cuts away time they would need to learn a new platform. They also offer data visualization through interactive dashboards, which eliminates solely relying on cookie-cutter reports and allows for managers to change the variables in their reports to get immediate and accurate data for decision-making. The ability to combine tables, charts, and graphs to identify business trends is quicker than their competitors.

8.4.9 Auditing

Auditing is a process that aims to provide reasonable assurance that a business is fairly presenting their financial statements and complying with set rules, regulations, and laws both internally and externally. Auditing is generally a long and arduous, as well as expensive process. AI-supported auditing software aims to combat these traditional drawbacks of the audit process. Accounting and audit firms use AI to reveal any risks or frauds during audit time. This saves the auditors time because they will not have to sort all the information manually and search for any errors or suspicious activity in the transactions. The perks of intelligent systems are they can help the accounting professionals see a larger picture by being able to predict and see the shift changes in consumer behavior, identify fraudulent behavior, and more all faster instead of having to do everything manually. Auditors can supplement their judgment capacities with AI analytical power to reach a better-informed decision and consequently provide a higher level of assurance. Initially, auditors will probably utilize AI in their analysis of big data.

A noteworthy smart auditing software is Jolt. It is designed as an entire operations suite with consistent forms, intelligent checklists, automated reporting, label printer, and more—all seamlessly integrated and organized together. Jolt is focused on accuracy of checklists and legal procedures in the workplace. For example, businesses can utilize scanning a (Quick Response) QR code on the device by an employee to verify that a certain procedure has been completed. This is a secondary method of verification without constantly having to oversee them. In addition, Jolt specializes in automated reporting as well. If there is a variable in the checklist, such as the temperature of a freezer, Jolt averages these numbers over time for managers to verify that their equipment is working over time.

8.4.10 Financial Fraud Detection

The continuous battle against fraud has driven companies to develop new and improved AI technology to detect it more efficiently. Techniques such as machine learning used for event monitoring, pattern recognition, continuous improvement, and anomaly detection are used by most companies. Kount Complete and Fraud.Net are some examples that employ the use of machine learning for fraud detection. Deep learning is considered one of the most helpful techniques as it offers an advanced approach which can search millions of transactions to detect any signs of fraud. There are various machine learning techniques including classification, clustering, prediction, outlier detection, regression, and visualization. Each of these techniques can handle different problems; however, classification has been used the most. The most frequently used techniques are logistic models, neural networks, the Bayesian belief network, and decision trees, all of which fall into the "classification" category. Risk Field and Similarity are two of the many software using AI and machine learning to detect fraud. Their software analyzes the customer's current methods of transaction and can quickly detect if there is a deviation. Such software is efficient, fast, and can give users more accurate results. Using tools such as machine learning or AI-based software prevents not only fraud but also provides a more secure platform for the customers as for the companies themselves.

8.4.11 Financial Risk Management

Of all the types of risks a company might face, financial risk has the most impact on a company's financial situation. Organizations manage their financial risk in different ways, but the key is to have a plan or develop a strategy based on the risk the company might get in the future, and IT is as well much needed in this field. To prevent any risk companies must also look over their credit, accounts receivable, and collections. The keys that help the system to assess risks and provide the right information are to access the right data and process transactional information, converting the data into business information, such as product data, client, entity, individual, etc. The third is to link the risk data to the finance process, and the fourth is to blend all financial or nonfinancial transactions that make sense to the business units. Zeb Control is one of the software dealing with the control over financial institutions. It reviews any investment activities, capital market, customer business, and property business. The software allows users to quickly generate risk reports and have a good overview of the test reporting system. Machine learning algorithms identify key patterns and simulations over individual transactions. It provides calculations based on coordinated transactions and market data.

With the use of AI and machine learning technology in accounting, auditing, or financing companies, it can vastly improve just about anything the company needs to do. There are many companies out in the world who are already using an AI- or machine learning-based system to improve their daily functions. Even if a business itself does not already have a platform in place that has AI or machine learning, there are other companies out there that keep those businesses up-to-date with the current technology and other improvements. There have been AI and machine learning technology to keep them in the market, and on the same level as all their competitors. AI and big data play important roles in companies like Intuit and Deloitte. Specific examples of this include Intuit's machine learning program and Deloitte Omnia, an analytics engine. In both cases, AI and big data are proven to create value in these companies and give them a competitive advantage in the accounting and auditing market.

Case 8.1: Intuit

Intuit is a company that provides accounting, tax filing, and budget counseling for both businesses and individuals. They are the parent company to QuickBooks, ProConnect, TurboTax, and Mint. Intuit was founded in 1983 by Scott Cook and Tom Proulx and made public in 1993. They work to power "prosperity around the world." With over 10,000 employees worldwide, with offices in 20 different locations in 9 countries, they ranked 11 out of 100 of the best companies to work for by Fortune, and one of the most diverse companies in America according to Forbes. As of 2020, they generated around $7.7 billion (USD); this was a 15% increase compared to 2019.

Intuit uses machine learning technology in all of their company programs, which allows for the websites to become completely customized for each individual customer. With the use of this technology in their programs, they have found that it creates a stronger connection between the customer and programs. This strong connection brings new and returning customers back to the websites. The AI programs that run behind the websites are not just a single algorithm or a single set of codes. Intuit actually has four main models that help run and feed the recommendation engine. First is the "training engagement model"; this helps to analyze the content from the users to help feed the recommendation engine (Stine, 2020). Second is the "Multi-Class Customer Profile Module," which looks at and assesses the user's product profile, and how they use each product. Third is the "User/Content Similarity Model"; this model is in place to assess similarities and differences in all user's behavior and interactions to help suggest new content based on the user's similarities. Last is the "Multi-Dimensional Categorical Model"; this helps to combine the data collected and combine it into like categories, creating a multidimensional program of new suggested content for each user (Stine, 2020). With these four models in place, it makes sure that the right content gets suggested to the right person, along with continual website enhancement for the users.

Intuit has created a competitive advantage by making it very simple for anyone to use their website for anything from filing one's taxes to making a budget for themselves or a business. Currently, Intuit is working on upgrading their machine learning programs to be able to use photos of financial documents, like somebody' W-2, to automatically fill in the needed information in the correct spots. If they are able to get this feature up and running, with little to no mistakes when transferring information, it would give them a serious advantage among other tax filing companies because people will be able to complete the task from anywhere using their mobile devices. Intuit is a very customer-driven company, which is why they are constantly trying to improve and keep their AI programs up to date. In a message from CEO, Sasan Goodarzi, he mentions that the company is going to work on improving their technology organization and website navigation for customers to help them complete tasks quicker and make them more successful. This gives them a competitive advantage over other companies because by putting your customers first, it allows the customers to be more successful, but also it brings them back to the company knowing that they will always be put first.

Intuit's globally used programs work to help make any customer who uses them successful when doing anything from filing taxes to creating a budget. Intuit states that they are "laser focused on our customers, live and breathe innovation" (Intuit, 2021). With this belief driving their company, this is why they work as hard as they can to have one of the best "AI-driven expert platforms" to help their customer succeed (Team, 2020). With the constant innovation being done to their preexisting system, Intuit is able to make their platforms completely customizable for each individual user. While the user is not able to do this physically by themselves, Intuit makes it possible by tracking the way they use the platform. While there is always going to be some distrust with customers not knowing where their information is going, Intuit makes sure it stays safe within their platforms and uses it to customize and fuel their suggestion engine.

Case 8.2: Deloitte

Deloitte LLP is a company that provides accounting, bookkeeping, and auditing services. Founded by William Welch Deloitte in 1845, Deloitte Touche Tohmatsu Limited merged with another company in America in 1989 to become the accounting and auditing giant it is known as today. In 2020, Deloitte generated $47.6 billion (USD). Also as of 2020, they employ 330,000 members of the company.

As a highly data-driven company, Deloitte takes measures to remain on the forefront of information systems and technology. As such, Deloitte uses artificial intelligence in many ways. The company writes a *State of AI in the Enterprise* report every year, which investigates other accounting companies and their use of AI over the past year. In 2020's edition, they found that "AI investments are increasingly leading to measurable organizational benefits: improved process efficiency, better decision-making, increased worker productivity, and enhanced products and services" (Ammanath et al., 2020). Deloitte's findings have influenced their own methods of application. Deloitte's Trustworthy AI framework is their answer to increasing AI usage. It includes six key dimensions: fair/impartial, robust/reliable, safe/secure, responsible/accountable, transparent/explainable, and privacy.

Some examples of how Deloitte's Trustworthy AI framework creates value from its processes include automating responses to certain repetitive tasks, placing online job ads, making product recommendations to customers, and even trading on behalf of its clients (an example of AI as a user agent). One of the major applications has been their implementation of an automated document-review platform, which uses "cognitive technologies to read and automatically identify relevant information within a set of documents" (Deloitte US: Market Development, 2017). Reviewing documents is a common, tedious task within the field of accounting and auditing. Auditors would often spend hundreds of hours reviewing relevant documents, contracts, and invoices for a company. In order to expedite this process, Deloitte developed the automated document-review system. This system was developed using natural language processing to comb over documents and recognize any patterns and also applies machine learning to identify relevant terms or information that is needed in the document. Each input subsequently improves the accuracy of the system as more information and data is run through it. The system is able to learn from the big data and previous inputs and can adjust itself to become more precise. An automated document review system has been very helpful within the organization, as Deloitte's teams have been able to process documents and any unstructured information with great speed and accuracy, "one team was able to increase the scope of their contract review effort by multiple orders of magnitude—processing more than 150,000 documents—using the application" (Deloitte US: Market Development, 2017). This automated document processing system is a very powerful system that can improve Deloitte's service quality with their clients, help analyze data and documents to bring valuable insights to the company, and enable workers at the company to spend more of their time on other important areas.

Deloitte uses a global audit platform that is digital, dynamic, and cloud based. Their analytics engine, called Deloitte Omnia, looks for hidden patterns, trends, and risks in large data sets and large entry populations. Omnia can also "curate publicly available financial information, such as disclosures and SEC comment letters, to perform more comprehensive risk assessments, and deliver industry benchmarking, perspective and visualizations" (Deloitte, 2021). Deloitte uses big data to gather information about its customers and use that information to influence their approaches to accounting for each individual customer. By gathering this data, they will be able to find patterns in customers' actions, anticipate what they will do next, and cater to their customers better. Another application of artificial intelligence used by Deloitte has been their development of an insight-driven organization (IDO) framework to help businesses achieve strategic goals. This IDO framework is able to analyze large amounts of data and provide feedback to make more informed financial decisions. The artificial intelligence system is able to translate "growing data volumes into measurable business value and creating long-term competitive advantage from existing data assets" (Zhang & Xiong, 2020). This IDO system is able to improve the quality of decision-making and also expedites the process, while at the same time reducing decision cost. Anyone with access to the framework can make better, more educated decisions regarding any accounting or auditing matters.

Using deep learning technology, Deloitte has also developed a voice analysis program, known as the Behavior and Emotion Analytics Tool (BEAT). BEAT is able to monitor and analyze any voice interactions, in over 30 different languages. BEAT has several key functions that help Deloitte increase competitiveness within their field. One of the functions is BEAT's ability to detect high-risk interactions, using natural language processing technology. This can help organizations with regulatory matters regarding their contracts, as the BEAT system can judge the preliminary data extracted from internal and external information and then determine the regulatory compliance of the signed contracts (Zhang & Xiong, 2020). BEAT is also fully customizable, so it can meet specific requirements set by the user to analyze the risk. One of the other functions of the BEAT technology is the ability to alert users to actions that may result in a negative outcome, such as complaints or behavioral issues. BEAT can then provide detailed information about the reasons for their occurrence. This is useful information for any organization, as they can analyze what sort of context results in negative outcomes and can adjust their strategy to try and avoid situations of that type in the future.

At the current stage of AI applications (analyzing additional data from smart devices and sensors), Deloitte is on the forefront of innovation but still has room to improve and create. All of these processes help Deloitte have a competitive advantage over other companies: by implementing its Trustworthy framework. By designing their AI to make fair, consistent decisions, to be completely explainable to participants, to include policies that clearly establish who is responsible, to be at least as reliable as traditional systems, to comply with data regulations, and to be protected from cybersecurity risks, Deloitte is ensuring that no matter what their strides are with artificial intelligence, they will put their people first.

8.5 Key Takeaways

The use of AI in the field of accounting can be beneficial and lead to more efficient/accurate results. Artificial intelligence can be used for things like enforcing corporate policy, streamlining data entry analysis, and other essential tasks. By having AI-based software available in the accounting and auditing sector, it allows more time for accountants to focus on their clients and potentially help them with larger purchases or investments. As previously mentioned, ensuring corporate policy is one of the advantages of having AI in the accounting/auditing field. "AI can scan employee receipts, credit card transactions and travel bookings to check if any purchases were made outside of the policy. This makes it possible for auditors to quickly assess errors and ensure employees are following all policies" (business.com). AI is also used for helping managers keep track of transactions that can be time-consuming, pulling data from receipt images and sorting them by spending category and then generating reports that can be reviewed in one place. Another way that artificial intelligence brings an advantage to the accounting/auditing field is by reducing the risk of fraud. "...it can predict patterns and detect a wide variety of irregularities in financial data. This allows auditors to fraudulent spending before the employees can be reimbursed" (business.com). This saves the accountants' time because it has the capability to check for any fraudulent transactions keeping everything efficient and safe for the company.

Studies have found that humans tend to perform poorly when it comes to complex tasks that carry large amounts of information from multiple sources, which can be overwhelming to take in. "...exposure to large amounts of information can potentially lead to increased ambiguity, information overload, difficulty identifying relevant information and patterns and, consequently, lead to suboptimal audit judgment" (Issa et al., 2016). When it comes to the non-routine tasks that come up, an AI machine would need to be able to adapt to the changes fast, which we are not that advanced yet. Therefore, accountants and auditors are still vital and can be assisted by AI technology to keep the consistency and efficiency for a company. Auditors can supplement their judgment capacities with AI analytical power to reach a better-informed decision and consequently provide a higher level of assurance. Initially, auditors will probably utilize AI in their analysis of big data (Issa et al., 2016). AI has progressively advanced, and its help in the accounting/auditing industry has resulted in fraud protection, company policy assurance, automatic populating and sorting, and others that make the more challenging jobs easier.

There are a few issues that come with big data and AI usage. Among the most notable, the main issue of big data in accounting and auditing is dirty data. Dirty data means inaccurate, incomplete, incorrect, redundant, or erroneous data. Ernst & Young, another accounting and auditing giant, has determined that unstructured data is the most pressing issue when it comes to the application of AI and that the solution is the standardization of data. Like Deloitte, Ernst & Young creates an annual report on technology in the accounting field, called the *EY Global Tax Technology and Transformation Survey*. In 2020, the report revealed that a typical tax team spends 40–70% of its time gathering and manipulating data, when this could be done in a fraction of the time by AI (EY Americas, 2020). This is proven to be difficult when there is unstructured data, so in order for AI to do difficult tasks in short amounts of time, data must be organized and standardized before being entered into an intelligence system. The implications for managers, then, are to make sure that the initial entering of data into information systems is flawless, structured, and standardized.

AI helps to minimize human error by being able to copy and paste information needed into the correct fields, along with performing simple to very complicated calculations. For example, Intuit's TurboTax uses auto-filling to make it very simple for their returning customers to complete their taxes each year. Once any customer using TurboTax fills in all their financial information, their program is able to quickly calculate their tax return balance for that year. If more companies were to add this into their existing systems, it would also help to lighten the workload on their current employees doing this work by hand and ultimately increase the output for the company. The implementation of AI in accounting and auditing firms also works to reduce fraud within the company. It is able to do so by being able to detect falsified transactions and detect any duplicate information that may appear. This would help the companies to keep things more organized in the long run by knowing there is only one location where each transaction or other vital information is going to be stored.

8.6 Conclusion

Through analyzing recent business practices, we continued to discover how accounting businesses use AI in assistance to uncover irregularities in auditing practices. Normally, auditing can be a very slow, monotonous practice that takes humans a very long time. However, this is a task that we are beginning to see getting taken over by AI, and it is benefiting these businesses tremendously. Along the same lines of identifying inconsistencies within the data, the implementation of AI into the accounting field is helping accountants discover fraud more easily. Human error is inevitable, but the use of AI will continue to close that gap of errorless accounting practices. It has become clear that efficient usage of AI and big data are essential for businesses to succeed. Both Intuit and Deloitte are utilizing big data and AI in impressive ways. In the future, this trend will become increasingly obvious. The world is turning to a new, digital forefront, and businesses need to keep up with the changing times in order to survive and thrive.

References

Ammanath, B., Kulkarni, A., Anderson, S., & Novak, D. R. (2020, October 28). *Conquering AI risks*. Retrieved from https://www2.deloitte.com/global/en/insights/focus/cognitive-technologies/conquering-ai-risks.html

Automated document review: Case study: Deloitte US: Market Development. Deloitte United States. (2017, November 29). https://www2.deloitte.com/us/en/pages/about-deloitte/articles/business-innovation-automated-document-review.html

Connell, N. (1987). Expert systems in accountancy: A review of some recent applications. *Accounting and Business Research 17*(67), 221–233.

Deloitte. (2021). *Audit Technology | Deloitte US*. Deloitte United States. https://www2.deloitte.com/us/en/pages/audit/solutions/audit-technology-solutions.html

EY Americas. (2020, November 17). *How artificial intelligence will empower the tax function*. Retrieved from https://www.ey.com/en_us/tax/how-artificial-intelligence-will-empower-the-tax-function

Finkle, L. (2020). *Not So Taxing: Intuit Uses AI to Make Tax Day Easier. NVIDIA Blog*. Retrieved from https://blogs.nvidia.com/blog/2020/07/10/intuit-ai-taxes/

Garg, Gupta, Prabhakar, Garg, & Trivedi. (2018). Optical Character Recognition using Artificial Intelligence. *International Journal of Computer Applications, 179*(31), 14–20.

Gray, G. L., Chiu, V., Liu, Q., & Li, P. (2014). The expert systems life cycle in AIS research: What does it mean for future AIS research? *International Journal of Accounting Information Systems, 15*(4), 423–451.

Gebauer, J., & Shaw, M. J. (2004, Spring). *Success factors and impacts of mobile business applications: Results from a mobile e-procurement study*. Retrieved from https://www.jstor.org/stable/27751105

Get a Free Demo. Adapt. (n.d.). https://adapt.online/company/company_index.html.

Intuit. (2021). *Intuit Company Info*. Retrieved from https://www.intuit.com/company/

Issa, H., Sun, T., & Vasarhelyi, M. A. (2016). Research ideas for artificial intelligence in auditing: The formalization of audit and workforce supplementation. *Journal of Emerging Technologies in Accounting, 13*(2), 1–20.

Katabat. (2021, January 05). *Katabat expands product reach by acquiring simplicity collection software*. Retrieved from https://www.prnewswire.com/news-releases/katabat-expands-product-reach-by-acquiring-simplicity-collection-software-301201227.html

Lee, C. S., & Tajudeen, F. P. (2020). Usage and impact of artificial intelligence on accounting: Evidence from Malaysian organisations. *Asian Journal of Business and Accounting, 13*(1), 213–240.

McCarthy, L. T., (1977). Reflections on TAXMAN: An Experiment in Artificial Intelligence and Legal Reasoning. *Harvard Law Review* 837.

Mehar, A. (2005). Simultaneous determination of inventories and accounts receivable. *Managerial and Decision Economics, 26*(4), 259–269. http://www.jstor.org/stable/25151374

Mincu, C. (2012). Innovative Operations Strategies for the Credit and Debt Collection Teams of the Non-financial Creditors. 1. Back to Business from Competition Policy Point of View 9, 141.

Mueller, H. (2021). *Debt collection software: Receivables Management: Digital debt collection*. Retrieved from https://ecollect.org/wiki/debt-collection-software/

Omoteso, K. (2012). The application of artificial intelligence in auditing: Looking back to the future. *Expert Systems with Applications, 39*(9), 8490–8495.

Peihani, M. (2017, March). *Financial regulation and disruptive technologies: The case of cloud computing in Singapore*. Retrieved from https://www.jstor.org/stable/44986444

Rainer, R. K., & Prince, B. (2020). *Introduction to information systems* (8th ed.). Wiley.

Stine, /. J. (2020, January 06). *How intuit uses AI and machine learning technology to power educational experiences for accountants*. Retrieved from https://proconnect.intuit.com/taxprocenter/practice-management/how-intuit-uses-ai-to-power-personalized-education-for-accountants/

Success & Insights. (2021). *Utilibill: Guiding utilities to the cloud through digital transformation*. Retrieved from https://www.insightssuccess.com/utilibill-guiding-utilities-to-the-cloud-through-digital-transformation/

Team, /. I. (2020, June 22). *A message from intuit CEO Sasan Goodarzi to intuit employees*. Retrieved from. https://www.intuit.com/blog/news-social/a-message-from-intuit-ceo-sasan-goodarzi-to-intuit-employees/

Zhang, Y., & Xiong, F. (2020). *The impact of artificial intelligence and Blockchain on the accounting profession*. IEEE Access, 2020.

Artificial Intelligence in Human Resources

9

Abstract

Artificial intelligence has been widely applied in managing human resources. This chapter introduces the evolution and applications of AI in human resources management. The key technologies covered include big data analytics and various machine learning algorithms. Some popular applications include AI in recruitment, scheduling, training, onboarding, turnover, retention, and performance management. A case study on Paradox Olivia is provided to illustrate the related AI applications.

Keywords

Human Resources Management · Human Resource Information System · Big data analytics · Machine learning · Convolution neural networks · Decision trees · Cased-based reasoning · Genetic Algorithms · Naïve Bayes classifier · Recruitment · Scheduling management · Training · Onboarding · Employee turnover · Retention · Performance management · Engagement management

9.1 Introduction

Artificial intelligence is changing the way in which all businesses conduct their operations and meet their strategic goals. Among some of the latest uses of artificial intelligence is in the human resources department, where human resource professionals conduct a variety of important tasks, including recruiting, interviewing, handling payroll, benefits, training, and employee relations. These are critical operations within a business, playing a significant part in the administrative functions within an organization. Introducing artificial intelligence into the daily operations of human resources can help professionals complete their work efficiently and with added creativity. The successful addition of artificial intelligence could provide accurate

L. Chan et al., *Applied Artificial Intelligence in Business*, Applied Innovation and Technology Management, https://doi.org/10.1007/978-3-031-05740-3_9

results and aid decision-making in areas such as the hiring process, calculating pay, creating efficient workspaces, and predicting the best actions to improve employee relations.

In the following sections of this chapter, we will introduce the functionality of AI in various components of human resource management. This includes recruitment, training, employee attrition, employee performance, engagement, benefits and payroll, and employee retention. First, we will start from the development of artificial intelligence technologies in human resources. Then, we introduce some related machine learning and neural network techniques, such as prototypical algorithms, decision trees, case-based reasoning, and regression analytics used in HR. Next, we analyze the different functional areas of HR that can benefit from AI technology. Lastly, key takeaways and challenges will be discussed.

9.2 Development of AI in HRM

Artificial intelligence technologies have been rapidly diffusing in the realm of human resource management. Many years ago, AI techniques were added as part of HR analytics into software packages. The application of AI into the human resource field can be dated back to the 1980s. The increasing demand for HR departments to adopt computer technology to process employee information efficiently resulted in an explosion in the number of vendors who could assist HR departments with hardware and software. The Human Resource Information System (HRIS), also known as a Human Resource Management System (HRMS), became widespread in the 1980s. HRIS is a software solution to automate and manage various HR functions such as recruiting, compensation, training, reporting, etc. These software packages were typically based on database systems to store, update, and retrieve information. HRIS was developed to plan more effectively, to improve efficiency and quality in HR decision-making, and to improve employee and managerial productivity and effectiveness (Marler & Parry, 2016; Jain, 2014). The introduction of automation through AI technologies significantly reduces the monotonous physical responsibility facing the HR personnel. In recent years, the unprecedented growth of big data has revealed the limitations of conventional HRIS. More advanced HR analytics need to be implemented through better algorithms and supported by systems that are more powerful.

The rapid growth in available data along with AI technologies has brought significant impact to the HR industry. Data analytics has driven important decisions in business' sales, marketing, customer success, and finance. Until recently, many companies did not have the technology to access, track employee data, and analyze other aspects of employee life cycle such as onboarding, hiring, hiring trends, vacation requests, workflow, engagement surveys, and performance management. Companies have implemented a wide range of digitization, and HR professionals have appreciated the benefits. Notably, the primary role of this technology is in the decision-making and risk reduction in both organizational success and talent management. Many HR managers argue that artificial intelligence has been adopted later and slower in the HR field compared to finance, accounting, and marketing. Some HR managers argue that it is due to the importance of keeping the human touch aspect and company morale, while others argue that there just has not been the same need for artificial intelligence as in other fields.

9.3 AI Technologies in HR

Human resources professionals use a variety of AI methods to analyze their data. HR analytics today includes machine learning, deep learning, neural networks, and some advanced algorithms. Software packages use machine learning and HR analytics by incorporating data from the human capital management platform to establish patterns and algorithms to predict trends. Also, with the help of an interactive dashboard, users can understand retention risks unique to their organization or in a specific department. By applying predictive analytics to the workforce database, better decision outcomes can be created. Through collecting past data, AI methods can create prediction models to evaluate each outcome. This is how human resources started to incorporate deep learning for effective data decisions.

Artificial intelligence's theoretical methods for HR are built on data analytics from various sources. For big data, some recruitment companies collect, normalize, and analyze millions of career information data sets across more than 100 different countries. They use the data to investigate different skills, jobs, positions, and industries for different profiles. Small data, on the other hand, is both internal and external data from HRIS, resumes, etc. It detects skills for employees and offers and enriches them dynamically, thanks to the analysis of millions of career paths. Machine learning will use this internal and external data for different career paths as a learning base and leverage different algorithms to deliver relevant and audacious matchings. The recommendations address important human capital management issues such as internal mobility, recruitment, or skill management.

Machine learning techniques, especially neural networks, are widely applied in HR analytics today. Convolution neural networks (CNN) are used to scan candidates for soft skills, possible dishonesty, and poor attitude all in attempts to determine if a candidate is a good match. Although CNN is a very powerful technique to recognize image processes and language translation, there is substantial amount of pushback from prospective job candidates. Many people fear that individuals will learn the prototypical algorithms desired by the AI and rig the system. CNN is also a powerful method in processing images, thus being used in AI-based interviews. In a multilayer process, an image is scanned region by region. A filter or kernel is applied to each region to determine the specific coordinates. Those are then mapped into a multilayer array and stored in an activation map. During each layer of CNN, the idea is to pool together areas with similar characteristics. This classification process allows CNN to depict items as small as an eyebrow curve in a picture. This technique paired with recurrent neural networks (RNN) makes for increasingly accurate image and language translation (Salkey, 2006). With deep learning, AI will try different solutions until it eventually gets the best results. Some ways that AI within HR is trying to evolve are by exploring the natural language, developing workflow automation, and mass personalization. Understanding the natural language will mainly be in areas like talent acquisition and training. AI is already communicating through bots in chats but still has a long way to go, to get a more human aspect of performing tasks.

Decision trees and case-based reasoning methods are traditional AI techniques that can be useful for HR analysis (Wang et al., 2017). Employee performance management can be analyzed using a combination of AI methods including decision trees, memory-based reasoning, and regression analysis (Buntine, 2013). Currently, there is a surplus of big data in HR departments. Companies are conducting and gathering immense amounts of data but are not sure how to properly utilize the data (Huichun, 2018). Data mining techniques can help turn some of this data into readable results. Decision trees can help companies turn big data into readable manageable results. This type of mapping can help companies visualize and draw conclusions. Memory-based reasoning is successful in processing big data as it draws conclusions based on previously stored information. If memory-based reasoning is applied to big data, it can help one use regression analysis to analyze current and past trends (Gotlieb & Marijan, 2017). These types of research methods are crucial in creating successful HR applications. Being able to assess employee performance can help determine potential problems early on.

Genetic algorithms scan input data such as resumes and videos looking for key patterns that are then weighted heavily in an individual's chances of progressing forward in the interview process (Liem et al., 2018). Certain keywords indicate that a candidate contains a profile that matches the company skillset criteria. Despite an individual's actual knowledge, if individuals can determine the keywords, there is fear that the wrong candidates will be screened through as the "perfect candidates" for a job role. Prototypical algorithms can help detect risks of attrition and help develop risk management plans to improve talent retention. These algorithms can handle large arrays of data, including results of employee surveys, and important demographic information (Asensio-Cuesta et al., 2012). Finding patterns of interest among employees can help find discrepancies in employee relations and detect problems within work culture proactively. An advantage to prototypical algorithms is the ability to create large amounts of unstructured data quickly and sort out individual comments and components. Ultimately, these algorithms can help monitor employee emotions toward company objectives, allowing companies to get an inclusive look at processes and specific issues.

The Naïve Bayes Classifier technique is a probability-based AI method that can be used to examine multiple characteristics of an individual during the hiring process (Valle & Ruz, 2015). This method can also be applied in employee performance prediction and turnover rate estimation. An important trait to continue monitoring while a person is employed is their likelihood of job-hopping. With the use of Sequential Optimization of Naive Bayesian, HR personnel are able to make increasingly accurate predictions of the likelihood of someone leaving their job (Kosylo et al., 2018). This method uses the idea of posterior probability by using prior probability and overall likelihood estimation. The algorithm can use various features (such as job start date, university, GPA, etc.) and give predictions of how likely someone is to engage in job-hopping. This type of analysis would be incredibly helpful in HR. Companies could use this tool to predict which employees are at risk and then determine trends, how to entice individuals to stay, and potential problems. Utilizing such technology can help augment many HR operations to help decrease the number of employees leaving and increase retention rates at companies.

Nowadays, many human resource management systems are holistic packages that incorporate a variety of AI methods to improve current human resource practices. These packages focus on tasks such as recruiting, performance analysis, onboarding, scheduling, timekeeping, payroll, and interviewing. While companies are increasingly investing in AI, human resource professionals are hesitant to adapt to this change. A very important topic to discuss regarding AI techniques is the difference between augmentation and automation. Augmentation is the idea of using AI to enhance human ability making their current task more efficient. Automation is the idea of removing the human element and making systems systematically automatic.

9.4 AI Applications for HR Functions

With big data and increasing amounts of data stored in the cloud, research shows that 40% of international companies with HR functions are using artificial intelligence applications. They are mostly US-based, but Europe and Asia are not far behind (Charlier & Kloppenburg, 2017). Here we focus on several major aspects within the HR field that will help us look closer at how AI is affecting human resource departments. These aspects are "talent acquisition," "employee turnover," "employee scheduling," and "employee training" (Fig. 9.1).

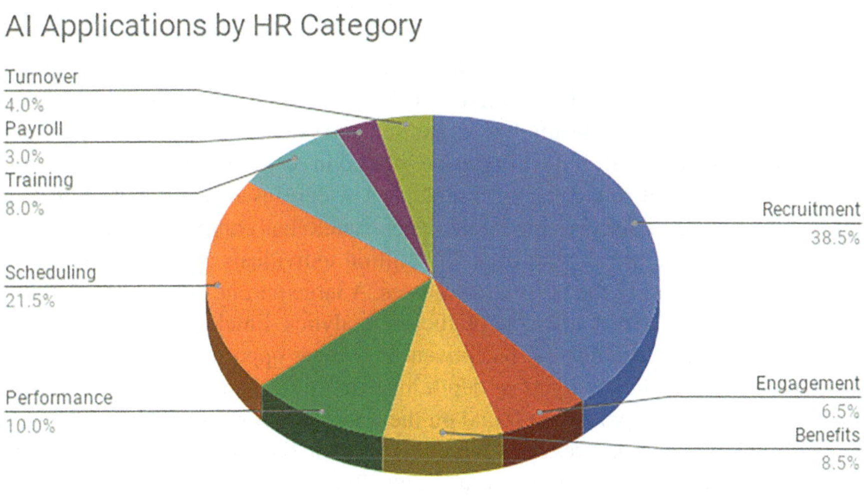

Fig. 9.1 AI applications by HR category

9.4.1 Employee Recruitment

Recruitment requires a lot of work such as reading resumes, scheduling, and meeting for interviews. AI can reduce repetitive tasks and make the hiring process automated. When searching for candidates, a system can filter, screen resumes, source candidates, and shortlist candidates which ultimately would cut costs and time and improve efficiency overall. AI can help streamline that process by pulling information through applicant processing systems. This works like keyword generators that pull out resumes that have a specific number of matching words or parameters set. Those resumes that are pulled move on to the next round. By setting specific parameters, managers can pair down long lists of resumes to a shortlist that contains candidates that are more likely a good fit for that position rather than sifting through them by hand and using personal judgment to make those decisions. A virtual partner could look up things not listed on a resume such as skills not mentioned, previous job performances at other companies.

Among the AI applications available, a common theme that has been evident is the cost/time decrease in the hiring process. Many of the resources are to assist managers for optimal decision-making in respect to the recruitment process. There are multiple sources that support our arguments about the positive effect AI can have in human resources within companies. More than one-third of the sources are related to how AI can positively affect the way companies go through the recruiting process in hiring new employees for their company. AI can be used to create automation systems to help speed up the recruitment process, saving time as well as making it easier to find more qualified candidates.

Chatbots use questions to screen for qualifications and can deliver updates about the "best-fit" and "non-fit" candidates to HR managers based on predefined screening algorithms (Sheth, 2018). It also takes in information about the desired location, salary, and promotion. As companies expand and technology advances, some large companies are introducing the idea of virtual interviews. Many well-known companies such as Facebook and Twitter are using AI to scan video interviews. A possible candidate will record an interview, upload it for a job listing, and progress further into the interview process depending on an AI's screening selection. Oftentimes a recruiter will validate the result that an automated system provided and make sure that every candidate analyzed was properly placed in respective categories.

As an example of this category, Entelo is a widely used recruitment tool that allows companies to discover top talent faster. Entelo has compiled the most comprehensive talent database, with over 500 million individuals around the world, to help employers identify the best-fit candidates. A large part of Entelo's AI technology is its products' ability to create predictive analytics. Entelo analyzes dozens of variables to predict candidates' receptiveness to new opportunities. Through the search tool, this application gets in-depth insights into each prospective candidate by surfacing key data points not found on the traditional resume, like a candidate's career highlights and progression, company fit, their likelihood of switching jobs soon, and the details yielding to their unique market value.

9.4.2 Employee Scheduling Management

AI can be used in many administrative tasks such as scheduling, vacation requests, and sick leave. It has become difficult for HR to manage employee vacation schedules without conflict, for instance, in situations whereby in 1 day more than two employees request the same vacation days and the HR department can only approve one of them. HR managers must consider how the absence of employees will affect the work. AI has brought practical planning steps, and HR managers can now use employee policies and vacation tracker tools to manage such situations (Aickelin & Dowsland, 2004). An AI vacation request system helps companies to track and plan for absences and engages in better decision-making, especially with regard to staffing levels. The AI works well in producing reports and compensation for vacation time and is less tedious and consumes less time as compared to keeping track of spreadsheets and files. However, a manual system may be useful for small companies, but the automated system for vacations works best in large corporations. AI also works well in the administration of sick leaves as HR can use AI to aid in diagnosing, treating, and prevention of illness. All of these processes are conveniently executed from the comfort of a mobile phone. AI can be used to cut down the sick days of employees because most employees prefer getting an opportunity to be off duty than to be working. Employees around the world overburden the healthcare system and worse when they are absent from work. AI ensures fast and confidential medical advice to individual employees, and this helps to address long-term employee issues that gradually cost organizations enormous resources.

AI systems can help human resources function in defining the appropriate time for a vacation for an individual. These applications store data about any person who applies for a vacation; they analyze the specific individual case and then recommend it just like a human resource employee could have done (Grudin & Jacques, 2019). They are efficient compared to humans since they never book a vacation. These systems accept data from the past concerning the medical conditions of the applicants. In the case of vacation applications, they accept data regarding the daily working hours of a person and holiday destinations, and sometimes, they will prescribe a vacation request on behalf of the workers. These applications have AI algorithms that are used to analyze all of these data sources. First, they search for data of interest. Then form a hypothesis, evaluate, and revise it before recommending either a sick leave or vacation request. The AI systems deliver schedules to the customers on how the sick leave and vacation requests will be made without affecting the smooth running of the organization. Some systems use Bayesian Network techniques, and in the case of sick leave, they can use a Phenom-Genome network that interprets the data that is fed to it.

HotSchedules is an application under this category. The data collected as the input for the software system including shift availability for staffing, tasks, and duties for staff positions, staff personal information, payroll information, message board, time and attendance, labor management, training and development, task and communication management, etc. The AI methods used in this application are prescriptive analytics for sorting and organizing information. Thus, the output result would be creating schedules that allow staff members including managers to assign shifts, tasks, check availability, and check on payroll items; make emergency announcements; find contact information for an employee; etc. HotSchedules' potential users are mainly restaurants, retail stores, and hotels or companies in the hospitality industry.

9.4.3 Employee Training Management

Training is a crucial part of the productivity, efficiency, and engagement of employees. Improper training may create errors and unproductive work, which will have negative effects on both the company and the employees themselves. Personalized learning and development using artificial intelligence can be a key factor in providing good and accurate training (Wilson & Daugherty, 2018). This type of technology uses data such as retention rate, lifecycle stage, competency level, position, employee's performance rating, and learning records to serve relevant and valuable content (Yano, 2017). By providing employees with learning content that relates to where they are in their careers and is constructed in a way that enables the employee to retain it, the employees will be more engaged and interested in following through with their learning (Gallup. 2017). Using artificial intelligence to train employees will be helpful to analyze and address skill gaps, create a learning route, track progress and certifications, and ultimately customize their training. It will be easier to hold everyone accountable for their learning and ensure that everyone is properly trained to do their job accurately (Davis, 2015). The AI application used in training is for the administration, documentation, tracking, reporting, and delivery of educational courses or learning and development programs.

Onboarding, as with training, is an important factor in the retention of new employees. If the onboarding process is not aligned with the company values and culture, the experience of disconnection can be damaging to the employee's overall engagement with the organization. According to statistics, only about 33% of US employees were engaged or enthusiastic about their workplace (Gallup, 2017). Onboarding is a holistic process involving not just the HR department but also many other functions in a company. By using AI, the different functions in the company can more easily communicate by sharing information and setting up specific tools for the new employee (He, 2018). When starting in a new company, workers may have many questions concerning their employment, and AI tools can help answer some of those questions in a quicker and more accurate manner than a human resource manager might. That way, the HR manager can focus their time on more important and strategic issues in the company. A lot of the onboarding questions and processes are very simple and mundane, which is why AI technology can be very beneficial by being more efficient, productive, and accurate (Jain, 2014).

AI applications for training software usually use similar types of input, while the output can be a little bit different. The most widely adopted input is to use data from the HR system, such as course titles, meta-data tags, schedule, etc., and transcript data, which tracks a user's course progression and completion. By using this input, cognitive learning- and machine learning-driven pattern detection can analyze skill gaps and needs, report progress, and decide which training and education to provide each person individually. The output is usually in the form of teaching content specialized for each, live reports to both employee and HR management showing current and past progress, and continuously developing new content to stay up-to-date.

A lot of the AI applications for onboarding are also connected with talent acquisition and the hiring process. Using information about the new employees, their job title, and the company database, many of these applications create personalized self-service portals that include messaging, videos, content, and documents personalized for them. Most of the widely used AI applications within onboarding use cognitive learning and chatbots to create more efficient onboarding processes.

As a case, the IBM Watson Education team is focused on using AI to improve learning outcomes and implement solutions that will help all learners to succeed. IBM uses a deep learning method to provide a better learning experience through making content more personalized for users. The package is more suitable for both businesses and schools because it focuses more on tutoring than the progress and continued learning an employee would need.

Mya Systems is another popular AI application for onboarding. This software supports a start-to-end employee life cycle, focusing on effective communication from the beginning of the hiring process to the end of onboarding and training. Mya captures meaningful information using semantic parsing, named entity recognition, and multiple intent classifications. The machine learning algorithms learn continuously from millions of interactions to continually improve the accuracy of responses and expand the breadth of knowledge. It also provides products for performance management for training, and time tracking, which goes under scheduling.

9.4.4 Employee Turnover and Retention

Artificial intelligence techniques can be applied in predicting turnover rates (Valle & Ruz, 2015). The AI system will be able to compute and evaluate a company's overall turnover rate. It can give an estimated timeline of how often employees are leaving the company. With this data, managers can have more time to plan scheduled recruiting to keep up with the outflow of employees (Rombaut & Guerry, 2018). Instead of having a lack of employees, or too many, managers can be able to keep it at a standard level. Secondly, AI will be able to break up the turnover rate, into a position-specific rate. This means it can identify the turnover rate of each job position, instead of all the positions combined. With this information, managers can hire candidates that they will need next, instead of blindly hiring someone because they know that a person will be leaving soon, without knowing who it might be. It is hard to be able to make that assumption, but with machine learning, it will come to be more accurate as time goes by. Thirdly, AI is also getting employee-specific with turnover rates that lead to predicting how long an individual employee will stay. This can be done by applying different variables to analyze each employee.

Such variables for individual employees could be work history in the company, time spent working, age, the previous number of jobs, how many cups of coffee drank per day, average arrival time, wherein the office they work, etc. There are many other variables that can be tagged and associated with each employee. With these projected turnover rates, AI can be able to detect trends and correlations and predict how long employees are staying. The most specific AI technique that is used within these situations is machine learning (Kosylo et al., 2018). Every time the program analyzes data, it gets a little smarter at picking up those trends. The desired results are all up to the initial company's discretion of what they wish to achieve from the data they created.

Predicting how long an employee in any corporation will stay with a company is essentially impossible from a human standpoint. However, machine learning can help to attain some sense of this. Many factors could create an answer to when an employee will leave, but it would take endless hours for a human to achieve this. Being able to analyze numerous variables with their different turnover rates that are supplemented with them is something AI is capable of accomplishing. By being able to identify tagged characteristics in a new hire, and compare them to the overall trend, AI can give an approximate timeline for how long that given prospect would stay with the company, thereby, helping the managers in the hiring process.

Retention rate is similar to turnover rate, and they both analyze turnover rates and different variables within an employee or set of employees. The difference however between the two is that turnover rate is more specific to a group, whereas retention rate is more specific to each individual employee. AI creates an opportunity to evaluate a huge amount of data in a short period. Some of the input data can be very interesting, and numerous variables can be examined, such as job satisfaction, promotions, time with current managers, years worked, age, marital status, etc. As far as data that AI would have to analyze, it is very similar to the input used for predicting turnover rates, but instead, the application would be processing a predicted timeline of how long this employee may stay with the company. Much like how AI predicts turnover rates, the major technique used in the calculation of these results is machine learning (Davis, 2015).

HiQ is one of the companies that provide their AI services to companies in turnover predictions. HiQ Labs is a company that provides AI services specifically to HR teams using their SaaS platform that is based on machine learning. Their business model is that they would charge a company a base amount depending on the service they would like, and then they would perform the analysis and provide the results. It is a smart business model because, for each client served, the SaaS program can become smarter which enables it to make better predictions in the future.

9.4.5 Performance and Engagement Management

Performance management evaluates employee productivity, conducts surveys, and evaluates performance statistics throughout the organization as a whole. Many of these tasks can be automated by AI to free the management of time (Smith, 2019).

Performance evaluations and surveys can also be done more frequently when automated. Instead of having to send out evaluations through emails to each employee depending on their job, an AI program can be programmed to automatically send a survey to specific people depending on their job. The majority of performance management applications using AI technologies use machine learning-driven pattern detection, neural network prediction, and intelligent anomaly detection to conduct frequent evaluations, providing both employees and HR staff with live performance statistics (Dhir & Chhabra, 2019). This way both the employee and managers will know when someone is falling behind, and they can figure out issues and solutions more proactively and quickly to ensure employee satisfaction and productivity.

Employee engagement can also be enhanced by AI. There are potential benefits when AI is integrated into communications (Jarrahi, 2018). AI within communication creates the ability to improve interaction with data (Hoffman, 2016). An AI-based virtual assistant could organize the relevant information, documents, and other materials for meetings and team interactions and then present those in collaborative sessions. It is more efficient and effective collaboration than traditional approaches. Many of these types of Groupware vendors are now building their products by using AI technologies like machine learning, chatbots, and natural language processing. The benefits of AI in collaborative sessions include transferring information more easily among globally dispersed teams. They can also offer real-time language translation through natural language processing, which enables global workgroups to communicate and collaborate in their native languages and receive native language meeting transcriptions. It can also lead to efficient schedules, such as calendar systems or meeting applications enabled to automatically schedule future calls based on a project's schedule and availability, without individuals having to manually search calendars for availability or exchange emails to find an appropriate meeting time.

There are some interesting AI technologies that can be used to better analyze employee engagement within their organization. The first one is sentiment analysis (Gelbard et al., 2018). This uses natural language and machine learning to analyze how emotionally attached an employee is to the company by the way they are communicating in their emails. The second application measures the mood of an employee as they enter and leave the workplace. By using AI-based facial recognition, the software can track the gender, age, and ethnicity and analyze the mood of the person. This data will be collected to evaluate and analyze the engagement level of the employees in the organization. There is not a lot of information on how far and technically feasible this type of technology is yet. There are still some questions as to whether or not facial recognition can go as far as to know who you are and fully accumulate mood statistics for each individual as well as the staff.

Case 9.1: Paradox Olivia: The AI Recruiter

Paradox Olivia has been a start-up success story. A company created in Phoenix, AZ, founders Aaron and Olivia Matos developed flagship AI Olivia in 2016 to address logistical hiccups in the human capital management sector. After three rounds of fundraising, Paradox Olivia is valued at $53.3 million. Olivia was developed as a 24/7 HR-oriented office assistant built to exemplify the firm's mission statement in mind—"we believe if you get the people thing right you can build teams that change the world. Our goal is to help you do it" (Paradox, 2021). The succinctness of the product offering and the firm's value proposition show why the firm has received strong financial support from investors.

In dissecting Olivia, there are three key technologies that make up the AI application. Olivia functions from the support of three pillars: personality data genome, direct-messaging hiring chatbot, and search engine optimization. In 2021, Paradox Olivia acquired Traitify and Spetz, companies responsible for the germination and cultivation of the personality data genome and the direct-messaging hiring chatbot, respectively (Crunchbase, 2021). Combined with Paradox Olivia's partnership with Google Analytics and its Search Engine Optimization (SEO) product, Olivia diversified its solution offerings. Olivia is able to manage hourly and salaried hiring, meaning the AI is able to differentiate the time characteristic of different positions when communicating with job candidates about the position they applied for/recruited for (Paradox Olivia, 2021). To help support this communication, Olivia is functionally compatible with different text and mobile communication platforms (i.e., Facebook Messenger, WeChat, WhatsApp). As a part of Olivia's recruiting solution, Paradox offers Olivia's human-like messages as a solution to create a smooth dialogue between candidates and the human HR personnel. What these solutions ultimately develop is an overhauled hiring process that is streamlined for improved communication and lessened bureaucratic burden of paperwork. For a firm's HR personnel, Olivia is an on-call 24/7 access point for candidates to ask questions and access certain documents. The AI also allows for the automatization of candidate search and outreach through tools like data mining.

Olivia's ability to help firms with their human capital management (HCM) systems targets what their clients value efficiency and effectiveness. As the main AI solution that Paradox Olivia offers, this 24/7 resource center and "middle person" has netted the firm an estimated $37.7 million in 2020 (GrowJo, 2021). This is an impressive revenue stream for start-ups. Another angle on Paradox Olivia's impressive revenue stream is the firm's approach to their customer needs and relationship. Paradox Olivia has identified a common issue among the four industries (restaurant and retail, financial services, health care, and trucking/logistics) the firm has had success with—high volume of information that needs to be processed (as documented and filed) (Crunchbase, 2021). This reason answers the key purchasing criteria potential clients have—why should the firm employ Olivia? This has created a very favorable subscription-based contractual relationship between Paradox Olivia and its clients.

Like any AI offerings, there is a unique cost structure for Paradox Olivia that has a flagship AI. The firm incurs costs according to the type of software, level of intelligence, the performance of the AI, the complexity of the AI, and how much data the AI needs to consume. Depending on the services required and the scale of the need, Paradox Olivia would incur different costs, so pricing is based on the client's need to affect the variable costs in offering Olivia. It is also worthwhile to note that some fixed general costs come from servers, software subscriptions, and salaries for specialized staff (e.g., programmers). The key activities of Paradox Olivia are centered on two types of projects—updating Olivia with changes with HCM practices and policies and maintaining Olivia's ability to work with new updates to mobile interfaces and HCM software. To achieve these activities, Paradox Olivia relies on servers and programmers who work with HCM partners like ADP to make sure Olivia stays relevant and useful in the HR industry.

Paradox Olivia has correctly identified the trend of technology in its market segment. Olivia should be able to continue its current success if the firm keeps updating the AI to be compatible with the latest mobile communications app and strengthen its user-friendly interface.

9.5 Key Takeaways

Artificial intelligence is mostly used to aid hiring processes and has been able to help make the process more efficient and personable. There are topics of discussion on the actual impact of technology within this practice. Part of the role of new technology focuses on screening the resumes of job applicants. There are complications sorting through them, as keywords within applications can become weighted heavier than if seen by a human eye. It may be easier for an applicant to cheat the system and input words and information to satisfy the AI. If artificial intelligence technology is used within an interview, such as a replacement for an interviewer, the applicant will receive less human cues and feedback on their performance. This can cause many interviews to have a less successful outcome, as being screened by technology can be intimidated and hinder typical performance. For most, it may be hard to judge performance when communicating with a machine or any non-human-like device. Understanding personality and judging how an applicant would fit into the culture of the workplace may also prove difficult, as training an AI to understand small movements along with phrasing is challenging given the state of technology nowadays.

A main challenge for the current technologies is the rigidity of parameters. Simply put, bots do not have the capability of making informed decisions if they have not yet been told to do so. While AI is a great tool to ensure accuracy and engagement, it may also hurt engagement because it hinders the human side of human resources. A typical problem with AI in HR is a lack of humanity. The technology has not been developed to mimic full human behavior, which makes any sort of automated intelligence the next best thing. In human resources, the human relational aspect plays a major role (Mittelstadt et al., 2016). Another thing computers lack is the ability to simulate human emotion. This is particularly important when looking at the way specific candidates embody the company's values, mission statement, and other core beliefs. Personality and charisma play a huge part in whether one candidate outperforms another in a job interview, and there simply has not been any meaningful work done to make AI superior in this field. Another issue with AI is that it lacks the human morals aspect of the job. Applying morals and the human touch to an HR position is mandatory when performing their everyday duties.

However, despite its inability, AI is improving its moral development through the advancement of neural networks and machine learning. It is far from perfect, but it is heading in the right direction.

The artificial intelligence technologies within HR are usually software that will extract patterns from data. As data volumes continue to grow, deep learning drives the automated creation of increasingly complex algorithms to capture more data. This also brings the concern of data privacy and ethical issues (Mittelstadt et al., 2016). HR departments keep sensitive information about employees, and using this data for analytics may reveal personal information to third parties. Tasks performed by machines can be difficult to trace. In the HR departments, this could be detrimental to a company as a large part of the information that a human resource company retains is private and personal. This can be a challenge that AI as a whole is facing.

HRM is now taking the advantage of AI by utilizing big data and analytics to open up opportunities for strategic value creation. From the discussions above, we can see that AI is able to influence many different aspects of HR, through recruiting, onboarding, training, and more. When AI assists in these tasks, it helps the company as a whole. Management and HR are closely related and work together on many tasks. Through AI, it takes a lot of stress off the management with employee-related tasks.

Many research efforts have already proven that AI is very useful when sourcing candidates. There are already products out there that can be used to evaluate the current workforce, where they can help employers make better decisions. These products are expensive, but over time they will save time and reduce costs to the human resource and managerial functions. By implementing AI into the recruiting process, it allows managers and HR representatives to be able to focus on more important tasks and less tedious work.

Workflow automation is an area where AI can affect the HR department significantly. In the past, humans have been doing most of the programming so that computers can work around it and understand it, but it is feasible that this can be automated by AI technology now. Examples are scheduling meetings with multiple team members, where this tends to get messy the more people involved. This used to be a time-consuming task, which can be taken care of as AI technology is applied.

Another area AI will influence HR is within mass personalization, here particularly around training and employee growth. AI can help train people and be their personal coach whenever it is needed, and will eventually save companies money, and be less time-consuming. AI software will recognize problems their employees are struggling with and help them through the difficulties.

HR functions are one of the important strategic planning functions. Management can provide the HR department with top-notch technology, which leads to the effective running of an organization. The future HR functions aim at developing an intelligent, employee-centered, and digitally supported work environment, and AI technology plays an important role in the implementation of future HR prospects.

The future trends and key priority for human resources management are the analytic transformations of talent leaders by using better AI technologies. Leadership in this digital era with AI will be less about leading people and more about creating the ecosystem of work. Future leaders need capabilities in agile thinking, digital skills, global operating skills, interpersonal, and communication skills. By applying AI methods and predictive talent models, it enables HR to be more effective in identifying an organization's current problem and in prioritizing future tasks. With the advancement of AI in HR, business leaders are prompted to transform their HR functions. HR operations are changing through using state-of-the-art AI tools and new processes. Applying AI technology to the core of HR function and machine learning being embedded into day-to-day HR functions allow predictive power to derive better business decisions.

9.6 Conclusion

AI in human resources is set up to assist human functions in the business process. The use of AI in HR is not a replacement for humans. Instead, AI systems will transform HR departments and remove redundancy in areas where it can easily be avoided. The main functions that AI will significantly assist HR departments in are recruiting, performance evaluations, and training and development. The AI systems can handle a majority of the bulk work when it comes to tasks like recruiting. Humans are still the ones ultimately deciding who works for the company, not the AI systems. AI in each of the HR functions helps eliminate many time-consuming activities so that employers can focus more on strategic issues. Almost every company with an HR department can benefit from adopting AI systems into their business process. The impact of AI in the human resource management area will be substantial. AI is affecting business at all levels ranging from the automation of tedious, time-consuming tasks to the augmentation of employee capabilities and the amplification of business functions. It is important for businesses to understand the impacts of AI on HR and to invest for long-term benefits.

References

Aickelin, U., & Dowsland, K. A. (2004). An indirect genetic algorithm for a nurse-scheduling problem. *Computers & Operations Research, 31*(5), 761–778.

Asensio-Cuesta, S., Diego-Mas, J. A., Canós-Darós, L., & Andrés-Romano, C. (2012). A genetic algorithm for the design of job rotation schedules considering ergonomic and competence criteria. *International Journal of Advanced Manufacturing Technology, 60*(9), 1161–1174.

Buntine, W. L. (2013). Decision tree induction systems: A Bayesian analysis. *arXiv [cs.AI]*. arXiv. http://arxiv.org/abs/1304.2732.

Charlier, R., & Kloppenburg, S. (2017). Artificial intelligence in HR: A no-brainer. *Pwc. at.*

Crunchbase. (2021). *Paradox – funding, financials, valuation & investors*. Crunchbase. Retrieved from https://www.crunchbase.com/organization/paradox-olivia/company_financials

Davis, P. J. (2015). Implementing an employee career-development strategy: How to build commitment and retain employees. *Human Resource Management International Digest, 23*(4), 28–32.

Dhir, K., & Chhabra, A. (2019). Automated employee evaluation using fuzzy and neural network synergism through IoT assistance. *Personal and Ubiquitous Computing, 23*(1), 43–52.
Gallup. (2017). *State of the American Workplace. Gallup Inc*. Retrieved from https://news.gallup.com/reports/199961/7.aspx
Gelbard, R., Ramon-Gonen, R., Carmeli, A., Bittmann, R. M., & Talyansky, R. (2018). Sentiment analysis in organizational work: Towards an ontology of people analytics. *Expert Systems, 35*(5), e12289.
Gotlieb, A., & Marijan, D. (2017). Using global constraints to automate regression testing. *AI Magazine, 38*(1), 73.
Growjo. (2021). *Paradox competitors, revenue, alternatives and pricing*. Retrieved from https://growjo.com/company/Paradox
Grudin, J., & Jacques, R. (2019). Chatbots, Humbots, and the Quest for Artificial General Intelligence." http://www.jonathangrudin.com/wp-content/uploads/2019/01/Chatbots-Humbots-and-the-Quest-for-Artificial-General-Intelligence.pdf
He, E. (2018). Can artificial intelligence make work more human?" *Strategic HR Review*. https://www.emeraldinsight.com/doi/full/10.1108/SHR-10-2018-146
Hoffman, R. (2016). Using artificial intelligence to set information free. *MIT Sloan Management Review, 58*(1), 20.
Huichun, X. (2018). Intelligent Management of Human Resources from the Perspective of Big Data. In *2018 11th International Conference on Intelligent Computation Technology and Automation (ICICTA)* (pp. 302–4). ieeexplore.ieee.org
Jain, A. (2014). Study on effectiveness of human resource information system at Vistaar technologies (Mumbai). *SIES Journal of Management, 10*(2).
Jarrahi, M. H. (2018). Artificial intelligence and the future of work: Human-AI Symbiosis in organizational decision making. *Business Horizons, 61*(4), 577–586.
Kosylo, N., Smith, J., Conover, M., Chan, L., Zhang, H., Mei, H., & Cao, R.. (2018). Artificial Intelligence on Job-Hopping Forecasting: AI on Job-Hopping. In *2018 Portland International Conference on Management of Engineering and Technology (PICMET)* (pp. 1–5). ieeexplore.ieee.org
Liem, C. C. S., Langer, M., Demetriou, A., Hiemstra, A. M. F., Wicaksana, A. S., Born, M. P., & König, C. J. (2018). Psychology meets machine learning: Interdisciplinary perspectives on algorithmic job candidate screening. In H. J. Escalante, S. Escalera, I. Guyon, X. Baró, Y. Güçlütürk, U. Güçlü, & M. van Gerven (Eds.), *Explainable and interpretable models in computer vision and machine learning* (pp. 197–253). Springer.
Marler, J. H., & Parry, E. (2016). Human resource management, strategic involvement and E-HRM technology. *The International Journal of Human Resource Management, 27*(19), 2233–2253.
Mittelstadt, B. D., Allo, P., Taddeo, M., Wachter, S., & Floridi, L. (2016). The ethics of algorithms: Mapping the debate. *Big Data & Society, 3*(2), 2053951716679679.
Paradox. (2021). *Paradox: The AI assistant for recruiting, Olivia*. Retrieved from https://www.paradox.ai/
Rombaut, E., & Guerry, M.-A. (2018). Predicting voluntary turnover through human resources database analysis. *Management Research Review, 41*(1), 96–112.
Salkey, J. (2006). HR for HR: Are your skills up to scratch? *Strategic HR Review, 5*(2), 2–2.
Sheth, B. (2018). Chat bots are the new HR managers. *Strategic HR Review, 17*(3), 162–163.
Smith, Cameron. 2019. "An Employee's best friend? How AI can boost employee engagement and performance." Strategic HR Review doi:https://doi.org/10.1108/shr-11-2018-0092.
Valle, M. A., & Ruz, G. A. (2015). Turnover prediction in a call center: Behavioral evidence of loss aversion using random Forest and Naïve Bayes algorithms. *Applied Artificial Intelligence: AAI, 29*(9), 923–942.

Wang, X., Wang, L., Zhang, L., Xu, X., Zhang, W., & Yingcheng, X. (2017). Developing an employee turnover risk evaluation model using case-based reasoning. *Information Systems Frontiers, 19*(3), 569–576.

Wilson, H. J., & Daugherty, P. R. (2018). Collaborative intelligence: Humans and AI are joining forces. *Harvard Business Review*. https://www.accenture.com/t20180828T222720Z__w__/ae-en/_acnmedia/PDF-84/Accenture-Collaborative-Intelligence-2018.pdf

Yano, K. (2017). How artificial intelligence will change HR. *People & Strategy, 40*(3), 42–47.

AI in Supply Chain and Logistics

10

Abstract

This chapter introduces the development and applications of artificial intelligence in supply chain management. The key AI technologies include genetic algorithms, artificial neural network, case-based reasoning, and decision model optimization. The features of AI applications in supply chain management include logistics, inventory management, scheduling, transporting, distributing, and digital freight shipping. Three cases are provided on Walmart, UPS, and Amazon.

Keywords

Supply chain management · Logistics · Forecasting · Genetic algorithms · Artificial neural network · Fuzzy systems · Case-based reasoning · Decision model optimization · Inventory management · Scheduling · Transportation · Distribution · Last mile delivery · Digital freight shipping · Electronic data interchange

10.1 Introduction

The primary reason people go into business is for one purpose to make a profit. A key concept that will enable a business to outcompete its competitors is to adopt artificial intelligence (AI) in its supply chain and overall operations. When we look at the supply chain sector, it is easier to just look at the big picture: one thing moving from one part of the world to another location; or from one state to another. What we often then forget is that for that object to get from A to B, we need a lot of steps or procedures in place to keep everything in order. Traditionally, this has been done through software and computers that track different steps of the process, but a lot can be improved when we use artificial intelligence to help us. Business leaders are

L. Chan et al., *Applied Artificial Intelligence in Business*, Applied Innovation and Technology Management, https://doi.org/10.1007/978-3-031-05740-3_10

actively seeking to increase their revenues, and they are investing in artificial intelligence. The trends prove that AI can increase efficiency and profits which is precisely why companies are investing millions into the technology. Companies recognized that by investing in AI, they can improve their forecasting, inventory space, and overall efficiency. These improvements help to optimize customer satisfaction which in turn will help with revenue. From the industry viewpoint, there are many positive trends for the future of artificial intelligence in the field of supply chains.

In the e-commerce world, there is a great amount of data that is available to increase the efficiency of operations. This is a critical area where artificial intelligence will play an impactful part. By using emerging technologies, companies can analyze the data and shorten delivery times while solving inventory problems at the same time. Another impact that will change the field is the ability to forecast. Traditional forecasting is done by methods such as moving averages, finding the trend, and linear regressions. AI can greatly increase the ability to forecast. Machine learning techniques in the supply chain have provided more accurate forecasting than the traditional methods listed prior. A reliable forecast is critical to recognize customer patterns which are an important aspect of a supply chain manager. The input data is commonly referred to as big data due to its sheer size. Inventory has and always will be an important aspect of the supply chain whether it be inventory space or shipping the inventory.

This chapter will delve into the applications of artificial intelligence in the supply chain, the technologies being used, the different subfields of the supply chain, and the future possibilities of AI technology in related fields.

10.2 Development of AI Technology in Supply Chain

Artificial intelligence has been hitting headlines with new applications throughout each subfield of supply chain management. Back a few decades ago, the biggest part of artificial intelligence was automation. It was primarily used for everyday activities like setting an alarm or using a personal assistant, like Google Assistant or Siri. Many companies used this for things like scheduling and making sure all supply chain things were running smoothly. It made it so that monotonous and annoying tasks could be done in seconds before forgetting about them.

Automation has changed the industry of truck driving, warehouse working, and management. It has made every part of this industry much easier. Artificial intelligence makes warehouse workers be able to track the shipments that are coming in and out, and it makes processing the shipments to be a lot smoother and quicker. Management benefits a lot from automation because artificial intelligence makes it so that management doesn't have to go from A-B-C-D. This makes for quick transactions and faster-processed orders. Nowadays, automation has been much improved. It has advanced to become a big part of all businesses. It is creating a time where we can manufacture without the use of manpower. There are three types of automation. The first is fixed automation; this is where companies will have warehouses and production facilities in which the sequence of processing operations is fixed by the equipment configuration. This means that there will be an assembly line of parts building and then moving the parts to the next station. This makes for quick assembly which will help companies save money on time and manpower. The next type of automation is programmable automation. This is where companies will make products by batch. This can range from a few dozen to a few thousand. Artificial intelligence in this subfield will make for a faster turnover rate of production. Programmable automation takes time, so flexible automation was developed. With each new batch of products, it takes time to reprogram and change over production equipment. With flexible automation, users can reprogram the equipment offline which can help produce new products faster than ever.

A new phase that is coming into the supply chain is self-driving cars. Self-driving cars are changing the way delivery is happening. Companies are slowly bringing this to life in recent years. Now people will be able to fulfill orders, load cars with products, and send the car out on its way to the buyers. Lately, there are developments in self-driving semi-trucks. This would allow the supply chain to excel even more than if there were self-driving cars. Self-driving semi-trucks would allow for more products to be packed for further shipments. Using both self-driving cars and semi-trucks, companies will soon be able to hit all locations of shipments, long or short without the use of manpower.

Another trend in supply chain management is the application of machine learning. This describes how machines are now collecting and interpreting data in this field. Michael Schmidt in an online blog says, "Machine intelligence teaches back to the human the reasons *why* things happen or will happen, arming users with the ability to make quick and justified changes in strategy. Machine intelligence, not 'big data,' offers the 'actionable answers' businesses need" (Schmidt, 2016). Machine intelligence will be a crucial piece in how companies succeed and take off. Owners and CEOs will be able to now see data of what is to come. They will be able to now look at how production can improve and what are the weaknesses in their supply chain.

There are so many new applications of artificial intelligence in each new or old subfield. When looking deeper into how these new applications will affect supply chain management, we will see how they change the efficiency and influence companies in a positive way.

10.3 Enabling Artificial Intelligence Technologies for SCM

Supply chain activities cover everything from product development, sourcing, production, and logistics, as well as the information systems needed to coordinate these activities (Sme, 2017). Artificial intelligence within the supply chain works in a different way, instead of robots or machines taking over, it works with humans. Artificial intelligence is ushering in a new era of supply chain optimization: an era where supply chain systems can think, analyze, present findings and recommendations, and learn from interactions with humans.

Forecasting is one of the biggest parts of supply chain management. Businesses want to know how much they need a certain product at a certain time. This has usually been done by trying to estimate and predict how big of a demand there will be for a product and by looking at how much of the market share the company predicts it will have and how much the market, in general, is growing. AI allows companies to make much more precise and accurate forecasts. AI has an advantage over humans because it can pull information from big data as well as looking at other external factors to predict how much is needed. This approach is revolutionary for the supply chain management industry because it cannot only make better and more informed forecasts but also much more efficient and reliable. Through IBM Watson's study of artificial intelligence through the supply chain, it works with humans through four steps: correlate data at an incredible scale and speed, provide predictive insights, facilitate decision-making, and drive automation. Through each step, AI is used precisely to retrieve and analyze the data and make predictions, then follow through with action after careful data collecting. These steps offer a new platform for bigger and better performance. AI technology is used externally and internally to gain insights and data from each perspective; this allows more confidence with decision-making.

One of the important AI methods for supply chain management is genetic algorithms (GAs). This process draws its inspiration from the theory of natural evolution first developed by Charles Darwin, or as it's better known natural selection. This process is colloquially known as "survival of the fittest," meaning that organisms who are better adapted to their environment will be the ones to survive to reproduce; hence, those same favorable genes will be passed down through generations to come. This process continues to repeat, ultimately resulting in a group of the fittest individuals (Whitley, 1994). Fascinatingly, now this genetic process can be replicated by machine learning and AI. In terms of utilizing a genetic algorithm, you start with a problem that you want to solve, be it inventory management, demand forecasting, route optimization, etc. You would likely have multiple ideas on how to solve the problem but be unsure which solution to pursue. Further, it is probable that the "proper" solution is a combination of components from each idea. This is where the GA takes over. It is coded to run simulations under each solution and from there execute the process of producing offspring under the same conditions of genetic reproduction. It combines components (genes) of each idea to generate new solutions based on the best parts of the previous simulation, creating an entirely new generation of solutions. This process then repeats and repeats until ultimately, the ideal solution to the problem is reached. For example, GA models can be applied to glass manufacturing lines. The process of smelting and refining glass is extremely dynamic, and there are a multitude of variables that contribute to the length of the manufacturing process. Further, the variables are inconsistent across individual pieces of glass making process performance evaluation and optimization extremely difficult. GAs could be introduced to assist in decreasing lag time and forecasting performance. Due to the strength of fast processing speed, the GA can perform multiple simulations and regression analysis over days and even months (Jeong,

2002). This allows manufacturers to make predictions and optimizations considering significantly more variables than any human mind ever could.

The next technology worth taking a look at is artificial neural networks (ANNs). We just concluded that computers are capable of making computations and decisions in a far superior fashion that any human ever could. But ANNs are inspired by the human mind and remind us that, despite the capabilities of machines, the brain also has a number of phenomenal abilities. As the name would suggest, neurons within the brain serve as the framework for ANNs (Mohiuddin et al., 1996). Obviously (at present at least), it's impossible to artificially create a neuron in all its immensely complex design. Resultantly, ANNs only manage a crude honoring of the "neuron" component of its name. Fortunately, though, this was never the intention, and ANNs present a fantastic new way for businesses and engineers to solve problems. One major application of AI in the supply chain is the use of ANN in forecasting how many supplies will be needed across certain periods of time. The continual adaptation of ANN in supply chain management is largely due to its ability to solve problems that are often left unsolved through traditional methods. As neural networks are computer programs designed to learn and make decisions in mannerisms similar to animal brains, they are able to cognitively learn and apply this learning process to model complex and poorly understood problems with sufficient data, serving as a useful tool for supply chain managers (Efendigil, 2008). The case study with artificial neural networks is especially interesting as it concerns the very pertinent issue of green practices. The ANN had to "think" through both the practicality of the traditional methods of supply and how they function with regard to environmental regulations (Kuo et al., 2010). Traditional supply methods tend to be less environmentally friendly as basically every tradition of the past is less friendly to the planet. ANNs are deployed in an effort to evaluate the practical components of our past methods and how they can be amended to take better care of the planet. In the discussion of GAs above, the solution being sought was binary, in the sense that the answer was effectively a number. However, problem-solving goes far beyond a simple black or white answer. ANNs try to create a thinking machine, one that learns from exploring the facts. It does this through a process called clustering, which again is inspired by neurons in the brain. Neurons, and therefore artificial neurons, are clustered together so information is sent through multiple checkpoints, each system learning from the other, and the data ends up being processed multiple times over before it is outputted. This is not quite the same thing as thinking, but it is one of the closest we can get with a machine.

In contrast, system modeling based on conventional mathematical tools is not well-suited for dealing with ill-defined and uncertain systems (Efendigil, 2008). To best counteract this, the use of fuzzy systems would be advised. Fuzzy systems are computer programs that employ the use of if-then rules to model the qualitative aspects of human knowledge and reasoning process without employing precise quantitative analyses. By using soft computing tools such as fuzzy logic, the clothing industry has been able to make decisions in materials required through the composition of fuzzy logic and neural networks to create neuro-fuzzy systems, combining an array of traditionally identifiable variables in the forecasting of materials with the cognitive learning process of their neural networks to produce better supply chain results, as textile-apparel companies deal with extremely competitive environments, making these improvements more urgent than many other industries (Thomassey, 2010). By improving on supply chain decisions in the past, artificial intelligence is now a pivotal and competitive aspect of the textile industry, alongside other competitive industries similar to textile.

As well as providing decisions based on the trend analyses present in neural networks, artificial intelligence is applied to assist in warehouse managerial decisions by a system called case-based reasoning (CBR). This system is designed as a tool for decision support in the application and availability of resources in the warehouse, and what their optimal use is across different warehouse operations, as it is designed to use its memory to decide on cases based on a data pool of previous cases at its disposal (Chow, 2005). The CBR system is a system that runs four tasks to sufficiently extract and apply cases from its memory and correct them as needed. These four tasks include retrieving, reusing, revising, and retaining information stored on past cases to apply to current and future cases. Through its reuse and revision stages, the system is able to make its computations, applying past knowledge from previous cases to the current case, providing a decision to supply the warehouse manager with regard to the application of resources. Through the revision stage, CBR then assesses the effectiveness of its decision and applies a formula to adjust the system, providing a more accurate response for future cases. Both retrieval and retaining tasks are simple tasks, involving selecting an appropriate case to retrieve and apply to the current one and inputting new data into it to find a solution (Chow, 2005). As a tool to assist in decision-making for warehouses, and not a means of reducing headcount, CBR is an example of how artificial intelligence can be used to improve the overall profitability of a company without having to reduce labor hours, as it provides metrics that otherwise would be unattainable due to its computational system while providing information and feedback to warehouse managers so that decisions made will continue to improve as time progresses and the CBR system continues learning.

In order to maximize profitability, expenses must be kept to a minimum. Regarding supply chain decisions, there are many expenses for suppliers to worry about, and many expenses for manufacturers to address and attempt to reduce. At the reduction of some expenses, oftentimes other expenses are incurred at different rates, allowing for decisions to be made at a point where an optimal balance is attained between two or more expenses. The more variables and expenses that are added to the equation, however, the harder it is for a human to decide on a proper trade-off without taking some risks. This is what the production/distribution model (PILOT) aims to solve. PILOT is a cost function, the mixed-integer mathematical program with a nonlinear objective function, and is one of the earliest successful programs in modeling supply chain problems. It determines the optimal stocking policy for manufacturers, deciding between many plant locations, distribution centers, and its own plant's production volumes to decide how often it should receive shipments of material and product, how many it should receive in each shipment, and from where to achieve the lowest cost to the manufacturer. While this model is very effective at these decisions, it is important to note that it is only practical when limited to a single manufacturing stage and considers only one objective function based on supply chain costs. As an early model of these supply chain issues, there is ample opportunity for expansion on this foundational model, which has already occurred, allowing companies to include more elements, such as emergency shipment to meet unforeseen demand (Safaei, 2013), ultimately allowing businesses to work toward achieving any goal with the use of artificial intelligence.

There is also an area where AI is being used in the supply chain sector that is less direct, but more a combination of different elements of AI technology being used to help. This is in managing warehouses. AI is being used to improve storing, sending, and processing products. It is also used to track the position of every individual product or item. Just think about how you can track your package when you order something from Amazon. This is a job that never could have been done by humans, as the volume of products and items would be way too much to keep track of. There are many other technologies used in supply chain management such as case-based reasoning and support vector machines (Watson 1994), but the ones mentioned above are the most commonly utilized and for the sake of brevity will be the only ones explored in this chapter.

10.4 Application Areas of AI in SCM

Now moving on to areas where supply chain and logistics can be applied, there are several application areas. Some such as inventory, transportation, warehousing, operations, etc. all play a critical role in how supply chain and logistics run for companies. In a globalized economy nowadays, the business stakeholders may be located in different countries or even continents. These include manufacturers, suppliers, distributors, retailers, and consumers (Fig. 10.1). If a company does not have sufficient chain management, that is money they are losing going right out the door. Great examples of companies with a strong sense of supply chain and logistics are UPS, FedEx, Expeditors International, Amazon, and many others.

Technology companies offer their services for companies who need to keep track of the information they use every day. AI has been seen in the past, present, and soon into the future. The necessity for AI is huge because employees need it at the touch of a button. In the past, AI would be used, but it was not really artificial intelligence since humans had to manually do certain parts. Microfiche or a microfilm reader would help managers read historical data. To read this and to figure out the company's future forecasting on inventory, they would have to insert the film manually. Currently, AI has sped up the process to where you can see the information in seconds. There is clearly an effect that artificial intelligence has on different areas in supply chain and logistics and that is what this section of the chapter will discuss.

One key area where AI can be used in supply chain and logistics is inventory. Inventory management is used for managing, storing, moving, sorting, arranging, counting, and maintaining the inventory, i.e., goods, components, parts, etc. Inventory management ensures that the right inventory is available as per the

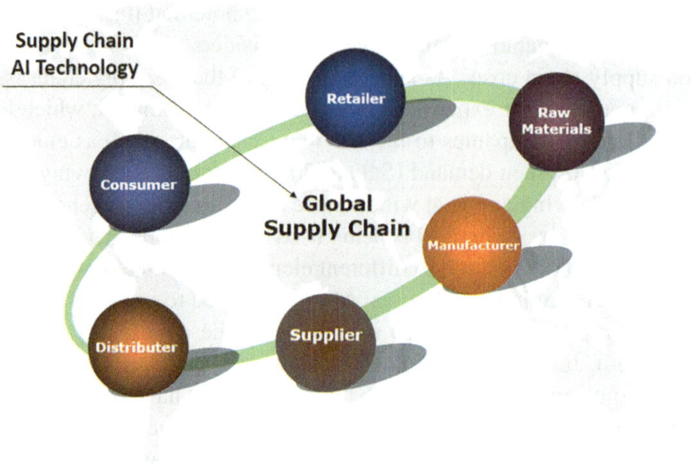

Fig. 10.1 Global supply chain and stakeholders

demand at low costs. Inventory management makes sure that the core processes of a business keep running efficiently by optimizing the availability of inventory. Inventory within a business is important because it is used to advocate optimization of inventory and helps a business run smoothly. As artificial intelligence changes frequently, so does the way inventory management is handled. For example, using robots instead of humans to do the job. Two of America's largest retailers are using robots as part of their inventory management. Over the summer of 2016, Lowe's introduced its LoweBot in 11 stores throughout the San Francisco Bay Area. These autonomous retail robots not only help customers but create real-time data by using computer vision and machine learning to scan inventory and look for patterns in product or price discrepancies. Instead of actual human workers doing the job of counting inventory and making sure product and price are correct, they have robots doing so now. Machine learning is starting to become the way businesses begin to run and manage the way to store things and help customers.

What AI does is that it enables companies to know what inventory they have on hand. For instance, many stores have handheld devices, and if you ask an employee about a product, they can check to see if they have it in stock through their database system. You can also ask about more than one item; the employee then can scan the barcode and instantly know if their store or even other stores have more than one item(s). Moreover, a real-life example is how AI tracks what you do online and what you look at. Say if you go online and research companies that make backpacks. You then figure out what you want and make your purchase after a week or so of promising results. Well throughout the research, those companies can have ads pop up anywhere on your devices such as through social media ads or even your email home page. This all happens because of AI; it tracks what inventory you are looking at and what you are interested in, and this is also how companies manage to make more sales as well. To take this a step further, in inventory, AI can predict and plan for future necessities. Through time, AI gains data and is constantly hungry for more data because AI can then forecast even better and have you prepped for the inventory that is required for the future, companies will look at this data and decide what they need with AI or maybe even go with a gut feeling. Car parts such as Paccar use AI systems constantly. They use it in their warehousing and distribution locations and when forecasting/estimating. If they do not keep a constant flow of parts coming in and out, they will lose business. AI tells them this is what the past looked like around that certain period and can make suggestions; a manager can then order parts for trucks that need to be fixed or trucks that are broken down during transportation.

Another significant area in supply chain and logistics where AI is used is transporting and distributing. Efficient ways are determined by the information system and can make determining a faster delivery route possible. It decides on a specific route depending on the time and day that companies have transported around the world. AI is also a huge money saver, really on the logistical side of supply chain management. Logistically, companies that use AI can predict how many modes of transportation they need. This aspect is how companies supply the goods whether it is through trucking, cargo ship hauling, or flying. Since businesses use this technology, the AI also figures out the best route and a minimal cost, but the route that can still get the goods to the destination on time and with quality. An even better money saver is the weight that the companies put on their modes of transportation. These transportation methods all have different weight settings, and the AI keeps track of all of this information. If UPS is flying freight out to China, there is only so many goods that they can put on the plane before it becomes overweight, slowing the transporting down and overall making the company lose money on that deal. Though with too little of weight, then the company will not deliver all of the goods on time, making them lose money and more than likely a customer/client. What AI is able to do is to track all of the weight that has been put on to modes of transportation. It then can see how long it took for the plane or cargo ship to get to its destination and almost do the "trial and error method" (Min, 2009).

Scheduling is another evolutionary project through artificial intelligence. Scheduling is a general technique to people when trying to plan for events, meetings, or appointments. It has become a way for humans to be able to stay organized and more time friendly. However, throughout time, scheduling has been a problem that encompasses a wide range of combinatorial optimization problems where the primary object is to temporally or spatially accommodate a set of entities. The benefits of proper scheduling may be tangible in the form of monetary profits or reduced environmental impacts. In other words, with a schedule that is efficient and correct, it brings benefits such as a form of profit and less impact on the environment. With that being said, it is effective to use machine learning techniques to better or create new processes when it comes to scheduling. Some of these techniques would be genetic algorithms, genetic programming, evolutionary strategies, and memetic algorithms in which are all derived from biologically inspired concepts that will still help solve scheduling problems (Dahal et al., 2007). The different techniques are still being explored and discovered in depth; from recent research, it is shown that the different techniques are effective when it is compared to other search algorithms. Effectively, within time, scheduling will transition from a daily problem to a problem many will no longer come across. For example, in the present time, we have applications such as "Google Calendar" or "Apple Calendar"; with each different application you are able to set a specific time and date for an important event or meeting. Also, with add-on features to allow it to send daily reminders or reminders days before the event to provide an effective way of reminding humans when something is scheduled.

Digital freight shipping is the digital services a traditional freight company provides to its customers, such as faster answers to questions via AI support. This technology gives a clearer picture of how much it costs to ship, and it helps to track the supplies shipped and gives a record of everything shipped. One of the companies that are using digital freight shipping is the company Freightos. They are using robots and digitization to make the shipping process smoother and simpler. The COVID-19 has accelerated the growth of e-commerce. AI enables freight shipping to be more efficient, more affordable, and more transparent by digitizing the whole process and making sure that the importers know precisely what they can get when they book the freight.

Looking into the future of AI in supply chain management, we can expect drones to largely take over the delivery aspect of the supply chain. Last mile delivery is the point from which a package has almost but not quite reached the customer—it is the last step of the delivery process. The problem is that this period in the delivery process can be quite time-consuming— sometimes delivery locations can be quite far apart, or traffic can make delivering packages slow. UAVs (anonymous unmanned aerial vehicles) can be a promising solution—they can decrease the cost of delivering during the last mile period and can make quicker deliveries than traditional options. It will reduce fuel emissions and allow for packages to be delivered quicker, as there will be no traffic for delivery vehicles to sit in. One of the key benefits of using last-mile delivery drones is that the AI-based software can calculate and find the most efficient route in terms of delivery. It will alert about, for instance, upcoming traffic, bad weather, or alternative routes that make it more efficient. It can allow for competitive advantage in businesses allowing for same-day delivery of items. Amazon is currently in production of a service called Amazon PrimeAir that will be able to deliver packages in 30 min or less to customers. The company is currently working on making the drones as safe as possible before releasing the service to the public though.

Overall, these few areas of supply chain and logistics are only the backbone of how a company operates. A business cannot have a slow supply chain, or they will not survive in the world economy. Since AI has been implemented, companies have been thriving and are hungry for more data and information. While AI is capable of replacing basic roles in the supply chain, such as number crunching or recording data from transactions between suppliers and vendors, its application is extended to assisting in larger strategic decisions, allowing supply chains to maximize efficiency and allocation of resources.

Case 10.1: Walmart

As one of the top retailers and e-commerce giants in the entire world, Walmart requires a top-tier supply chain and logistics management system. Without it, they would not be the force in the market that they are today. Walmart utilizes several systems that will be discussed in this section which heavily support their supply chain and logistics: electronic data interchange (EDI) and vendor managed inventory system (VMI), and finally, this section will analyze how Walmart is using artificial intelligence to improve their ability to have a successful supply chain as well as improve their customer experience. The use of EDI for Walmart could be the most essential component in making their supply chain run smoothly as it works to automate simple processes. EDI technology is able to exchange documents between servers in real time, which allows for rapid communication, loads of data, and automated data entry into their system. Rapid communication is essential for Walmart because they need to be able to communicate with their suppliers in order to be on the same page regarding their stock and other necessities. Therefore, Walmart utilizes VMI, so that their suppliers can look at their stock in real time to see if Walmart needs more goods. With the capabilities of having so much data within one system, Walmart is able to see exactly what is happening within their supply chain in real time with complete transparency. This transparency can be seen with another addition that EDI brings to Walmart supply chain management, improved warehouse logistics through the use of barcodes. EDI gives Walmart the ability to utilize barcodes to track shipments throughout their supply chain. This tracking allows not only for Walmart to be fully aware of their shipments but also gives their customers the knowledge of when their products will be delivered or in stock. The use of the EDI system and the real-time communication allows for them to see exactly where these packages are in real time because of the barcodes. This creates a completely transparent system for Walmart and its suppliers.

The last emerging ability, which may be the most important, is third-party logistics. Third-party logistics, or 3PL, allows Walmart to receive products from a third party rather than their suppliers. It could be more cost-effective or quicker than trying to use their warehouses. This is ultimately improving the customer experience because they are able to receive their products faster than if it was coming from a Walmart warehouse. This is certainly a growing part of the e-commerce industry because EDI will continue to aid in making third-party logistics more effective for companies like Walmart. Moving slightly away from EDI, we can look at this rapid delivery process enabled by the usage of 3PL that Walmart has begun to use and see how artificial intelligence is aiding in the delivery and supply of the products available in this process. Of course, as a customer begins to place items in their virtual shopping cart, the site is using information to make assumptions on what they might want or be interested in. The artificial intelligence system calculates route time, scheduling a driver, a time slot, even scheduling a time for the items purchased to be packed, and finally, making sure the items purchased are tagged out of the system.

The EDI system, the VMI system, and the artificial intelligence that Walmart incorporates into their supply chain and logistics management are all reasons why they are mentioned in the top tier of retailers and e-commerce companies in the world. They will continue to innovate and use these tools to their advantage in order to become an even more dominant force within the market.

Case 10.2: United Parcel Service

The United Parcel Service (UPS) is the world's largest air and ground package delivery system, delivering over 20 million packages and documents per day to customers in 220 countries and territories (Rapier, 2020). Annually, UPS invests about $1 billion in technology that will enhance efficiency and customer service, as well as support increasing consumer demand for faster delivery times. The utilization of various information technologies and innovations in AI have proven crucial to improving UPS' logistics and supply chain management, thus bearing the responsibility for its success today.

One of the most well-known technologies is the On-Road Integrated Optimization and Navigation (ORION) device. This device utilizes sophisticated algorithms to map out the best route available to drivers based on a variety of variables—traffic, weather, accidents, and road conditions to name a few—to assist drivers as they make almost 100 deliveries per day. This feature is responsible for the commonly known "no left turn" policy at UPS, as left turns tend to slow down deliveries, use more gas, and increase chances of getting into an accident. This technology took nearly a decade to fully complete, but since its full implementation in 2016, this technology alone has reduced miles driven by UPS trucks by nearly 100 million miles.

Where ORION operates as a means to optimize delivery routes, Enhanced Dynamic Global Execution (EDGE) operates as a means of optimizing internal operations (Marr, 2018). This program, consisting of a collection of various different projects used throughout the organization, analyzes immense amounts of data—collected across its facilities over the last several years—regarding operations to seek to maximize efficiency. This umbrella program is projected to save $200–$300 million dollars per year by advising the company on key operations, such as how the trucks should be loaded and when they should be washed. This has led to various improvements within the organization. One such improvement is a small, Bluetooth device fitted into UPS trucks that emits a loud beep when a parcel is placed in the wrong vehicle; a different beep is emitted when a parcel is placed in the correct vehicle. This reduces delays and the chances of misplacing a package. Another such improvement is the use of a simple technology that relies on color-coded conveyor belts to help organize packages in distribution centers, thus allowing employees to scan a package, and quickly determine which conveyor belt to put the package on based on the reading from the scan (Woyke, 2020).

Another cost-saving innovation is the Delivery Information Acquisition Device (DIAD), used by every driver in the UPS fleet. This device can access wireless or cellular networks to access the drivers' route, capture signatures, and provide pickup and delivery instructions. Once a package is delivered, the drivers then use this device to update the status of the package immediately, informing the customer that their package has been delivered. This device, which is connected to the automated package tracking system, is also utilized as a means to reroute packages throughout the delivery process.

While there are many more technologies utilized by UPS, for the sake of brevity, there is only one more that will be discussed: drones. The Federal Aviation Administration approved UPS' request to operate a drone airline in 2019 (Hodge, 2019). This technology is only being utilized on a small scale immediately—such as delivering goods to small islands, rural communities, or campuses—and UPS assures its fleet of over 400,000 drivers that this technology will not be used to replace them. These drones are being programmed to autonomously deliver parcels to consumers, all while the driver is still making deliveries, and then returning to the driver after the drone completes its delivery.

Taking advantage of its sophisticated and centralized package tracking system, and mobilizing it in the form of EDGE and DIAD allowed UPS to improve their transparency with their consumers; similarly, ORION and drones work to improve delivery times and the execution of UPS' services. UPS utilizes a multitude of IT and AI technological innovations to continue to improve its logistics and supply-chain management and to continue to prove that they remain on the cutting edge of the industry and a fierce competitor in the global market.

Case 10.3: Amazon

Amazon is known for being the best online store in the world. Amazon is constantly coming out with new services like Amazon Echo, Amazon Music, and Amazon Prime. Not only does Amazon provide a variety of products for their customers, but they also employ thousands of people all over the world. Their jobs consist of operating in warehouses, distribution centers, hub lockers, and as delivery drivers. In other words, a large part of their jobs is in logistics.

Amazon's supply chain management is vital to its online business. When orders are made, and the warehouses process the orders, employees pack up their branded vans and set forth to deliver each package to the customers. To help deliver packages even faster than same-day delivery, Amazon is working to provide working drones—also known as Amazon Air—to deliver these packages. This would benefit the company and the customer. The company would be able to cut down on delivery drivers and save more money by doing so, and the customers would be able to select the option of getting their package delivered in just 30 min. This would be a first for any delivery service company to come out with. Despite owning warehouses all over the world, Amazon makes it a priority to ensure supply meets demand at all times. Inventory is constantly being restocked and kept an eye on at all times. Logistics in Amazon is a large part of what makes the company so successful. For example, the transportation system is one of the main reasons customers buy off of Amazon. They are able to buy products from the Amazon website and get it delivered whenever they want and prefer. There's a wide variety of customer products available on the Amazon website. These items are available at all Amazon's warehouses. This is what makes Amazon so easily accessible.

The AI and machine learning systems in Amazon are very brilliant and important for the company. A recent AI system that Amazon created is called the Amazon

Echo. This technology is used as a virtual assistant through the speakers of a device. The Amazon Echo allows users to ask any questions, activating the trigger score by saying "Alexa" before asking their question. This AI system is the first of its kind and has other companies developing similar technology since it's so unique and popular. Alexa's foundation from the beginning had been a combination of machine learning and data. As the amount of data it collects gets denser, its ability to learn and use AI also increases with its popularity. One of the most prominent features Alexa uses that also increases its competitiveness against other voice-controlled digital assistant devices is its ability to take data that was a mistake and learn it so that it does not repeat the second time it happens. Another function Alexa has acquired through machine learning is the ability to register follow-up questions without the need for consumers to repeat the system's wake word. In addition, Amazon has also implemented an active learning technology so that the device knows where it needs assistance from a human expert. This allows the device to understand its errors and catch them before they can occur, significantly reducing the number of times it makes inaccuracies. Amazon also uses the system called transfer learning to help the device reduce the amount of errors it makes in a year. This system enables deep learning, which can be a more advanced algorithm to model many different fields and use those domains to transfer and enhance it as a new skill. Alexa now has many capabilities that put it far ahead of its competition. By continuing to use AI and machine learning in their systems, Amazon has upgraded the device to do many tasks, such as communicate with different people at the same time, understand different languages, and the ability to learn from its users' preferences and needs. There is no doubt that Amazon's Alexa device will be the most dominant voice-controlled digital assistant device in the world. So far, they have shown tremendous capabilities, and it only continues to become more smarter and consumer-friendly from here.

Amazon Rekognition device is an artificial intelligence (AI) solution that allows users to integrate picture and video analysis into their apps. Amazon Rekognition detects objects; recognizes individuals, places, events, and words; and recognizes improper material. The device is extremely accurate in facial analysis and identification, allowing it to compare different faces and provide correct user authentication. The reason why Amazon Rekognition is helping their business increase competitiveness boils down to the simple use of the product, provision of rapid responses, how inexpensive it is to acquire, and it can be used to analyze millions of items, shapes, and products. Amazon Rekognition's future depends on the inclusion of more data and the continuous inclusion of machine vision. Specifically, common cases for using Amazon Rekognition include searchable image and video libraries, face-based user verification, detection of personal protective equipment, sentiment and demographic analysis, facial search, unsafe content detection, text detection, and custom labels. While technology has a long way to go, it is believed that Amazon's AI gadgets will have fast advancements in the next few years.

Amazon Web Services and development teams have created easy-to-use and powerful AI tools and services that have been vital to their business environment's success. According to Bezos, AI is a primary driving force behind Amazon's success that customers benefit from speedier delivery of Amazon's products and services, thanks to AI gadgets such as Alexa and Rekognition. These AI capabilities have also enabled Amazon customers to analyze data, identify photos and graphics, and interpret voice without the need for costly high-end computer systems. Amazon is continuously growing and improving their AI technology. It has claimed itself as an AI company and has benefited a lot from the latest technology. With advanced AI, their inventory is always stocked, they have a good idea of what customers are looking for, and they are staying at the top of their game as the best online store in the world.

10.5 Conclusion

Artificial intelligence and big data within the supply chain management industry are continuing to be utilized at a rapid pace as time goes on. While relatively new to the work field, SCM is embracing big data for a variety of reasons. The consumption of big data allows for the integration of greater technologies to be studied and developed further, allowing the processing, manufacturing, and distribution sectors to be capitalized to their fullest potential. Despite the challenges that accompany big data analytics currently, there is ample evidence for exponential growth within SCM due to the number of opportunities that can arise within the industry. It is evident that big data utilization will continue to flourish within related industries due to the sharp competitive edge it provides, as well as allowing the logistics industry to grow at its fastest pace since it first came about.

References

Chow, H. K. (2005, September 6). *Design of a RFID case-based resource management system for warehouse operations*. https://www.sciencedirect.com/science/article/pii/S0957417405001454

Dahal, K., Tan, K. C., & Cowling, P. I. (2007). *Evolutionary scheduling*. Springer.

Efendigil, T. (2008). A decision support system for demand forecasting with artificial neural networks and neuro-fuzzy models: A comparative analysis. https://pdfs.semanticscholar.org/f576/e82f0c77ccc58f0623ba67fa79a00ff61a0c.pdf

Hodge, R. (2019). UPS lands broad FAA approval for drone deliveries.

Jeong, B., Jung, H., & Park, N. (2002, February 15). A computerized causal forecasting system using genetic algorithms in supply chain management. *Journal of Systems and Software, 60*(3), 223–237.

Kuo, R., Wang, Y., & Tien, F. (2010). Integration of artificial neural network and MADA methods for green supplier selection. *Journal of Cleaner Production, 18*(12), 1161–1170.

Marr, B. (2018). *The brilliant ways UPS uses artificial intelligence*. Machine Learning and Big Data.

Min, H. (2009). Artificial intelligence in supply chain management: Theory and applications. *International Journal of Logistics Research and Applications, 13*(1), 13–39. https://www.tandfonline.com/doi/abs/10.1080/13675560902736537

Mohiuddin, K., Mao, J., & Jain, A. K. (1996). Artificial neural networks: A tutorial. *Computer, 29*, 31–44.

Rapier, G. (2020). UPS delivered over 21 million packages on average every day in the second quarter thanks to the coronavirus pandemic.

Safaei, M. (2013). An integrated multi-objective model for allocating the limited sources in a multiple multi-stage lean supply chain. https://www.sciencedirect.com/science/article/pii/S0264999313004458

Schmidt, M. (2016). *Clarifying the uses of artificial intelligence in the enterprise*. Techcrunch.com, Retrieved from https://techcrunch.com/2016/05/12/clarifying-the-uses-of-artificial-intelligence-in-the-enterprise/.

Sme, S. (2017). What is Supply Chain Management (SCM)? | Supply Chain Resource Cooperative | NC State University. https://scm.ncsu.edu/scm-articles/article/what-is-supply-chain-management-scm

Thomassey, S. (2010). Sales forecasts in clothing industry: The key success factor of the supply chain management. https://www.sciencedirect.com/science/article/pii/S0925527310002598

Watson, I., & Marir, F. (1994). Case-based reasoning: A review. *The Knowledge Engineering Review, 9*(4), 327–354.

Whitley, D. (1994). A genetic algorithm tutorial. *Statistics and Computing, 4*(2), 65–85. Retrieved from https://link.springer.com/article/10.1007/BF00175354.

Woyke, E. (2020). *How UPS delivers faster using $8 headphones and code that decides when dirty trucks get cleaned*. MIT Technology Review.

Artificial Intelligence in Manufacturing 11

Abstract

This chapter introduces the development and applications of artificial intelligence in manufacturing. Some of the key technologies include the semantic web of things for the Industry 4.0 platform, computer-aided manufacturing systems, intelligent agents, fuzzy interference, decision-making systems, time-series forecasting, and others. Three case studies are provided to illustrate the AI applications in John Deere, DataProphet, and Bright Machines.

Keywords

Manufacturing · Industry 4.0 · Smart factory · Semantic web of things · Computer-aided manufacturing · Intelligent agent systems · Fuzzy inference engine · Decision-making systems · Time-series forecasting · Recurrent neural networks

11.1 Introduction

Artificial intelligence (AI) is rapidly developing and taking over many industries and departments to make the procedures more efficient to maintain consumer demands as the market continues to expand globally. Manufacturing must address and create products at a reasonable rate and cost for the company so their consumers will remain satisfied with their purchases and business performance. The benefits and risks have continued to be monitored as this technology is new and upcoming in many areas of the world, but with the amount of data and automation AI can provide for manufacturing departments, there is a high chance it will only keep expanding. More companies within other industries will begin to implement this technology to better allocate the resources available and use the time of production wisely. In this chapter, we will explore how AI has revolutionized manufacturing, where and

L. Chan et al., *Applied Artificial Intelligence in Business*, Applied Innovation and Technology Management, https://doi.org/10.1007/978-3-031-05740-3_11

what forms of technologies are applied today, and the advantages of AI in the manufacturing sector.

The surge in manufacturing has been overwhelming for production plants throughout recent years as more consumers have access to the global market. Due to globalization, there is a need for distribution and production performance boost to adapt to the current pressures. Industry 4.0 or the Fourth Industrial Revolution drives the investment value in the economy. Smart factories and equipment can potentially bring many benefits to the manufacturing sector in areas with high demand and time constraints. In countries such as India, the high demand for products has created supply chain time constraints. Implementation of AI technologies and machine learning in their operations could improve productivity and reduce human error by incorporating intelligent machines to assemble and work the supply chain (Rizvi et al., 2021). The noticeable challenge for businesses, especially in developing countries, is investing in the equipment and skilled people needed to execute this technology properly. Although investing in AI can be challenging based on the specific economy or potential rate of return, old equipment failure or maintenance can be more costly. Therefore, it is crucial to understand how this technology developed over the years and what outcomes can be expected.

11.2 Development of Artificial Intelligence in Manufacturing

The manufacturing industry has gone through several distinct changes in the last century. From Henry Ford's creation of the assembly line to the Toyota Production System, the goal of companies has been to increase their efficiency and decrease errors in manufacturing systems. Craft production, an early stage in manufacturing during the 1900s, is done by hand, either with or without the aid of tools (Katana, 2019). The second stage, mass production, centers on creating a standardized product using automation or assembly lines, while the late stage, lean production, focuses on reducing waste from the manufacturing process. However, some researchers believe that manufacturing is on the verge of a fourth stage, AI-powered production.

The evolution of AI in manufacturing started with people using assembly lines and some automated machines to create products. The manufacturing industry has moved beyond that and started to improve equipment and programmed it to complete tasks by itself. Automation became a popular concept that could help industries create great products using only machines that could perform movements and actions on their own. Now, sensors and the Internet of Things (IoT) devices are used to track and monitor the actual state of the machinery and see what needs to be fixed before anything catastrophic can impact the line of assembly. This AI technology allows maintenance workers to actively view the state of the equipment and predict potential equipment failure before it occurs (Bukkapatnam et al., 2019). As a result, productivity increases, and production levels are maintained and managed appropriately.

In 1970, the first-in-line palletizing systems were designed and put to use along assembly lines. Automated palletizing enabled stacking of containers in alternating patterns on top of a palette (iGPS, 2018). In the 1980s, the use of robotic arms came onto the palletizing scene. These robotic arms were able to handle packages or products individually, allowing for greater palletizing flexibility (iGPS, 2018). The automation of palletizing improves safety, speed, and efficiency while maintaining flexibility of controls (Palletizer, 2021). The 1980s also showed the beginnings of computerized automation development, and in the 1990s, the movement carried towards digital programs (ThinkAutomation, 2021).

Artificial intelligence (AI) has become more and more ubiquitous in recent years. Within the manufacturing industry, new types of technology have been increasing productivity, reducing downtime and human error, and improving production yields. Back in 1913, Henry Ford's design of a moving assembly line for his factory significantly decreased the amount of time it took to produce cars (Britannica, 2021). Adding AI to the classic assembly line model improves company performance even more.

11.3 Application Areas of AI in Manufacturing

There are many areas within manufacturing where AI can serve well. Some of the key areas for AI integration are fault diagnosis, remaining useful life (RUL) prediction, and quality inspection (Ding et al., 2020). Manufacturing AI is able to identify machine output errors and run algorithms according to ideal manufacturing specifications and make suggestions about repairs or other necessary steps in order to correct the mistakes.

AI gives companies the ability to perform preventative maintenance on multiple levels of manufacturing processes before large issues arise from failures or faults. AI can also be used by manufacturers to run quality control specifications without the need for specialized employees by incorporating algorithms that run functionality tests on finished or in-progress products according to company standards (Tsolakis et al., 2021). These systems also help manufacturers improve production standards due to their real-time tracking and analysis of production process patterns.

Warehouse management and other production storage and organization of raw materials as well as finished goods will greatly benefit from AI incorporation in the process. Nowadays, in most industries there are machines that assemble the product; however, correct and organized storage and feed of materials are required for successful assembly work. This work may still be performed by human workers. However, like the packaging process, machinery with sensors can use visual imaging to distinguish which materials are placed in certain facility areas. Also, the machine could count the specific quantity needed or be programmed to do other tasks. There are still many human workers in the inventory management area, responsible for packaging the product quickly and carefully. AI technologies may assist those employees and ease their packaging duties, improving productivity and shortening time to market. The use of AI in warehouse management may lead to decrease in equipment and labor costs, while changing duties of warehouse management and production employees to machine support, observation, and maintenance.

11.4 AI Technologies in Manufacturing

There are a few technologies already being used in the production plants worldwide that have helped industries flourish. Applications of machine learning and the Internet of Things, use of automation, and intelligent robotics can improve manufacturing, quality of produced goods, and overall productivity as well as facilitate R&D, reduce errors, and maintain the supply chain through demand forecasts and simulations (Rizvi et al., 2021)

Recent trends of technological, informational, and data exchange and automation revolution in manufacturing, a so-called Industry 4.0, have driven manufacturers to enhance connected and smart manufacturing through vertical integration, connected discrete operational systems in horizontal integration, and end-to-end integration in the entire supply chain (Patel et al., 2018). AI technologies fit perfectly for enhancements to automation, flexibility, design, and interoperability of manufacturing systems. In manufacturing, companies are implementing AI for organizational flexibility, enterprise resource planning (ERP), better market response, and improvements to changes in business conditions (Butler, 2018).

Due to complex interactions in large datasets in manufacturing, AI models in manufacturing have to learn a large number of variables and their interaction in the system. The data for training AI should reflect the process and those interactions, with samples that are sufficiently representing process complexities and lower data bounds ranging from a few hundred to several thousand historical cases (Stork, 2019). Another important issue to stress is the representation of data with respect to time, i.e., the data should be sufficiently recent and corresponding to periods of operation to allow AI to learn about sustainability of the operating regions and effects from one process node to the next (Stork, 2019). AI in manufacturing should feature a robust data validation layer for dealing with location and elimination of inconsistencies. Data consistency and reliability are some of the key AI in manufacturing data requirements, since the model should be fed with current, constant, reliable data for correct model outputs.

11.4.1 Semantic Web of Things for Industry 4.0 (SWEeTI) Platform

Augmentation of Semantic Web, AI, and analytics are general methods in support of building smart IoT applications for the Industry 4.0 platform (Patel et al., 2018). This platform's data-analytic layer relies on a distributed data lake, with an opportunity to add industrial analytics through AI algorithms, leveraging such platforms like Predix (predix.io/catalog) for predictive maintenance, anomaly detection, and intelligent edge algorithms, Microsoft's AzureML (studio.azure.net) and AzureAI gallery (gallery.azure.ai), and Siemens MindSphere (siemens.minsphere.io; hosted on AWS).

11.4.2 Interoperative STEP-NC Computer-Aided Manufacturing and Intelligent Agent Systems

Current developments in AI allow automation of computer-aided manufacturing (CAD) and computer numerical control (CNC) interface with the arrival of integration standards (STEP). Nassehi et al. proposed a novel manufacturing chain based on the STEP-NC standard, with agent-based manufacturing decision-support system (Nassehi et al., 2006). Distributed artificial intelligence methodology is implemented through intelligent agents (autonomous intelligent entities with sensors for the surrounding environment, goals and agendas to follow, and effectors to evoke changes in the environment) (Nwana, 1996; Woolridge, 2002; Nassehi et al., 2006).

11.4.3 Fuzzy Interference, Relational Databases, and Rule-Based Decision-Making Systems

In earlier stages of the product development process, manufacturing issues could be assessed with AI tools, which could enable savings in costs, improvements in quality, and reductions in manufacturing time. Authors Munguía et al. (2010) described the AI-based rapid manufacturing (RM) system in their research article, proposing an integrated RM selection system. This system is composed of an expert system (with a series of if-then-else statements), a fuzzy inference engine (representing all the goals and constraints as fuzzy sets and mapping the membership values on the user-defined selection of linguistic variables), and databases (one-for RM process parameters and individual machine information and the other one – materials database) for qualitative and quantitative data support (Munguía et al., 2010).

11.4.4 Time-Series Forecasting and Recurrent Neural Networks

Since manufacturing deals with high volumes of raw materials and finished goods data, the data-driven algorithms should scale up properly with the increase in data. Time-series forecasting has been applied for predicting past and present sales numbers, for example, machine learning ARIMA (autoregressive integrated moving average) algorithms for univariate time-series data (Gardner, 2006; Pole et al., 2018; Chatfield, 2000; Chen et al., 2021). While standard forward-feed neural networks do not proliferate the information through time, the recurrent neural networks (RNNs) are more suitable for preserving temporal information by incorporating memory modules according to the future predictions of input data sequences (Chen et al., 2021). While RNNs have some issues with vanishing gradients, proposed long short-term memory (LSTM) mitigates the issue in a long-sequence dependency learning (Chen et al., 2021).

11.4.5 Other AI Technologies and Applications

There are high expectations that AI will change production and manufacturing paired with other key digital technologies like cloud computing, big data analytics, Internet of Things, robotics, and additive manufacturing (Tekic et al., 2019). A recent survey conducted by Forbes in 2018 shows that almost half of the respondents from the automotive and manufacturing industry characterize AI as "highly important" and "absolutely critical to success" to the manufacturing in the next 5 years. In manufacturing AI could improve the manufacturing process by better monitoring, early detection of problems and their solution, creating smarter supply chains, improving quality standards, and performance safety (Tekic et al., 2019). Some other bright examples of AI use for improvement of manufacturing processes include incorporation of robotics by Amazon (Kiva robot automation in retail logistics), GE Oil & Gas using additive manufacturing, and Local Motors (www.localmotors.com) using multiple microfactories in manufacturing of low-volume open-source motor vehicles (Tekic et al., 2019).

Case 11.1: John Deere

John Deere, a company that is almost 200 years old, is applying AI and machine learning in all aspects of its business. Deere is the first mover in the agricultural industry in implementing AI into its products and operations. As a pioneer in adopting AI, John Deere has gained a large competitive advantage over its traditional competitors.

In 2013, Deere revealed its "Farm Forward" campaign, a program focused primarily on implementing AI into its machines to create an array of enhanced technology-driven machinery. One example of this advancement is the development of the solely automated self-driving tractor, which is capable of not only driving itself around, courtesy of AI, but is also capable of identifying how much herbicide to spray. John Deere also developed the Autonomous Drone Sprayers. The drone sprayer flies over the fields using a weed scanner and a sprayer to precisely apply pesticides to the crops where it needs to go. Having the weed scanner be able to read and analyze how much pesticide to use on certain parts of the field is a great idea. This is a new way to cut down on the amount of chemicals used on growing crops and, at the same time, decrease cost. Furthermore, Deere is using AI to gather first-hand data to enhance their ability to accurately optimize the advice it gives to farmers. Over time, this will increase the farm's general efficiency, likely increase their revenues, and increase Deere's competitive advantage (Sarnecka, 2019).

In 2017, Deere acquired a Silicon Valley company Blue River which specializes in computer vision and image recognition. This move has allowed Deere's machinery to interpret images captured by cameras installed in machinery and enable autonomous decision-making using AI technology. This increases the rate at which the plants survive, as the machinery has become more accurate and effective at aiding the plant in surviving than the farmer.

Welding is a high-demand industry that suffers from many challenges. AI and machine learning can benefit the agriculture industry and companies like John Deere. Think about the sizes of the agricultural machinery, and even bigger combines and balers that farms use, one could imagine that fixing these large machines may take extreme welding. The pieces of iron could be thousands of pounds to lift and hold in the right spot while a high-strength weld is completed. The engineers came up with a new idea to use Intel's artificial intelligence technology to solve a costly problem in the process. The solution also uses computer vision to automatically spot common defects in the automated welding process in its manufacturing facilities. Considering the volume of welds that Deere must produce every day the facility is running, there are bound to be some mistakes. One of the most common problems is when cavities in the weld medal form caused by trapped gas bubbles as the weld is cooling down. These cavities weaken the strength of the weld. With AI technology, Deere and Intel developed an integrated end-to-end system of hardware and software that can generate insights in real time, at levels beyond the human sense's capability (Sarnecka, 2019). When using a neural network-based inference engine, the solution logs defects in real time and automatically stops the welding process. The automated system allows Deere to correct the issue in real time and produce the quality products that Deere is known for. To put into other words, this technology allows the AI welding machine to sense and stop whenever there has been a mistake in the recently finished welds that are cooling, allowing Deere to fix the problem before it has even been put out into the field and malfunctions.

John Deere is a machinery-based company, and implementing AI into their business is something most people would not think of connecting. The technology they produce becomes patented and is often improved upon. The technology itself will give Deere a competitive advantage over those who resort to traditional, human-based methods.

Case 11.2: DataProphet

Artificial intelligence in manufacturing is fast developing to change how we create products across many industries. The implementation of AI has become the central part of improving efficiency and productivity, aiming to reduce costs and product defects. AI and machine learning acknowledge more data and perform tasks quicker. DataProphet is a machine learning and artificial intelligence company (AI-as-a-service company) located in Cape Town, South Africa, focused on applying artificial intelligence in a factory setting. This company is optimizing complex manufacturing processes with its AI capabilities.

DataProphet gathers historical production data in various formats from all sectors in organization and uses predictive modeling for identification of optimal operating parameters as well as defects and errors. The company's AI-as-a-service deep learning solutions target improvements to key performance indicators throughout the production line and to the company's ROI with prescriptive changes and continuous production optimizations without the overdependence on human experts (Dataprophet, 2021).

The company differentiates several products-solutions in their suite: DataProphet CONNECT, DataProphet PRESCRIBE, and DataProphet DETECT (Fig. 11.1). DataProphet CONNECT prepares the manufacturing process for AI-guided optimization by displaying and organizing production data from multiple sources within the operating facility. DataProphet PRESCRIBE (deep learning Expert Execution System) analyzes process variables and guides their correction towards continuous improvement. DataProphet DETECT focuses on faults and weaknesses in the production system, providing technicians with deep diagnoses, aiming to prevent large issues or system breakdowns (Dataprophet, 2021).

DataProphet has already helped many different companies achieve this goal. For example, BMW and Volkswagen, the car companies, hired DataProphet to reduce stud welding defects by 75% with the aid of artificial intelligence. DataProphet aims to assist the companies using their own production data. They also help the company save 2% on costs after making the required adjustments to the process performance indicators.

The company works with several industries: automotive, semiconductor, rubber, and foundries. In foundries, for example, the company emphasizes application of advanced supervised and unsupervised machine learning methods, relying on their

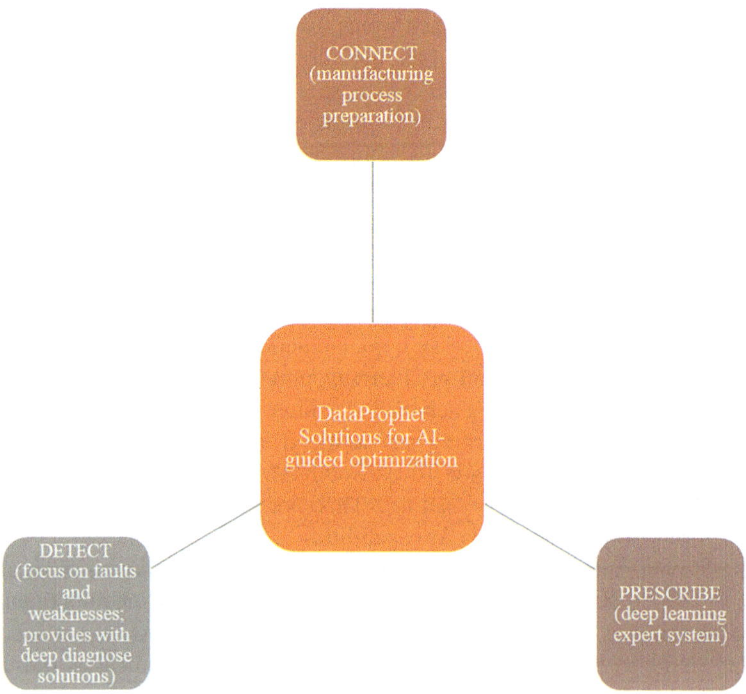

Fig. 11.1 DataProphet solutions with AI

Expert Execution Systems to produce deep learning prescriptions for operators, engineers, and managers to maintain optimal global performance. DataProphet has sensors within the plants to help relay live feedback to the "hub." This helps to improve plant stability, enhance key plant metrics, meet production targets, and maintain strong operational efficiencies. The company applies its AI-empowered prescriptive analytics in the areas of mold sand mixing, mold production, core sand mixing, core sand production, metal production, metal casting, and cooling. Their product solutions collect large volumes of data through hundreds of control parameters and quality measurements, learning about parameter interactions and influences, while prescribing optimal machine settings aiming at defects reduction and achievements of high yields (Dataprophet, 2021)

DataProphet stays ahead of their competition because of their innovation capabilities towards process optimization. It generates great value with cutting-edge AI technology, harnessing prescriptive analytics and innovating with deep learning techniques.

Case 11.3: Bright Machines

Bright Machines is an AI manufacturing company that focuses on a software-first mindset towards creating machinery used in manufacturing. By using AI software within the machines that they create for companies, Bright Machines products allow companies to create automated assembly lines that are fast and agile and can be used to monitor and improve upon production processes. The company specializes in creation of "microfactories" that are AI-run assembly lines that automate simple assembly processes and can also run inspection tasks at a high degree of accuracy, without human error or fatigue.

Microfactories are easily designed and can be created to fit the needs of manufacturing processes such as assembling, fastening, welding dispensing, pressing, labeling, vision, and certain testing. Their ease of design comes from their diagnostic approach towards the way their machines are created for companies. Assembly machinery is created from a problem within a company's manufacturing process, the machinery is then made for its intended purpose and is implemented with Bright Machines manufacturing AI software, Brightware. All of its functions are coded within Brightware which is used by their operator to perform its assembly tasks. Another highly regarded aspect of Bright Machines products is that their assembly lines can be easily reconstructed or reprogrammed to perform different tasks, or even to the assembly of a whole new product.

Typical microfactories include robotic assembly machines that perform tasks such as screwing in place screws on a motherboard. These robotic arms perform at an amazing accuracy and efficiency and greatly reduce production costs and time associated with assembly problems, for example, the microfactories used in the automotive industry with regards to the assembly and inspection of rear and front media hubs. The insertion points of several pieces used to manufacture these media hubs have to be done at specific angles with great precision or else it can cause defects in the final product. Microfactories made by Bright Machines used robotic arms to perform these intricate assembly tasks through AI technology by giving the machines the ability to perform to exact specifications as well as have vision on how to assemble the product within these exact specifications. This gave the company a 98% production yield rate, increased productivity of assembly by 60%, and increased units of production per hour by 40%.

Bright Machines offer companies the opportunity to improve their overall equipment efficiency by incorporating this kind of AI- and machine learning-led manufacturing into their production processes. Typical assembly tasks can be incredibly time-consuming for manufacturers to hire out human workers, often leaves them with a much higher chance for errors within their production, produces less consistent products, and can waste company money that is associated with dealing with these previous dilemmas. Bright Machines' microfactories can perform these tasks with a high degree of accuracy while also running diagnostics of production that can allow businesses to gather crucial data that can lead toward the improvement of manufacturing processes.

Another example of this improved efficiency by Bright Machines AI manufacturing products comes from their involvement with the creation of assembly lines for a single-cup coffee maker. This company was experiencing problems with assembly of their products, not only maintaining enough employees to do the required tasks but also with human errors of assembly. Bright Machines created a microfactory that uses a vision device to precisely analyze the areas of the product that need the assembly, target this area, and perform assembly with great accuracy and control, improving production yield to 98% from 60% and increased units produced per hour by 50%.

Bright Machines is currently only developing AI in manufacturing for the back end of production such as assembly, testing, and inspection but hopes in the future to work with companies to produce AI systems in a broader aspect of production such as the creation of new and improved product/assembly processes. They currently serve over 50 companies in over 8 sectors of manufacturing.

11.5 Key Takeaways

The idea of incorporating artificial intelligence into business is becoming more influential. Now we have started to use it to better our manufacturing processes to keep up with demand. The evolution of AI has transformed how we do business and how workers complete their tasks. There are many advantages of having artificial intelligence techniques in any manufacturing field. Applying artificial intelligence technology in manufacturing can help with an increased level of performance, allow calculated outcomes to be done within a fraction of the time, and help provide the best display model for the products of a store. Artificial intelligence does not replace the need for a worker, but instead increases the outcome of the worker getting the correct answer even the first time.

The major benefit of having AI in manufacturing facilities is that you can track everything you can access within the plant. The information and data give you the best possible predictions based on information provided to keep personnel updated about any potential damages or problems they can fix ahead of time to prevent any potential product delays. Another benefit associated with AI is the ability to build the product using factory equipment to lift big pieces or place them in the correct spot in an efficient manner. One machine can do multiple tasks, creating a simple one-way stop when assembling a particular product. There is less risk of error and a higher chance of lowering costs since the machine could perform repetitive tasks over a prolonged period of time. It is effective because the machine needs a program to work correctly, and if inputted right, the equipment will build the products correctly without any delays or mishaps.

11.6 Conclusion

Nowadays, the manufacturing sector of business still has not fully realized the potential for production plants worldwide. In developed countries, people are continuously trying to implement AI into their facilities to improve productivity further. Items like sensors and IoT devices are becoming more common in daily life and in the business world as we try to allocate our resources and employees to more critical tasks. Corporations need to invest in these new technologies to succeed in the global market. More consumers are subject to purchase items, and social connectivity to intercontinental markets is likely to expand. Nevertheless, AI will continue to grow and prosper in manufacturing because of how quickly technology can be adapted and programmed to complete specific tasks.

Having an AI system will also help manufacturing companies stay at the top of their competition. Over time, AI developments in manufacturing have led to cognitive computing – where "every piece of your supply chain was accounted for in terms of how they affect various processes, production shifts, supplier changes, and equipment maintenance weeks in advance, updating in real time" (Hitch, 2017). Such changes in automation software optimize employee time and work, leading to resource savings (ThinkAutomation, 2021).

Overall, the innovative technologies of AI and machine learning have reimagined the manufacturing industries for many companies and industries. The innovation of sensors and gathering data has become an advantage to a multitude of people because it can provide you with time-saving information, solutions to potential problems, indications of possible maintenance, and many other features we could never have gathered with manual labor. Automation and AI are ideas of the future that every industry will want to have embedded in their system for a better supply line. Technology will always be a part of our lives. Businesses applying this technology to their everyday tasks have proven how much our lives can be more accessible and convenient for many employers and employees. People can focus on what is most important and place their resources into areas that need improvement for the sake of their company.

References

Britannica. (2021). *History of work organization.* Retrieved from Britannica Encyclopedia. https://www.britannica.com/topic/history-of-work-organization-648000/Division-of-labour-in-the-workplace

Bukkapatnam, S. T. S., Afrin, K., Dave, D., & Kumara, S. R. T. (2019). Machine learning and AI for long-term fault prognosis in complex manufacturing systems. *CIRP Annals, 68*(1), 459–462. ISSN:0007-8506.

Butler, R. (2018, November). Front of mind: AI in manufacturing. *Control Engineering Polska.*

Chatfield, C. (2000). *Time-series forecasting*. CRC Press.

Chen, Y. C., He, B. H., Lin, S. S., Soeseno, J. H., Tan, D. S., Chen, T. P. C., & Chen, W. C. (2021). Demystifying data and AI for manufacturing: Case studies from a major computer maker. *APSIPA Transactions on Signal and Information Processing, 10.* https://doi.org/10.1017/ATSIP.2021.3

Collins, M. (2015, January 5). *Artificial intelligence in manufacturing.* Retrieved from Forbes. https://www.forbes.com/sites/mikecollins/2015/01/05/artificial-intelligence-and-manufacturing-part-one/?sh=639522b63458

DataProphet. (2021). *Leading provider of AI solutions for global manufacturers.* https://dataprophet.com/about-us/

Ding, H., Gao, R. X., Isaksson, A. J., Landers, R. G., Parisini, T., & Yuan, Y. (2020). State of AI-based monitoring in smart manufacturing and introduction to focused section. *IEEE/ASME Transactions on Mechatronics, 25*(5), 2143–2154.

Gardner, E. S., Jr. (2006). Exponential smoothing: The state of the art – Part II. *International Journal of Forecasting, 22*(4), 637–666.

Hitch, J. (2017, December 4). *A brief history of AI: From Fun & games to manufacturing genius.* Retrieved from Industry Week. https://www.industryweek.com/technology-and-iiot/media-gallery/22024672/a-brief-history-of-ai-from-fun-games-to-manufacturing-genius/slideshow?slide=15

iGPS. (2018, 11 8). *What is palletizing?* Retrieved from iGPS: This Way Forward. https://igps.net/blog/2018/11/08/what-is-palletizing/

Katana. (2019). *Craft production: How to make it in the craft business.* Retrieved from https://katanamrp.com/blog/craft-production/

Munguía, J., Lloveras, J., Llorens, S., & Laoui, T. (2010). Development of an AI-based rapid manufacturing advice system. *International Journal of Production Research, 48*(8), 2261–2278. https://doi.org/10.1080/00207540802552675

Nassehi, A., Allen, R. D., & Newman, S. T. (2006). Application of mobile agents in interoperable STEP-NC compliant manufacturing. *International Journal of Production Research, 44*(18–19), 4159–4174. https://doi.org/10.1080/00207540600786723

Nwana, H. S. (1996). Software agents: An overview. *The Knowledge Engineering Review, 11*(3), 205–244.

Palletizer. (2021). *Palletizing systems.* Retrieved from Palletizer.org: http://www.palletizer.org/palletising-systems/palletising-systems.html

Patel, P., Ali, M. I., & Sheth, A. (2018). From raw data to smart manufacturing. *IEEE Intelligent Systems, 33*(August), 79–86.

Pole, A., West, M., & Harrison, J. (2018). *Applied Bayesian forecasting and time series analysis.* Chapman and Hall/CRC.

Rizvi, A. T., Haleem, A., Bahl, S., & Javaid, M. (2021). Artificial Intelligence (AI) and its applications in Indian manufacturing: A review. *Current Advances in Mechanical Engineering: Select Proceedings of ICRAMERD, 2020*, 825–835.

Sarnecka, D. (2019). *John Deere-using AI to reimagine farming.* Digital Initiative. Harvard Business Review. https://digital.hbs.edu/platform-digit/submission/john-deere-using-ai-to-reimagine-farming/

Stork, J. (2019). Data requirements for AI in manufacturing. *Foundry Management & Technology*, 27–28.

Tekic, Z., Cosic, I., & Katalinic, B. (2019). Manufacturing and the rise of artificial intelligence: Innovation challenges. *Annals of DAAAM and Proceedings of the International DAAAM Symposium, 30*(1), 192–196. https://doi.org/10.2507/30th.daaam.proceedings.025

ThinkAutomation. (2021). *A history of automation: The rise of robots and AI.* Retrieved from ThinkAutomation. https://www.thinkautomation.com/bots-and-ai/a-history-of-automation-the-rise-of-robots-and-ai/

Tsolakis, N., Zissis, D., Papaefthimiou, S., & Korfiatis, N. (2021). Towards AI driven environmental sustainability: An application of automated logistics in container port terminals. *International Journal of Production Research*, 1–21.

Woolridge, M. (2002). *An introduction to multiagent systems*. Willey.

Part III

Artificial Intelligence for Industrial Applications

Artificial Intelligence in Insurance

12

Abstract

Artificial intelligence and big data techniques have been widely used in the insurance sector nowadays. This chapter explores various insurance technologies including chatbots, natural language processing, robotic process automation, computer vision, telematics, and predictive analytics. The AI-based insurance applications include claims processing, fraud detection, and personalized policies. Case studies are provided on Allstate, Liberty Mutual, State Farm, and Progressive.

Keywords

Insurtech · Insurance technology · Medical insurance · Automotive insurance · Chatbots · Natural language processing · Robotic process automation · Computer vision · Telematics · Predictive analytics · Claims processing · Fraud detection · Personalized policies

12.1 Introduction

Insurance is a huge part of our lives because everyone wants some form of insurance, such as insurance for vehicles, health, land, and life. To keep us safe in case of potential incidents, insurance is required. Insurance is a form of risk management, mostly used to counteract potential losses. An insurer charges the insured a premium for its financial protection. To do this, an insurer must calculate the worth of what is being insured and the risk involved. This is done by collecting information and assessing different aspects of it, so in a way, the insurance industry has always used data. Therefore, it is a natural progression for them to implore the use of artificial intelligence and big data.

L. Chan et al., *Applied Artificial Intelligence in Business*, Applied Innovation and Technology Management, https://doi.org/10.1007/978-3-031-05740-3_12

This chapter introduces the impact of big data and AI on the insurance industry. The following section details the many possibilities that big data and AI have brought to the insurance industry. The focus is on the AI technology and tools used. AI and machine learning have made the insurance sector more efficient. This chapter provides examples to show how and why they were used. In the final section, everything is wrapped up. It includes challenges and suggestions of actions that should be taken. It also states the trend and future of using AI in insurance.

12.2 The Development of Insurance Technology

Insurtech (Insurance Technology) is a new word coined after Fintech to specifically represent the technological innovations to improve the efficiency of the insurance sector in recent years. The insurance industry provides important support to businesses, homes, and individuals in many aspects of the economy. However, the business process of insurance could involve lengthy form filling, low transparency, and high risks for the stakeholders.

With the development of AI and big data, many insurance companies notice that the role of information technology is very essential to the management, risk, price, product design, market, customer service, organization, and operation. Insurtech revolutionized the traditional complex business process, liberating the labor force in the insurance sector. Big data and AI are becoming the new routines with the rise in population and policyholders to store data and ensure the accuracy of information in order to deter fraud and manage risks.

AI is being used for medical insurance in the healthcare industry. Insurance companies utilize both AI and big data to provide helpful intel for health service providers and patients including procedure price variations by the region and doctor. Patients can then view their desired provider through reviews based on their regions (Daim et al., 2009). This process saves the user and the company lots of time and is more efficient. AI-based Insurtech works to simplify claims data intake to search millions of data points to detect holes, miscodes, and misdirected treatment. Capturing and fixing these mistakes makes life faster and more efficient for those in the healthcare sector, saving time and resources and improving the standard of treatment.

Automotive insurance is another key area adopting a lot of AI applications. Many new cars today are built with a bundle of sensors and computing chips that can detect and transmit real-time data about the car's condition, speed, location, and so on. With the deployment of smart devices, such as chatbots and GPS route advisors, cars have gained better capabilities in data collection and analysis. The data can be transmitted to insurance carriers for risk assessment and control using machine learning algorithms or other AI methods. The output can help insurance companies to provide a variety of personalized services for customers.

Insurtech has been life-changing for many insurance carriers due to its ability to improve customer satisfaction and help businesses make better decisions. AI has been proven to make processes easier and are becoming increasingly used in insurance companies across various types of businesses from car insurance, travel insurance, property insurance, and medical insurance. Some key carriers have already applied AI tools to enhance user's experience during their business processes.

12.3 Enabling Technologies of AI for Insurtech

Automation is seen throughout the insurance industry in several different ways. Robotic process automation (RPA) is employed for simple repetitive tasks; natural language processing (NLP) is used to extract meaning, intent, and key information from text or audio; computer vision is utilized to provide instant assessment of damage through photographs or video clips, while chatbots are used to gather information, provide answers, direct customers, and much more. An insurance carrier also needs to decide on the type of AI platforms; some will choose a public cloud, while others will go private. Some other challenges are whether to build AI or deploy AI or to use supervised learning or unsupervised learning or machine learning or deep learning. While the differences seem similar, the approaches can be fundamentally different. The companies' choices will shape the foundation for how the industry works.

12.3.1 Chatbot and Natural Language Processing

Chatbots require NLP since they deal with recognizing the meaning within the input voice data, as well as responding to users with a certain language. NLP is a subcategory in AI that deals with input data such as voices, languages, and sounds. AI-embedded software detects and analyzes voice data and converts it into useful information with meaning. This process involves text mining through large databases. One of the business areas that are experiencing the greatest change is customer experience, especially with insurance claims. AI is often used to enrich customer experience by helping resolve service issues faster than a pure human interaction by using an extended database of information to treat the issue. Chatbots are always accessible and they have been proven to enhance customer loyalty and experience. Experience with claims is the number one priority for most insurers because it is where they begin to gain the trust of customers. AI technology has now made the experience of statements more personalized and simpler than ever before to use. This is done through data collection and analytics to find pain points in consumer encounters and make the process of customer engagement more fluid and personalized. AI can be used to improve marketing effectiveness by tailoring products to individual preferences. Think of Netflix recommendations based on shows that users have already watched. That concept is used to give a customer the most effective health insurance plan.

12.3.2 Robotic Process Automation

According to IBM, AI has the potential to transform the business model of an insurer by improving the speed at which tasks can be carried out with RPA. This technology is great for repetitive and simple tasks, and it will free up agents to handle other items. For more complicated tasks, one would need "trained AI." Then insurers will be able to use former communications to enhance and improve services to customers, brokers, and other third-party vendors. AI creates operating efficiencies by streamlining the application process. An example of this would be a prefilled homeowners' application. AI can facilitate better claims processing by applying machine learning algorithms to outcomes for more accurate results. RPA improves efficiency in the insurance industry, simplifying assignments, finding more efficient ways to handle problems, and saving both time and money.

12.3.3 Computer Vision

Computer vision employs machine learning techniques which enable machines to detect patterns within pictures and videos. The input data in computer vision systems can include satellite maps, surveillance cameras, facial recognition, fingerprint sensors, and all types of image data. The machine vision system can recognize the existence of different entities in real time and run image analytics on them. For example, auto insurance providers can allow customers to upload pictures of car damage into their information system. The machine learning algorithm will analyze the damage and estimate the cost for repairs, which can significantly facilitate the claim process and related decisions.

12.3.4 Telematics

Telematics is a behavioral intelligence technology of monitoring drivers, automobiles, or any moving objects by using remote sensor systems. With the Internet of Things (IoT) technology, telematics (or a telematics system) deploys data gathering tools to collect information about car mileage and driving habits. Telematics data is typically captured by either a mobile app or a small device attached to a car provided by an insurance company. Telematics may also help users to save money on car insurance. Risk assessments such as Fitbit and Apple Watch are telematics, which are examples of telematics being used in insurance. These devices capture a wide range of lifestyle data that could contribute to better predictive and diagnostic analytics, such as heart rates and health improvement. AI can be used to improve company solvency (ability to meet expenses) through the ability to assess risk more accurately. Insurers will not overestimate the value and overpay for the loss of insured items, causing loss for the company. AI reduces fraud for insurance companies through better identification techniques.

12.3.5 Predictive Analytics

Predictive analytics use machine learning algorithms to analyze historical and available databases to make predictions. Risk assessment, task automation, and behavioral intelligence are the most popular areas being analyzed using AI algorithms in the insurance industry. AI-based predictive analytics can be very useful in disease prediction and forecast for health insurance. Customers' medical records, family health history, individual behaviors, and even regional population trends can all be used as factors for prediction. AI programs will consolidate such input data and compute probabilities for the future. The output can inform and support business decisions for insurance companies. Text analytics can identify potential "red flag" trends across reports and flag new reports that are likely to be fraudulent. Machine learning and big data boost effectiveness and decision-making, while AI processes can greatly speed up the handling and payment of claims.

12.4 AI Applications in the Insurance Industry

An effective AI platform can streamline the business processes for insurance carriers. This includes, but is not limited to, customer feedback assessment, checking how a policy is selling, assessing customer response to sale techniques, gauging the effectiveness of promotions, and determining which policies have the highest number of claims (Ortiz, 2020). The list of possible ways for AI to be used within the insurance industry is ongoing. This technology has reshaped the insurance industry, changing the way things are done, and the time it takes to do them. It is through AI that insurance carriers can more accurately underwrite, assess risks, and incentivize risk reduction, as well as improve customer experiences, reduce processing time, and personalize products and policies to meet customer needs.

12.4.1 Claims Process

The claims process is usually quite cumbersome. The claims process spends most of its time on rigorous auditing. Using artificial intelligence and big data, it is possible to analyze the liability of both parties in an accident and confirm whether a customer is insured or not. If there is a problem in which case, then the fraudulent case can be handed over to manual audit, which not only improves the audit efficiency but also enhances the service awareness. Using AI in this process also saves cost. Computer vision programs can read and digitize the documents such as the claims forms. It can also assess car damage and repair cost through scanning the photos uploaded by users. Machine learning algorithms can be used in text mining for retrieving claims information. IBM Watson provides customizable applications which can be used in claims adjustment.

12.4.2 Fraud Detection

As we know, the insurance industry is an intangible industry, has a lot of loopholes, and needs more regulation. This is not entirely possible with traditional labor. Consumer fraud is one of the problems in the insurance industry. AI and big data can help companies to identify fraud by using face recognition, voice recognition technology, and anomaly detection techniques to improve the efficiency of anti-fraud protection. According to the FBI, the total cost of insurance fraud (non-health insurance) is estimated to be more than $40 billion per year (FBI, 2020). With the use of machine learning algorithms, a large amount of data can be checked in a short amount of time. It includes a variety of AI solutions, such as social network analysis and telemetric analysis. This is the strongest weapon insurers can deploy for the detection of fraud.

12.4.3 Personalized Policies

Insurance providers can target customers according to their different behaviors and then predict which will appeal to them most. An insurance company with AI-based data analytics provides essential personal positioning and is often in a better position than its competitors in the marketplace. IoT devices on cars have sensors which can collect driver's data and transfer to remote cloud platforms, allowing safe drivers to pay less for auto insurance. The same mechanism can also be used in healthcare where people with healthier lifestyles can save money for health or life insurance. The benefits of personalization are clear for insurance companies. It supports sales, customer loyalty and engagement, and higher success rates for cross-selling.

All of these AI applications and tools serve to improve efficiency and increase customer satisfaction, which is very important, especially when customers will be dealing with an increasing number of automations instead of people. Therefore, making sure that there is already a relationship between insurer and insured would be smart, as that might be the only reason they do not leave for another company.

Several large established insurance providers began to deploy AI-based applications in recent years, including Allstate, Liberty Mutual, Progressive, and State Farm. Let us take a deeper dive to explore their AI initiatives in the following cases.

Case 12.1: Allstate

One insurance company that uses artificial intelligence to its advantage is Allstate. According to Forbes, analytics and algorithms, dealing with large amounts of voice data and free-form text, are very well integrated into Allstate claims handling, billing inquiries, technical helpdesk, and agent interactions (Bean, 2018). Allstate collects about 11,000 terabytes of data from 1.2 million people every day, with the goal of providing personalized experiences to each, according to a report in Insurance Business. "Allstate is not an insurance company, we are a data company - a customer-centric data company" (McKendrick, 2019).

Allstate originally used a tool for digital estimation: Colossus. The Colossus program was first licensed and popularized by Allstate in the 1990s. Allstate turned to Colossus because they wanted to standardize their claims. Allstate also turned to this program because it was billed as a means to save money on payouts. Allstate was using Colossus to estimate the value of claims through the use of AI. In 2010, Allstate was fined $10 M for the Colossus' computer claim handling process. It was said that the claims made by the program were insufficient and the program was not large enough to properly cover all of the content provided by Allstate accurately. That year Allstate began renovating the Colossus program and formed some small analytics subsidiaries such as Arity to gather more data to create an even better system than Colossus, which could make more accurate claims. In 2010, Allstate created Arity. The goal was to build a team and technology to create and gather driving data to price insurance more accurately. Arity put telematics devices in cars while giving users insurance discounts for sharing data. Arity claims that this method of tracking user driving patterns is the most predictive way to most accurately assess the risk of a driver. This component proves that if someone has specific behaviors, those behaviors are going to lead to losses.

Allstate used machine learning to turn the company around after a major employee turnover within the company. Allstate focuses on customer relations; they use collected data to gain valuable insight into their customers, which helps keep customers satisfied, improving business outcomes. In its most recent quarter, the company reported a revenue of $8.94 billion, which increased by 6% from a year earlier. Hadoop and AI provide them with new competitive advantages. Instead of focusing on traditional small sample data, they focus more on market segmentation, accurately understanding the target customers, instead of randomly picking customers. In addition, Insurtech gives them good sales strategies, such as identifying fraudulent claims and developing better marketing and sales activities. Therefore, they can make better decisions. Allstate's use of artificial intelligence and big data has been driving the success of the company and will continue to do so, as long as Allstate keeps developing its AI alongside its competitors.

Case 12.2: Liberty Mutual

In January 2017, Liberty Mutual announced plans to develop automotive apps with AI capability and products aimed at improving driver safety. Solaria Labs, an innovation incubator established by Liberty Mutual, has launched an open API developer portal which integrates the company's knowledge and public data to inform how these technologies will be developed. An Application Programming Interface is essentially a toolkit that provides the blueprint for building software applications. The insurance company is reportedly experimenting with a new app to help drivers involved in a car accident quickly assess the damage to their car in real time using a smartphone camera. The app's AI component would be trained on thousands of images from car crashes and as a result could also provide damage-specific repair cost estimates. This is a timely initiative considering that motor vehicle deaths in 2016 peaked around 40,000, the highest amount recorded in nearly a decade. In May 2016, Liberty Mutual announced the launch of its $150 million venture capital initiative, Liberty Mutual Strategic Ventures (LMSV). The early-stage venture fund will focus on innovative technology and services specifically designed for the insurance industry. The VC firm has invested in companies such as Snapsheet, a smartphone application that reportedly allows users to receive auto repair bids from local body shops within 24 hours. Snapsheet's president C. J. Przybyl has stated that AI and machine learning are used to support the company's data analysis process.

Liberty Mutual Insurance is taking advantage of technological change and believes in the opportunities presented by technology. They are working with MIT on AI technologies to improve visual discrimination, data analysis, and image recognition. Liberty Mutual has an AI program whose components have been trained to recognize thousands of accident images, and customers can assess damage to their cars from their smartphones. Similar to Progressive, Liberty Mutual also built an app based on telematics. This software helps consumers, using only their phone camera, to record car damage in real time. The AI component is trained to identify most types of damage and can even provide estimates of repair costs as soon as needed.

Case 12.3: State Farm

State Farm is headquartered in Carthage, Illinois. The company collects and analyzes customer's driving behavior through their mobile app and in-vehicle systems through their Drive Safe & Save Program. This program allows customers to earn rewards and discounts for safe driving and avoiding phone use while driving. Customers will also earn discounts by having good driving habits such as avoiding rush hours and will not be fined if they have a bad turn, for example. This is a very efficient way for a car insurance company to monitor their customers and provide incentives while encouraging them to drive safe.

In an effort to explore the ability of computer vision to identify distracted drivers, State Farm launched an online competition in 2016. The competition resulted in 1440 participants and the company offered a total of $65,000, divided into three prize levels. The dataset provided by State Farm consisted of photos of drivers described as "2D dashboard camera images." Participants were challenged with the task of classifying the perceived behavior of each driver using a list of ten categories including safe driving, texting, operating the radio, and talking on the phone. Competition scores were calculated using a log loss metric ranging from a minimum value of 0 to a maximum value of 1. The goal of a machine learning model is to achieve a score that is as close to zero as possible, which indicates the level of accuracy of a given model. The first place application which achieved a score of 0.08739 utilized two neural network models and focused image classification on two main photo regions: the head region and the bottom right quarter where the driver's hand normally appears. From a business strategy perspective, a patent application and the company's Drive Safe & Save program provide evidence which suggests that driver data collection and interpretation will play increasingly important roles in State Farms' approach to customizing insurance options and providing customer discounts. This improved use of data is consistent with one of the most important broad trends in AI and insurance.

Case 12.4: Progressive

Progressive is another example of an automobile insurance firm incorporating AI into its scheme. Snapshot, a gadget that allows drivers to record driving habits by simply plugging it into their vehicle, was invented by Progressive. Progressive Insurance gives discounts to safe drivers enrolled in Snapshot, which is a telematics device that plugs into a vehicle and sends driver data. They use a machine learning algorithm to decipher the data and learn how that person is driving. If their customers have steady, good driving habits only from the first month, the business will observe the data and provide savings. This encourages healthy driving practices and may be a money-saving deal for customers. Insurers such as Progressive generally use telematics data to offer personalized driving feedback, safe-driving rewards, or potential cost savings on your car insurance policy for safe driving. AI is used to more accurately estimate the value of a price risk and financially incentivize risk reduction. Telematics allows insurers to collect real-time driver behavior data and combine it with loss data and insurance premium data to provide premium discounts efficiently and effectively.

Progressive uses AI to analyze consumer preferences and monitors the customer's level of driving and safety through its snapshot program that tracks the driver's activity through a device plugged into the dashboard. The program allows drivers to drive less and safer, which means bigger discounts for consumers. The ways they collect data are also very diverse. The company has a lot of structured data in relational databases using DB2 or Oracle and also collects a lot of real-time unstructured data. They store it in centralized data warehouses and analyze it in different ways through software packages such as Hadoop and Tableau. Although Tableau cannot save costs for Progressive, it is not convenient to collect and process data with traditional tools. Tableau has achieved a qualitative leap in work efficiency and achieved a limit beyond which traditional methods cannot be broken.

12.5 Key Takeaways

From the cases, we can see that the insurance carriers have been using Insurtech to transform their business. AI can minimize human interactions and maximize users' experiences. The big question in the insurance industry is "How will AI impact the future?" The answer is simple. It is already happening now. Artificial intelligence makes it possible to personalize customer experiences, give insight into customer behaviors, streamline the claims process, prevent fraud, improve underwriting, and much more. Allstate and other insurance agencies are able to more accurately provide claims in a timely manner due to collection of user data. Accuracies in claims save insurance companies large rates while still paying their policyholders "fair" amounts. In the future it will only become more complex and accurate as data systems and their methods of interpretation are refined.

Despite the many benefits of using AI in insurance, there are some potential challenges that may arise. One problem could be managing the real-time data flow. AI requires mass amounts of data to be collected, tracked, and stored. There are potential threats involved with AI in the insurance sector, along with the positive developments. The main challenge is bringing consumers to trust AI and the technical processes it conducts. Security and secrecy, on top of that, may be a worry that people feel more debatable and unsure of trusting the system. In the business world and the insurance industry, competition also plays a major role, especially as AI is beginning to show great business outcomes in the insurance industry. The positive benefits, however, still outweigh the risks because insurance carriers can take advantage of big data to use diagnostic and predictive analytics to predict the behavior of potential policyholders and take action based on the outcomes (OECD, 2020). AI and intelligent systems replace human work and make it incredibly easy to gather data and maintain endless quantities of data. For some smaller insurers, the complexity and volume of data can be a barrier. The algorithms used to synthesize big data lack transparency and may be biased. Highly personalized interest rates lose the benefits of risk concentration. In the face of these challenges, the insurance industry has to adopt AI more carefully, rethink how to use it correctly, under what circumstances, how to protect consumers' privacy during the use process, and how to improve the vulnerability of Insurtech.

12.6 Conclusion

In conclusion, artificial intelligence and big data are important in the insurance industry as they help insurers improve fraud detection rates, offer more accurate quotes, and reduce claims processing time. But the technology faces big challenges, especially with regard to customer privacy. Insurance companies also need to pay a lot of energy to master this technology. After all, big data and artificial intelligence technologies are constantly growing. Only by keeping pace with the times and following the changes in the market environment can they serve the industry better. Insurtech is the future of the insurance industry, a must-have for anyone in it. Insurers must make sure that they have the capabilities needed to utilize these technologies. That means new code frameworks, change methodologies, and ultimately, a culture shift for insurers. Making these changes will be expensive but is necessary. Not all changes have to be done at once. Prioritize the changes that are most beneficial and complete them over time. If done correctly, this will have a favorable outcome for all. Insurtech is expected by the insurance industry to thrive in the long term. Big data and AI are capable of doing things that would not be practical for individuals to do. Technologies in the insurance sector also help save lives, make lives simpler, raise sales, and boost consumer service, in addition to providing better interactions with insurers and policyholders. Although there is still more space for growth, AI is still growing and will continue to have a significant influence on the insurance industry's future.

References

Bean, R. (2018, November 11). *AllState's data-driven business transformation initiative*. Retrieved from Forbes Magazine, https://www.forbes.com/sites/ciocentral/2018/11/11/allstates-data-driven-business-transformation-initiative/?sh=73faa68b4d9e

Daim, T. Chan, L. Amer, M. Aldhaban, F. (2009) Assessment and adoption of web-based health information systems. *International Journal of Behavioral and Healthcare Research, 1*(3), 274–292.

FBI, Insurance fraud, 2020.

McKendrick, J. (2019). *Every Company A Data Company, Eventually*. Retrieved from https://www.forbes.com/sites/joemckendrick/2019/01/08/every-company-a-data-company-eventually/

Nelson Ortiz, *What health care consumers should know about artificial intelligence*, 2020.

OECD. (2020). *The impact of big data and artificial intelligence (AI) in the insurance sector*.

Artificial Intelligence in Credit, Lending, and Mortgage

13

Abstract

This chapter presents AI technology development in the credit and mortgage industry. It explores AI applications in various areas of the industry like predictive analytics applications, customer service chatbots, robo-advisor, credit scoring and others. Types of AI technologies used in credit and mortgage include machine learning (deep learning, supervised and unsupervised), natural language processing, expert systems, virtual agents, machine vision, speech processing, digital footprint analysis, and accounting automation. Case studies on lending platforms and related implementation of artificial intelligence tools include Upstart, Affirm, and Monedo.

Keywords

Mortgage applications · Machine learning · Natural language processing · Expert systems · Virtual agents · Digital footprint analysis · Accounting automation · Cloud-based solutions · Credit analysis · Credit scoring · Cybersecurity · Chatbots · Robo advice · Machine vision · Robotics · Speech processing · Deep learning · Supervised · Unsupervised · Risk assessment · Risk verification · Decision-making processes · Credit Risk · Data mining

13.1 Introduction

Artificial intelligence and big data are becoming a huge part of our everyday lives and in the business world. In recent years, credit and mortgage companies have tried to find ways of improving their business and becoming more competitive within their industries. AI can help in more thorough analysis of creditworthiness of clients by looking at traditional and nontraditional data sources, engaging innovative and robust lending systems and scoring models. In addition to the well-known FICO

L. Chan et al., *Applied Artificial Intelligence in Business*, Applied Innovation and Technology Management, https://doi.org/10.1007/978-3-031-05740-3_13

score, for example, and taking into consideration factors, such as payment history, amounts owed, and credit mix, modern mortgage companies are now using artificial intelligence and machine learning algorithms to improve upon these old credit determinant factors.

AI and big data are making it easier to detect fraud and protect against it, assess risk, improve operational efficiency, predict performance of a loan, enhance consumer/borrower experience, and solve customer issues. In this chapter, we will explore the evolution of AI applications in the credit and mortgage industries. We will discuss major AI technologies used in these fields and delve into some case studies of related companies.

13.2 Technology Development

Computerization of the credit and lending industry in the 1990s led to reduced loan processing times, more sophisticated projections with various empirical models, and automated underwriting systems. This had brought changes in the evaluation of credit risk and credit policy. Such great advances in information technology and data processing capabilities also gave a push for rise in mortgages from out-of-state from 10% to 20% in 1990 to around 60% over a decade (Foote et al., 2018).

In 1990, credit and mortgage lenders began using AI to evaluate mortgage applications by using a set of "knockout rules" which would either qualify or exclude an application. The system would take into account loan-to-value ratios and debt-to-income ratios. Such implementations helped speed up the process of reviewing mortgage applications. This method seemed to work for evaluating applications that checked all the boxes; however, AI back in this day was just not advanced enough to compete with human underwriters with their experience and human intuition. The introduction of credit scores was the next big development in making AI more precise when assessing mortgage applications.

Also, in the 1990s, AI began to grow faster in the credit and mortgage industry since the rapid growth of capabilities, affordability, and processing power of personal computers. As credit scores became more relevant, debt-to-income (DTI) ratio has actually become less important. In the 2000s, this allowed people with high debt-to-income ratios to get bigger mortgages than they should for their income. As we all know, this helped lead to the crash of the housing market in the late 2000s. The accuracy of the AI-enabled processing of mortgage applications keeps advancing. It has helped increase the turnover rate of applications while costing mortgage companies less money. AI continues to move forward at fast rates which makes the industry ever evolving and keeps companies pursuing to gain the edge on each other.

13.3 AI Applications in Various Areas

There are a variety of AI technologies that lending and mortgage companies have utilized since the emergence of artificial intelligence in recent years. Simple methods of analyzing credit and approving borrowers for certain loan amounts are a thing of the past. These technologies have made business operations much more efficient for the companies. Specifically, credit and mortgage companies are using AI technologies such as machine learning, natural language processing, expert systems, virtual agents, and digital footprint analysis to improve their business.

The importance of AI-based technologies can help make functions such as credit management more efficient and cost-effective. This technology can also be used to minimize risk and predict loan performance. AI uses many different computer programs that are able to generate cognitive functions. The methods AI uses are superior to statistical methods in dealing with credit risk evaluation problems. AI is able to track hundreds of indicators and make unbiased decisions, which allows humans to look at the information being collected from the machines and see who is and isn't a credit risk. Fraud detection systems with AI are also implemented in the credit and mortgage industry.

A company that has been using AI in accounts receivable and pushing the capabilities AI is known for in the credit sector is BlackLine. BlackLine is an accounting automation software. The beginning of this month, April 1, 2021, they unveiled BlackLine AR Intelligence which is the latest offering in its portfolio of accounts receivable. The goal for their AR intelligence is to broaden its financial operations management platform. The AI enables customers to manage financial risks and opportunities by providing access to real-time data which allows them to use the information to impact strategic and operational decision-making. BlackLine uses cloud-based solutions to help move companies to a more modern approach of accounting by unifying their data and processes, automating repetitive work, and driving accountability through visibility.

Credit analysis in the past was considered by lenders under only a few circumstances. It used to be that credit score, purchase history, and income were the biggest factors when banks considered lending money to borrowers. However, with the rising use of AI technologies and the ability to analyze much larger portions of data, credit companies can analyze a person's entire life, specifically their digital footprint. Lenddo, a startup company formed in 2011, was created to track all of these underlying factors that may influence the creditworthiness of an individual. They can track factors such as social media use, Internet browsing habits, and over 12,000 other factors to formulate a complex credit score that banks can use to assess borrowers. The global credit agency FICO has just recently partnered with Lenddo to use their machine learning algorithm in their credit scoring.

Mortgage companies have also found practical applications for artificial intelligence in their line of work. The emergence of young adults fresh out of college looking for loans to buy houses has led to massive amounts of data that must be collected to assess the worthiness of borrowers in this age group. Typically, traditional credit scores for young people are lower and harder to analyze due to less credit history. However, the company Upstart has started pairing with mortgage companies to assess the stature of younger generations, by looking at more than the traditional methods used to obtain credit scores. It takes education, SAT scores, GPA, field of study, and job history into account to predict their creditworthiness. This provides lenders with a better understanding of individuals who may not qualify for a loan under conventional credit standards.

AI technologies are used in various aspects of the mortgage and credit industry (as shown in Fig. 13.1). Customer engagement in banking is effectively done through chatbots, tackling common tasks such as balance inquiries and statement assessment, while robo advice aims to understand and analyze the financial health and history of the client as well as give appropriate as well as specific recommendations towards the product/service/loan. General-purpose and predictive analytics with natural processing applications look at the patterns in data for possible lending/sales opportunities, metrics, key indicators, and operational data that is tied to direct revenue and profits for the lending provider. Cybersecurity systems can be significantly improved by using AI algorithms, examining the previous threats and

Fig. 13.1 AI technology applications in credit and mortgage

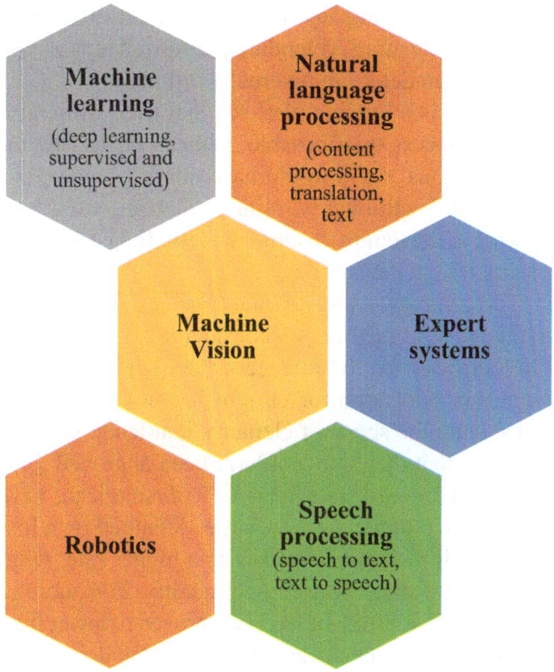

Fig. 13.2 Types of artificial intelligence technology in banking, mortgage, and credit

patterns to prevent cyberattacks, as well as monitoring internal and external threats and suggest corrective measures. Innovative lending systems with AI (for example, in companies like Affirm and GiniMachine) can help analyze various data sources to determine the creditworthiness of clients.

The banking and credit industry was one of the first industries that adopted AI with anomaly detection technology for automated fraud prevention and protection. Natural language processing in search and discovery along with the digitization process of the documents can speed up application processing and loan underwriting.

Machine vision (a combination of image sensors, cameras, and other hardware with image processing software) – a type of artificial intelligence system – can help in the recognition of handwritten signatures, information location in documents, and font and formatting differences and therefore expedite processing of documents in mortgage processing (Fig. 13.2). AI applications also help with automating compliance processes and various data privacy regulations. The next focus of AI in the industry is centered around the categories of cost reduction, risk reduction, and revenue improvement. The use of AI in credit scoring can help with reductions in costs of load origination and decision-making in cases with low complexity, as well as improve the scalability of the process.

Case 13.1: Upstart

One of the leading companies to implement AI technologies into their company is Upstart, and their innovativeness may drastically change the credit and mortgage industry. The company was founded in 2012 by current CEO Dave Girouard. Upstart is a leading AI lending platform that uses unconventional yet accurate measurements in determining creditworthiness.

Upstart is a lending platform that uses artificial intelligence that is designed to improve access to affordable credit to those who might be a certain demographic that traditional ways would have made it harder for these individuals to get a loan approved. Traditional ways are still being used because we are comfortable with looking at the length of someone's credit history and making the decision if they are qualified to get an amount of money from a bank or a lending company.

The company uses machine learning algorithms along with artificial intelligence to take several factors into consideration when deciding how creditworthy a potential borrower is. It considers components such as one's specific occupation, employer, education, or current institution where they may still be in school. In broadening the scope of elements that lenders can use, borrowers can be approved for loans that they may not have been approved for under traditional FICO considerations. Girouard stated that 45% of Americans have access to bank-quality credit, yet 83% of Americans have never defaulted on a loan. Upstart used this as motivation to help borrowers qualify at a higher rate, which they did successfully. Their model has been proven to help qualify 27% more consumers than standard credit practices. In addition, it has been proven to lower interest rates by an average of 3.57 points. The alternative data that Upstart collects to determine creditworthiness have had some consumers concerned about invasion of privacy. However, the company has made it clear that under fair lending laws and ethical business practices, the information that they gather is strictly confidential and in no way could put consumers at risk.

The machine learning algorithms that Upstart is using are always improving. This could mean adding more uncommon variables to an algorithm to better assess the risk to a possible user. Upstart is trying to be able to make machine learning the way to approve loans. In 2019, 67% of the loans that had gotten approved were fully automated through the machine learning underwriting process. As machine learning in this industry gets further training and receives more information, it will be more common to see conventional banks and loan companies adopting these algorithms. To start this new wave of getting more people in business, they need to eliminate any unwanted biases that us as human beings have.

Upstart can increase its accuracy with the risk assessments because the algorithms are always evolving and adding new or changing variables. This has helped Upstart face lower default rates at similar approval rates. This also helps Upstart be able to accept more applicants that apply for loans and get accepted at the same loss rate. Due to the success of Upstart and similar companies, I believe it will lead to a huge shift in the finance sector of the business world. The banks that do not see the change from human to AI will become obsolete in a sense because the approval rates are much higher with companies like Upstart. Companies like Upstart are targeting the younger generations and allowing them to get an amount of money even though they have the lack of credit history typical lenders require/want and they do not have an absurdly high interest rate that shy people away from getting a loan altogether.

Analysis of this kind was never possible before the introduction of artificial intelligence and machine learning. Algorithms that can examine these factors in a matter of seconds have elevated business for Upstart and other companies that plan on utilizing the evolving technologies. As COVID restrictions begin to lift and young adults with low credit scores begin to look for loans for new homes, cars, and other big purchases that their generation will be looking for, Upstart will have much of an advantage over lenders who are still using conventional credit analysis methods. Young borrowers with less credit history know that companies using traditional FICO methods may reject them, whereas through Upstart they have a much better chance of getting approved for that loan. As the competitiveness begins to rise within this industry, it is very likely that every credit and mortgage company will eventually evolve towards using artificial intelligence and machine learning in their business practices.

Case 13.2: Affirm

The company that we will discuss under the credit and mortgage industry is Affirm. They are a financial lending company which offers loans and payment options to customers. Most of Affirm's customers come from online shopping platforms. They allow shoppers a way to afford products despite not having all of the money on hand. Although this business model can become handy for consumers, it can be very risky. It is easier for customers to buy products without having to pay the money upfront, which is why it is risky for Affirm. This is where artificial intelligence is important to protect Affirm by deciding the customers who are more likely to pay their loan back.

Affirm uses data from customers to assess how likely customers are to repay their loans. They do this using an algorithm known as risk verification which comprises artificial intelligence. They use their online testing system and break it down into two areas. The first is risk service which uses network requests, database queries, and remote procedure calls. This is where their raw data is generated from risk-related data such as repayment data, fraud reports, and credit reports. The second component uses a set of rules such as underwriting decision, feature extraction, and credit report parsing. This is from their library which creates derived data. The library uses the raw data from the service which it can then use to measure all risk-related derived data. This would consist of things like repayment features, fraud scores, and FICO scores. "Many of our derived data points are used as input features for our machine learning algorithms'" (Shnayder, 2018). This is how Affirm can improve their future decisions on whether to make loans to customers based on the risk to the company. This is all done by artificial intelligence when deciding if a customer should get a loan. The customer's information is run through a series of algorithms where the customer has to meet a list of criteria. If the customer does not meet all of the areas required, then they will not get a loan. An example of this could be if they do not have a good enough credit score, then the AI will decide they are too risky for the company to give them a loan. After each decision is made, the computers keep track of the raw data from the risk service, the derived data from the library, and the business logic DAG. The DAG is called a risk log and that is what keeps track of if they accepted or denied the loan. All of this information is then heavily encrypted and transferred over to an offline world where it is stored. The company has a lot of valuable information, so it is very important that it all stays protected for the sake of the customers and the company. Affirm can use the data stored offline to test and improve their algorithm. For example, if they want to change their algorithm, they can test it on their stored data offline to make sure the algorithm will catch an application and either accept or reject it. They can run a series of different tests on their data for their machine learning to improve from the various results. This is very important for a company to continue to grow in a competitive market.

Affirm uses machine learning to stay ahead of their competition in a couple different ways. The first being that they have been able to detect numerous bugs while testing their offline data before using these algorithms on their actual customers. This has helped keep their name as a reputable company by minimizing risks while still improving their risk verification system. The second is that they have been able to process applications at faster speeds than their competitors giving them a better turnaround speed. This overall improves the company's income. Finally, artificial intelligence has allowed them to improve their risk verification system. This has allowed them to grow as a company and keep an edge on their competitors in a very competitive industry. As you can see, artificial intelligence is a key element in Affirm's business model which has allowed them to continue to grow and be competitive in their market.

Case 13.3: Monedo

Monedo is a German fintech that is an alternative online lending. Starting in 2012, this company was backed by many influential people such as Peter Thiel and JC Flowers (Hinchliffe, 2020). Since its foundation, the company has provided more than two million loans and served over one million customers (Clarke, 2020). In the first half of 2020, another online lending provider company by the name of Kreditech underwent the process of rebranding its name to Monedo but in September the company filed for bankruptcy. Monedo has used artificial intelligence and machine learning to bring greater financial freedom for their customers as well as use it to make better customer lending and credit risk decisions and underwrite loans.

Monedo's use of artificial intelligence and machine learning allows them to acquire data from as many data sources as possible in comparison to traditional lending banks that verify income based on information provided by credit bureaus. This data is then made into thousands of attributes that describe the customer and fed into a machine learning model, allowing for the company to underwrite more efficiently and achieve a much better performance than banks that utilize traditional methods to underwrite. Monedo uses an API called Kontomatik that enables financial institutions to verify customer's identities and access their banking activity, as well as a loan management and servicing platform built by Mambu. This service platform provides cloud solutions for banks and lending businesses (Hawkins, 2020).

Compared to traditional banks, Monedo has a competitive edge due to their use of AI and machine learning. Not only does its machine learning processes allow for more efficient underwriting, but their AI-driven credit scoring technology is fully automated, meaning that their customers can receive personalized loan offers and payouts at any time of day online (Clarke, 2020). Traditional banks can take days before their customers are given a decision, and with them being physical locations, they are often closed at certain times of the day such as in the evening and on weekends. Monedo, on the other hand, is online and allows for customers to work with loans at any time of the day as well as at any location due to smartphones.

The use of AI and machine learning further allows the company to automate a series of decision-making processes and leads to serving their customers better. The increased speed of production caused by using AI and machine learning also speeds up the processes for customers and applicants. The company's e-commerce technology enables the company to open up new possible online retailers and provides more flexibility for their online shoppers. (Clarke, 2020). Especially due to the lockdown caused by COVID, traditional banks are not offering some form of online methods for their customers, so they cannot compete with a completely online lender such as Monedo. Monedo's use of AI and machine learning technology is assisting the company to simplify and speed up the application process for customers as well as processing data to understand their customers better.

Just like many other companies utilizing AI and machine learning, Monedo's use of technology is allowing for data and decisions to be processed more efficiently while increasing the convenience for both the company and the customer. Compared to their competition, by using machine learning technology, the company can underwrite loans at a faster and more efficient rate than other companies, and their AI technology allows for their customers to have the major convenience of being able to interact with the loans at any time of day at the push of a button on their phone or computer. Monedo utilizes AI and machine learning technology to provide a competitive advantage to their online lender business.

13.4 Key Takeaways

Artificial intelligence is being used by all kinds of companies to their advantage. There are many cases where AI has increased the convenience for businesses and customers alike, and there are also many cases where AI has increased the accuracy of certain processes because it avoids human error. By using AI techniques, businesses can operate faster, more convenient, and more accurate. This applies to the credit and mortgage industries as well. Artificial intelligence techniques provide many advantages to companies that handle credit and mortgage.

One advantage that results from applying artificial intelligence techniques to credit businesses is the ability to use machine learning for credit risk. Credit risk is the possibility of a loss due to the borrower failing to make the required payments to a de bt and it's one of the largest risks for any company that deals with credit. One of the earliest uses of machine learning was to calculate credit risk for companies.

While statistical learning can figure out the credit risk using linear data, machine learning can use "non-linear relations among the financial information contained in the balance sheet" to calculate credit risk (Bussmann et al., 2020). Using both statistical learning and machine learning when calculating credit risk and using the data gained from these calculations to prevent credit risk are faster and more convenient and allow for more information than traditional credit risk calculations.

Banks are using artificial intelligence to provide many advantages for them by using it to serve customers better. Banks are utilizing AI to curb fraudulent practices and improve customer services. Machine learning, deep learning, and data mining are being used to combat money laundering by analyzing internal, publicly available and transactional data within the customer's wider network (Vedapradha & Ravi, 2018). Chatbots are used as automated service assistants to customers, allowing greater convenience in resolving their problems via online messaging systems. These artificial intelligence techniques are providing clear advantages to banks and other companies that manage credit.

13.5 Conclusion

AI can greatly benefit the companies in credit and mortgage industries. In the coming future, the mortgage industry will eventually shift to a more AI-based system. AI will help benefit this industry in multiple ways; one of the biggest things is that it helps change the existing loan process. Rather than relying on outdated methods of determining one's credit score, AI removes human bias and error and streamlines the entire process. Instead of going off traditional FICO and credit scores, lenders will look at a consumer's digital footprint to determine their creditworthiness. AI is also utilized to find potential borrowers of money, helps to identify risks, and looks for opportunities to lend. This takes away the need to hire tons of employees and enable automation from AI. Artificial intelligence and big data are evolving the customer experience and giving more control to the consumers. We are only at the beginning of this new technological era and the customer experience with artificial intelligence and big data will only improve.

References

Bussmann, N., Giudici, P., Marinelli, D., & Papenbrock, J. (2020, September 25). *Explainable machine learning in credit risk management*. Retrieved from https://link.springer.com/article/10.1007/s10614-020-10042-0

Clarke, G. (2020, August 20). *Behind the Idea: Monedo*. Retrieved from https://thefintechtimes.com/behind-the-idea-monedo/

Foote, C. L., Loewenstein, L., & Willen, P. S.. (2018). *Technological Innovation in Mortgage Underwriting and the Growth in Credit: 1985–2015*. Federal Reserve Bank of Cleveland, Working Paper no. 18–16. https://doi.org/10.26509/frbc-wp-201816.

Hawkins, L. (2020, July 1). *Monedo: The future of digital lending*. Retrieved from https://www.fintechmagazine.com/company/monedo-future-digital-lending

Hinchliffe, R. (2020). *German fintech lender MONEDO files for bankruptcy*. Retrieved from https://www.fintechfutures.com/2020/09/german-fintech-lender-monedo-files-for-bankruptcy/

Shnayder, A. (2018, September 10). *Verifying risk decisioning changes by testing against production data*. https://tech.affirm.com/verifying-risk-decisioning-changes-by-testing-against-production-data-431279176351

Vedapradha, R. & Ravi, H. (2018, December 07). *Application of artificial intelligence in investment banks*. Retrieved from https://ideas.repec.org/a/aic/revebs/y2018j22vedapradhar.html

Artificial Intelligence in Tourism and Hospitality

14

Abstract

This chapter presents the enabling technologies for AI in tourism and hospitality highlighting expert systems, voice chatbots, query engines, artificial neural networks, belief networks, sentiment analysis, fuzzy logic systems and virtual reality. The major applications of AI in tourism including smart tourism, demand forecasting, and customer data analytics are explored. Case studies include Henn Na Hotel, Hilton Hotel, Airbnb, and Expedia.

Keywords

Tourism · Hospitality · Web Portals · Customer service · Automation · Service automation · Social media analytics · Business tourism · Expert system · Chatbots · Artificial neural network · Pattern recognition · Belief network · Forecasting · Sentiment analysis · Scenario predictions · Data mining · Opinion mining · Fuzzy logic systems · Fuzzy set parameters · Virtual reality · Augmented reality · Smart tourism · Demand forecasting · Customer data analytics · Robots · Text mining · Natural language processing · Smart pricing · Machine learning · Personalization · Virtual agent

14.1 Introduction

Tourism is an important part of peoples' leisure activities. Tourism can range anywhere from a road trip, camping, dining, sightseeing, or even flying to staying at a hotel in a different state, country, or continent. There is a lot of technological advancement in recent years with things like AI hotel receptions and self-driving cars among other things, and we will discuss the kind of effects this might have on different companies in the tourism sector.

L. Chan et al., *Applied Artificial Intelligence in Business*, Applied Innovation and Technology Management, https://doi.org/10.1007/978-3-031-05740-3_14

What is truly captivating about artificial intelligence is its capability to outperform humans in a way that previously had not been possible. AI is fascinating because it has the ability to execute tasks that have traditionally required human cognitive function. In the tourism and hospitality industry, AI has become especially useful because it can save businesses time and money while potentially eliminating human errors and allowing tasks to be completed swiftly and effectively. Hotels and resorts rely heavily on providing excellent customer service to build their reputation and AI technology can assist with this in an extensive range of different ways. AI can, for instance, improve personalization, by customizing recommendations and guaranteeing fast response time, even in the absence of human staff. Artificial intelligence is continuously progressing to become increasingly advanced because through communicating with customers, the technology is smart enough to learn from every individual encounter which will help improve future interactions. There is, as mentioned, a wide variety of methods where AI can be useful. Especially when it comes to big data analysis, which this particular industry depends on quite copiously.

Tourism and hospitality include very broad subjects, so we would like to discuss the most influential areas of AI in the sector. A few detailed topics that we will look at include, but are not limited to, AI development in tourism, hospitality, traveling, dining, and related fields.

14.2 Development of AI in Tourism

While AI has a heavy influence on what customers see when searching online for the best deals and options of their vacation, marketers are using AI behind the scenes to best target audiences. AI is involved in the behind-the-scenes curation of tourist marketing content. The tourism industry, with a special emphasis on travel agencies, hotels, and destination marketing organizations, has had to face challenges in adjusting their business models due to the rise of the Internet platforms. The development of information technology has provided this industry with new opportunities, such as improvement in communications, distribution channels, and transactions. This gave travelers and tourists the means to research destinations, transportation, accommodations, and leisure activities and the ability to purchase all these services online.

Many tourism marketing organizations have access to big data that serves as inputs for AI systems. One example of this kind of data hub is Brand USA, which is an organization specialized in marketing data collection in the United States. Smaller destination marketing organizations may have access to that information and typically use it to get the most value for their budgets while bigger organizations tend to use the database to create multifaceted marketing plans (Richey, 2015). This puts into perspective truly how much data marketers have access to and how much that can influence the way they market to consumers. Having access to big data makes it possible for tourist companies/marketers to see where they stack up compared to others. Rather than only having data from their company websites, they have something relative to compare to. As a result of increased data availability, tourism has been ranked as one of the foremost in the industry in terms of the volume of online transactions. The data and information are largely unstructured because they are scattered throughout numerous sources, there are data redundancies, and there could be false data, such as a rival company leaving a negative review on their competitors' product or service. Due to the sheer amount of time and energy it would take these companies to sort out relevant and useful information, AI can alleviate the workload and make the process more efficient. The Internet and mobile platforms have become the most important marketing communication tools for tourism organizations by providing five important functions such as communication, promotion, product distribution, management, and research (Akehurst, 2009). Tourism organizations can also enhance the four Ps of the marketing mix of product, place, price, and promotion using the four Cs of customer solution, cost, convenience, and communication.

Hospitality services influence where and how tourists will stay during their trips. Tourist experiences determine whether they want to travel again. A main component of hospitality is to make tourists feel more comfortable at the destinations. How tourists stay at hotels or resorts which will influence their travel experience. There are many hotel chains that want to lead in competition and that depends on the experience or services they can provide. AI is changing the hospitality industry, rapidly creating the environment in which hotels need to catch up with consumer-oriented markets and know-how consumers react to hotel services. In order for hotels to understand their target market, they have to use some form of AI technology to support their research of what their customers like, so they can provide solutions for customers' needs and wants. For instance, a Las Vegas resort may determine that its customer base is largely comprised of younger adults, so it may host a popular national hip-hop star's concert in its auditorium to attract more visitors (Pal, Website). This type of personalization creates experiences for customers so that they "may also enable travel businesses to generate repeat business through loyalty and to get more word-of-mouth referrals" (Pal, Website). AI allows companies to determine why customers are more likely to choose their competition over them, which in turn allows these businesses to determine marketing and services to gain and retain customers. "The lifetime value of a customer is a much-talked-about subject for hotels, as over 30% of travelers visit the same hotel annually. Data analytics give hotels decision-making power about which customers to invest in" (AbsolutData, 2019).

The tourism industry has been growing rapidly with the use of web portals such as TripAdvisor, Yelp, and various others allowing customers to exchange information, opinions, recommendations about destinations, products or services, and the option of allowing customers to share their experiences and leave reviews. This trend of the online platforms allowing customers to share their experiences and recommendations has ballooned outside of these travel websites into countless blogs all over the Internet. As a result, these tourism organizations can sift through these blogs and websites and collect information involving industry trends, market data, research, and technical developments (Akehurst, 2009). The related companies can use these blogs for customer profiling, customer acquisition, customer engagement, brand awareness, brand reinforcement, and customer management.

Another trend in the tourism and hospitality sector is using AI-embedded robots to improve automation. One approach is the use of chatbots to commence online communications with customers rather than human employees to save time and money. Robots, artificial intelligence, and service automation (RAISA) are already in use in various tourism services such as online check-ins, self-check-in kiosks, automated border control gates with biometric passport/ID card readers, and mobile boarding passes (Ivanov & Webster, 2017). The benefit of using these devices to improve automation is that although it can be expensive at first to install, these devices can save money in the long term. This is because companies can save money on labor costs by running 24/7, perform repetitive tasks, and communicate in different languages.

Tourism is not only for the leisure of individuals but also for businesses and groups. Business tourism is a significant portion of the tourism market, but the use of social media analytics is not as common. Business tourism is recovering after the pandemic influence and becoming increasingly popular in the tourism market, in particular MICE tourism (meetings, incentives, conventions, and exhibitions). Through the analysis of tourism marketing and effective strategies, business tourism marketers can maximize their impact as well. Through effective use of company portals and Facebook, there are certain strategies tourism marketers should utilize to maximize their reach and the user's experience. Some strategies for hotels to attract business tourists include creating personalized websites and photos, staying active on Facebook, building loyalty programs, and providing services specific to MICE rather than leisure tourism (Vaid & Kesharwani, 2018).

14.3 Enabling Technology for AI in Tourism

There are a variety of AI technologies that can be applied in the tourism and hospitality industry. This is because tourism is largely related to customer experience and services. Here we introduce some of these key technologies.

14.3.1 Expert System

Expert systems are widely used in the tourism industry. These are rule-based decision-making systems that consist of compiled knowledge from experts. The computer is capable of searching the database very quickly to retrieve the requested information. Human experts provide their expertise to knowledge engineers, who then convert the information to a set of if-then rules. The expert system is able to search through its "knowledge" when queried and find the information that it thinks will be most relevant to the query. This allows users who may not be experts to access information that was provided by real-life experts, even though it may not be directly. Expert systems are good for situations where there may not be too much AI "thinking" required. A good example of an application of an expert system in the tourism and hospitality industry could be a software or an app that tells tourists information about certain landmarks or historical facts about a city or town. An expert on a certain landmark could tell an engineer important information about their landmark, and the computer would then be able to pull that information when prompted by a user. Another example could be a travel assistant that gives you information about your itinerary: what gate your plane is at, what time your taxi will be arriving, what the weather will be at your destination, etc.

14.3.2 Chatbots

Voice chatbots and query engines are AI programs that are capable of listening to a user, process what they said, and return information in a way that a human assistant would. There are several real-world examples of voice chatbots that are already widely in use today: Apple's Siri, Google Assistant, or Amazon's Alexa. Chatbots work in a similar way to an expert system, except there are extra layers added to the process. Voice chatbots receive queries in the form of speech, convert that speech to text, use that text to search for information, and then return what it found in the form of output data. Voice chatbots are good for replacing interactions that people like to have human interactions with. The perfect application of this technology in tourism would be customer service. By automating customer service through chatbots, efficiency can be improved drastically, and costs can be reduced radically. The cost of an AI customer service system is much lower than a full-time staff of real people.

Chatbots with AI technologies are widely used in the hospitality and tourism sector. A typical application of chatbot is intelligent travel assistants. Intelligent travel assistant chatbots, or online customer service, are all very similar and all have the same function, to make the lives of the consumer easier. There are also many different actual applications of the intelligent travel assistants, including helping make decisions based on price and availability. For hotels and other businesses in the industry, one of the most exciting uses for AI is for aiding customers online. There has already been widespread adoption for the purposes of powering chatbots on social media platforms, as well as instant messaging apps. Research is now also experimenting with AI-powered robot concierges to work at hotel receptions. As an example, Sam is a chatbot developed by FCM Travel Solutions that blends AI with the expertise of consultants to deliver personalized, relevant information to travelers' mobile devices. Sam proactively supports the individual traveler at each stage of their trip, to give the traveler a more enjoyable experience while on the move and reduce the stresses and strains of traveling on business. You could ask the app to schedule flights for you, arrange transportation to and from the airport, and give you warnings about weather or other local events. Apps like this are in use already, and there will be more improvement in the future as AI becomes better.

14.3.3 Artificial Neural Network

A neural network (or neural net) is an AI system that attempts to recreate the human cognitive process by learning and recognizing patterns. It does this by having multiple layers of data input and then a number of hidden functions that change the data, followed by an output. The computer then tweaks the inputs to achieve what it considers to be the optimal output. These systems can get very complicated, with multiple hidden layers and multiple inputs as well as outputs. Neural nets are good for things that require pattern recognition and are therefore efficient at doing tasks related to forecasting, where predictions are key. A good example of an application of a neural net within the tourism and hospitality industry could be something like an app that recommends destinations for tourists to visit and stay, based on other tourists' experiences. In such a case, the input data would be what landmarks or activities are available, the hidden layers would be variables of how well the tourist enjoys the combination and order of activities, and the output would be the overall satisfaction level from the tourist. By changing inputs and given enough data, a neural network would eventually be able to suggest optimized day plans for tourists and even be able to create specific plans for tourists with different preferences such as less walking, more thrill, high budget, and low budget.

14.3.4 Belief Network

Belief networks are complicated tree layouts of various events, with the probabilities of each event happening. Each event has relationships with other events in the tree. By giving the computer the probabilities of each event and how they relate to each other, it is capable of making very complicated scenario predictions. The output will be a single probability, which is much easier for managers to work with than a large number of other events and their probabilities individually. Belief networks are good for situations where you need to make a prediction but involve a high number of variables. Like neural nets, one of the primary applications of belief networks is forecasting. An example of belief network application in the tourism and travelling industry could be an airline trying to get maximum value out of all the seats on an empty flight. There are a lot of variables that go into how many people will book a seat including price, what the current season is, how early the ticket purchase is, and whether or not people will cancel their ticket. A belief network would be able to look at the probabilities of all of the factors, and how those factors will affect other factors, and make a good prediction. This would allow the airline to maximize the value it gets out of each flight, ensuring that their plane gets filled, with each passenger paying the maximum amount they would be willing to for the flight.

14.3.5 Sentiment Analysis

It is also noteworthy to discuss the significance of sentiment analysis in the hospitality industry. Machine learning tools and applications have enabled hotels to become "smarter" in how to increase their performance and competitiveness by informing, automating, and transforming their business functions and processes such as marketing, sales, customer service, and facility management (Gretzel et al., 2015). Many tourists with a smartphone share their experiences and photos on social media and on review apps and sites. This is a large pool of valuable data that hotels can analyze to improve their services. One approach is with the use of "opinion mining" as opposed to traditional "data mining" to find relevant consumer views and opinions. The maturity of natural language processing and sentiment analysis allows for adopting accurate analytical tools without time-consuming data gathering and mining.

AI technology in tourism grows rapidly with widespread use of social media and blogs. This is because there is a large volume of data that these companies must go through contained in these various formats on the Internet. Big data can come from various sources and contexts. Data does not always come in the form of numbers and statistics but can also come from analyzing the picture post. In a study conducted in Italy, tourists were analyzed through the pictures posted. In the article "Using social media to identify tourism attractiveness in six Italian cities," they talk about the methodology behind this. Using the Mathematica software, tourist marketers were able to both analyze photos to determine the object in them and organize them by categories. Through these analyses it was discovered that tourist marketers are able to identify dynamics among tourists as well as one that links the economic and cultural environments of a city, examining real-time data extracted from social media (Giglio et al., 2019).

Sentiment analysis also uses real-time sensor data to analyze users' behaviors, facial expressions, and voice tones. The output can be used to adjust environmental settings and services that make users more comfortable. The range of sentiment analysis applications in the tourism and hospitality industry is huge. For example, hotels can use sentiment analysis to customize room interior environments such as temperature, lighting, and other service settings. The amount of sensor data and information gained through this technology can be used in an unlimited number of ways when it comes to services in hospitality, tourism, and traveling.

14.3.6 Fuzzy Logic Systems

Another approach that has arisen in tourism technology is the use of AI in forecasting models such as fuzzy time series and grey theory. In the case of these AI systems, data can be input into the model, and with fuzzy set parameters, the model can forecast tourism demand. For example, such models can be used at predicting the number of arrivals of US tourists. With the fuzzy time model, the variation in the current year is related to previous years. Historical numbers and statistical values are used as inputs, and these inputs are combined with many current influencing factors or restrictions. The system applies fuzzy set parameters in the machine learning process and computes different probabilities. The linguistic values are translated into fuzzy numbers and the prediction variation value will be converted back into numerical value. The grey theory is a decision-making approach that deals with incomplete or uncertain information and constructs a short-term time period and predicts future trends (Yu & Schwartz, 2006). These forecasting models allow the tourism companies to organize seemingly unorganized data into helpful information to predict future trends.

14.3.7 Virtual Reality

As technologies such as virtual reality (VR) further evolve and be applied in the tourism industry, it will become easier to find out what consumers' needs are with the use of virtual environments. One instance of this is using a system interface with the use of a virtual reality engine to render a 3D visualization of a certain environment (Burger, 2007). This method can further combine with augmented reality (AR) tools to attract potential customers. Hotels can use both VR and AR to provide a virtual tour for customers to experience the environment and services. The AI technology tools can gather users' first-time impressions before implementing the environment into real-world application. With this type of AI applications, businesses can save cost and time by developing travel and tourism destinations that they have already received positive feedback before the service is even brought into the real world.

14.4 Applications of AI in Tourism

The major applications of AI that go with the subfields of tourism and travel have an infinite amount of uses that have not been discovered yet or the technology has not been made, as it is a newer part of artificial intelligence. As the technology and subfields expand in the coming years so will the major applications, not only expanding the industry with new applications but also improving what is already around.

14.4.1 Smart Tourism

Smart tourism is an advanced stage of tourism informationization. It consists of digital, intelligent, and virtual tourism based on digital, intelligent, and virtual technology. Smart tourism is sort of an umbrella term for the progression of technology in the travel and tourism industry and its goal is to gain and use information relating to travel and tourism that can be instantly implemented to raise the efficiency of the tourism sector. In hospitality, we can see contactless keys replacing traditional hotel keys already. Smart devices such as cameras and sensors provide better services that are personalized and programmed for individual guests. IoT smart devices allow for massive amounts of big data to be collected and transformed into business value propositions.

Tourism recommendation systems take anything a user may have searched online or even said in some circumstances and then provides recommendations on flights, accommodations, and even activities while in the area. AI can further help tourists by providing information on nearby restaurants, theme parks, and hotel recommendations. The information that is used when making these recommendations is not only taken from one individual's searches but is also used by thousands of other people that took similar trips. This type of information provided by AI allows hotels to better use their facilities and prepare sufficient resources when needed. Tourism companies can use AI algorithms to recommend relevant service packages or products to consumers based on group behaviors and trends. AI software also enables smart pricing for service providers. Smart tourism has allowed companies to redefine their business models to operate more efficiently and remain profitable.

14.4.2 Demand Forecasting

Demand forecasting is a process commonly used across multiple sectors in the business world. What AI allows us to do in terms of demand forecasting is that it can determine the level of demand that may be generated, which helps marketers, managers, and planners by reducing the risk of decisions regarding the future.

We have always known that vacationing has been restricted by time and income, but with AI technology we are now able to weigh in noneconomic factors, such as psychological, anthropological, and sociological factors, that have not previously been analyzed in the traditional econometric travel demand studies, which allows a greater amount of data to be analyzed in the process of demand forecasting. The perishable nature of tourism products and services and the information-intensive nature of the tourism industry makes accurate forecasting of tourism demand highly necessary. Demand forecasting allows companies to take information from previous years, months, or even days and use that to predict what may happen in the future. This is a vital part of tourism and travel for the future because it allows people to receive information that they otherwise would not have and that leads to saving money and time. The forecasting applications work in areas more than booking flight tickets. The main one can be hotel/hostel prices. Hotel prices are constantly changing and can be a pain to book when there happens to be a rise in price because of some sort of convention or holiday. No matter what area it is, forecasting has many applications when it comes to tourism and travel and is just another keyway where artificial intelligence improves this field.

14.4.3 Customer Data Analytics

Present day customers often use online service and search for potential hotel candidates that could greatly accommodate them when it comes to "services, location, room, price/value, food and beverage, image, security, and marketing" (Xiang et al., 2015). However, one consumer's bad experience could be a factor in another consumer's decision-making when it comes to the same hotel. Hotels are becoming innovative when it comes to using AI to make themselves a competitor in their industry, but AI is also helping consumers become innovative on their own. They are able to create and find reviews which generate impact on hotel sales because "user-generated reviews provide a reliable source of material that can be used to understand the drivers of hotel satisfaction and, accordingly, change hotel offerings to meet future demands" (Liu et al., 2017). Hotels have an ongoing battle when it comes to satisfying its consumers because more often than not, negative reviews attract more attention on generated reviews than positive reviews do. On a positive note, these reviews also help hotels understand their target market so they can offer services and better identify its strengths and weaknesses.

Taking a broader look as to how many consumers can influence one another, TripAdvisor claims that as of late 2013, there were more than 150 million reviews and opinions generated on its website alone covering more than 3.7 million accommodations, restaurants, and attractions worldwide. Not only do consumers use TripAdvisor but they use Expedia as well. In late 2012, Expedia's collection of verified reviews reached a total number of more than 7.5 million (Xiang et al., 2015). Based on this information, it is important for hotels to pay attention to the needs and wants of their target market so they can keep flourishing in the tourism industry. AI also allows hotels to view factors that make them inefficient when it comes to marketing, or services provided, and how these can be transformed and updated so there is a return from investment.

Case 14.1: Henn Na Hotel

Japan's Henn Na Hotel opened in 2015, boasting a staff consisting of a workforce of 243 robotics. The creation of this hotel was made to combat potential societal issues in Japan, where it was predicted that during the 2020 Olympics, there may be a shortage of up to 3000 rooms, and robot-staffed hotels may be a potential solution to the problem. Henn Na Hotel or "Strange Hotel" opened its door in 2015 in Nagasaki's Huis Ten Bosch amusement park, with another hotel opening in 2018 in Tokyo's high-end shopping district, Ginza. The hotel's parent company, H.I.S, announced plans to construct eight more hotels, four in the Tokyo area and the others in Kyoto, Osaka, and Fukuoka.

The robots in the two hotel locations serve various purposes from directing the guests to check in on touch screen kiosks to mowing the grass. Important background on why this hotel employed as many robots as they did is because they value efficiency above all. An example of this detail to efficiency is the hotel's special development of pillows and sheets. The hotel found this task to be too time-consuming and, after they implemented the new bedding, found that it took about

10 seconds to make a bed. The robot workforce accentuates this importance of efficiency, with a robotic orchestra in the lobby, numerous vending machines (offering amenities), and a concierge robot at the front desk that can provide the guests with directions to restaurants, as well as tourist hotspots. Some of the other specialized robots are a robotic arm at check-ins for coats and luggage, a robotic trolley that delivers the luggage to the guest's rooms, vacuuming robots, facial recognition on the doors, and a communication robot in the room that answers the guest's questions.

Some ways in which this robotic workforce can provide business value is they provide guests with a homogenous experience in which each guest is provided the same level of service. Another benefit that relates to this is the decrease in human emotional labor. This is because there are no human employees that are required to provide excess hospitality based on a customer's frustrations. Also, a staff of ten human employees has their tasks more specialized, instead of being tasked with low-effort, repetitive tasks. Some of the specialized tasks include repairing broken down robots, driving cars to pick up and taking guests to and from the hotel, and accounting tasks. With these changes, the human labor force can focus more on creative tasks that the robots don't have the capacity to complete.

Limitations in today's technologies impede the efficiency that the robots provide, sometimes creating more work than they save. To this effect, the hotel is seen more as a novelty and less of a place housing state-of-the-art technology. As a result, the human staff hides so that the guests don't choose to interact with them over the robots. Also, the hotel can have difficulty with hospitality because the robotic receptionists can't detect subtle human facial expressions that are showing distaste in hotel services. The robotic staff also cannot look directly at humans when interacting with human customers, because of the uncanny valley effect. This effect details how humans are uncomfortable with robotics that resemble humans too much. The stage of technology has resulted in the human staff constantly having to repair the robots (such as the robotic trolleys consistently getting stuck) and aiding guests with directions and check-in. The limitations in AI implemented in the hotel have resulted in the communication robots unable to answer the guest's questions regarding a business's hours, airline flight times, and directions. All of these issues have accumulated to the hotel firing over half of its robotic staff in early 2019.

Case 14.2: Hilton Hotel (Connie)

Hilton Hotels has started to use an AI-powered concierge robot called "Connie," named after Hilton's founder Conrad Hilton. Connie is powered by IBM's Watson. This is the first Watson-enabled robot to be developed for the hospitality market. Connie supplements the role of the hotel concierge, by helping to answer routine questions, allowing human hotel concierge staff to focus on more advanced services. Things that require local knowledge, like hot spots for nightlife, would be an example of a task that would stay under the responsibilities of the human concierge.

Connie is powered by IBM's Watson, an AI supercomputer that is capable of answering questions posed in natural language. As a demonstration of IBM Watson capabilities, IBM set up a mock jeopardy game, where Watson competed against some of the top human Jeopardy champions. Watson was able to win easily and by a very large margin. Watson uses deep learning to build a neural network to try and predict what the best option is based on other information. Watson can be fed prior knowledge as well and does not necessarily need to learn all of its information from scratch. One of the main advantages of Watson is how fast it can process and retrieve data. This makes interactions with it feel natural and humanlike.

Connie is able to supplement the role of the traditional hotel concierge by automating several processes, such as answering common questions from guests, checking in guests, providing basic information about the local area, and providing a fun lobby environment for the guests. An important thing to note is that the CEO of Hilton said he has no plans to replace concierge workers with AI or robotics. By implementing systems like Connie, the role of the concierge can shift from doing routine tasks to more interesting, specialized work, such as giving guests local knowledge. A great example of this could be where the hotspots are for nightlife, or where the secret local shopping spots are.

Setting up Connie takes some time at first. Hilton works with IBM to feed Connie info about the hotel – where the facilities are, what the hours for certain services are, what is on the room service menu, etc. An outside AI firm called WayBlazer feeds Connie info about the surrounding area – what the local restaurants are, where the local points of interest are, what the tourist attractions are, etc. Connie then can learn based on experiences it has and improves itself as it goes. Another source of information for Connie is facial expressions. It has cameras that are able to detect facial expressions and make decisions based on them.

Each Connie unit costs about $9500. It adds value by assisting the concierge and improving the overall experience of hotel guests. While a human concierge may only be available at certain hours of the day, Connie can be available 24/7. Another aspect that Connie helps is consistency of service. When a guest talks to Connie, they will receive the same service as the next guest. Connie also differentiates Hilton from other hotels. It adds a new gimmicky aspect to Hilton, and perhaps customers will choose Hilton over its competitors just to get the chance to experience this new kind of AI.

At this point, it is unclear whether or not technologies like Connie will become popular in the hotel industry. Hilton's CEO was adamant that the hotel industry is a hospitality industry, and hospitality should involve human interaction only. It is still a new technology, and it will keep improving year over year. In the future, our hotels may be entirely run by AI robots like Connie.

Case 14.3: AI at Airbnb

Airbnb was founded in San Francisco, California, in 2008, and it became a publicly traded company after the 2020 IPO. The company reported a revenue exceeding $3.3 billion in the same year. Airbnb's current market cap is about $100 billion. Airbnb has a revolutionary business model that transforms the travel industry by offering regular people an opportunity to rent out their homes or apartments to travelers for an affordable price, allowing them to stay for a prolonged time and in a larger space. This is a great alternative to a hotel and the platform manages millions of users daily. Airbnb's hosts span over 100,000 cities worldwide. Through online platforms and mobile apps, millions of hosts allow for different experiences ranging from rock walls to golf courses to private on-site chefs. This innovative business model has been proven to be trusted and deals with problems quickly and efficiently. Airbnb is more than a mobile app that just allows people to rent out or rent a home. The use of artificial intelligence and big data analytics is widely acknowledged. Here we will introduce how Airbnb applies AI to improve its business.

One of the best tools to analyze the information using AI is sentiment analysis, which analyzes customers and their feelings toward products, services, and facts. Airbnb appraises opinions from the reviews that were posted on the application. Airbnb uses natural language processing technology that analyzes the review boards or the message boards through sentiment analysis, which helps Airbnb understand the true feeling behind the reviews. The results show how consumers made their decisions and what made them stay at a particular place in that region. With such analysis, patterns and themes were gathered to make Airbnb aware of what behaviors or feelings were provided to the consumers. In turn, Airbnb provided their hosts with discoveries to potentially improve their amenities or services within their accommodation based on what the results displayed. The use of sentiment analysis is everywhere in Airbnb as there are numerous sensors and real-time data being collected every day from the users. And overall, these inputs created a more functional environment that allows for endless possibilities for both the company and its users.

Text mining is the process of transforming unstructured text into a structured format to identify meaningful patterns and new insights (ibm.com). Text mining was used in Airbnb to extract valuable information from guest reviews through a tool called Rapid Miner, which uses AI algorithms to identify patterns and understand meanings from texts such as customer feedback. The mining processes include data preparation, machine learning, and predictive model deployment. The software system first performs sentiment analysis using ALYIEN and then Rapid Miner conducts correlation analysis on discoveries based on words, aspects, and visualization findings. The software can automatically process a variety of texts and languages. AI monitors everything so patterns can be reported and studied and once again put into use by Airbnb. Text mining has provided Airbnb with new information that was not taken into consideration or examined before. By identifying common trends in the reviews, hosts can identify where they are among the competitive listings by seeing what their competitors are doing better with the aim of replicating those aspects into their own service. Additionally, Airbnb can use this information to give insights to hosts about their strengths and weaknesses, which allows the hosts to do a SWOT or competitor analysis so that they can emphasize the relevant points in marketing and strategic decision-making.

Smart Pricing is an AI-based software package that Airbnb developed to help hosts set the best price for their properties. Since Airbnb's hosts and properties are distributed diversely all over the world, varied in room size and locations, with drastically different amenities and services, it is next to impossible to have a fixed rate for all. If the hosts set the price too low, both Airbnb and the hosts will lose revenue. If the price is set too high, the property is likely to be left vacant because the customers will go elsewhere to other providers. Considering more influencing factors such as competing properties nearby, seasonal demand shifts, and special festival events, pricing can be a challenge for both Airbnb and its hosts. The Smart Pricing software considers all such factors as inputs and provides a dynamic pricing solution for each property. The software comes with Aerosolve, which is a machine learning algorithm developed to interpret complex input data with intuitive computational models. The results are presented as dynamic pricing features on a calendar with different color codes to indicate the probabilities of renting a room at different price levels. The Smart Pricing software was proved to have grown revenue by 8.6% for hosts while decreasing rates for guests by 5.7% (Barron et al., 2020). With Airbnb's split-fee formula for revenue distribution, the AI application appears to be a win-win-win solution for hosts, guests, and the company (Owen, 2021).

This Airbnb case shows how AI is used in Airbnb to analyze information from various sources in order to improve business efficiency and guest experiences. Machine learning algorithms are used in Airbnb to help identify common trends between hosts and their listings. AI is useful not only for Airbnb but also for other businesses because it helps reveal patterns and behaviors relating to the market and customers. Consumer feedback offers important information for businesses because it can also help predict demand, improve pricing, and can predict the maintenance of facilities or equipment. In the future, AI technology will see an increase in popularity in the hospitality industry and also for other businesses in general because it will help companies strategically place themselves in a market based on data.

Case 14.4: Expedia

Expedia Group is a leading online travel company that provides leisure and business travel to customers worldwide. Expedia owns a large amount of travel fare aggregator and travel metasearch engine websites. Popular Expedia Group sites include Expedia.com, Vrbo.com, CarRentals.com, Hotels.com, HotWire.com, Trivago, Orbitz, and Travelocity. Expedia is a global company that offers services to companies around the world. Expedia wanted global users to find what they were looking for in an effective manner with the support of technology. They also wanted to allocate resources such as sites or infrastructures, so they were faster and closer to customers. Expedia found the solution to these needs by using technologies including cloud computing, big data analytics, and machine learning. Expedia is a client of Amazon Web Services (AWS), which is one of the most comprehensive and widely adopted cloud platforms, offering a variety of fully featured computing services from data centers globally.

Expedia uses AI and machine learning tools for big data analytics through AWS applications. There are so many ways that data is created without people knowing it at times. When it comes to tourism, there are so many different checkpoints over the course of a trip including the planning and conclusion of the trip. Through each phase of the process, such as initial research, booking, your stay, checking out, etc., there could be an interaction with computing technology. When doing initial research about where to go, computers store cookies and track users' activity. During someone's stay, they may take a picture and post it along with a geotag, geofilter, or a hashtag; that picture and location are now usable data. If travelers get to the end of their trip and decide to extend their stay, that is usable data. Expedia uses all of this data to inform the way their service works as well as how they market to customers. AWS extracts and gathers its data in similar ways that it is created. They are able to aggregate the data they gather by different categories and groups. For example, they could gather data based on customer location. If they are interested in what people in a certain geographic location prefer, this ability may come in handy. They can also acquire data from past customer activity. If someone has an account, they can book multiple trips through, and they can track where they go and what time of year. They also can look at overall trends in customer activity. AWS has many tools they offer that Expedia benefited from. For example, by using AWS, Expedia was able to drastically decrease their latency of response time. One of the tools Expedia used through AWS is the Amazon Elastic Map Reduce. This helps Expedia analyze and process streams of data coming into Expedia Group. Analyzing raw data through machine learning gives Expedia the insight into consumers' needs and wants when it comes to travel. This includes preferences, suggestions, popularity, and even personalization as mentioned throughout this chapter. Personalization that comes from data of consumers is a more thorough approach because much of the time, consumers might not know what they are looking for that would satisfy their needs and wants. AI-based personalization allows Expedia to stay on top against competitors because they can analyze and know how to create a satisfying experience for its customers.

Expedia has invested heavily in AI in recent years. The company reports that its research and development funding is above one billion dollars every year. Through Expedia Partner Solutions (EPS), the company further provides B2B technology solutions for business partnerships. EPS reaches out to both upstream suppliers and downstream service providers, including financial institutions, hotels, car rental companies, loyalty organizations, retail travel agents, and online travel dealers. Using virtual agent technology, Expedia helps tourists to arrange amenities like meals and parking services for hotels or changing a flight if needed. The AI-enabled virtual agent technology also helps travel agents save time by allowing them to easily cancel bookings or check the status of a customer's refund. Incorporated with AI and machine learning algorithms, virtual agents interact with customers and travel agents in real time. The software also learns from historical data and actions from other travelers to decide the optimal course of action to solve a specific problem from a traveler, which means the system is capable of learning and improving. EPS is using deep learning models to improve the computational process. There is a three-stage process starting with a deployment algorithm sorting properties for its rapid API to deliver to different partners, whether airline, retail store, or perhaps corporate travel partner. Then, the second stage is about real-time sorting of the properties according to who is searching on a partner's website so that relevant results are presented whether the customer is a corporate traveler or family or another traveler type. In the third stage, the system will be launching a recommendation API, which kicks in with similar properties that might be a better fit while the traveler is exploring a property they like. Overall, the improvement in the booking process for the end consumer is a win-win for Expedia and its partners (Fox, 2019).

AI has enabled Expedia to develop applications more efficiently, process large quantities of data, and troubleshoot problems quickly. The outputs of software systems helped Expedia to develop strategies to reach, engage, and convert consumers with sophisticated targeting and metrics such as click-through-rate and returns on ads. The faster Expedia can provide actual time-to-market information, the more consumers they are able to attract due to their efficiency and accuracy. AI gives Expedia better knowledge of all its consumers through the processing of the data. This allows for Expedia to be among the top competitors in the travel industry. The benefits can be wrapped up in the efficiency that consumers receive due to how fast data is processed to ensure time-to-market service and how well data is transformed to fit the needs and wants of consumers in the travel industry.

14.5 Conclusion

AI is having a stronger influence on the tourism sector in recent years. It is common to see AI when it comes to finding deals and prices on flights and hotels and even using AI for marketing. With AI technologies, businesses are able to offer a wide range of information to their target market and can combine many services to attract tourists, which can make the business more competitive. AI technologies also help customers share their interests so that businesses know who to target and how and overall let businesses know whether their services made an impact. This can be either positive or negative to the contributors of the tourism industry. Which is why we take a look at the different contributions of tourism. In this article, we look at airfare, hotels, and marketing strategies implemented by AI.

As technology advances and businesses rely on technology to increase profit, status, and power, questions about how exactly companies use consumer data and privacy become prominent. Big companies use data for a variety of reasons. In the future, it is almost impossible to not use AI in favor of a business. AI can be fundamental toward the growth and success of any tourism company.

Overall, artificial intelligence has made massive leaps in tourism and continues to grow at a rapid rate. By narrowing our scope and focusing on a few new advancements in the field, such as forecasting and smart tourism, we are able to see the already massive impact AI has made on one of the largest world industries. With these advancements, an increase in both customer savings and company earnings will arise and only increase the growth that the industry consistently sees.

References

Akehurst, G. (2009). User generated content: The use of blogs for tourism Organisations and tourism consumers. *Service Business, 3*(1), 51.

Barron, K., Kung, E., & Proserpio, D. (2020). The effect of home-sharing on house prices and rents: Evidence from Airbnb. *Marketing Science, 40*(1), 23–47. https://doi.org/10.1287/mksc.2020.1227

Burger, H. (2007). *Opening New Dimensions for e-Tourism*. n.d. Accessed 22 Mar 2019. https://search-proquest-com.ezproxy.plu.edu/docview/223129837?accountid=2130

Fox, L. (2019, April 12). *How expedia is using deep learning to improve the hotel booking process*. Retrieved from: https://www.phocuswire.com/Expedia-Partner-Solutions-machine-learning

Giglio, S., Bertacchini, F., Bilotta, E., & Pantano, P. (2019). Using social media to identify tourism attractiveness in six Italian cities. *Tourism Management, 72*, 306–312.

Gretzel, U., Sigala, M., Zheng, X., & Koo, C. (2015). Smart tourism: Foundations and developments. *Electronic Markets, 25*(3), 179–188.

Ivanov, S. H., & Webster, C. (2017). *Adoption of robots, artificial intelligence and service automation by travel, tourism and hospitality companies – A cost-benefit analysis*. https://papers.ssrn.com/abstract=3007577

Liu, Y., Teichert, T., Rossi, M., Li, H., & Hu, F. (2017). Big data for big insights: Investigating language-specific drivers of hotel satisfaction with 412,784 user-generated reviews. *Tourism Management, 59*, 554–563. https://doi.org/10.1016/j.tourman.2016.08.012

Owen, R. (2021, October 4) *Artificial Intelligence at Airbnb – Two Unique Use-Cases*. Retrieved at: https://emerj.com/ai-sector-overviews/artificial-intelligence-at-airbnb/

Richey, E. (2015, April 24). *How big data is giving local tourism organizations a big boost*. Retrieved from https://www.forbes.com/sites/centurylink/2015/04/24/how-big-data-is-giving-local-tourism-organizations-a-big-boost/#165a4ba540cb

Vaid, J., & Kesharwani, S. (2018). Role of big data analytics in social media marketing of MICE tourism. *Global Journal of Enterprise Information Systems, 10*(1), 55–61.

Xiang, Z., Schwartz, Z., Gerdes, J. H., & Uysal, M. (2015). What can big data and text analytics tell us about hotel guest experience and satisfaction? *International Journal of Hospitality Management, 44*, 120–130. https://doi.org/10.1016/j.ijhm.2014.10.013

Yu, G., & Schwartz, Z. (2006). Forecasting short time-series tourism demand with artificial intelligence models. *Journal of Travel Research, 45*(2), 194–203.

Artificial Intelligence in Transportation 15

Abstract

This chapter introduces the application of artificial intelligence technology in transportation. We focus on the new applications in autonomous vehicles, ships, and drones. Some important machine learning techniques are introduced, including deep learning, swarm-based fuzzy controllers, wireless sensors, and actuator networks. This chapter also provides several case studies of applying AI in the transportation sector, including AI in Tesla electric cars, Uber's AI Platform, and AI in WeRide.

Keywords

Artificial IntelligenceTransportationAutonomous · VehiclesSelf-driving CarsMachine · LearningNeural · NetworksGenetic · AlgorithmDeep LearningSimulationWireless · SensorActuator · NetworksSwarm-based · TrucksAutonomous · Fuzzy ControllerSelf-driving · ShipOpenAIElectric VehicleHardwareAutonomy · AlgorithmsCode · AlgorithmDeep LearningSimulationWireless · FoundationsEvaluation Infrastructure

15.1 Introduction

With the digital transformation from artificial intelligence technology, we will see more and more everyday devices having some sort of automation, and in some instances, devices will be completely controlled by AI. In this chapter, we will focus on the implementation of AI in the transportation industry. The industry of transportation ranges from everything to riding bikes and buses, to flying 600 miles an hour at 35,000 feet on a commercial jet. Transportation is such a large field, with so much data flowing through it all. The transportation industry has huge coverage of many

L. Chan et al., *Applied Artificial Intelligence in Business*, Applied Innovation and Technology Management, https://doi.org/10.1007/978-3-031-05740-3_15

different areas and applications of AI, so this chapter will explore AI applications for autonomous vehicles.

Autonomous vehicles are vehicles that use AI to navigate without any human interference. With AI technology always improving, people wondered how far technology can improve and how it will affect generations to come. Now that autonomous vehicles are becoming a reality, car manufacturers are racing to become the first to bring the dream to reality. Even today there are some vehicles already out there with assisted driving and some with a self-driving option. With cameras and sensors around the car, these devices are able to take in these input data and make specific real-time decisions based on the situation. Through machine learning, the AI systems in an autonomous vehicle will be able to navigate and learn with experience, and hopefully, we can get to the point where most vehicles on the road are autonomous (Puthanpura et al., 2015). Although many of such vehicles are still in the testing phases, autonomous vehicles are up and coming in the market with several big corporations investing billions of dollars into research and development. There still needs to be more years of testing for fully autonomous vehicles, but these types of vehicles are the next evolution of vehicles that will reshape our society (Gadam, 2018; Zhang, 2014).

15.2 Development of Autonomous Vehicles

Autonomous vehicles have been researched and developed for decades by different scientists and engineers in advanced nations. In the 1980s, there were two types of autonomous vehicles tested in the United States. Since 1961, the first autonomous car air-cushion vehicle (ACV) has been invented by William Bertelsen, and the autonomous car had a dramatic development in the past 40 years.

The Autonomous Land Vehicle (ALV) was a military-funded vehicle that used a camera to look at the color of the pixels that the camera was taking in, and this would adjust the steering of the vehicle. In 1984, a team by the name of Strategic Computing, a one-billion-dollar program funded by the US military, had the task of coming up with the first autonomous-driven vehicle. The 10.4-million-dollar defense contract was to be completed in only 9 months after the project was given to Strategic Computing. The demo was to have a vehicle be driven completely autonomously on a 2-km, obstacle-free, stretch of road. The ALV team put together a vehicle large enough to house all the generators, computers, and cooling systems. The team then put a colored video camera on the top of the vehicle. The team had to figure out how to keep the vehicle on the road using only the images coming from the video camera. They decided to use the pixel colors in the image to steer the vehicle. Since the color of road pixels are usually different from sky pixels, the team ignored the location of the pixels on the screen and instead focused on the color. They then organized the pixels in a red and blue color space. Mathematical equations were then used to organize the color of the pixels in each distinct color group. The team ended up being successful with their demo, but the vehicle only traveled 10 km an hour. This method was later named the analytical method of autonomous driving vehicles. The method had many flaws, and the ALV project was shut down early. Although this was the case, this project gave way to the later ALVINN (Autonomous Land Vehicle in Neural Network) in 1989 (Pomerleau, 1989).

There was a leaping revolution in the development of autonomous vehicles in 1989. Dean Pomerleau and Todd Jochem, both from Carnegie Mellon University, decided to start their own autonomous vehicle-driven project. They named their vehicle ALVINN (Autonomous Land Vehicle in a Neural Network). Their approach to this project was different from the approach Strategic Computing used. Instead of using formulas that looked at the color of pixels coming from the color video camera on the top of the vehicle, they instead decided to put a whole entire neural network in the vehicle. The vehicle then had to be built big just like the ALV to house all the computers and machines inside. The neural network took all the processes that the ALV's algorithms did and made it simpler. The neural network first learned how to drive from a driver being behind the wheel. It then looked at the image that was coming in from the color camera and looked at the degree the steering wheel was at relative to that image. It took hundreds of riders from the neural network to finally learn how to drive on its own. Dean Pomerleau called this approach to teach the neural network how to drive "supervised learning." When it could drive on its own, the ALVINN actually looked for lane markers on the road without ever being programmed what lane markers even are. This method of supervised learning in an autonomous vehicle was known as the empirical method. The empirical method took quite a while to obtain enough data for the system to work efficiently, but after the network had enough data, this approach proved quite successful. This method however is now not used by major autonomous vehicle manufacturers because of how long it takes to get sufficient data for a fully autonomous-driven vehicle to operate. Dean Pomerleau later created a vehicle that drove across the United States 98% autonomously.

In the new century of the 2000s, many large established corporations in different countries began to step into the autonomous vehicle industry (Chan & Daim, 2012). Google started its own autonomous-driven vehicle project in 2009. This project was headed by Sebastian Thrun, a Stanford professor with whom Google had close ties in regards to artificial intelligence. Thrun later worked on Google projects like Google Glass and Google Street View. Thrun started this project at Stanford University with a faculty and student team that was already working on robots and cars. The team started out with designing autonomous-driven systems into six Toyota Priuses and an Audi TT. The team then hired individuals with perfect driving records to sit behind the wheel of the cars that Google designed. Google's cars use high-tech sensors, cameras, radar, lasers, and GPS systems. The technology in these vehicles can detect cars, objects, bikers, and construction zones up to two football fields away. In just 1 year, the seven cars drove more than 140,000 miles. That same year, the team hired more engineers to make the cars even better. In 2011, the team switched from having six Toyota vehicles to having 23 Lexus vehicles. By 2014, Google said that the cars had gotten a lot better. They saw improvement in urban situations that before caused the vehicles to have problems. A year later, Google released their own autonomous-driven vehicle that had no steering wheel, brakes on the driver's side, or gas pedal. All Google put in the vehicle was a button to turn it on. The vehicle however only went 25 miles per hour. In 2016, the first autonomous-driven car made by Google got into an accident. It was in Mountain View, California, but luckily the car was only going 2 miles an hour. In 2017, the Google self-driving car project was renamed Waymo. Waymo later went on to test out a self-driving taxi in Phoenix, Arizona.

Autonomous vehicles are classified to have different level designations. The National Highway Traffic Safety Administration (a subset of the DOT) adopted a six-level system for designating vehicle automation levels. Most vehicles on the road are at level 0 or 1, where minor lane assistance, flexible cruise control, and other small assistance are available. In these two levels, the help of automation is limited. The driver should control the car at any time. In level 2, the driving assistance system assumes steering and speed acceleration. For example, Tesla's vehicles are level 2 – they can perform many automated functions based on their environment but require a decent amount of human interaction. At this level, automation can help drivers do some basic operations, for example, lane-keeping cruise control. Audi's Traffic Jam Pilot is at level 3. Drivers still need to be able to intervene, but on an ideal trip, there would be no human intervention. The most advanced autonomous vehicles of level 4 and 5 designations are fully automated machines. Companies involved with R&D for these kinds of vehicles predict road readiness within a decade. For now, though, we are going to focus on the artificial intelligence technology that is currently being used for these vehicles (Daim et al., 2018).

15.3 AI Technology in Autonomous Vehicles

In the autonomous vehicles that are being created today, there are many different AI technologies. Techniques like voice recognition, gesture controls, eye tracking and other monitoring driving systems, and mapping and safety systems are all ways that AI is implemented in autonomous vehicles and even some "normal" vehicles today. In this section, we explore several major AI technologies of autonomous cars. These include some advanced machine learning algorithms such as artificial neural networks, deep learning, and genetic algorithms. These AI technologies are combined with the use of sensors and controllers to help autonomous cars achieve self-parking, anti-collision, and speed command.

There have been many types of machine learning methods used in autonomous vehicles and even normal vehicles that we have today. In most autonomous systems, the main feature of the system was the inclusion of neural network algorithms. This allowed the vehicle to "learn" from the inputs it is receiving. One of the things that the vehicle can learn is to look for lane marker patterns and traffic signals. Cameras and sensors are heavily used so the automated car can figure out where it is and its surroundings. Machine learning techniques like neural networks and genetic algorithms are implemented to allow the vehicle to learn through experience and then make decisions. This allows autonomous vehicles to make decisions on their own based on previous data that has been collected and this will lead to increased safety and all the other potential benefits of autonomous vehicles. Neural networks (NN) are biologically inspired systems consisting of a massively connected network of computational neurons. By adjusting the weights, neural networks can be trained to approximate virtually any nonlinear function to a required degree of accuracy. A learning algorithm would then be used to adjust the weights in the network so that the network would give the desired output. Genetic algorithm (GA) is an algorithm based on the principle of survival of the fittest. The algorithm starts with a randomly generated initial population of individuals, and each individual represents a potential solution to the problem. Then each solution is evaluated to give some measure of the "fitness," which means the algorithm determines which individuals or solutions are the best fit for the situation. Then a new population is formed by selecting the more "fit" individuals. Within this new population, some members undergo alterations by means of mutation to form new solutions, and after some number of generations, it is expected that the algorithm comes to an optimum solution.

Deep learning is a subfield of machine learning concerned with algorithms inspired by the structure and function of the brain called artificial neural networks (Brownlee, 2016; Goodfellow et al., 2016; Hippe et al., 2021; Si et al., 2021). The reason why deep learning has been used in autonomous cars more widely than other technologies such as rule-based learning is that compared to using other machine technologies, the improved speed of learning is superb when deep learning is used. Even though engineers put countless data in other machine learning technology, it reaches a plateau in learning at some point. However, when deep learning is used, it does not reach a plateau in learning. In other words, the performance of learning keeps getting better and better as more data is added in deep learning technology. Then how are deep learning techniques applied to the autonomous car? The answer is "simulation." Engineers set up simulators for deep learning and make software to be simulated with several million repetitions. Waymo is one of the big companies that have applied deep learning simulators to their autonomous vehicles. According to Waymo, "they are heavily investing in simulation and have collected in excess of one billion miles generated through computer simulation" (Grzywaczewski, 2017). Therefore, as the simulation progresses, the software learns to make reasonable decisions when facing many different situations that the car could encounter on the road. Because making autonomous cars have the same driving behaviors as humans is the most important task in that field, developing deep learning technology can be a thing that many companies and engineers should develop more. Deep learning technology can be applied to various levels of autonomous vehicles. It can be applied to level 4 or 5 autonomous vehicles which are fully autonomous driving. However, it can also be applied to level 2 or 3 autonomous vehicles which still need human drivers to drive. Although a deep learning system is not used as the main agent to drive a car, the system can be used as the assistance of drivers in level 2 or 3 autonomous vehicles. Nowadays, we can easily find the use of the deep learning system as the assistance of drivers in the real world.

Wireless sensor and actuator networks (WSANs) consist of a group of sensors that gather information about their environment and actuators. The most important factor of this system is the coordination between the wireless sensor and actuator networks. When this system is in an autonomous car, the sensors on both sides of the vehicle will measure the distance between the vehicle and barriers. Then the vehicle's main computer actuator networks which are located in the truck will analyze data from the sensors and compare its stored map to give the order to control the vehicle to avoid a collision. WSANs can sense, reason, and react as a group with distributed intelligence, without any intervention from the back end and despite the hardware limitations of sensor nodes. A CMOS sensor is used as a path recognition sensor to extract the lane centerline through image analysis, and speed feedback is introduced to form a closed-loop control. The camera in the autonomous cars will take the image of the road, and then a fuzzy control system can control vehicle traffic along the road.

A swarm-based fuzzy controller (SBFC) is used to search for the designed fuzzy controller parameters and the parking time (the elapsed time in following the intended path trajectory) that achieves the nearest generated path to the desired one with minimum errors (Mohamed Hanafy, Development of a technology for car's auto-parking using swarm search-based fuzzy control system). This system can generate an optimal parking path based on parking space, surrounding environment, and parking time and then control the speed of each wheel of a vehicle to ensure the vehicle can achieve auto-parking by following the optimal parking path.

These AI-based systems allow autonomous vehicles to learn and to "think" of solutions and make decisions based on these algorithms and neural networks. Besides the technology built in the vehicle, another important factor is experience. The key to such an experience is data inputs. As for the data or information used to support AI, they can be classified in two parts. The first part is the external data or information; these data from the outside can be the map, road condition, outside image, or traffic condition. This information comes from the input sources to help the main computer of the autonomous cars to make decisions based on actual circumstances. The second part is the internal data; this is the data manipulated by an algorithm or formula. These data are calculated by the autonomous car's computer, and these data can help autonomous cars analyze the driving conditions. For example, in auto-parking, there are a lot of data to support AI technology, and auto-parking can be split into three parts. The first step is using a sensor to detect the distance from the car to the parking space and make the 2D map. In the second step, the optimal parking trajectory is planned based on this 2D environmental map. In the last step, the auto-parking controller executes the real-time vehicle motion path estimation and the planned parking trajectory-tracking control. So in this case, the 2D map is the external data, and the algorithm to search the optimal parking path is using the internal data or information.

The vehicles that corporations like Uber, Google, or Tesla have created are primarily level 3 and 4 autonomous vehicles, which means they still have features where a person is able to control the car. In order for society to implement level 5 autonomous vehicles, which are fully autonomous vehicles with no self-driving features, years and millions of miles need to be tested with these vehicles because these neural networks and genetic algorithms need to get enough experience and information to make real-life decisions. As mentioned above, this technology within autonomous vehicles will determine life and death, and it is important for these algorithms, neural networks, and other AI systems to be trained and build up experience as much as they can so that they can learn from all the input data and develop solutions for every situation on the roads.

15.4 Applications of AI in the Transportation Industry

Artificial intelligence will have effects that span all sectors of transportation (Antony, 2017; Sadek, 2007). It will have effects on how sectors such as trucking, airlines, railroads, marine logistics, public transportation, and ride-sharing are handled. Traffic will be significantly decreased with the help of autonomous vehicles on the road. Some of these effects may be good for consumers, as they will help make our lives easier, as that is what artificial intelligence is designed to do. However, it also may have adverse effects, where it could lead to an overreliance on AI and could lead to a loss of jobs with companies such as Uber.

One industry that autonomous vehicles will help to improve is the trucking industry. The trucking industry currently has a massive truck driver shortage. The United States faced a deficit of nearly 45,000 truck drivers in 2015 (Fagnant & Kockelman, 2015). In another report done by the American Trucking Association, it states that because of retirements and individuals leaving the industry, trucking companies will need to recruit nearly 100,000 new drivers a year over the next decade to keep pace with the country's growing freight needs. This is obviously a massive issue for the industry and is certainly something autonomous vehicles would help to alleviate. The need for autonomous trucks will only grow as the economy becomes more global and we will need to ship freight interstate/internationally. This revolution has already begun. In April 2016, Uber acquired Otto, a start-up company that developed a kit to convert conventional trucks into self-driving trucks (Mittal et al., 2018). This shows that big-name companies such as Uber want to be able to grab a piece of the pie that is autonomous trucking, as it will no doubt be a moneymaker in the future. In fact, mining company Rio Tinto is already using 53 self-driving ore trucks, having driven 2.4 million miles and carrying 200 million tons of materials (Maurer et al., 2016; Mittal et al., 2018). They may not be used to traveling interstate in the United States, which would most likely be more difficult and will take more time, but it shows that companies are already doing this to increase efficiency.

One thing that the world could go without is traffic, and hopefully, autonomous cars will be able to reduce or even eliminate traffic. Traffic is often caused by human drivers who unwillingly create it by following too closely behind another car. When the person in front of them brakes, so do they, and the person behind them does too, and the shockwave goes back to all the cars on the road. Autonomous cars are smarter than humans, so they will be able to sense what is best, therefore giving the optimum amount of space between them and the car in front of them. A further point to touch on is if autonomous cars were to be interconnected, it would mean optimum efficiency on roads, which would help to minimize traffic congestion. As stated in Science Daily, "Connected vehicle technology can also further increase the efficiency and reliability of autonomous vehicles" (Bagloee et al., 2016; Elliott et al., 2019). If autonomous vehicles were to be interlinked and be able to communicate with each other on where they all were going and at what speed, this would be a fascinating concept. It would help to eliminate crashes and decrease the amount of time spent in traffic.

AI has numerous impacts in this industry to make it safer, reduce costs, and make driving just a whole lot easier. With an AI-driven car, long drives by individuals will be a thing of the past. Instead, the user can sit and relax while the car does all the work. This also has the added bonus of rarely stopping for breaks unless to fill up on gas. The overall safety of driving will also be higher than it is now. There are studies that show fully autonomous-driven vehicles actually have a higher safety percentage than under human-driven vehicles. There is a lot of trust that goes into having just a computer drive for someone, but the studies do show that it is better. In the trucking industry, AI can reduce costs for big corporations by not having to hire as many truck drivers to haul freight.

Not only can autonomous vehicles run on roads, but they can also fly in the sky (drones) or cruise on the water. Rolls-Royce Commercial Marine has been working hard in the last decade to create a fully autonomous ship. Rolls-Royce is a key part of Kongsberg Marine, a well-known Norwegian technology company. Kongsberg Marine is in the fields of marine automation, satellite navigation, and dynamic positioning systems, which are very useful knowledge to know when creating the world's first fully autonomous ship. On December 3, 2018, Rolls-Royce performed the world's first fully autonomous voyage in Finland on a 1-mile-long route. The company used a state-run ferry during the test, and with the utilization of artificial intelligence, the ferry avoided obstacles in the mile-long course and was able to dock successfully. Thanks to the AI systems installed on the ship, it was able to navigate rough waters in snow and strong winds during winter. This was an amazing feat that Rolls-Royce was able to pull off and they will continue to progress artificial intelligence in the near future.

With the developments towards the unmanned ship, a lot of technology and artificial intelligence has to go into creating such a large, smart machine learning piece of technology. Rolls-Royce (not the car company) has been trying to perfect this kind of technology for more than 10 years. The goal is to have fully autonomous ships developed by as early as the 2030s. Rolls-Royce will be able to do this with the help of machine learning and by teaming up with both Google and Intel. Since the advancement in technology has changed so rapidly in the past few decades, the enhancement in artificial intelligence algorithms will help with the ship's machine learning system, specifically the image recognition system that is in place. What this system will do is help recognize what is in front of the ship while out at sea. The sensors, which will be all around the boat, will determine the danger level of objects and will be able to dodge when need be and even classify the objects to how hazardous the object(s) is or are. Furthermore, this daunting task seems near impossible, but Rolls-Royce is figuring it out. It is not similar when comparing a self-driving car because there is only one person that is needed to be replaced, whereas, on container ships, it takes a 20-man crew to have the ship running and protected. There is navigation and observation for both, but with ships, there is also a focus on what goes on inside, down below deck. Cargo handling and security would need to be replaced also, these are critical in order to keep everything in order on board and secure from any people such as pirates that would want to hijack the ship. The machine learning will use a neural net-based software that is powered by Google's voice and image recognition system/search applications. More specifically, this means that the ship will already know what to do when it sees a hazardous object. The ship(s) will already know what to do because of machine learning and the help from sharing data between autonomous ships. Artificial intelligence will have the ability to share data with other vessels all over the world and have other options to consider very rapidly before dodging an object or even adjusting course. With positives, there are sometimes negatives which are the challenges that Rolls-Royce will face. Some include figuring out navigation, programming, and teaching the artificial intelligence to guide 100,000 tons of container ships to the docks and finally the legislation such as national, international, and private laws.

Artificial intelligence is changing the shipping industry in a big way that will impact the future of supply chain and logistics, for companies especially. For example, faster shipping will be offered because companies will be able to cut costs and can deliver with expedited shipping. Companies will be able to provide better accuracy on delivery time. Another is that artificial intelligence can predict any risks or future problems with the help of historical data. Since weather is difficult to predict, artificial intelligence can predict weather patterns and whether or not the shipping season will be slow or fast. A major cost that will be reduced with the help of artificial intelligence will be fuel consumption. By knowing the best route to take, dodge objects, and not get held up by weather, clearly, fuel will be immensely saved through this process. AI will help companies who deal with the maritime industry become more efficient in every way possible in and around the company.

Case 15.1: AI in Tesla Cars

Tesla has quickly become the name of the game in the autonomous vehicle market. Technology entrepreneur and engineer, Elon Musk, joined the company as an early investor, leading the Series A financing and taking on several other roles as well. Their plan was to start with a high-margin, high-performance sports car, with the goal of shedding the stigma around electric vehicles, after GM's failed attempts in the late 1990s and early 2000s. "As a tech pioneer with a significant interest in the race to build and market autonomous vehicles, it makes sense that today they would be deeply interested in artificial intelligence," writes Bernard Marr of Forbes, and in January 2018, Elon Musk publicly announced that they were working on their own AI hardware. The future of AI in the travel sector currently belongs to Tesla, until other companies step up, because along with autonomous cars, Elon Musk has more plans to enhance the travel experience through technologies and building developments like the Hyperloop and The Boring Company's tunnel.

Elon Musk tends to be very outspoken when it comes to matters of his investments, using social media as a tool to share snippets of his business ventures, so it should come as no surprise that Musk and Tesla are working on their own AI technologies. Musk is the cofounder of OpenAI, a research organization dedicated to ensuring that AI is developed and deployed in a safe, manageable way so as to minimize any existential risk robots may one day pose to humanity. Although very few details are known about Tesla's AI technologies, sources connected to Forbes believe it will process the thinking algorithms for the company's Autopilot software which currently gives Tesla vehicles limited (level 2) levels of autonomous driving capability. Musk said that he believes his cars will be fully autonomous (level 5 autonomous) by the early 2020s. Although the current electric vehicle (EV) market segment is 1–2% of the total vehicle sales worldwide, the anticipated growth is massive. Recent projections show that EV sales are expected to surpass those of traditional vehicles by 2038, while the global fleet of EVs is expected to surpass one billion by 2047 (Daim et al., 2018).

Tesla took a risk by dipping its toes in the electric vehicle market and AI market, but it has paid off immensely. In the data-gathering department, Tesla is crushing all competition. In fact, every vehicle ever sold by Tesla was built with the potential to one day become self-driving. Tesla crowdsources its data from all of its vehicles as well as their drivers, with internal as well as external sensors which can pick up information about a driver's hand placement on the instruments and how they are operating them. The data they gather is then used to generate highly data-dense maps showing everything from the average increase in traffic speed over a stretch of road to the location of hazards that cause drivers to take action. Tesla's machine learning takes care of educating the entire vehicle. It is clear that Tesla has always been a company that focuses on and takes pride in data collection, analysis, and development.

With all of the technology being developed by the Tesla team, Elon Musk thought to go even further with it. He is doing this through other companies that he started, including The Boring Company and SpaceX. The idea of The Boring Company was one of Musk's that people weren't sure exactly what it was. He created the company to explore any weird or crazy ideas that he happened to think up, including a flamethrower. One day while sitting in traffic, he had the idea to create a tunnel system underground that allowed people to travel in cars much faster than they normally can. This idea is now in the making and even has a finished test tunnel built which Musk rode in himself. The technology behind this is the same AI as used with the current Teslas. The car is driven onto a platform, the platform then begins to go down like an elevator taking the passengers into the tunnel. The technology then takes over and becomes fully automated through the tunnel, traveling at what they hope to be over 120 miles per hour. After arriving at your destination, the platform then rises back up to the surface and you can continue driving on the regular road.

Tesla's self-driving capability has hardware that allows for short and long trips without requiring any action from the driver. All you have to do is sit and say where you want to go. And if you don't say anything, it will gather information from other apps like your calendar and assume that's the destination. It will navigate through traffic lights, stop signs, and even freeways with heavy and fast traffic. When you arrive at your destination, you can simply get off the car, and it will enter a park seek mode and park itself wherever there is a spot. And all you have to do is tap on your phone and it will come back to you.

Tesla's autopilot uses AI technology, which we know controls steering, acceleration, braking, and automatically stopping at stop signs and lights. They achieve their goal of developing self-driving cars through advanced AI, which they use for vision and planning. Multiple different components of AI go into creating self-driving cars ("Artificial Intelligence & Autopilot", n.d.):

- Hardware.
  - Build silicon chips that power the whole self-driving software from functionality to performance. The program communicates multiple different tasks with these chips.
- Neural networks.
  - Involves 48 networks that predict other cars or pedestrians, even what drivers would do by correlating past and future actions. They train neural networks, which are basically implemented for perception and control and to detect objects. The bird's-eye view neural network takes videos of the road layout and 3D objects.
- Autonomy algorithms.
  - Used to create data obtained from the sensors in their cars. This data is then used to build systems in the car that operate in any real-world situation.
- Code foundations.
  - The codes are used to capture high-volume data from the sensors and share it with other systems, even consumers. They simulate the real-world environment that feeds autopilot software.
- Evaluation infrastructure.
  - These are tools that Tesla uses to track performance and improvements.

Another function inside the Tesla cars keeps the pets safe and comfortable when their owners have to leave them in the car for grocery shopping or something else. This function helps maintain the temperature in the car, which is important for pets during the summer because of high temperatures, and it can be adjusted even when the car is off (Entrepreneur en Español, 2020). Owners can monitor the temperature with the app on their phones. A message on the screen pops up when you set it to dog mode to warn anyone passing by and inform people that the pet is safe (Entrepreneur en Español, 2020).

There are disadvantages to applying AI to Tesla's autopilot system. Many consumer reports show that certain features work inconsistently. For example, the autoparks did not park straight between lines, and other cases have shown Tesla ignoring carpool lanes on the highways; it stayed in one passing lane for a long time, and it drove on the wrong side of a parking lot (Monticello & Barry, 2020). These are functions that can be better controlled by drivers without their car on autopilot, but customers fail to understand that the drivers still need to have their hands on the wheel even if their Tesla is on autopilot. This is something Tesla needs to clear out with the drivers for their own safety.

Tesla's advanced hardware and AI system give them a huge competitive advantage in the market. Tesla's competitors like GM don't have such advanced technology for their cars (Wayland & Kolodny, 2021). In order to make sure that the Tesla cars are up to date and function properly, there is software update like over-the-air update, which improves stop sign control, traffic light, and even camera (Fortuna et al., 2020). Through updating their AI system, they're able to gather information and analyze images from their customer's cars to better improve and train neural networks.

Case 15.2: Uber AI

In March 2009, Uber was launched in San Francisco and became the world's largest ride-sharing company. Uber has a mobile app where a passenger who needs a ride can connect with independent drivers. So, when the passenger requests a ride, a driver nearby accepts the request and the app estimates when the driver will arrive at the pickup location and when the customer will be arriving at the destination. One of Uber's most valuable assets is data, which has been a key competitive edge of Uber's business. Therefore, Uber is arguing that the company is a technology platform and not a pure transportation company. Uber is committed to developing technologies such as AI and machine learning to fulfill the vision of creating seamless, impactful experiences for the customer when Uber's core business is serving as a technology platform.

Uber is one of the leading companies in the transportation industry when it comes to putting AI to work as AI powers many of the technologies and services underpinning Uber's platform. This allows the engineering and data science teams to make choices that make the user experiences much better throughout their business model. At the forefront of Uber's effort for developing and applying advanced artificial intelligence is the Uber AI research platform. This AI platform deploys software programs in machine vision, deep learning, optimization algorithms, NLP (natural language processing), intelligent sensor positioning, etc.

Uber AI's projects span across different platforms from mobile to back-end server stacks in order to enhance the coverage, accuracy, speed, and heading of vehicle locations. These programs have gone beyond the restrictions of GPS and provided more precise location information for drivers and riders to find each other. This is all possible because AI moves at such a high pace where it can outwork most GPS systems and give a better understanding of what to do with the data found. The recent development of Uber Heat Map has impacted the business the most. Being able to understand the demand in a certain area allows Uber to strategically place drivers in spots that will attract the most drivers. Uber can estimate the demand depending on the time and the location. The intelligent system helps drivers to be aware of when and where there is the highest demand in a particular region, and the system ensures that there are enough drivers in the demanded area. The estimate of the demand also allows the app to increase the prices in peak hours. It is also important for Uber to use this technology to ensure customer retention because the customers do not want delays on their daily rides and take a ride from another service if they cannot get from Uber. Uber makes the most money when they can pick up and drop off a rider with another rider ready to be picked up within the same location. AI helps and speeds up the process of finding riders that are close to the end location of the last ride. Uber noticed that when they began to implement these technologies, they saw improvements in demand prediction and much better pickup experiences for their customers.

Uber utilizes machine learning when (for example) the customer taps a destination, the app already has suggestions based on the customer's latest traveled destinations and ride history. Machine learning can discover meaningful patterns in data to help the customer get a better experience. Another factor which has a big influence on the customer's choice is the expected time of arrival. Customers do not want to waste their time in traffic jams. Machine learning can address this issue by forecasting demand and then putting drivers ready in the forecasted demanded areas. Uber's AI-based system offers estimated times of arrival (ETAs), reduces rider and driver cancellations, and makes the business process operate much more efficiently. The reliability and accuracy of the ETA are other features of Uber's platform. When choosing an application/company to use, customers want the most accessible and easy-to-use platform and that is what Uber offers by using AI. Uber uses a conversational AI platform to help the support teams solve the customers' issues as quickly and accurately as possible. This AI platform is also helping the driver not to get distracted while driving by communicating with the riders via hands-free pickup and one-click chat.

By using advanced machine learning and AI technologies, Uber has enhanced their product in multiple ways including transportation, mobility, and driver-partner navigation. Uber is also using artificial learning for fraud detection, risk assessment, safety processes, marketing spend and allocation, and matching drivers and riders. This establishment of AI within Uber has allowed them to be much more competitive throughout the marketplace and is why they sit at the top for (taxi services). Companies that have not implemented these technologies will be left in the dust and never be able to compete with a company like Uber. In the future, Uber wants to make visions of self-driving cars, urban aviation, and optimized cities a reality while making streets safer for road users and pedestrians with artificial learning and machine learning.

Case 15.3: AI in WeRide

In addition to the cases of Tesla and Uber, this section introduces another top self-driving car company – WeRide. WeRide was established in 2017, with its global headquarters in Guangzhou and branches in China (Beijing, Shanghai, Shenzhen,

Zhengzhou, Nanjing, etc.) and the United States (San Jose, California). The team has more than 800 people and is engaged in technology research and development, commercialization, and corporate operations. In addition to that, WeRide also has rich practical experience internationally (by 2021, WeRide's autonomous mileage has reached over 8,000,000 kilometers while the number is still escalating every day). As the world's leading L4 autonomous driving technology company, WeRide is committed to creating new species, new models, and new experiences for smart cities. Moreover, it is the world's first start-up company to carry out autonomous driving testing in both China and the United States.

WeRide focuses on the Iron Triangle strategic cooperation with car companies and platform parties, forming a three-product matrix of driverless taxis (Robotaxi), minibuses (Mini Robobus), and intra-city freight vehicles (Robovan), providing online car-hailing and multi-scenario services of on-demand buses to same-city freight, exploring the commercialization of autonomous driving (Fig. 15.1).

Similar to Tesla, AI and big data are widely used in WeRide. For example, it uses service from their partner Alluxio for its Cross-Region Hybrid Cloud Storage Gateway for Machine Learning and AI. The WeRide company uses a local Alluxio cluster to process the road test data. By doing that, engineers can use the data immediately from the local Alluxio cluster, while Alluxio uploads the road test data to the cloud S3 in the background. Engineers in different offices can quickly obtain the data through the Alluxio cache, thereby further reducing time to get data from the cloud S3. "Data orchestration for WeRide via Alluxio is now a critical component of connecting in-office machine learning applications with data in the cloud," said Haoyuan Li, founder and CEO.

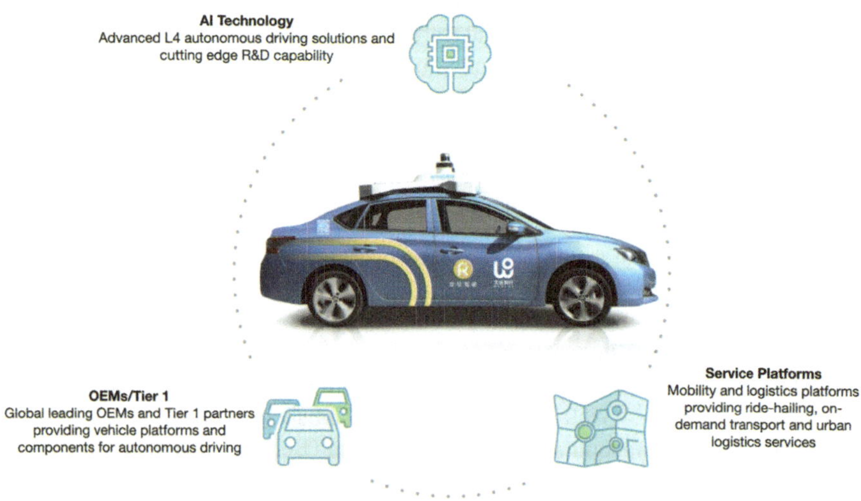

Fig. 15.1 Triangle strategic cooperation from WeRide

15.5 Future Trends

With more and more autonomous vehicles on the roads, we can identify future trends or developments that will bring changes to the world. The market for autonomous vehicles right now is still relatively small compared to other markets. It is estimated that by 2026, the global market for autonomous vehicles is estimated to grow to $556.67 billion with a compound annual growth rate of 39.47%. The reason for this growth is that many big corporations are investing millions, even billions, of dollars to create and develop AI technology to be used in autonomous vehicles. Although Google and Tesla are huge players in this market, other corporations like Amazon, Apple, Uber, BMW, and Audi are investing money into artificial intelligence and implementing this technology into vehicles. Along with these huge corporations, the US government has also invested in this technology. In 2018, the Trump administration passed a bill to spend $100 million on research and development for autonomous vehicles. One of the government's main focuses with this bill was to assess the safety of these vehicles. This technology is relatively new, and it is still in the testing phases. The market growth for autonomous vehicles is very high, and many corporations and even the US government see the huge potential of AI on vehicles (Marr, n.d.).

The ride-sharing industry could massively use autonomous vehicles in the future. For example, Uber uses ride-sharing now to have their employees pick up people and take them to where they need to go. This company and industry could be potentially reshaped by autonomous vehicles, as this would eliminate the need for them to hire employees to take people places. They could just have a set of cars do it for them. A Columbia University study suggested that with a fleet of just 9000 autonomous cars, Uber could replace every taxicab in New York City, and passengers would wait an average of 36 s for a ride that costs about $0.50 per mile (Business Insider). This would be a huge change in our country and something that will send shockwaves throughout our society. Uber CEO has come out and said publicly that he will replace all of his drivers with self-driving cars.

Another trend is that ownerships of traditional owner vehicles will fall. The technology that is used in autonomous vehicles will change our world where we would be moving towards a future where people do not own cars. Autonomous vehicles would be accessible in most highly populated places, whereas rural areas may not see such a change. Having a subscription service for self-driving vehicles is one of the ways where this possibility may come into effect. Not only will autonomous vehicles help those who transport to places a lot, but they will make life easier for people with disabilities or even children. For those who may not be able to drive on their own, an autonomous car will be able to do that task for them. For example, if an elderly person must get to the grocery store but cannot drive, the autonomous car will be able to take them there, the individual gets what they need from the store and then the vehicle will be able to take them home safely. This same type of example would apply to children when parents may not be able to take them to their sports practice, for instance. Another lifestyle change that may occur because of AI in vehicles is that people may change where they live. The reasons why people live close to work or families and live close to school are because long commutes take a toll every day when they make long journeys while driving. Autonomous vehicles will get people to a destination without having to do much where you can relax in the car. Along with these future trends, there are so many other ways that may change our society for the better and AI is a key technology that we will have to adapt to in the future.

15.6 Conclusion

Artificial intelligence technology is revolutionizing the transportation industry. Since this industry is a huge part of society and driving is an everyday use, autonomous vehicles or self-driving cars will change our world with the many applications that they can be implemented into. For decades, it has been a developing thought but it will soon be a driving force in people's lives. There are also many safety and regulation concerns where there have been fatalities while in the testing phases of autonomous vehicles. The use of AI in transportation has achieved many more pros than cons and there are lots of future ideas where AI can be used in our world today to make life easier. Since AI is still developing rapidly, it will influence autonomous vehicles as well. These vehicles will be ultimately fully automatic, and once they are cleared to be safe, our future in the transportation industry will be bright.

References

Antony, A. (2017). *How will AI impact the transportation industry.*

Artificial Intelligence & Autopilot. (n.d.). Accessed December 25, 2021. https://www.tesla.com/AI

Bagloee, S. A., Tavana, M., Asadi, M., & Oliver, T. (2016). Autonomous vehicles: Challenges, opportunities, and future implications for transportation policies. *Journal of Modern Transportation, 24*(4), 284–303.

Brownlee, J. (2016). *Deep Learning With Python: Develop Deep Learning Models on Theano and TensorFlow Using Keras. Machine Learning Mastery.*

Chan, L., & Daim, T. (2012). Sectoral innovation system and technology policy development in China: Case of the transportation sector. *Journal of Technology Management in China, 7*(2), 117–135.

Daim, T., Chan, L., & Estep, J. (2018). *Infrastructure and technology management.* Springer. ISBN-13: 978–3319689869, ISBN-10: 331968986X.

Elliott, D., Keen, W., & Miao, L. (2019). Recent advances in connected and automated vehicles. *Journal of Traffic and Transportation Engineering (English Edition), 6*(2), 109–131.

Entrepreneur en Español. (2020). Tesla vehicles have a 'Dog Mode' function and this is the photo that left users shocked. *Entrepreneur.* November 27, 2020. https://www.entrepreneur.com/article/360525

Fagnant, D. J., & Kockelman, K. (2015). Preparing a nation for autonomous vehicles: Opportunities, barriers and policy recommendations. *Transportation Research Part A: Policy and Practice, 77*(July), 167–181.

Fortuna, C., Waterworth, D., & Crider, J. (2020). *Tesla's 5 biggest competitive advantages – CleanTechnica.* July 16, 2020. https://cleantechnica.com/2020/07/16/teslas-5-biggest-competitive-advantages/

Gadam, S. (2018). Artificial intelligence and autonomous vehicles. *Data Driven Investor.*

Goodfellow, I., Bengio, Y., & Courville, A. (2016). *Deep learning*. MIT Press.

Grzywaczewski, A. (2017). *Training AI for self-driving vehicles: The challenge of scale*. Available from Internet: Https://devblogs. Nvidia. Com/training-Self-Driving-Vehicles-Challenge-Scale. https://developer.nvidia.com/blog/training-self-driving-vehicles-challenge-scale/

Hippe, Kyle, Cade Lilley, Joshua William Berkenpas, Ciri Chandana Pocha, Kiyomi Kishaba, Hui Ding, Jie Hou, Dong Si, and Renzhi Cao. 2021. "ZoomQA: Residue-level protein model accuracy estimation with machine learning on sequential and 3D structural features." Briefings in Bioinformatics\\Soppdysprfs01.spitech.com\production\04_EDITORIAL\Copyediting\Work_Area\Spr_DD\513784_1_En_Chan\04-Style-QA\Chapter 15\, . https:\doi.org\ https://doi.org/10.1093/bib/bbab384.

Marr, B. (n.d.). The future of the transport industry-Iot, big data, Ai and autonomous vehicles. 2017.

Maurer, M., Gerdes, J. C., Lenz, B., & Winner, H. (2016). *Autonomous driving: Technical, legal and social aspects*. Springer.

Mittal, N., Udayakumar, P. D., Raghuram, G., & Bajaj, N. (2018). The endemic issue of truck driver shortage – A comparative study between India and the United States. *Research in Transportation Economics, 71*(November), 76–84.

Monticello, M., Barry, K. (2020). Tesla's 'full self-driving capability' falls short of its name. *Consumer Reports*. September 4, 2020. https://www.consumerreports.org/autonomous-driving/tesla-full-self-driving-capability-review-falls-short-of-its-name-a1224795690/

Pomerleau, Dean A. (1989). *ALVINN: An autonomous land vehicle in a neural network.*

Puthanpura, A., Khalifa, R., & Chan, L. (2015). Assessing emerging automotive Technologies for the Future, Portland international conference on management of Engineering & Technology, Portland, IEEE.

Sadek, A. W. (2007). Artificial intelligence applications in transportation. *Transportation Research Circular*, 1–7.

Si, Dong, Andrew Nakamura, Runbang Tang, Haowen Guan, Jie Hou, Ammaar Firozi, Renzhi Cao, Kyle Hippe, and Minglei Zhao. 2021. "Artificial Intelligence Advances for de Novo Molecular Structure Modeling in Cryo-electron Microscopy." Wiley Interdisciplinary Reviews. Computational Molecular Science. doi:https://doi.org/10.1002/wcms.1542.

Wayland, M., & Kolodny, L. (2021). Tesla vs. Lucid: Here's how the EV rivals are and aren't alike. *CNBC*. March 2, 2021. https://www.cnbc.com/2021/03/02/tesla-vs-lucid-heres-how-the-ev-rivals-are-and-arent-alike.html

Zhang, B. (2014). *This study revealed the staggering potential of self-driving cars*. Retrieved November 9: 2015.

Artificial Intelligence in Real Estate

16

Abstract

This chapter explores AI technologies like machine learning, artificial neural networks, predicting algorithms, and others in real estate. It covers AI-powered real estate platforms like Houzen, Homesnap, and NeighborhoodScout. Three case studies are presented in this chapter. The first case analyzes Zillow's incorporation of machine learning algorithms, data processing, and mining tools to gain competitive advantage in the real estate industry. The second case is about Redfin and its use of AI technologies that assists buyers in the home-searching process. The third case is about Compass and the use of analytical marketing and AI-powered recommendation platforms in the real estate industry.

Keywords

Artificial intelligence · Big data · Real estate · Expert systems · Forecasting · Artificial neural networks · Home pricing · Hedonic pricing theory · Customization · Personalization · Augmented reality · Virtual tours · Python programming language · Customer engagement · Platforms · Valuation · Zillow · Zestimate · Amazon web service · Redfin · Listing recommendations

16.1 Introduction

Finding a dream home can be a very difficult, expensive, and lengthy process. Future homeowners will hopefully spend the rest of their lives in the house and will want to make a good investment in their property. With the assistance of a real estate agent, customers will need to determine an affordable price, ideal neighborhood, and school district along with ways the home will be personalized to a customer's preferences. Future homeowners will seek real estate agents to help point them in the right direction, but individuals do not realize that most of the pertinent

L. Chan et al., *Applied Artificial Intelligence in Business*, Applied Innovation and Technology Management, https://doi.org/10.1007/978-3-031-05740-3_16

information can be obtained through mobile applications such as Zillow, Houzen, NeighborhoodScout®, and Redfin. All applications use artificial intelligence (AI) to explore a large body of real estate property data, which will lead future buyers to enhance their decision-making process and optimize their investment.

Utilizing artificial intelligence within the retail housing market brings about a world of possibilities for users to grow their businesses and obtain other desirable benefits. The retail housing market has online websites that offer their listings and available for sale houses. Making retail housing into an e-commerce business can be beneficial as the business can collect a variety of relevant data including customer's click data, their browsing history and interests through stored information sources such as web browser cookies, as well as other customer preference data that may help tailor specific retail properties to their specific needs. Such data sources can also be utilized to provide a convenient way to shop and search through the available inventory of retail housing offered in the market making the process smoother and more convenient for them.

There are many ways to use technologies such as big data and artificial intelligence in the retail housing sector. Businesses can leverage them to improve revenue and sales, keep current and accurate status of products and optimize inventory management, identify new sales opportunities, and differentiate their offerings from competitors within the same market. The use of AI and machine learning to reveal customer behavior patterns is a good strategy for improving revenue and sales. Machine learning is harnessed to devise appropriate strategies for placement and promotion of for-sale houses and listings, which overall helps satisfy customer needs and increase sales. Using AI algorithms allows for more efficient inventory management, as it collects accurate status data for each house and available for sale listings in a real-time manner that is always maintained and updated. If businesses can use recommendation algorithms to personalize profiles and listings, based on customer browsing history, then they can identify new sales opportunities which creates a competitive advantage for the real estate business.

AI is currently changing the competitive landscape of many industries, which can, and will, have major impacts on the value generation of businesses. With big data and AI, the marketing scope in real estate has changed dramatically and in ways that can take the industry in many new directions that further the marketing potential for sellers but also have an impact on real estate buyers all over the world. Within this chapter, we will look at how artificial intelligence is used in the real estate industry and examine some of these impacts.

16.2 AI Technologies for Real Estate

In the real estate business, the use of market forecasting is fundamental and important. A scholarly article entitled, "Using Expert Systems and Artificial Intelligence for Real Estate Forecasting" by Peter Rossini, explains this concept well. According to the article, historical real estate transactions become important factors when making forecasting decisions for the future. There are several techniques for determining the prices of properties. However, over the last decades, there have been huge changes to the forecasting techniques that are available to analysts (Rossini, 2000).

Advanced methods are available for routine use as well as advanced econometric models which are often a solution to forecasting problems. Some researchers believe that the use of better systems instead of better forecasting techniques will lead to better forecasts in general (Makridakis et al., 1982). The research included forecasting over 1000 different time series and using 24 different methods (Rossini, 2000). They concluded that more sophisticated methods did not produce any better results than simple methods. However, the research highlights those systems with simple artificial intelligence and expert systems (ES) can produce better results and be more efficient. These systems can even be an advantage and provide assistance to less experienced real estate practitioners.

The most deployed AI technique in forecasting for properties is artificial neural networks (ANNs). ANNs work similarly to how the human brain functions but uses a digital algorithm for learning properties of a data set. An ANN consists of a series of interconnected neurons, similar to the way the brain is organized. Using the ANN for forecasting is similar to other forecasting methods such as multiple regression. The ANN and multiple regression are similar when it comes to how data is input to the model and how the ANN solves a forecasting problem and generates model output data. Both methods use a series of coefficients in the process and each attempt to minimize errors in a similar manner. To measure the forecasting ability, both methods use a standard approach of withholding samples. However, the internal process of the artificial neural networks is more complex and harder to reproduce and explain. An interesting fact is that people without forecasting experience tend to be able to make better predictions using the ANN method (Rossini, 2000).

Forecasting is extremely important in many aspects of a real estate practice. Valuation and appraisal are forecasting activities and numerous facets of real estate rely on forecasting methods. For example, in property development, fund and investment managers as well as property and facilities managers use the forecasting of supply and demand, growth, value, and economic activity (Rossini, 2000). Forecasting is very important, and the article states that it is surprising that the use of artificial intelligence and expert systems is restricted. Further, the article explains the use of AI and ES in general in real estate practice. There are numerous examples of useful applications of expert systems. Some examples include leases, forms, and the preparation of documents. ES can be used by both clients and managers to assist with computer software; the preparation of property descriptions and reports, budgeting, and the cost estimation of development projects'; and solving property and facilities management problems.

Housing prices can be predicted with the use of machine learning algorithms. Home pricing has been studied extensively through the perspective of the theory of hedonic prices (Pérez-Rave et al., 2019). Pérez-Rave et al. (2019) state that the theory of hedonic prices shows the market price of a home "is a function of the utility of structural characteristics, of neighborhoods, and environmental characteristics." Hargrave (2020) adds to the definition of hedonic pricing theory by stating "the price of a building or piece of land is determined by the characteristics of both the property itself...as well as characteristics of its surrounding environment." For example, an internal factor of a home would be the number of rooms it has, and an external factor would be the type of neighborhood the home is located in. These hedonic attributes are typically examined under multiple regression analyses, with a more econometric framework (Pérez-Rave et al., 2019). Pérez-Rave et al. (2019) combined hedonic pricing regressions and machine learning to predict the prices of homes. Hedonic pricing can provide inference analysis where machine learning cannot (Pérez-Rave et al., 2019). In other words, Pérez-Rave et al. (2019) claim that machine learning can predict housing prices, but it can't learn about the data generation process (Doring, 2018). Combining both hedonic pricing regressions and machine learning to predict housing prices could avoid the weaknesses of either tool. Winson-Geidman and Krause (2016) show the type of data within the real estate industry that could be used to predict the price of a home. Winson-Geidman and Krause (2016) explain three types of real estate data: financial, transactional, and physical. Financial data refers to real estate-related stocks, transactional data refers to data such as mortgages and leases, and physical data includes locational data and structural characteristics (Winson-Geidman & Krause, 2016). These three types of real estate data make up the big data available for companies in order for them to use machine learning and artificial intelligence to predict the value of a house.

Real estate companies analyze, collect, and interpret big data from all of their information gathering sources. This could be from security measures, like logins and passwords, or emails and names collected from customers creating an account with a company. Financial information is gathered based on subscription information or signing up with a real estate agent. Once basic knowledge about a person is gathered, big data in real estate allows companies to begin customer profiles through tracking all of the information about a person based on the devices they use to access real estate websites and mobile device applications. This data tracking takes into account a person's location, memorizes price ranges, what kind of home that person is looking for, and what sort of school district he/she/they prefer for his/her/their children. The data is processed and then analyzed by companies with creation and analysis of customer profiles and preferences to better sell customers what they are looking to buy. Although raw data might not be valuable by itself, the information we can extract from it can be of a major source of value to realtors and real estate developers. Contextualizing data is what ultimately adds value to information derived from multiple sources, which can be done through advanced analytics. An article by McKinsey & Company illuminated how advanced analytics can be implemented in real estate through swift identification of focus areas and assessment of a particular land parcel's potential. Hyperlocal community data and land use data, as well as market forecasts, can be accessed by a developer to analyze and help to select the real estate development areas, appropriate neighborhoods, or relevant buildings (Asaftei et al., 2018). Big data can also help illuminate prime site locations and optimal types of buildings for real estate developers by combining important information from multiple sources using advanced analytics.

The major potential application area for big data and AI is the customization of real estate listings. An article published by Innovation Enterprise explains how big data and AI can help brokers and realtors cater their content to their audience and deliver the listings, blogs, videos, and other information that matters most to each individual reader (Sanders, 2020). It goes on to explain how gathering, categorizing, and analyzing data related to past home purchases and annual household income can help create customized recommendations for clients, who receive listings tailored to their preferences (Sanders, 2020). This is mutually beneficial for buyers and sellers, in that it narrows the search for clients while simultaneously cutting costs for sellers by providing a more efficient search process.

Another aspect of the real estate industry that can be improved through AI and AR (augmented reality) is the concept of virtual tours. Today, people looking to purchase a home can view videos that simply showcase the house in a two-dimensional video clip. AI can advance this experience through virtual tours, which would allow potential buyers to experiment with the home by taking a wall out or changing the paint on the walls. This technology would allow people to picture themselves in a home, as opposed to simply viewing it in its current state. Creating such a personal connection between a product and a buyer will likely have a persuasive influence on sealing the deal, as it gives them a sense of personal customization prior to making the purchase.

A great number of real estate AI application software are programmed in the Python programming language. Different data analysis tools are available in Python libraries for complex data manipulation, mixing and matching of datasets (Kirzhner, 2017). It is important to understand that having large quantities of data means that only some of it is relevant to specific tasks. Python is an object-oriented, semantically structured programming language that is great for scripting programs and connecting other programmable components (Kirzhner, 2017). These characteristics make it a great tool for data analysis in the real estate world, where it is used to find relationships between property features.

16.3 AI-Supported Real Estate Platforms

AI and big data have impacted the way consumers interact with businesses by changing the platform engagement model at the user end. Customer engagement initiatives are "defined as organizational initiatives that facilitate firm–customer interactions to foster emotional or psychological bonds between customers and firms" (Meire et al., 2019). This concept helps platforms become tailored to the preferences of the customer or user which, in turn, makes them use the app more frequently. Personalization allows the app to be fit to the customer preferences, while customization allows the customers to be more engaged with the app by engaging them to make their own content. For example, customer engagement is improved via rapid messaging when customers need help. Now, apps can provide centralized searches, which allow customers to pick the type of housing, location, bedroom or bathroom specifications, and a variety of other features. The end user is important in platform accessibility, particularly as it pertains to different types of platforms such as Android, iOS, and Windows 10 (Interactive Session). This provides easier and more efficient service to customers that are trying to find the right home. Research has shown that "40% of consumers follow their favorite brands on social media [this leaves a] sizable opportunity for firms to leverage … surrounding customer interactions to influence the sentiment of digital engagement" (Meire et al., 2019). Customer engagement is important within a business because it helps companies determine their customers' needs and to make improvements to meet those needs. Over time, businesses can use customer satisfaction data and company feedback to evaluate customers' needs to keep their business functioning and viable for generations to come.

16.3.1 Houzen Real Estate Platform

Houzen company is an example of how artificial intelligence is used by internal agents in the real estate industry in the city of London in the United Kingdom. It is an intelligent platform that works towards matching residential properties with the right tenants within 24 h. Houzen's goal is to change the leasing industry while being careful to avoid turning people into just numbers on a page. Houzen advertises itself as a simple, fast, and safe way for landlords to connect with local expert real estate agents (Mire, 2019).

Houzen works by having the customers first enter their postal code and then expert local agents are determined. Houzen further filters and selects agents based on three criteria: local expertise, professional accreditation, and success history. After the evaluation and selection, the customer speaks with the agents online about particulars and rent. Once expectations have been set, the agents find tenants while the customer watches their progress online. Finally, an offer is made and the customer can choose to accept the new tenant for their property. Artificial intelligence creates an equation based on the dataset as it grows from a single sample to a population. As the data increases, the AI has a greater opportunity to learn from the outcomes of the equation.

As of July 2019, London offered around 150,000 property units, and around one million tenants and buyers searched through these units each month (Mire, 2019). Therefore, Houzen built a data-backed recommendation equation by matching properties with potential tenants and buyers. An interesting observation is that over time the equation has been becoming more accurate due to the influx of data captured for both supply and demand. This results in a higher match quality, which leads to deals being closed faster than previously. While the theory is simple, the execution has proven to be more difficult, which is why this new technology is groundbreaking.

In previous years, it would take a significant amount of time for a landlord to manually find tenants through real estate agents. Companies like Houzen that are using artificial intelligence to revolutionize the real estate industry have made this process more efficient. However, it is important to remember that real estate agents have acquired important skills in socializing with people to provide a more personal touch to individual transactions. Many areas can be improved with AI, but some areas should remain as they are. For example, due to either discomfort or a need for familiarity, many people prefer to speak to a human agent rather than a machine. While the searching capabilities of real estate agents could be replaced with machines, their occupation cannot be entirely replaced. This is because most people prefer to get to know the real estate agent and work with the agent on a more personal level. Chemistry is very important, and it is often favorable to be kind, caring, and social. There is no machine or AI system that will ever replace human interactions. Artificial intelligence can serve as a beneficial asset for real estate agents, but there should not be too many concerns about job losses in the future.

16.3.2 Finding a Home Through NeighborhoodScout

Having a home brings people security and it is a life necessity that realtors are responsible for helping customers find. They can use a variety of platforms and companies that make it easy for customers to find their perfect home. "NeighborhoodScout provides additional information about an area, such as crime rates and school data" (PR Newswire, 2018). NeighborhoodScout displays information on the average house value, local school information, demographic data, crime rates, traffic data, and more. Dr. Andrew Schiller, founder and CEO of NeighborhoodScout, explains, "We've completely transformed the NeighborhoodScout platform." They have expanded on their previous reports and can now indicate crimes more specifically, providing information that includes murder, robbery, assault, burglary, and car theft (PR Newswire, 2017).

Through this platform, NeighborhoodScout is able to provide home buyers with robust data for a monthly subscription. This data allows homeowners to ignore the stereotypes of a particular neighborhood and determine if the property is a good investment. The information offered through the monthly subscription is not available to any other individuals on other applications. Through NeighborhoodScout, homebuyers are presented with conventional big data. The conventional information provided by NeighborhoodScout will be able to provide concrete evidence to support any previous claims or stereotypes individuals might make of a particular community. Through artificial intelligence individuals are able to determine the expected economic property value by viewing the values of houses sold in the area in previous years. The combination of NeighborhoodScout and artificial intelligence enables future homeowners to leverage their current assets and potentially use it to negotiate a better deal with sellers.

16.3.3 Homesnap App

In February 2020, Homesnap released Sell Speed, a proprietary artificial intelligence algorithm, which allows agents to identify potential deals earlier than their competition, amplify their market knowledge, advise sellers on the likelihood to sell and pricing strategy, assist in buyer negotiations, and enhance listing presentations with pricing acumens (PR Newswire, 2020). Sell Speed is available to Homesnap Pro and Homesnap Pro+ users.

Homesnap will also use a predictive algorithm that will leverage artificial intelligence to find patterns and predict properties that might be placed on the market soon. Having Homesnap coordinate with real estate agents through the use of big data enables both partners to identify potential buyers and sellers as soon as they enter the market. This may lead to a quicker turnover time, decreasing the amount of time a property will be on the market.

Case 16.1: Zillow

Innovation is an important part of every company's present and future endeavors. The Zillow Group incorporates innovation in a remarkable way by utilizing a special model. The real estate giant introduced an interesting way to upgrade their Zestimate. The Zillow Prize is an AI competition in which the goal is to gather the best ideas for improving the Zestimate. The Zestimate is Zillow's name for their estimated property value. Since Zillow's launch in 2006, they keep improving the accuracy of the Zestimate. The main idea of the Zillow Prize competition is to improve the machine learning algorithms of the software for predicting home values. Yearly participation is over 3700 teams from about 90 different countries. From its launch in May 2017, the prize grew from one million US dollars to 1.2 million attracting a plethora of participating teams. In 2019, the winning team introduced a software tool that trains convolutional neural networks with photos of properties, learning visual cues of homes, and is able to accurately value their "curb appeal" (Schlosser, 2019). The winning team also had to show the proper machine learning algorithms in action and how it could be implemented as a new and improved tool. Zestimate is compared to real market data for error estimates. It's important to note that buying a home is an emotional decision and the Zestimate will never be 100% accurate.

Zillow is one of the largest names in the online retail housing market and its ability to grow comes from big data. The emergence of corporations like Zillow was spearheaded on the ideas of a new online real estate service providing their customers with a way to view all the homes in their area and explore what is available to fulfill their specific individual needs. Zillow collected \$2.7 billion in revenue in 2019 and \$3.3 billion in 2020 (Zillow Group Annual Report, 2020). Zillow had 36 million users during just the month of October 2021 and continued to shape the real estate market (Fig. 16.1) (Statista, 2021).

When customers sign up and use the online services provided by the company, their website usage data is used for internal and external analysis by the organization. Zillow deals with large data encompassing data creation, data acquisition, info processing, data analytics, and value generation.

One of the largest and most important Zillow datasets is its clickstream data. The clickstream data set is composed of web activity (page requests, actions, user clicks, and others) logged for the millions of Zillow customers and site visitors

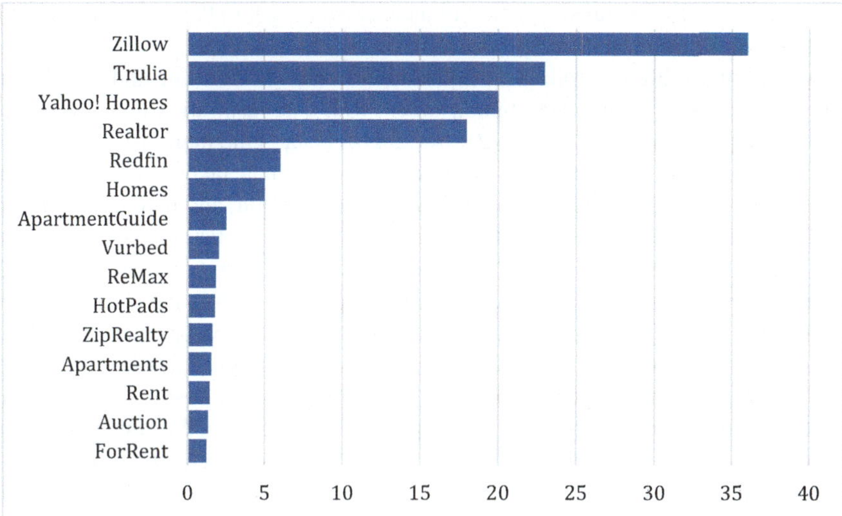

Fig. 16.1 Most popular real estate websites in the United States, based on unique monthly visits, million (October 2021). (Source: Statista, 2021)

(Krishnamurthi, 2018). This data is used in various ways to generate actionable insights, particularly for analysis of user behavior, recommendations, product initiatives, personalization, and machine learning (Krishnamurthi, 2018). External clickstream data is gathered by Zillow through Google Analytics.

Zillow processes several terabytes (TB) of data per day. The company gathers web activity data, produced through Zillow Group web platforms and mobile apps. The source system consists of separate data sets of daily logs from each web platform or mobile application (Krishnamurthi, 2018). Since timely processing of large datasets is crucial for the company dealing with a massive amount of data, in order to meet the demands of the internal stakeholders, Zillow had to go through several iterations and enhancements of their data parsing and processing. The earlier processes included the use of Amazon Redshift for their data warehouse and query platform, addition of multithreading, and introduction of Apache Hadoop. Their fourth version of a data pipeline is making data available in the Data Lake with Spark replacing Hadoop, Elastic MapReduce (EMR) cluster, Apache Airflow, and Amazon Web Service S3 technology (Krishnamurthi, 2018).

Zillow has used a scalable cloud service provider – Amazon Web Services – to help in the storage and processing of large amounts of data since 2015. AWS is used to manage the Zillow Group Data Lake. The image below shows the process that clickstream data goes through in order to reach the data lake.

Raw and available clickstream data is exported into JSON format. The Amazon Elastic Cloud MapReduce cluster is used for data processing and the movement of the raw JSON-formatted data to a Raw Zillow Group Data Lake S3 bucket. Spark is then used on EMR for transformation of data, converting it to Parquet and placing it in the Zillow Group Datalake S3 bucket.

According to Zillow's website, "Zillow is the leading real estate and rental marketplace dedicated to empowering consumers with data inspiration and knowledge around the place they call home" (Zillow, 2020). Data is the main driving force to Zillow's popularity within the real estate industry. Zestimate takes into account public and user-submitted data, as well as home facts, location, and market conditions (Zillow, 2020). The house transactional market data such as listing price, sales history, and tax assessments, as well as physical data (property characteristics), get evaluated for the estimate (Zillow, 2020). As of present, Zillow has data from 110 million US homes and publishes estimates for 95% of those properties. Zillow applies a sophisticated neural network-based model to analyze this big data.

The machine learning technology that Zillow uses for the Zestimate can understand facts and figures such as the listing price of a home as well as the quality and curb appeal of a home (Schlosser, 2019). The algorithm design was inspired by a human brain interpretation of scenes, objects, and images (Schlosser, 2019). Thomas (2019) points out that Zillow reported a median error rate of 2%. Although the median error rate of homes currently listed for sale is 2%, the median error rate for off-market homes is around 7.5% (Zillow, 2020). The accuracy of the Zestimate depends on the amount of data that is available for off-market homes. The more data is available, the more accurate the Zestimate will be (Zillow, 2020).

The Zestimate makes it easy for homebuyers and homeowners to understand the value of their home or potential home at any given time. Zillow's Zestimate is a clear example of how the real estate industry is using artificial intelligence and big data. Zillow gained a competitive advantage leveraging artificial intelligence in home value analysis within the retail housing market.

Case 16.2: Redfin

Redfin is a Seattle-based real estate brokerage company that uses artificial intelligence and big data to help revolutionize the online home-searching process for consumers. Rather than focusing on the needs of sellers, Redfin narrows in on the consumers and what they want in their future homes. Redfin uses AI technologies that assist the buyer in the home-searching process. The company wanted to figure out how to find the best possible homes for their customers taking into account their unique tastes. They managed to accomplish this with the help of machine learning and big data.

Redfin uses AI to augment human real estate agents, off-loading some labor-intensive tasks, and uses AI to automate property recommendations to users who might be interested in real estate and match them with their new future homes. Redfin has increased its average visitors on their website to more than 20 million in 2017, which was 40% more than the prior year (Redfin, 2017; Moubarak, 2018). Machine learning and artificial intelligence allow the company to generate more traffic on its website, while other next-generation technologies (map-based real estate search, cloud computing, streaming technologies) help it to perform computationally intensive home comparisons and customer notifications and increase productivity of their staff (Redfin, 2017). Redfin uses a full-stack approach to address the complete value chain end to end and to control their customer experience with their services (Moubarak, 2018). This full-stack approach has advantages in scalability, flexibility, and holistic thinking.

The company pairs their agents with its technologies embedded in listings-search website, mobile application, and machine learning for listing recommendations. This reduces marketing costs, increases efficiency and productivity of agents, and provides immersive, faster, and better experience for the customers. Redfin constantly evaluates and measures the cost-effectiveness of their digital media marketing channels (search engine optimization [SEO], targeted email campaigns, paid-search advertising, and social media marketing) in order to boost company engagement with customers.

Machine learning is used for Redfin Listing Recommendations, Redfin Estimate, and Redfin Hot Homes (Redfin, 2017). Redfin Listing Recommendations algorithms learn which listings are visited, toured, or bid on by a customer and suggest personalized and better-fitted properties, complete with agent follow-up. Redfin Estimate is a proprietary technology that provides valuation of properties and guides customers in home values and enables marketing teams to target customers for a listing consultation. Redfin Hot Homes proprietary algorithm detects the properties that are most likely to sell quickly and, combined with alerts of on-demand tours and offer deadlines, provides customers with a first-mover advantage in home buying. The company believes in the valuable potential of data science and machine learning to bring customers, gain market insights, and improve competitive advantage in real estate (Redfin, 2017). AI technologies allow Redfin and many other companies to analyze a large amount of data. The higher the quality of the data that is available to Redfin to analyze, the better the outcome. This leads to more accurate predictions of customer needs and home listings. Machine learning allows the technologies that Redfin developed to learn from what customers choose and click on. These machines do not need to be told exactly what to do, which is the beauty of machine learning. Rather, they are constantly learning and adjusting in response to customer behavior! Redfin's approach ties into a popular marketing concept that we have probably all heard variations of at some point in business courses. With AI and big data, the business could understand consumers and what they want better than they even understand themselves and what they are looking for. Let's say you are looking at apartments in downtown Seattle with two bedrooms, wood flooring, and recently updated appliances. When you look at many other real estate websites, you plug in the city or zip code you are interested in seeing listings from. You then choose the attributes you want in the homes you are looking for. Generally, the results you are going to get returned will be exactly what you asked for and nothing more. Redfin changed this by developing an algorithm to help predict what their customers are looking for before they even ask for it. Redfin is able to do this with their algorithm dubbed the "Redfin Matchmaker." Customers get results that they did not even realize they were interested in. Rather than just focusing on what attributes the customers explicitly select, Redfin focuses on the data regarding a person's online activities and behavior. During an interview, Redfin's Chief Technology

Officer, Bridget Frey, was quoted saying "When Redfin recommends a home, customers are four times as likely to click on that house as they are on a home that fits the criteria of their own search" (Frey, n.d.). Buying and renting a new home is a big and often emotional decision, and it helps to have someone there to talk to about it. Redfin's technology exists to assist agents in the services they are able to offer to customers. The interactions between agents and customers make the experience more meaningful and personal.

Case 16.3: Compass Real Estate

Compass, a New York-based real estate technology company, is making its mark on the real estate industry as a forefront of technological innovation. Their advanced set of analytic and marketing technologies help real estate agents with more accurate property pricing, workday optimization, and market timing for property listings (Compass, n.d.). Their app, Compass Real Estate, is a visual workspace that allows agents and clients to collaborate with one another in real time, subsequently offering a more streamlined and user-friendly experience for both parties. In addition to the app, Compass recently announced several new product enhancements to further the potential of their search-and-sell platform. In this case study we will be exploring some of these new additions and discuss how they align with the value-generating aspects of AI implementation within the real estate industry.

The Compass app provides both agents and homebuyers with accurate real-time housing data. Compass launched the Compass Collections app, which serves as a visual real-time collaborative workspace for agents and clients, a dashboard of real estate marketplace with status and price updates, discussions, and organized listings (Compass, n.d.). One of the most intelligent additions to this platform over the past year has been the implementation of AI-powered recommendations. Compass has newly launched the recommendation features "Recommended for You" and "Similar Homes," similar to the technology used in Netflix's algorithmic structure. These features utilize machine learning and artificial intelligence algorithms as a way to deliver the most relevant listings to consumers across the platform. This new element supplements the overall user experience by shortening the search time on the consumer side while simultaneously creating a tailored experience for each individual user by offering them listings that accommodate their wants and needs.

The "Similar Homes" feature displays listings that are similar to the customer's viewed listing in attributes of location, price, bed/bath count, square footage, and other property features. The "Recommended for You" tool, on the other hand, generates recommendations based on the customer's search and viewing history on the site (Compass, n.d.). Compass has created an algorithm that distinguishes features of a home you are looking for (e.g., 2 beds/2 baths) and generates suggestions by comparing data points across thousands of listings on their site.

The added value of these new additions echoes the potential of AI in other areas. Real estate companies and brokerage firms capitalize on the value-generating potential of AI in real estate. An article published by *PR Newswire* quotes Compass' Chief Technology Officer, Joseph Sirosh, who states that "AI and machine learning have revolutionized entire industries and real estate is no exception (PR Newswire,

2019). The Company invests significantly in AI technologies and advancements in these technologies, providing an end-to-end software platform and building predictive technology to empower both consumers and agents" (PR Newswire, 2019).

16.4 Conclusion

AI and big data have made a large contribution to the real estate industry. Advancing the technologies allows realtors to use new AI technologies to analyze big data to determine the cost of a home. It supports realtors to advise and match consumers with real estate listings that fit their criteria most closely. The use of AI technologies and building of straightforward end user platforms gives an opportunity to better analyze consumer behavior and customer needs. While AI and big data have drastically changed the real estate industry, there are many limitations and drawbacks to some of their aspects. Some of those downsides include biases towards types of customers. The computer engineers and system designers might construct the system based on limiting criteria or data, or target a specific type of consumers. This can leave out consumers of certain budget limitations, renting or ownership history, credit scores, or length-of-stay records. Data scientists and programmers need to reevaluate whether their models are inclusive of various customer segments and are not discriminatory to some populations. Other recommendations for AI involvement might include areas of additional advising platforms and better access to virtual tours.

Both big data and artificial intelligence are extremely influential in the real estate industry. We have yet to experience the full effects of their influence, but the potential is immense. The magnitude of possibilities for these technologies are enormous, and it is exciting to see that this industry will be able to harness these possibilities to create a more efficient market and increase its growth. Machine learning allows different web platforms to learn customer needs and tailor results to facilitate the right responses to satisfy their criteria in home-buying. Combing through large datasets, machine learning algorithms present customers with customized listings. The benefits are not just for the customers, but for the stakeholders on the other side of transactions as well: real estate agents, real estate developers, real estate companies, general sellers, investors… the list goes on. Understanding property characteristics, neighborhood factors, what people want, when people will want it, and what the future holds are just a few of the things that these new technologies can help us understand. Understanding patterns in data to answer these questions helps users make better and more informed decisions.

The retail housing market has been completely revolutionized since the addition of new companies using AI in their business. These new technologies will continue to shape how we conduct research and do business in this sector. The prospects that AI yields for the real estate market is exciting; however, there is continuous maintenance, new algorithms, and much improvement that needs to be done before they can efficiently and effectively be used to their fullest potential.

References

Asaftei, G. M., Doshi, S., Means, J., & Sanghvi, A. (2018, October 8). *Getting ahead of the market: How big data is transforming real estate*. McKinsey Insights. https://www.mckinsey.com/industries/capital-projects-and-infrastructure/our-insights/getting-ahead-of-the-market-how-big-data-is-transforming-real-estate

Compass. (n.d.). *The compass foundation. Our technology*. https://www.compass.com/app/agents-compass/technology

Doring, M. (2018, December 07). *Inference vs Prediction*. Retrieved December 06, 2020, from https://www.datascienceblog.net/post/commentary/inference-vs-prediction/

Frey, B. (n.d.). *AI-bridging the human element*. https://www.cioapplications.com/cxoinsights/aibridging-the-human-element-nid-1399.html

Hargrave, M. (2020, November 18). *Using hedonic pricing to determine the factors impacting home prices*. Retrieved December 06, 2020, from https://www.investopedia.com/terms/h/hedonicpricing.asp

Kirzhner, E. (2017, December 18). *Big data applications in real estate analysis*. https://codeburst.io/big-data-applications-in-real-estate-analysis-502accc54dc8

Krishnamurthi, K. (2018, April 6). *Building a big pipeline to process clickstream data*. https://www.zillow.com/tech/pipeline-to-process-clickstream-data/

Makridakis, S. et al. (1982). The accuracy of extrapolation (Time Series) methods: results of a forecasting competition. *Journal of Forecasting*, (1), 111–153.

Meire, M., Hewett, K., Ballings, M., Kumar, V., & Van den Poel, D. (2019). The role of marketer-generated content in customer engagement marketing. In *Journal of marketing* (Vol. 83, Issue 6, pp. 21–42). SAGE. https://doi.org/10.1177/0022242919873903

Mire, S. (2019, July). *AI in Real Estate use case #3: Houzen*. https://www.disruptordAIly.com/AI-in-real-estate-use-case-houzen/

Moubarak, M. (2018, June 4). *Inside Redfin – A Closer Look at how Redfin is using "next-generation" technology to compete*. https://roof.ai/blog/redfin/

Pérez-Rave, J. I., Correa-Morales, J. C., & González-Echavarría, F. (2019). A machine learning approach to big data regression analysis of real estate prices for inferential and predictive purposes. *Journal of Property Research, 36*(1), 59–96.

PR Newswire. (2017, March 2). NeighborhoodScout® launches revolutionary scout vision™ appreciation trends & forecasts in its all-new platform, offering dramatically enhanced analysis for real estate decision-making. *PR Newswire US*.

PR Newswire. (2018, February 12). Neighborhood scout® reveals the top 100 safest cities in the U.S. for 2018. *PR Newswire US*.

PR Newswire. (2019, October 9). Compass launches new consumer experience, AI capabilities. *PR Newswire US*. https://www.prnewswire.com/news-releases/compass-launches-new-consumer-experience-ai-capabilities-300934558.html

PR Newswire. (2020, October 26). Homesnap introduces sell speed tool for real estate agents. *PR Newswire US*.

Redfin. (2017). *Annual report*. https://investors.redfin.com/static-files/1eb74f28-960e-44a1-b13e-7163443b80a2

Rossini, P. (2000, January). *Using expert systems and artificial intelligence for real estate forecasting*.

Sanders, A. (2020). *The impact of big data and AI on real estate*. Retrieved from https://tweakyourbiz.com/business/marketing-strategy/real-estate-data

Schlosser, K. (2019, June 27). *Zillow launches retooled Zestimate that uses AI to analyze photographs and 'see' value in homes*. Retrieved December 06, 2020, from https://www.geekwire.com/2019/zillow-launches-retooled-zestimate-uses-AI-analyze-photographs-see-value-homes/

Statista. (2021). *Most popular real estate websites in the United States as of October 2021, based on unique monthly visits*. https://www.statista.com/statistics/381468/most-popular-real-estate-websites-by-monthly-visits-usa/

Thomas, D. (2019, July 1). *Zillow uses AI to hone its Zestimate tool.* Retrieved December 06, 2020, from https://www.bizjournals.com/bizwomen/news/latest-news/2019/07/zillow uses-AI-to-hone-its-zestimate-tool.html?page=all

Winson-Geideman, K., & Krause, A. (2016, January). Transformations in real estate research: the Big Data Revolution. In *Proceedings of the 22nd Annual Pacific-Rim Real Estate Society Conference, Queensland, Australia* (pp. 17-20). http://www.prres.net/papers/Geideman_Transformations_in_RE_Research.pdf

Zillow. (2020). *What is a Zestimate? Zillow's Zestimate Accuracy*. Retrieved December 06, 2020, from https://www.zillow.com/zestimate/

Artificial Intelligence in Education 17

Abstract

This chapter highlights the implementation of AI technologies in education with particular interest in personalization of educational ecosystems, development of online learning, and adaptive learning. The chapter explores evolution of AI in education and application of AI in online learning platforms. Features of AI in education include learning personalization, teaching personalization, effectiveness, smart content, and big data-driven system implementation. Case analyses comprise Realizeit, Nuance, and Civitas.

Keywords

Education · Personalization · Educational ecosystem · Online learning · Data mining · Natural language processing · Robotics · Learning platforms · Student success intelligence platform · Learning assistant · Adaptive learning platform · Audio processing · Virtual backgrounds · Video compression · AI assistant · Cloud-based technology · Teaching customization · Machine learning · Smart content · Big data · Learning management system · Virtual assistant · Just-in-time systems · Intelligent learning systems

17.1 Introduction

The implementation of artificial intelligence (AI) technology in multiple industries has proven to be beneficial to those who have incorporated it into their everyday use. Among said industries, education is one of the most significant and challenging fields that influences generational career prospects. Due to the historic nature of education, there is a large reservoir of information that AI and machine learning can use to benefit the academic atmosphere. AI has already been used to create tools that help students develop essential skills and facilitate academic testing systems.

L. Chan et al., *Applied Artificial Intelligence in Business*, Applied Innovation and Technology Management, https://doi.org/10.1007/978-3-031-05740-3_17

It fosters efficiency and personalization in the educational ecosystem, which in turn provides teachers the flexibility to develop an understanding and adapt according to their students' needs. Artificial intelligence introduces a customized experience among diverse learning groups, teachers, and tutors. In general, machines struggle with uniquely human capabilities, although advancing AI technology is capable of transforming the way we teach and learn (Plitnichenko, 2020).

In educational assistance, AI can open a new avenue to personalized development for students who require additional help to succeed. Businesses that are trying to help the way students are taught and improve the education system can heavily benefit from this pursuit. A significant area of assistance for AI to target is the ability to level the playing field for students that may be disadvantaged in the current educational system. It is no surprise that everyone learns at a unique pace and faces different challenges along their academic journey. AI can help by accommodating those who may need a different style of learning to retain necessary information. The overall learning experience for a student can be modified upon recognizing patterns of behavior and identifying weak areas that impair their ability to improve. The data gathered from these learning programs can provide valuable information to both the student and the teacher, giving an opportunity to adjust their educational plans accordingly. In this chapter, we will be exploring the applications of AI in education by analyzing the available platforms and identifying the many possibilities it has to offer.

17.2 Evolution of AI in Education

While artificial intelligence (AI) platforms have not existed for as long, educators and students have been using computers and the World Wide Web to accomplish massive advances in research faster and communicate more effectively. Over time, AI has gradually extended itself into education, gathering relevant information on a wide array of students' learning capabilities. To truly appreciate the degree at which computational technology has grown, one must learn about the initial introduction in the twentieth century, the accelerated evolution in the twenty-first century, and the subsequent expansion in the present day.

Over the years, technology has been accelerating in advancement, meaning the timeline for breakthroughs became shorter with each passing decade. In 1983, the Apple Lisa, an abbreviation of "Local Integrated Software Architecture," became the first personal computer with a graphical user interface (GUI). This was a monumental milestone that allowed users to interact with their electronic devices using visual components and graphical icons. During the same year, the Gavilan SC was released, and it became the first portable computer featuring the same laptop design we use today. After the establishment of the graphical user interface and an increase in consumer interest, the Apple Macintosh was announced to the world in a 1984 Super Bowl commercial. Around this same time period, several other companies were racing to release their own personal computer operating systems and hardware. In 1985, Microsoft released Windows, providing another user interface for people to use on their personal computers that is still popular today. While the capability of compiling and analyzing data using computational devices improved, there were limitations to communication that made a barrier to their use in education. It was not until 1989, when Tim Berners-Lee submitted his proposal for what became the World Wide Web, that communication entered the stage. Since the invention of the World Wide Web, the Google search engine and Wi-Fi were created before entering the twenty-first century (Williamson, 2021). At that point, educators and students had already begun adopting the technology for research and developing learning platforms.

In general, an AI machine can perceive, recognize, and react accordingly, which is meant to simulate human intelligence. In the twenty-first century, a significant amount of AI research in education has been done to provide educators with up-to-date knowledge on the rapid changes occurring in the field. Additional digital resources have generated and expanded online learning platforms. To put that evolution into perspective, K-12 USA students registering for online courses grew by 3 million between the years 2008 and 2011 (Woolf, 2015). Cloud computing provides a means of communication for students and instructors, allowing teachers to check in on progress and overall well-being. Google Docs is an excellent example that is currently a popular method of collaborative work among students and professionals worldwide. It tracks the contributions of the people working on a given project and teachers can evaluate the progress their students are making. This form of data mining is allowing efficient performance feedback and can distinguish which students are struggling or excelling in specific topics. From there, the teacher can either incorporate more challenging work or spend more time with a struggling student. This way, students can either avoid boredom with more mental stimulation or catch up with the rest of the class.

In the most recent years, machine learning algorithms are being used in developing practical software for computer vision, speech recognition, natural language processing, robot control, and other applications. In the past, processing speed was a primary limitation to the acquisition of AI and machine learning. Now, processing speed has reached the point where machine learning can take in large quantities of information that humans would not be able to accomplish on their own. Learning data is extremely useful in aspects such as machine learning and AI so that we can make applications that are more accurate, personalized, and overall, more beneficial for learners. For example, educational robotics provides students with a learning environment that has the potential to successfully integrate concepts within science, technology, engineering, and mathematics (STEM) into learning environments in class, after school, or for robotics competitions. Educational technology (EdTech) has since been developing rapidly with the influx of available information in the twenty-first century.

17.3 Applications of AI in Learning Platforms

There are a variety of ways artificial intelligence (AI) can help students learn and give companies a competitive edge in the education industry. Some AI programs help students by focusing on their learning strengths and weaknesses, while others have one-on-one tutoring with AI tutors that eliminate the need for human tutors that may or may not be completely knowledgeable on a subject.

Applications of AI in education can be divided into online learning platforms and standalone software packages on users' digital devices. The learning platforms usually collect and analyze the data from users through the Internet or computer networks. Users log into the web portals through registration, participate in learning activities, and can save previous learning content through the background. Through the learning platforms, learners can not only watch video courses but also can carry out human-machine dialogue, testing, and other learning content. Learning platforms are more popular than standalone software because of increased network bandwidth and telecommunication speed. In Table 17.1 below, we focus on exploring some of these AI-supported learning platforms:

Naviance is a, "college and beyond," planning software used by many school districts around the United States. It integrates a variety of metrics and data points to help project possible careers based on a multitude of measures. Naviance was uniquely useful because it included grades, courses, and instructors for the user to navigate. Analytical processing is the backbone of their software, and it is feasible to see that their use of AI could provide students with a multitude of options that could fit their interests.

Civitas Learning is a student success platform that integrates AI at the university level. Their goal is to use "predictive analytics to guide student engagement, advising workflows, course evaluation, and institutional management" ("Harnessing the power", 2019). Civitas uses a Student Success Intelligence Platform (SSIP) to collect information on student data to be used for student support systems and create an interactive cycle of learning. It can be used by individual students but works best using its integrated platform at the university level. Their integrated platform

Table 17.1 Learning platforms

Learning platform	Website	User	Category	Purpose
LinkedIn Learning	www.linkedin.com/learning	Adult	Higher education	Professional education
Best College Review	www.bestcollegereviews.org	Students	Higher education	Decision-making in education, ranking
Common Sense	www.commonsensemedia.org	Children	Family	Education access
Netex Learning	www.netexlearning.com	Adult	Personal	Educational technology
Carnegie	www.carnegielearning.com	All age	Personal and business	K-12 solutions

includes a campus scheduler and a portal to campus resources, and it can be used to make strategic decisions with its insights function. Their software uses thousands of data points to give advisors the edge in career planning and future planning for their advisees. Texas State University uses the platform for automated scheduling and planning for a more effective registration process for students, as well as better course availability and future demand planning ("Scaling New Student", n.d.).

Quizlet is an online learning platform that uses AI. The company launched the Quizlet Learning Assistant which, "combines machine learning technology and learning science principles to create study experiences that adapt to each learner for better recall and deeper understanding" (Quizlet, 2020). This new adaptation creates a more personalized study path and progress insights and brings in smart grading, helping students reach their learning goals quicker and with more success. The learning assistant is especially useful during the pandemic times since there is less in-person interaction, which impacts a personalized learning experience. Quizlet focuses on a personalized study path, based on a short diagnostic, and adapts this path to the correct challenge level for each learner. Other features of the learning assistant include smart grading and progress dashboard. Smart grading is based on harnessing natural language processing technology to interpret and evaluate the meaning of student answers, while a progress dashboard presents a full view of their learning activities, mastery of the course, and insights for improvement (Quizlet, 2020).

Cognii is a company based out of Boston, Massachusetts and was established in 2013. It is an AI in the field of online and scalable personalized education and corporate training powered by AI technology (Cognii, 2021). Cognii has won several awards for their groundbreaking technology in education. They use AI for both education and corporate training; thus, their products are applicable to both adults and students at all levels. Cognii is unique and has different ways of helping students and educators in teaching. Their main product is called Conversational EdTech, which is their virtual learning assistant that employs conversational technology to lead students in discussion and improve critical-thinking skills. The virtual assistant is essentially a tutor that can respond with timely feedback, providing rich learning analytics, and can be customized to each person's needs. Cognii virtual learning assistant is an intelligent tutoring system that uses natural language processing algorithms, which analyze syntax, semantics, and hierarchical structures of students' questions and answers (Fig. 17.1).

Knewton is a company that uses AI to enhance student knowledge and fill gaps in learning. They created an adaptive learning platform for higher education through a program called Alta. They identified gaps in a student's knowledge to then provide relevant coursework for the student to make sure they are on track for college-level courses (Knewton, n.d.). Knewton focuses on STEM (science, technology, engineering, and mathematics) courses in particular. The program is currently being used for math, chemistry, statistics, and economics. Knewton's new product Alta provides personalized learning experience through adaptive learning technology (Fig. 17.2). Three pillars of this technology are depicted in the figure below. Their

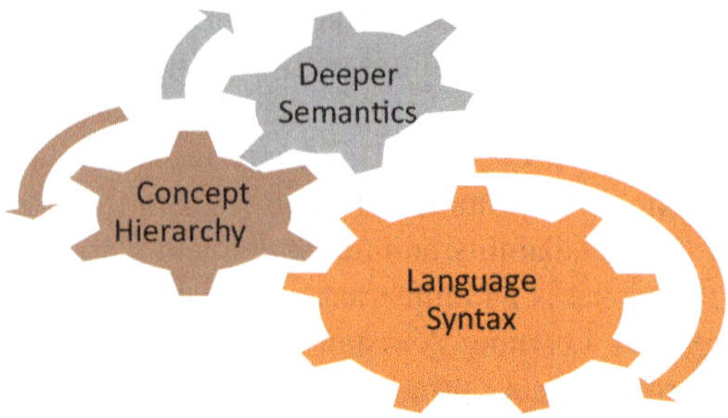

Fig. 17.1 Natural language processing compounds

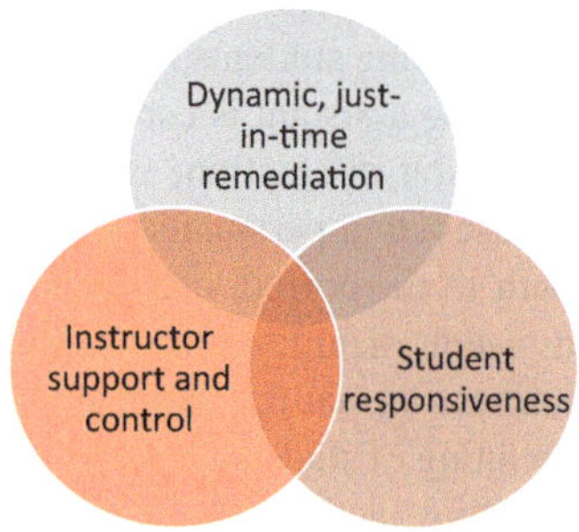

Fig. 17.2 Adaptive learning technology for Alta from Knewton

focus is on accessibility and affordability of this technology as well as adaptability and dynamic remediation in recognition of knowledge gaps.

Another company that uses AI in the education industry is Knowre. The company is located in New York. It developed a personalized math learning program that helps identify any gaps in student learning. Knowre employs Knowre Success Score (KSS) that analyzes student performance and measures student achievement as a function of student utilized support, and the Teacher Dashboard allows data management across curriculum, classroom, and student. Knowre is able to customize the curriculum for each student using their unique machine learning algorithm. The personalized Walk Me Through support collects data or learning gaps of an individual student for personalized math instruction and lesson support. This technology also provides engaging feedback graphics that help keep the student focused, interested, and supported. The platform is also easy to use for instructors and students with personalized math instruction and immediate intervention and support. Knowre also shares the data with teachers to help inform them which students may require more attention.

Carnegie Learning is also a well-known company that built its software to help students and teachers in the fields of math, literacy, and world languages. Their solutions provide new creative lesson plans and textbooks with collaborative, blended, and personalized learning. MATHia is an intelligent math software, providing real-time feedback and assessments for students as well as insightful data and individual student support. The learning is set up to be deeper and conceptual through the combination of cognitive and learning science, research, and practical instruction. This learning is engaging students in real-world examples, encouraging collaboration, and developing one-on-one support and group activities, as well as providing formative assessments with learning adjustments to accommodate the needs of the students. MATHia maintains a student's day-to-day progress, growth, and future predictions of where they would stand at the end of the year. They also created a live facilitation tool, LiveLab, that was named "Best Use of Artificial Intelligence in Education" in the 2019 EdTech Breakthrough Awards. LiveLab alerts teachers when their students may be in need of further assistance or have reached milestone objectives. The tool primarily lets teachers examine and manage the student performance in MATHia.

Zoom is an online audio and web conferencing platform. Since the Covid-19 pandemic, many schools have been relying on Zoom for online teaching since meeting in person was not safe. Artificial intelligence is at the core of the Zoom platform (Fig. 17.3). With its cloud-based technology, optimized connections, audio transfer, and video compression, Zoom also uses AI to augment the experience and user interaction and provide additional features for its users (Bresler, 2021).

Most learning platforms introduced above are expanding their product and solution offerings and will grow as the market for AI in education continues to evolve. We will see some of these products gain more traction in future education and it should improve learning experiences for all learners.

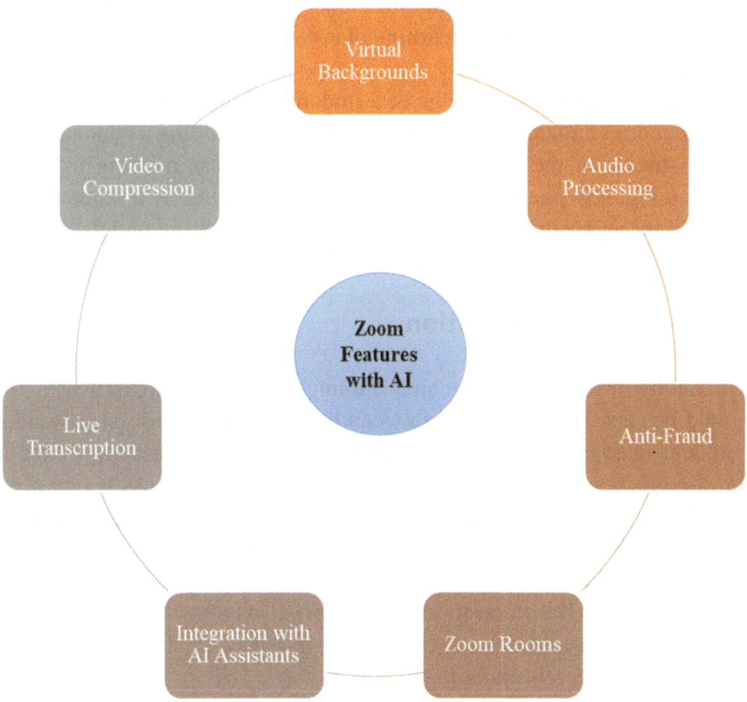

Fig. 17.3 AI aspects in Zoom

17.4 Features of AI in Education

No matter how reasonable the teacher-student ratio is in the school, it is difficult for the teacher to make an objective analysis of every student's problems and make a targeted learning plan suitable for every student. AI technology could aid teachers in school in creating a more personalized approach to learning. With AI aiding in the background, the teacher can preview the content before class and the reviewed content after class is sent to AI. Students can consolidate the learning content through AI and predict the new learning content in advance. Through feedback, the teacher adjusts the lecture content to effectively improve the students' learning effect in class. AI can also complete tasks assigned by teachers in other ways. For example, students could use the chat program of AI as an additional support, when the teacher is not available or before an actual dialog or conference with the teacher. The AI can extract effective information through the dialogue content and quickly gives feedback to the teacher.

17.4.1 Learning Personalization

AI may not only help abled students with their study but also helps disabled students with their needs. Independent use of the system can also ensure the independence of students' learning. AI can store and analyze the learning process of a student. Students can adjust their learning plans at any time according to their learning situation.

AI helps figure out the knowledge of a student and the gaps. It helps track down what a student does and does not know. AI can help in building a personalized study schedule to focus on the gaps in learning and the areas needing improvement. Artificial intelligence platforms can be tailored according to a student's specific needs, which increases the student's efficiency in learning and understanding.

17.4.2 Teaching Customization

Artificial intelligence (AI) and machine learning (ML) help with improving the education field because teaching programs can be customizable for each student. Not every student learns the same way as another or has the same knowledge as one another; therefore, customization will make the learning process better, since students can learn at their own pace without being stressed that they are behind, or ahead, of their classmates. It is easier to notice any trends of what students may need to learn about more and also which teaching methods can work best for any particular student or group. Based on the feedback of AI on students' learning situation both inside and outside the school, educators will have a relatively objective understanding of students' performance.

17.4.3 Effectiveness

Compared with traditional education, the efficiency of learning using AI education technologies can be greatly improved. With the aid of AI, information between educators and students can be exchanged. AI will collect data from both sides and effectively propose new plans for the next step of learning. In this process, the educator will also need to update the knowledge structure and improve the teaching skills. We can even speculate that, with the deepening of AI into the teaching process, the time for students to receive education in school may be shortened due to the high efficiency of education. Due to the limited time or resources, the teacher cannot make an overall and individual evaluation of each homework. AI may aid in checking homework and might help in conserving time and minimizing the error rate. AI-based educational applications can help educators to guide students both inside and outside the school.

17.4.4 Smart Contents

From grade school to college, AI can apply digital textbooks and personal customization learning digital interfaces to students. The smart content platform allows teachers to formulate a curriculum according to subject outline and teaching purpose. Curriculum comes in many forms, including audios, videos, and even an online assistant. AI is also reflected in the dialogue and interaction with students. The virtual assistant with AI technology may not only offer educational support but also give personalized feedback. In science and technology, AI can stimulate learners' interest and satisfy their curiosity, cultivate habits and hands-on ability, and promote the comprehensive development of learners.

17.4.5 Big Data Driven

Big data is making a huge impact on the educational world. Big data has greatly promoted the education development of AI. There are systems being implemented to collect information on all students, including their test scores, strengths, and weaknesses, as well as suggestions for teachers. Big data allows for instant communication between teachers, students, parents, and staff. Schools generate a massive amount of data, effective use of which can promote pedagogical goals and change patterns of educational management (Blau & Presser, 2013). Student academic achievement is positively related to continuous monitoring of achievement and instruction since monitoring ensures that specific educational goals remain the driving force behind a school's actions (Waters & Marzano, 2009).

Case 17.1: Realizeit
Realizeit is an adaptive learning platform that provides solutions to enhance the learning experience through curriculum development. Realizeit was invented by

instructors and researchers with the intent and belief that every student can realize their full potential if they are given the right tools to do so. Their platform serves K-12, higher education institutions, and corporate learning. They work with the faculty to provide a unique learning path for students and easy integration with any learning management systems. This platform specifically features embedded analytics that constantly measure, calculate, and collect teaching- and learning-related data. With that data, there are analytical dashboards that provide real-time reports and trends to gauge the students' progress and also the educators' teaching and content effectiveness.

What Realizeit specializes in is creating a seemingly one-on-one learning experience. It has a system that is constantly learning and adapting to what the needs of the individual student. Using all the current and building up data, the platform is able to understand the knowledge and ability of each student and then is able to create and shape a unique learning map for each student. This in turn reduces the amount of "busy work" because the work that gets assigned will be work that the student is struggling with or will struggle with. The optimized pathway will allow students who understand to progress faster through material because they will not have to review information that they already know.

Case 17.2: Nuance

Nuance is a computer software technology company that provides speech recognition and artificial intelligence to support not only the education sector but financial services, law enforcement, healthcare services, and many others. Nuance implements an AI-powered software called Dragon Speech Recognition. In the classroom, this means students and teachers can freely express themselves. Teachers are able to prepare lesson plans faster and easier as well as present more detailed feedback for students with just the sound of their voice. Dragon is targeted towards students that struggle with writing and those who are slow at typing and take longer because they have a hard time with spelling. These students are able to speak effortlessly without losing their thought process while Dragon transcribes for them up to 160 words per minute and gives them supportive feedback when needed. While working on their essays, students can use voice recognition to search the Internet for questions. Dragon can also help with communication between students and teachers by sending emails entirely by voice. Overall, Nuance puts artificial intelligence to great use in assisting students through an area where most would find challenging things like writing. Landmark College integrated this software to help students with learning disabilities to help them achieve academic success. Studies have shown that voice recognition promotes improved spelling and word recognition when students watch the words they speak get transcribed, word by word, on a computer screen. Other research also validates that technology is useful in increasing writing ease and fluency, including Landmark College, which has used Dragon's software as a teaching tool to help students with learning disabilities.

Case 17.3: Civitas

Another company that uses AI and big data to benefit education is Civitas. Civitas Learning is a learning platform that works with over 400 colleges and universities and reaches over 8 million students by providing them with a "scalable, transparent platform." The software gives "comprehensive insight about students, activities and programs." This supports strategic planning and day-to-day student success work. It also allows advisors to access data which allows them to more actively manage their students (progress and caseloads). They impact students with academic, career, and life trajectories. One of their many features is a dashboard that allows schools to access the impact analyses of any student success initiative at their institution. Being able to track what is allowing students to be more successful in the classroom allows for professors and school administrators to implement and stick with these tools and ways of learning which leads to a higher graduation rate. One of the many schools that benefited from this software is Florida Atlantic University. After using the Civitas Learning software, they saw an 18% boost in their 4-year graduation rate. Florida Atlantic University also ended up being ranked at the very top of the performance funding model after only 2 years of using Civitas.

Data is created within different software like Nuance and Civitas by using different assessments within their software for students to test their ability in the different segments of education. Another way data is created is by having teachers and students input data through the different applications within the software. This data is stored in an institution's student information system and a learning management system. This kind of software has insight analytics infrastructures for data collections and predictions. These predictors are for distinct segments, which are feature and point variables contributing significantly to the success or challenge of the given segment (Civitas Learning).

17.5 Key Takeaways

AI's involvement in education is more of an up-and-coming process. While there are not too many companies that are implementing AI in classrooms, there are some that are using it to allow students a better learning experience as well as aid.

17.5.1 Impacts on Learning Style

With the aid of artificial intelligence, students can learn activities anytime and anywhere. Education is no longer limited by place and time to study. Learners can freely arrange learning activities. For elementary school students, parents can keep synchronized learning with the help of an artificial intelligence approach.

17.5.2 Impacts on Teachers

AI brings teachers not only advanced technology but also challenges traditional ways of teaching. Teachers should adapt to changes in the era of AI and receive the training needed for education activities anytime and anywhere. For certain courses, educators can acquire the required knowledge and content at any time through AI. Artificial intelligence technologies may help educators deal with diverse student populations, their specific learning needs, and aspirations. A teacher's professional development is a never-ending process; the teacher must adapt to the development trend of new technologies. Teachers are no longer merely imparting knowledge, but also meeting the individual needs of students in this new information technology era with the growth and implementation of customized learning solutions.

17.5.3 Impact on Business

The potential for business impacts is large. Just looking at the education system today, we do not see many changes in the teaching style. We cannot deny that there have been technological advances in the education sector such as improvements from blackboards to smartboards. However, the overall system is still the same where usually one teacher is overloaded with around 30 students in one classroom and lectures in front of the board. Teachers alone do not have the time to be able to check up on every single student to pinpoint their struggles and needs. AI can revolutionize how students get help. The applications of machine learning will know what areas the student needs help on and what parts they understand to create a new lesson that is not repetitive but instead adheres to their needs. The data can also show the teacher which concepts students struggle with, so they can plan their lessons accordingly. This makes large classrooms more manageable and allows the teacher to easily understand the progress of all the students.

The areas of education that can benefit the most from these machine learning programs would be schools and classes that have a high student-teacher ratio. This assistance for the teachers would be greatly utilized in the future. Then the next area of help would be for classes and programs for students that need extra help and accommodations. There would be programs that would seamlessly bring these students of need up to speed with their peers by having specialized assistance with the parts of education that they are struggling with. Applications of AI technologies in the educational system would focus more on new and needed learning. This would allow students who need a little extra help to catch up as well as students who are ahead to excel. AI could enable more services for students with better intelligent tutoring systems as well as 24/7 assistance for schoolwork.

17.6 Conclusion

AI technology and big data are evolving every day, which is creating an opportunity for the educational world to grow. With these advances, both educators and students mutually benefit from the new capabilities the technologies have to offer. The collection of data and information brings a new insight into tracking student growth and comparing it over the course of time. Overall, big data and technology will only increase and improve the world of education.

When it comes to using AI in the education world, there is a realization of how the technology can enhance the learning process and effectiveness. As the world is changing, we believe it is important for education to change as well. And we are seeing that now, with the use of AI, companies and universities are able to implement new strategies to keep students engaged and learning in a more focused, tailored, and personalized system. Further case studies have shown that AI is here to stay in education as these studies have proven that there are many benefits to technology integration in education.

Along with the 5G technology, Internet of Things, cloud computing, big data, and AI, more intelligent learning platforms are emerging. With the support of AI, the way students receive education has become increasingly diversified. Students can be motivated to learn more after class with additional AI-enabled feedback and adoption learning mechanisms.

There are several major AI-enabled applications in the areas of personalized learning and virtual assistants, tailored just-in-time systems that are succeeding in aiding educators and breaking barriers. Artificial intelligence is our future; it is so important for educators of today to learn about these technologies and really understand how to apply them to better their teaching. Although the presence of our teachers and professors is irreplaceable, AI and machine learning have come a long way to help them where they struggle most. Artificial intelligence is making learning more accessible and personalized for each individual student. Many educational companies have used AI to provide extra assistance, including voice support to communicate with students when their teachers are not around. Online learning with AI-enabling technologies breaks learning barriers and gives accessibility to education for students all over the world who may have learning disabilities, language differences, or illnesses, as well as anyone who cannot make it to the classroom, especially during times like COVID-19.

AI and big data allow the creation of learning management systems, personalized courses for students, and career path assistance along with many other advancements. Artificial intelligence uses big data to understand students and teachers in a way that supports their weaknesses and celebrates their strengths. This is especially important during various crisis situations such as the COVID-19 pandemic, where much of student interactions are limited, and most learning is done online.

Educational reform caused by intelligent learning systems is deepening, and significant changes have taken place in every aspect of teaching activities. In the near future, natural language processing, knowledge management systems, chatbots, big data, cloud computing, and deep learning will be more widely used in education and will have profound impacts on teaching modality, educational management, and talent training approaches. Future education not only calls for technological innovation, but also requires universities to constantly explore new business models of training and educational services.

References

Blau, I., & Presser, O. (2013). e-Leadership of school principals: Increasing school effectiveness by a school data management system. *British Journal of Educational Technology, 44*(6), 1000–1011.

Bresler, T. (2021, April 23). *How Zoom leverages AI to provide the best video conferencing experience.* Retrieved from https://digital.hbs.edu/platform-digit/submission/how-zoom-leverages-ai-to-provide-the-best-videoconferencing-experience/

Cognii. (2021). *Cognii – Artificial intelligence for education and training*. Retrieved from https://www.cognii.com/

Cognii Virtual Learning Assistant. (2021). Retrieved from https://www.cognii.com/technology.

Harnessing the power of data in the field of education: Civitas Learning. (2019, October). *The Silicon Review*. Retrieved from https://thesiliconreview.com/magazine/profile/harnessing-the-power-of-data-in-the-field-of-education-civitas-learning

Knewton, A. W. B. (n.d.). *Alta's adaptive learning technology*. Retrieved from https://www.knewton.com/the-power-of-altas-adaptive-technology/

Plitnichenko, L. (2020, May 30). *5 main roles of Artificial intelligence in education*. Retrieved from https://elearningindustry.com/5-main-roles-artificial-intelligence-in-education

Quizlet. (2020, September 9). *Quizlet introduces new AI-powered learning assistant to streamline studying*. Retrieved from https://www.prnewswire.com/news-releases/quizlet-introduces-new-ai-powered-learning-assistant-to-streamline-studying-301126669.html

Scaling New Student Registration to Personalize Academic & Career Guidance. Learning Brief. Texas State University. (n.d.). Retrieved from https://media.civitaslearning.com/wp-content/uploads/sites/3/2020/02/Texas_State_University_Learning_Brief-1.pdf

Waters, J. T., & Marzano, R. J. (2009). Works: The effect of superintendent leadership on student achievement. *Educational Leadership and Administration, 2*, 131.

Williamson, T. (2021). *History of computers: A brief timeline. Live science*. Future US Inc.

Woolf, B. (2015). AI and education: Celebrating 30 years of marriage. *AIED 2015 Workshop Proceedings, 4*.

Artificial Intelligence in Healthcare

18

Abstract

This chapter explores the AI technologies in healthcare. We start with emphasis on a backward-chaining expert system MYCIN and IBM Watson for Oncology cognitive technology-incorporating and AI-integrating project. Then we describe the current AI technologies in healthcare like machine learning, artificial neural networks, computer vision, human unstructured natural language processing, and others. AI applications in healthcare like virtual nursing assistants, robot-assisted surgery, fraud detection, dosage error reduction, connected machines and clinical trial participant identifiers, diagnosis applications, and wearable tech are explored. Case studies include COTA Health, Babylon, and wearable technologies supporting AI in healthcare.

Keywords

Electronic health records · Medical chatbots · Virtual nurses · Robotic surgery · Robot-assisted surgery · Backward-chaining expert system · Data mining · Healthcare management · Natural language processing · Feedback tracking · Evidence-based treatment options · Machine learning · Artificial neural networks · Computer vision · Smart devices · Wearable technologies · Diagnostic applications · Research applications · Quality-of-life applications · Personalized exercise programs · Virtual nursing assistants · Connected machines · Dosage error reduction · Precision analytics · Deep learning · Remote monitoring

18.1 Introduction

Artificial intelligence is an up-and-coming technology that is being applied through all sectors all over the world. One of the most fascinating applications of artificial intelligence is in the field of healthcare. In the healthcare industry, people need

L. Chan et al., *Applied Artificial Intelligence in Business*, Applied Innovation and Technology Management, https://doi.org/10.1007/978-3-031-05740-3_18

accurate results quickly and any delays in urgent care or resources required could cause a problem to become much worse. We are now seeing AI implemented into healthcare in many areas. There have been advances in everything from electronic health records, decision-making tools in healthcare, and online medical chatbots in the form of virtual nurses to cancer diagnostics and treatment plans, to robotic surgery, and everything in between (Mudavadi et al., 2016). The use of AI in healthcare could help pave the way to a healthier world. Advances in disease cures, noninvasive surgeries, and the solutions to many problems doctors and healthcare experts have been searching for are beginning to be answered by AI. It is the future of the industry.

18.2 Evolution of AI in Healthcare

One of the first utilizations of AI in healthcare was a backward-chaining expert system MYCIN, created in the early 1970s at Stanford University to identify bacteria that causes life-threatening infections and blood clotting diseases, and recommend a weight-based dosage of antibiotics. MYCIN had a knowledge base of a large number of rules and an inference engine, querying a physician with a series of text-based and yes/no questions and providing with a probable diagnosis, reasoning of it, and recommended drug treatment options (Shortliffe, 1976). While in experiments MYCIN had a 65% success rate for correct medication prescriptions, it was never used in a routine clinical setting due to poor acceptance among physicians and its inability to recognize its own limitations (Coats, 1988). Nowadays, expert systems such as these are becoming prominent in the healthcare field. Today most of the research for AI and healthcare surrounds the oncology domain. The incorporation of AI in oncology, the study of cancer, could be imperative in discovering new treatment options and even cures. These AI technologies are able to look at data from research studies, academic journals, doctors, and field experts to form billions of usable data points. Every time a patient is diagnosed, AI can look at X-rays, CT scans, blood work, and patient health history to gain full knowledge of the patient's health and condition. AI in healthcare could also be a part of data mining applications focused on the evaluation of treatment effectiveness, customer relationships in healthcare, detection of fraud and abuse, and healthcare management (development of better diagnosis and treatment protocols, identification and management of chronic disease and high-risk patients, reduction in the number of hospital admissions, and decrease in patient length of stay (Koh & Tan, 2011)). The use of AI (e.g., IBM Watson for Oncology) has the potential in the improvement of cancer care to patients (Muhsen et al., 2018). AI systems can aid doctors with the set of applicable treatment options and possible treatment outcomes of similar cases. While researchers indicate that integration of AI into medicine is inevitable, it should be done cautiously, well-validated, and focused on the improvement of patient care (Muhsen et al., 2018).

IBM Watson for Oncology is one of the leading AI-integrating projects in healthcare. It incorporates cognitive technology similar to human unstructured natural language processing and feedback tracking and learning. Watson for Oncology combines expertise of leading oncologists in cancer care with the speed of IBM Watson to help clinicians decide on individualized cancer treatments for their patients. Watson has been trained to compare patient's medical data against treatment guidelines, patient's medical record and genetic data, as well as published research for selection of the best evidence-based treatment options (Doyle-Lindrud, 2015). The system integrates both the healthcare provider and health insurance, which allows fast processing and approval times and ability to standardize care. When oncologists input a question into the system, Watson presents them with a list of hypotheses with the ranking numbers and confidence levels aiding the doctors in identification of the most appropriate treatment options (Doyle-Lindrud, 2015).

The accuracy of AI technology applications similar to Watson depends on the amount of good-quality data of applied treatments and outcomes and other important care information in the field, gathered and available for learning by those systems.

18.3 Current AI Technologies in Healthcare

The research surrounding AI in healthcare is growing and there have already been many groundbreaking technological advances in the healthcare field. One of the pioneering implementations of AI in the healthcare field has been in robotic surgery. The AI components reduce tremors in the robot, providing a possibility for a less invasive surgery. AI-enabled technologies also help surgeons perform surgeries. The combination of the four main AI subfields (machine learning, artificial neural networks, natural language processing, and computer vision) and their synergy, when utilized correctly, has a potential to accelerate the capabilities of AI in augmented surgical care and empower surgeons to improve the quality of care (Hashimoto et al., 2018). Another popular AI utilization is in administrative healthcare. Collection of patient health history and demographic information, along with current health data and visit information, allows the AI technology to assist patients in scheduling and informing the doctor on the urgency of care needed by the patient. These technologies have already changed the way we look at healthcare and will be continually advanced and improved.

Newly introduced healthcare devices allow fast and convenient monitoring of valuable data like glucose levels, blood pressure, cholesterol levels, and heart rate. Now patients can receive medicine reminders, appointment reminders, and information on their next visit on their smart devices. Patients no longer have to stand in long queues or make numerous phone calls to set up an appointment with the doctor. Online consultations have gained popularity due to streamlined implementation of healthcare technologies. Big data analytics has changed the way we manage, analyze, and leverage data in any industry. Healthcare analytics implementation has the potential to reduce costs of treatment, predict outbreaks of epidemics, avoid preventable diseases, and improve the quality of life in general. Health professionals, just like business entrepreneurs, are capable of collecting massive amounts of data and look for the best strategies to use these numbers.

Artificial intelligence is used in many aspects of the healthcare industry. AI involvement in the industry is also focused in the area of prevention of chronic and acute illness, drug development, and organization of clinical trials (patient recruitment, adherence monitoring, data collection, and analysis). AI is able to analyze complex medical data, learn from it, and arrive at ranked/probable conclusions, without any human input. This could help doctors spend more time with their patients and focus more on the clinical care aspect of their jobs.

18.4 Major Categories of AI in Healthcare

AI is making significant impacts in diagnostics, research applications, data collection, wearables, and applications for quality-of-life improvement. Data collection plays a significant role in the world of healthcare. AI can also help in the process of data collection. Reviewing literature from top experts and receiving inputs from doctors and experts in the field of healthcare and data science (Chan & Daim, 2018). AI can aid in processing and sorting the data. Data collection in healthcare needs to be done with appropriate accuracy, privacy, security, ethics, relevancy, and comprehension.

Diagnosis applications are becoming very popular. The AI using expert systems can now identify what health concern a patient has based on their symptoms or from looking at images that are related to the issue (Stephenson et al., 2019). AI synergy allows doctors to work on treatment plans in collaboration with the healthcare application. Research applications are also becoming important in healthcare, especially surrounding drug development. Through the use of data collection and machine learning, AI can continue to aid in the development of new drugs and treatment programs.

Wearable tech and quality-of-life applications are much more consumer based and are used by people who want to take their health into their own hands. The quality-of-life applications may review health records and create personalized exercise programs and diets tailored to the customer's health needs. AI applications can help consumers make lifestyle changes and follow up with changes and updates for a continuous process of healthy living (Chan & Liu, 2020). The wearable tech also provides consumers with feedback while tracking their steps, heart rate, oxygen and blood sugar levels, etc. and can alert of any apparent health issues (Hogaboam, 2018; Hogaboam & Daim, 2018, Daim et al., 2016). People are willing to invest in their health and this is the next big trend in the consumer marketplace. Samsung, Huawei, Xiaomi, Garmin, Fitbit, and Apple hold a large portion of the wearable technology market. Tech companies will continue to invest resources into the space as long as there is still a demand present from the consumers.

According to an Accenture analysis report, the top three estimated high-value AI applications by 2026 in healthcare include robot-assisted surgery (mainly orthopedic), virtual nursing assistants, and administrative workflow assistance. Other AI

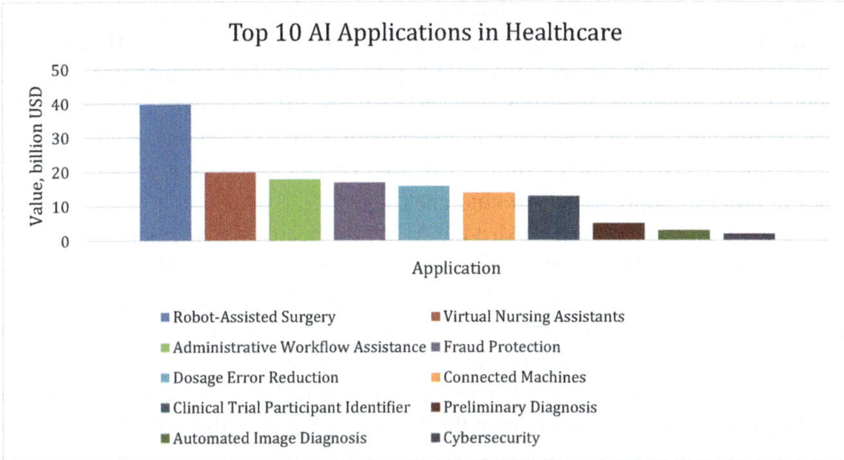

Fig. 18.1 Top 10 AI applications in healthcare

application areas with projected high yields are fraud detection, dosage error reduction, connected machines, and clinical trial participant identifiers (Fig. 18.1).

There are so many current applications for healthcare and these subcategories could be divided even further. Healthcare is focused on benefits to patients.

Case 18.1: COTA Health

One of the healthcare applications in clinical data curation and oncology analytics is COTA Health. COTA aims to empower patients, doctors, and providers with data analytics and decision support tools to drive more cost-effective and meaningful value-based care. COTA transforms and generates meaningful insights using electronic health records and their components (X-rays, CT scans, lab reports, blood samples, patient health history, and doctors' notes). COTA classifies data using the CNA (COTA Nodal Address®) system based on the clinical expertise and claims data. The CNA is a proprietary system created by COTA that codifies specific details of a patient's diagnosis (cancer type, location, tumor type, phenotype, therapy type, and number of progressions). Providers analyze data using the CNA platform and are able to make more informed treatment decisions as well as provide the patient with all of the information related to their condition using the company's data visualization tools. COTA also empowers researchers with their cured data analytics, accelerates drug development, aids in new trials design, and enables better decision-making towards accurate treatment options.

COTA provides two products for life sciences companies: Focus (for focused real-world data cohorts) and Vantage (disease-based real-world data populations). Data elements for their applications are defined by their medical experts and key industry leaders. Key dashboards include visualizations on demographics, diagnostics, performance data, molecular markets, labs, treatments, and outcomes data.

Their proprietary abstraction technology paired with oncology expertise creates insight by curating de-identified longitudinal and meaningful data (COTA, n.d.).

In November 2020, an investment and collaboration deal with Varian provides enabling data analytics, decision support, and cost-effective care (Varian, 2020). Their Intelligent Cancer Care™ tools and initiative are focused on the creation of a technology ecosystem, fueled by information, collaboration, and artificial intelligence in order to improve patient outcomes.

Another fruitful collaboration driving AI in healthcare implementation happened between COTA and IBM Watson. The artificial intelligence of IBM Watson, combined with the medical databases of COTA, was focused on joining big data analytics, precision analytics, machine learning, and artificial intelligence with an aim to improve clinical outcomes and reduce the costs of care.

COTA uses a multitude of artificial intelligence technologies and uses them in collaboration with each other to give the best information to the patient. First, there are expert systems that are used to generate outputs from expert data that has been collected over time from healthcare experts, doctors, and past results. Machine learning is used during the CNA process to determine treatment options, payment options, and clinical operations plans. The process uses hypothesis testing and a simplistic neural network to generate the best outputs for providers to use and reduce cost.

COTA has a strong business model that is not currently at full capacity. As of now, a majority of customers are oncology facilities/ wings in hospitals which are utilized by cancer patients. They are selling the propriety of their patented CNA system. Investors are Boston Millennia Partners, Horizon Blue Cross, IQVIA, EW HealthCare, and Kettering Cancer Center, with the possibility of a buyout by IBM COTA's top competitors, Syapse, ARIEL, and DNAnexus. A possible alliance could be the acquisition by IBM Watson for Oncology as they are more treatment focused with more cost reduction combined with treatment.

Case 18.2: Babylon

Here we chose to focus on the virtual nursing application Babylon. Babylon is helping millions of people to get affordable doctor's appointments from the comfort of their home. In our project, we put this AI application in the quality-of-life category. We felt that this was a fitting place for this application since it makes users' lives easier. Babylon is a mobile app for both IOS and Android that makes it easier to contact a doctor if you are ill and cannot get out of your house, or if you do not have time to skip work for going to the doctor. Babylon's trial came when they partnered with UK's National Health Services and offered this application to all of the UK's population. When a user wants to use Babylon, they just simply install the app from the App Store or Google Play Store. Then the user opens it and creates an account that corresponds with their UK Social Security number. When this is done, they simply just book an appointment with choosing what type of service they need, a normal checkup, a specialist, or a therapist. Then you choose your desired time for your appointment and desired method, either through phone or video. Babylon also offers an alternative where you just type in what your problem is and an interactive chatbot window will be opened, where the user answers a few short multiple-choice questions to diagnose the patient.

Babylon collects four main categories of information. First, it collects data of who the user is: name, date of birth, address, and email address. The second category collected is the user's medical records: symptoms, treatments, appointments, sessions, medications, and procedures. The third category collected is how the user interacts with the application; here they collect video and audio appointments, so the user can rewatch the media if there was something they missed. The final category collected is, with the user's consent, the normal behavior in the application to make the service better. This, in turn, improves the power of the AI and gives the user a better service.

Data is processed with the use of external service providers. These data operators are bound by strict confidentiality and data security provisions and can only use the data in ways specified by Babylon. Data is also given to medical service providers when it is necessary, services like NHS, their doctor, hospital, and emergency services. Data is also given to insurance companies if their access is funded by the insurance company.

The output given to the user is pretty simple; it's mainly a fitness overview, that logs how many times you have contacted your doctor and the medical results from that consultation, like blood pressure and weight. This, in turn, gives the user full control over the results, which means that they don't have to contact their doctor each time they wonder what their blood pressure was the last session.

Babylon's AI system has been created by experienced scientists using the latest advances in deep learning. It is much more than a searchable database, and it assesses known symptoms and risk factors to provide users with informed, up-to-date medical information.

Babylon's business model is still in growth. The major customers are BUPA, NHS, and WeChat. They offer a pay-as-you-go model or a monthly fee for people outside of the UK. Their investors are Hoxton Ventures, Kinnevik AB, and the founders of Google DeepMind. Babylon just closed a huge deal with the Chinese company WeChat for an undisclosed sum. That integrates the Babylon symptom checker into WeChat. The main competitor for Babylon is Qikwell, which was just bought by Practo and Push Doctor.

Case 18.3: Wearable Technologies Supporting AI in Healthcare

Wearable technology is nothing short of a remarkable concept. These products, such as smart watches, were introduced to the market as a way to track athletic activities. Slowly but surely, they have transitioned into something much more than that. Smartwatches are being utilized beyond their initial design. The healthcare industry is employing an ample amount of data collected from wearable technology to implement preventative and predictive healthcare initiatives.

To understand what wearable technology does, it must first be understood what wearable technology is. Wearable technology or wearable gadgets are defined as technology worn by the human body that includes sensor technology that can collect and deliver information, usually in relation to tracking a user's vital signs and data related to health and fitness, location, and biofeedback including emotions. Such data is detected from an ECG monitor (electrocardiogram monitor), a blood pressure monitor, a fitness tracker, daily activity tracker, and a GPS tracker. The technology of wearables has gone so far as Apple creating a movement disorder manager to monitor Parkison's tremors and dyskinetic symptoms. On March 16, 2019, researchers from the Stanford University School of Medicine presented preliminary results of the Apple Heart Study, an unprecedented virtual study with over 400,000 enrolled participants. The researchers reported that wearable technology can safely identify heart rate irregularities that subsequent testing confirmed to be atrial fibrillation, a leading cause of stroke and hospitalization in the United States (Stanford Medicine News Center, 2019). This technology has the potential to save lives and promote a more mindful consumer when it comes to monitoring their health.

Even though this technology has so many beneficial attributes, it also carries some drawbacks. It is not the device that is the issue, but the actual collection of data. With the vast influx of data, it is immature to assume it is not being utilized and possibly not for our own benefit. "In fact, smart watches collect enough data to be able to create profiles of their users to predict future actions, habits, and preferences." This idea of monitored predictability is broadline invasive. Beyond that, who now owns this data? The obvious answers would be Apple and Android, but what about the actual telephone providers, such as AT&T and Verizon. Third parties are becoming privy to this information, whether it be insurance companies, employers, and data analyzing platforms. This creates a conflict of interest for the consumer; on the one hand, they may be very interested in having their information shared with a medical provider, presenting them with what can be presumed as an accurate reading of certain vitals, but now this information is also being utilized beyond the original objective. Beyond the idea that our information is being utilized past our consent, the consumer must be weary of the fact that data breaches do happen and could continue happening, ultimately exposing personal information. We are currently in a period where many people are willing to give up their data without measuring the cost (Maddox, 2015).

To provide insight into how these systems operate, we looked at a company called Medial Earlysign that has been producing AI technology geared towards the healthcare industry. They developed machine-learning-based tools that find generally hidden layers of information in standard medical data. The company's main focus was on preventive care as their algorithmic platform essentially took vast amounts of data and began to be able to predict who, among a population, would be most likely to suffer chronic disease. This is then used to begin preventive care measures. While these measures are a wonderful way in which to help prevent people from developing chronic illness, it relies heavily on information that is already in the healthcare databases. This information is put into the databases as patients are seen on a regular basis (Hogaboam et al., 2014). How do we prevent disease or monitor those that do not regularly see a physician? This is where the idea behind either remote monitoring or wearable devices comes into play.

Remote monitoring of patients can be done at home or wherever life takes them. One such company that has taken over this form of AI is called Current. Their wearable system allows for both patients and doctors to be alerted as new symptoms arise so they may be treated before it becomes a serious issue. Their device just received its second FDA clearance in April of 2019. This clearance allows for the device to be used at home with a patient. The Current device collects data and analyzes it, alerting the patient's physician if need be. The device is equipped with a "chatbot" that can communicate with the patient and record responses. The ease-of-use features of this device have shown an over 90% utilization rate among patients. This is a huge step for patients that normally have to write down their symptoms or check their vital signs on their own, most fail to do so. This company, Current, has now partnered with many health institutions to deliver accurate care at home.

We are familiar with these devices, but not with the specifics on how they actually work and are able to transmit information to a healthcare provider. This field is quite diverse, but the associated technologies actually share some similar components. While it may seem to be quite easy, such as the device needs to have sensors that measure data and also be wireless to communicate the information, it is a little more complex than that. Shared data storage for the information conveyed is crucial and so is the software that analyzes the data. It is this software that will offer treatment recommendations as well as alert your physician. Abbot created one of the first monitors (cardiac) that utilized a smartphone app to record data and send it to the provider. However, this technology required a phone to work with it, which is why several companies (such as Current) have developed newer models.

The question arises then, of how this information can be transmitted to your healthcare provider. The research indicates that most data management is utilized on the device itself with SD cards, through a mobile phone (intermediate node), or by storing data directly on computer nodes. The newer technology that is being created, such as the Current device, suggests that data storage and management be done directly on the cloud. There are some companies such as Pachube or Nimbits that are cloud-based services that are dedicated to storing sensor-based data. These are online database service providers that allow developers to connect sensor data to the web. It is a real-time data cloud-based infrastructure that supports the IoT (Internet of Things). According to research performed by Doukas et al., the cloud-based services will enable users to build IoT products and services that can share, store, and deliver real-time sensor data from patients.

Figure 18.2 helps to visualize the way in which not only remote health monitoring through wearables but also several other types of data are taken through a certain pathway. The data warehouse in the case of most remote monitoring is the "cloud." Once information is stored, it can then be analyzed through the use of AI to be then turned into an "outcome" or information for the health service provider. One issue that concerns many is privacy when sending such personal information to a data warehouse. This is where there must be a distinction between a public and a private cloud network. According to Dash et al., the "Healthcare industry has not been quick enough to adapt to the big data movement compared to other industries. Therefore, big data usage in the healthcare sector is still in its infancy" (Dash et al., 2019). This also allows for patients to become wary of security issues. Eric Wickland writes that the National Institute on Standards and Technology is asking for help "to

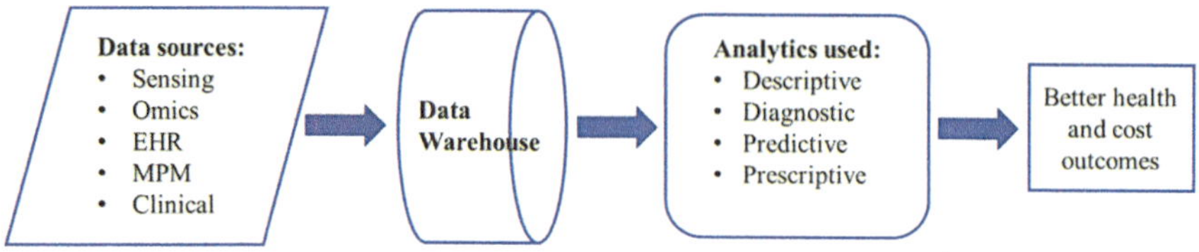

Fig. 18.2 Remote health monitoring pathway with AI

provide an architecture that can be referenced and guidance for securing a telehealth remote patient monitoring (RPM) ecosystem in healthcare delivery organizations (HDOs) and patient home environments, including an example solution that uses existing, commercially, and open-source available cybersecurity products" (Wicklund, 2019).

This comes as a concern because remote patient monitoring is utilized in a patient's home or elsewhere. When this occurs, there can be third-party platform providers. This means that a patient's information could very well be going to another site before it reaches the database warehouse used by the medical facility. The NIST is requesting this to be taken care of because as recently as May 2019, there are still challenges in securing an outside remote patient monitoring platform. As stated earlier, big data in healthcare is still considered to be in its infancy. As it grows larger and more complex, it is very important to ensure that the entire infrastructure is designed to maintain confidentiality and to ensure the safety of patients.

18.5 Key Takeaways

AI while still having issues is overall beneficial for healthcare. First, AI allows for more accurate prognosis and diagnosis of patients because the computers can analyze data and have perfect calculations and deeply analyze the details. These accuracies, while may be very close to that of a doctor, are still slightly stronger allowing confidence in the results. Second, AI is time and resource efficient (Mannix, 2018). The results of an AI analysis come back much faster than a human could ever do. Also, the doctor would be able to see other patients rather than spend his or her time looking at and analyzing images and bloodwork and other patient data. That could all be done by a computer freeing up the doctor to see more patients. Finally, while the research does come with a cost, the overall cost of operating with AI is going to greatly cut costs and allow money to be used more efficiently. And the best part of all of this is that AI would not be replacing doctors but rather working in conjunction with them. The AI system would give suggestions and levels of confidence that do not make the final decisions that would still be up to the doctor along with patient interaction (Saxena, 2018). It is easy to see that AI will become more integrated with healthcare as the research broadens, and it will be interesting to see new benefits that arise as a result.

AI in the healthcare field has many realized and unrealized benefits. But as with anything that is moving away from traditional practice, there are some issues that have arisen. First, AI has the ability to almost eliminate the need for administrative assistants at healthcare offices. All patient data including signs, symptoms, and judgements of how soon the patient needs to be seen by a doctor could all be collected and distributed via AI systems. It would only take simple computers instead of people and imaging and basic questions rather than being looked at by the receptionist. This would pose a major problem in terms of job loss as well. And although this would cut costs, it may not be beneficial as you lose that empathy and human touch that are felt when you are greeted by a human who has real concern for your health. Second, there are certain circumstances where the AI system would not be beneficial, and a doctor would be needed. The most common example used is that of an ineffective treatment plan. The AI would still give the same recommendation for treatment as the patient's data is all still the same. There would be no recognition of need for an alternative that may not be considered the ideal treatment (Tu, 1996). Doctors would be able to use logic and the human decision-making process to run trial and error on different plans in order to find a possible solution. Finally, the healthcare industry is a service-oriented field that needs human interaction to be sustainable. While AI systems may be more accurate, they are not able to provide empathy or relate to the patients. This is important because patients want to know the people treating them actually care. Also, many people still do not trust computers and may not be open to using a treatment plan that was determined by AI (Khan et al., 2017). All of these things will get better with time and as new technologies come about but for now these are very prominent issues in the world of healthcare and AI.

18.6 Conclusion

AI is taking over the healthcare world. Everywhere we look we see more and more research and implementation of artificial intelligence in medicine. As all of these amazing advancements are occurring, we are also seeing where the technology may fall short in terms of being a successful attribute to a business. Healthcare is a service-oriented industry where people's lives are on the line and it is very important to have that human connection. The empathy and the calming words that are required by a doctor cannot be matched by any AI system. However, we are slowly seeing many facilities adopt the practices of AI to aid the healthcare process. By working in collaboration with the human touch, we are seeing resources more efficiently used and also seeing costs cut dramatically. The biggest win for AI in healthcare is the time and resources that are saved by utilizing such technology.

As a manager, it will be important to look at all the aspects of the business. What areas can humans be replaced by an AI system and what areas need to maintain that human interaction. Also, it is important to understand that this implementation has to be gradual and should be very clear to all of the personnel as to what is going on within the business. It may be difficult for some people to work with a computer, and it is your job as the manager to ensure proper training and to make sure all of the doctors and patients feel comfortable with AI helping in the decision-making process regarding patient health.

With such a new technology there must also be policy in place to control such a powerful system. First, we believe in human control. This means that the patient should have the option to choose whether or not an AI system is consulted in determining their diagnosis and their treatment plan. It is their health, and if they would rather only have a provider examining them and their results, then that should be at their discretion. Second, we believe that personal privacy is very important. Just because people's results could help out machine learning, it should be at their discretion whether or not those results get released. Also, with personal privacy, those systems must be secured and encrypted to avoid any possible hacks or breaches. Third, we believe that human values are important. These AI systems need to be programmed with human values in mind. People come from many different cultures and beliefs, especially regarding medicine and those things need to be considered when making decisions for treatment. Finally, we believe that there is responsibility of the AI system and it should be held accountable for mistakes and other things that are caused due to the system. These policies could greatly increase the acceptance and the benefits of implementing AI into healthcare.

Finally, we are seeing trends within AI in healthcare. Currently, there are many technologies and research surrounding wearable health products, big data, and health analytics. These things are all focused on outcome-based care, focused on providing the best opportunity for the patient to get healthy and doing it with the most efficient use of time and resources. These will continue to get stronger, and we are also starting to see the beginning trends of robotics and augmented reality. This would focus more on preventive care that would stop all problems before they even start. All of these trends are big in the success of healthcare and it will be interesting to follow the future of these technologies within the industry.

References

Coats, P. K. (1988). Why expert systems fail. *Financial Management, 17*(3), 77–86. https://doi.org/10.2307/3666074

Case Study: Ochsner Health System – AI-powered Early-warning System Saves Lives: AHA. (n.d.). Retrieved from https://www.aha.org/case-studies/2018-06-27-case-study-ochsner-health-system-ai-powered-early-warning-system-saves

Chan, L., & Daim, T. (2018). A research and development decision model for pharmaceutical industry. *R&D Management, 48*(2), 223–242.

Chan, L., & Liu, D. (2020). Policy planning to support technological innovation in the pharmaceutical industry. In *Disruptive technology: Concepts, methodologies, tools, and applications* (pp.779–801). IGI Global. https://doi.org/10.4018/978-1-5225-9273-0.ch039

Daim, T. U., Behkami, N., Basoglu, N., Kök, O. M., & Hogaboam, L. (2016). *Healthcare technology innovation adoption* (Innovation, technology, and knowledge management). Springer.

Dash, S., Shakyawar, S. K., Sharma, M., & Kaushik, S. (2019, June 19). *Big data in healthcare: management, analysis and future prospects*. Retrieved from https://journalofbigdata.springeropen.com/articles/10.1186/s40537-019-0217-0#Sec39

Doyle-Lindrud, S. (2015). Watson will see you now: A supercomputer to help clinicians make informed treatment decisions. *Clinical Journal of Oncology Nursing, 19*(1), 31–32.

Hashimoto, D. A., Rosman, G., Rus, D., & Meireles, O. R. (2018). Artificial Intelligence in Surgery: Promises and Perils. *Annals of Surgery, 268*(1), 70–76.

Hogaboam, L. S. (2018). *Assessment of technology adoption potential of medical devices: Case of wearable sensor products for pervasive care in neurosurgery and orthopedics* (Doctoral dissertation). Portland State University.

Hogaboam, L., & Daim, T. (2018). Technology adoption potential of medical devices: The case of wearable sensor products for pervasive care in neurosurgery and orthopedics. *Health Policy and Technology, 7*(4), 409–419.

Hogaboam, L., Ragel, B., & Daim, T. (2014, July). Development of a Hierarchical Decision Model (HDM) for health technology assessment (HTA) to design and implement a new patient care database for low back pain. In *Proceedings of PICMET'14 Conference: Portland International Center for Management of Engineering and Technology; Infrastructure and Service Integration* (pp. 3511–3517). IEEE.

Khan, O. F., Bebb, C., & Alimohamed, N. A. (2017). Artificial intelligence in medicine: What oncologists need to know about its potential—And its limitations. *Oncology Exchange, 16*(4), 8–13.

Koh, H. C., & Tan, G. (2011). Data mining applications in healthcare. *Journal of healthcare information management, 19*(2), 65.

Maddox, T. (2015). *The dark side of wearables: How they're secretly jeopardizing your security and privacy.* Techrepublic.com. Retrieved from https://www.techrepublic.com/article/the-dark-side-of-wearables-how-theyre-secretly-jeopardizingyour-security-and-privacy/

Mudavadi, C., Hogaboam, L., & Daim, T. U. (2016, September). A hierarchical decision model (HDM) for exploring the adoption of electronic health records. In *2016 Portland International Conference on Management of Engineering and Technology (PICMET)* (pp. 2770–2781). IEEE.

Muhsen, I. N., ElHassan, T., & Hashmi, S. K. (2018). Artificial intelligence approaches in hematopoietic cell transplantation: A review of the current status and future directions. *Turkish journal of haematology : official journal of Turkish Society of Haematology, 35*(3), 152–157.

Mannix, B. (2018). Benefit-cost analysis and emerging technologies. *Hastings Center Report, 48*, S12–S20. https://doi.org/10.1002/hast.817

Saxena, A. (2018). Enterprising artificial intelligence: Aiding patients as well as the healers. In *Biotechnology products in everyday life* (pp. 55–73). Springer.

Shortliffe, E. H. (1976). *Computer-based medical consultations: MYCIN.* North-Holland.

Stanford Medicine News Center (2019). *Apple Heart Study demonstrates ability of wearable technology to detect atrial fibrillation.* Stanford.edu, Retrieved from https://med.stanford.edu/news/all-news/2019/03/apple-heart-study-demonstrates-ability-of-wearable-technology.html

Stephenson, N., Shane, E., Chase, J., Rowland, J., Ries, D., Justice, N., Zhang, J., Chan, L., & Cao, R. (2019). Survey of machine learning techniques in drug discovery. *Current drug metabolism., 20*(3), 185–193.

Tu, J. V. (1996). Advantages and disadvantages of using artificial neural networks versus logistic regression for predicting medical outcomes. *Journal of clinical epidemiology, 49*(11), 1225–1231.

Varian. (2020). *Varian Medical Systems Invests in COTA, Inc. to Help Drive Faster, More Accurate Data-Driven Cancer Care.* Retrieved from https://www.varian.com/about-varian/newsroom/press-releases/varian-medical-systems-invests-cota-inc-help-drive-faster

Wicklund, E. (2019, August 29). *NIST seeks security guidelines for remote patient monitoring programs.* Retrieved from https://mhealthintelligence.com/news/nist-seeks-security-guidelines-for-remote-patient-monitoring-programs.

Artificial Intelligence in Energy

19

Abstract

This chapter introduces artificial intelligence technology and related applications in the energy sector. It explores different AI techniques and useful applications for energy conservation and efficiency. The key machine learning techniques covered in this chapter include deep learning, artificial neural networks, expert systems, and fuzzy logic. We also provide several related case studies such as AI applications in smart home devices and an energy company E.ON.

Keywords

Artificial intelligence · Energy · Renewable energy · Smart meter · Smart home · Sensor · Ambient sensors · Smart grid · Energy efficiency · Energy consumption · Energy storage · Machine learning · Fuzzy logic

19.1 Introduction

AI in energy is a field that is very active and projected to grow immensely globally. Applying AI technologies in energy can be so far-reaching and impactful. Energy can be in different forms: electromagnetic, thermal, mechanical, chemical, nuclear, kinetic, solar, hydro, wind, tidal, gravitational, etc. All these fields can be impacted by AI in energy; however, the types that regulate the production of electrical energy are the most benefited from AI as they impact everyone in every country. In most industrialized economies, energy is mainly used in the form of electricity from simple things such as electric lights, electric heating, and electric pumps for running water to complex objects such as electric cars, among many other examples. AI can be used to automate and regulate systems that are currently monitored inefficiently by humans and render them more energy efficient by mitigating waste and excess usage (*AI Impact on Reliability and Safety Within the Energy Sector*, n.d.).

L. Chan et al., *Applied Artificial Intelligence in Business*, Applied Innovation and Technology Management, https://doi.org/10.1007/978-3-031-05740-3_19

The impacts and trends of AI in energy are seen most notably in our daily lives, through industries and production, grid management, and energy storage (Kumar, 2018). An example is the impact potential renewable energy power storage has on our current electrical grid system, as it can save reserves of excess electrical energy for later use. The way in which we live our lives, the amount of energy we use, impacts our planet wholly, a fact which many people do not realize, or simply choose to ignore. We should be investing in ways we can help improve our planet. It is a simple fact that electricity is one of the greatest technological advancements made in human history; almost all modern technologies owe their existence to the advent and implementation of large-scale electrical production. So, it is not a stretch to say that electricity is not going away; it is only going to continue to become more prevalent as more of the world powers are on. Thus, it is important that as a society we invest in ways of mitigating losses, increasing efficiencies, and reducing our carbon footprint; all of these can be achieved with the implementation of AI in the energy sector (Daim et al., 2018).

Some examples of how we may do this include smart transportation options such as electric cars, biking or walking to work, and smart home technologies. AI in energy can help reduce costs and energy consumption through a smart home device (elaborated in more depth in subsequent sections), which can turn the lights off when no one is home. Another way we could help is to implement more reusable energy, such as solar panels on top of homes and buildings; with AI helping point them towards the sun to optimize energy production in peak conditions. Companies and residential homes have, in recent decades, switched to using more solar panels because they see the cost-cutting potential through electricity savings, and it does so with a carbon-neutral footprint. If we do not think about ways in which we can live a cleaner and more sustainable way of life, specifically in energy, our planet will see a greater impact on climate change that has the potential to be catastrophic in the near future. In this chapter, the advent of AI in the topics of smart homes, smart grids, and renewable and nonrenewable energy production will be discussed, and the benefits explained.

19.2 Evolution of AI in Energy

The first application of AI in energy was ECHO IV, or the "Electronic Computing Home Operator." It is the first commercialized smart device in energy. This machine was created in 1966 by an engineer from Westinghouse. ECHO IV was a home automation system, hand-crafted with surplus electronic parts and enclosed in wooden cabinetry, that computerized many of the household chores formerly undertaken by the homeowner. ECHO IV had the ability to store recipes, compute shopping lists, track family inventory, act as a family message center, control home temperature, and predict the weather (*History of Computing*, n.d.).

In 1972, Ted Paraskevakos developed a digital monitoring system for fire, security, and medical alarm systems. It was also capable of reading utility meters. The technology Paraskevakos used to develop this system was derived from the automatic telephone line identification system, known today as "Caller ID" (Tamarkin, 1992). For this technology, Paraskevakos was awarded a patent in 1974. He launched a new company, Metretek, Inc., three years later. Metretek, Inc., produced the first fully automated commercially available remote meter reading and load management system. It was a breakthrough for utilities because the energy sector has been searching for a method to match energy generation with consumption. Originally, gas and electric meters measured total consumption and did not provide information about when the energy was used. This new smart meter measured site-specific data, which provided electricity suppliers and consumers with knowledge about energy usage. The electric suppliers used this new information for monitoring and billing.

Moreover, the commercialization of automated meter reading began in 1985 when some impactful projects were realized. Hackensack Water Company and Equitable Gas Company were the first two to commit to the operation of automated meter reading on water and gas meters. In 1987, Philadelphia Electric Company was faced with a large number of inaccessible meters, and to combat this dilemma, thousands of distribution line carrier automated meter reading units were installed. The automated meter reading was becoming more viable every day. The "Advances in solid-state electronics, microprocessor components, and low-cost surface-mount technology assembly techniques have been the catalyst to produce reliable cost-effective products capable of providing the economic and human benefits that justify the use of automated meter reading systems on a large, if not full-scale, basis" (Tamarkin, 1992). As the modern era of AI arrives, new breakthroughs in robotics, finance, healthcare, robotics, etc., are shaping the future of the world. Now, countless energy or utility companies are exploring the possibilities of incorporating AI in their business, for energy efficiency. AI in energy today largely deals with energy storage, accident management, grid management, energy consumption, and energy forecasting.

Energy storage emerged to boost sustainability and efficiency. For example, Athena Energy, Inc., uses AI to highlight energy usage. This allows customers to track energy fluctuations to have more efficient energy storage solutions. Accident management is a major area for AI in today's world. Machine failures and accidents are of common occurrence in the energy sector. Without AI, human errors may lead to massive equipment failures and significant losses. AI can be used now to detect faults continuously in equipment. This allows for timely detection of these failures and faults. It saves time, money, and lives. To illustrate this, companies such as SparkCognition use sensors and analytics to forecast possible failures of their infrastructure. Furthermore, modern power grids retrieve energy from numerous sources such as solar, wind, and coal. Managing and operating these power grids is very complicated for humans. By using AI, power grids are able to increase stability and efficiency by analyzing large datasets in a short frame of time (Kumar, 2018). Energy consumption is another major issue faced at this moment globally. For more sustainable consumption of energy, AI is now monitoring businesses and individuals' energy consumption (Chan & Daim, 2012). An example of this is the Nest thermostat, in which homes averaged 12% savings of electricity used for heating

(Bailes, 2015). In addition to the above information, a company called Energex is forecasting energy by using data mining with AI. As the world continues to move through time, we are now entering the Fourth Industrial Revolution. The wave of the industrial revolution is "The increase in productivity due to artificial intelligence and hyper-connectivity. Diverse new technologies are being proposed that integrate the physical, biological, and digital worlds and new technology will be embedded, even in the human body" (Yoon, 2017).

19.3 Features of AI Applications in Energy

Some AI technologies currently being used in the energy sector are machine learning, including deep learning, neural networks, expert systems, and fuzzy logic. In the first few chapters, we have gone over the general ideas of techniques in big data and machine learning techniques, and these technologies are used in many ways, to predict the amount of energy that will need to be produced and circulated through the power grid as well as lower the energy bill in your home. An example of machine learning in energy is Numenta's machine learning system. This system predicts energy consumption patterns and the likelihood that a machine such as a wind turbine is going to fail. Machine learning is also used to forecast supply and demand, in real time for utility companies. Google's DeepMind has teamed up with National Grid to predict the supply and demand peaks and hopes to minimize national energy consumption by 10% (Mooney, 2018). Although AI in energy is still in the early days, it will soon revolutionize the energy industry. This will limit the environmental impact of consumers and businesses while increasing efficiency. This saves time and money while providing sustainability (*8 Ways AI Can Help Save the Planet*, n.d.; Helmenstine, n.d.; IEEEadmin, 2017).

19.3.1 Smart Grid

A smart grid is an electrical grid that includes a variety of operation and energy measures including smart meters, smart appliances, renewable energy resources, and energy-efficient resources. Smart grids have led the way in developing more and more ways that data can be collected and used. The meters are used to track information and record the necessary data. Various appliances can serve many different purposes in order to benefit the research involved in the field as well as make certain objectives easier.

Smart grids use AI to improve the communication, automation, and connectivity of the various components of the power network. By analyzing energy data, power generation plants are able to better predict and respond to periods of peak demand. Data is usually collected using smart meters that record the consumption of electric energy and communicate the information to the electricity supplier for monitoring and billing. Smart meters encourage more efficient use of energy and power sources, but they do have some privacy concerns. Utility companies analyze the data through statistics, pattern recognition, and machine learning. Analyzing the energy consumption data is the basis for discovering valuable information and supporting decision-making (*History of Smart Meters*, n.d.).

The smart grid is an upgrade to the current outdated energy grid that all countries use to get power from today. Currently, the United States generates most of its power from nonrenewable energy sources, like natural gas or coal. The power plants then use these resources to generate power as demanded by current usage. This is a very antiquated system that can lead to many problems such as blackouts with ramp-up events in which more power is demanded. AI can be implemented in this antiquated grid system to create what is known as the smart grid. The smart grid can be outfitted with AI technologies, such as ambient intelligence and fuzzy logic, to help bring it into the twenty-first century. In the past decade, the smart grid has seen tremendous technological advancement and has been continuing to grow fast. Smart grid could allow integration of diverse power generation, such as the implementation of renewable power generation, thus allowing more storage options to store excess power generated at low demand for later use. This can also help reduce losses associated with power demand fluctuations, improve efficiencies in generation, increase grid flexibility, reduce power outages due to high demand, allow for competitive electricity pricing, and allow the integration of electric vehicles (Raj, 2018). A true fully automated smart grid does not yet exist, as this is potentially too cost-prohibitive to implement on a massive, say national, scale; however, several technologies have been implemented in recent decades to help monitor the existing grid and help reduce demand fluctuations. Demand fluctuations can be both predictable and unpredictable in that demand is a variable that is subject to constant change. Daily, demand for power increases as the sun sets; more people are in their homes using electricity. However, there are peak demand events that can occur in direct correlation with weather events, such as a heatwave which might lead to more air conditioner usage which leads to increased demand, temporarily. These fluctuations can be very costly for power companies as they must increase power output to keep up with demand, and as quickly as demand increases, it decreases, and the power plants are then generating excess power at a net loss. With a smart grid, the system can detect an influx of power consumption and use its reserves in storage to meet demand until the plant can get up to capacity; conversely, as power consumption begins to decrease, the smart grid system can store the excess power generated by the plant until it can reduce output, thus minimizing losses (*Here's How AI Fits into the Future of Energy*, n.d.).

19.3.2 Smart Homes

Smart homes are a more recent advent of AI in energy; they are ever increasing in popularity with cheaper and better products coming to market all the time, most recently with products like Amazon's Alexa, Google's Home Hub, and Apple's HomePod. Smart homes generate data that can be transformed into insights for city planners. The data collected by customers' smart homes and devices spread across a city can be shared and aggregated. A smart home consists of many smart appliances connected to the Internet of Things, which together make a home automated. These devices allow you to control certain features of your home with your voice; the temperature, the lights, and the garage door, among a multitude of other features, are just some of the things possible thanks to this technology (*The History of Smart Homes*, n.d.). However, the possibilities of AI in smart homes go far deeper than asking Alexa to turn the heat up. These devices use sensors that are typically built into other smart appliances connected to the smart home hub; these appliances can be anything from smart light bulbs to smart refrigerators or any other device connected to the Internet of Things that can communicate to the rest of the smart home. With ambient sensors built into appliances like smart thermostats, the thermostat can detect the presence of humans and turn devices such as the heater, or the air conditioner, to a less than comfortable temperature until needed, thus saving energy and money (Lu et al., 2010). Using fuzzy logic, the AI system can decide what a "comfortable" temperature is and adjust the home's climate accordingly. These sensors, coupled with ambient intelligence, can make decisions to reduce energy consumption, mitigate waste, and save money.

Ambient sensors are also capable of much more than turning down the heat. These sensors use radio waves to measure the movement in the room and then use fuzzy logic AI to determine if the data is within acceptable parameters. These sensors can help reduce energy costs by turning on or off some electrical devices such as heaters or air conditioners. Home security is another major advantage with the advancement of the smart home. Never has it been easier and more energy-efficient to make sure your home is safe and secure. Other sensors in the home, like smart smoke detectors, coupled with AI technology can use an algorithm that checks the validity of a fire alarm by measuring the variations in temperature, humidity, and carbon monoxide levels, thus determining if a particular emergency needs the assistance of the fire department before making the call.

19.3.3 Renewable and Nonrenewable Resources

Using AI can improve the efficiency of using renewable energy. For example, solar electrical energy generation is a big part of renewable energy. Based on different observation data sources and models, AI can analyze the temperature and adjust for different weather conditions. Recent research illustrated the use of image recognition and machine learning to determine the best sites to place rooftop-based PV arrays, allowing local decision-makers to assess the potential solar power capacity within their jurisdiction. The computer receives the geodata, and then AI will make the best position to output irradiance simulation and power generation potentials, which can be used to determine the best sites for PV panels.

AI can be used in the renewable energy sector as it can decrease variability and help mitigate the effects of ramp events in power output. Those are the key challenges to energy system operators due to the impacts on system balancing, power reserve management, scheduling, and commitment of generating units. AI can be used when installing new renewable energy sources, like wind turbines and solar farms, as the system can be automated to turn the turbines or the solar panels to the most efficient position for maximum power generation. In the case of overproduction, the AI system can divert excess power away from the grid and into storage for later use during peak consumption times. This is all part of the larger smart grid system. Recently, technologies such as these have drawn the interest of utility companies and researchers toward developing state-of-the-art forecasting techniques for forecasting wind speeds and solar irradiance over a wide range of temporal and spatial horizons (Jha et al., 2017).

Lastly, AI has even more potential in nonrenewable energy as well since this is currently the biggest contributor to the global energy grid. One of the biggest contributors is oil; the problem is finding oil and drilling wells to extract it as it can be both expensive and wasteful. AI can help mitigate these losses until a more sustained alternative can be reached. AI can help find the optimal spot to drill the well and maximize extraction. The uses for AI do not end here either, as variables change with depth with drilling, so do the optimum drilling variables. The deeper the drill bores, the more changes need to be made in order to extract the oil without waste; therefore, constant parameters when drilling will waste both time and money, which could be immensely improved with the use of dynamic drilling parameters. These dynamic drilling parameters can change the rate of penetration, weight on the bit, and drill speed in order to maximize oil extraction. All are automated with AI technologies that can monitor the changing ground conditions and adjust the machinery accordingly, much faster and more accurately than its human counterparts (Self et al., 2016).

Case 19.1: Smart Home Devices

The products that make up a smart home consist of devices that can control various functions in a user's home and connect via Wi-Fi to the central hub, or a smartphone app, to be controlled. These devices act like tools for the central smart home hub, as they use the smart home hub's AI to decide whether to turn the heat on, turn off the lights, or alert the authorities if an alarm is triggered. These devices that are integrated into the smart home can control a variety of things: thermostats, lights, garage doors, cameras, alarms, and even door locks. Many of these devices can work on their own if the user has a smartphone to control them. However, they all can be connected into a smart home hub, which can centralize all the various functions these devices are capable of. These devices can have built-in sensors which can relay information to the smart home hub, to help the AI better make decisions and execute functions. Figure 19.1 shows images of different smart home devices by researchers from the Pacific Lutheran University (Smith, n.d.).

To illustrate this, a Nest thermostat has a built-in ambient sensor that can detect if the user is home or not. This information is sent to the smart home hub which will determine if the thermostat should be turned down, so as to not heat an empty home. This data is sent to parent companies of these smart home hubs, like Google or Amazon, who can use this big data collection to gain more information about a user. Nest has many other products as well that work exclusively with Google's smart

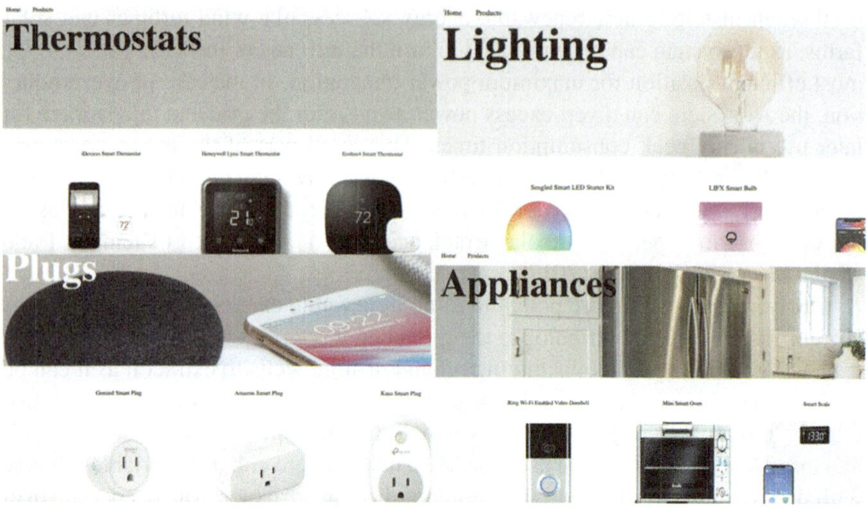

Fig. 19.1 Examples of different smart home devices

home system. These include thermostats, cameras, video doorbells, alarm systems, door locks, smoke + CO alarms, and Nest Aware. Nest video doorbell works by detecting when someone is approaching a user's door, or if they ring the doorbell; it will then send the user's smartphone a notification, containing the clip (if not live video) of the occurrence. The user can also push the doorbell feature and will video call the user's smartphone, so they can talk to the person as if they were at home. If the user cannot pick up, they can have a prerecorded message which could tell the delivery service to put your package in a specific place. A limitation of this product is that the Nest video doorbell cannot detect whether someone nearby is either a bug, raccoon, bee, or someone jogging by. This sends many false alert notifications to the user, forcing them to go through all the clips just to be sure if it was legitimate.

The next example of smart home devices, which connect to a smart home hub, is the Philips Hue smart light bulbs. These bulbs are sold in a wide variety of sizes and shapes, so they fit into almost any light fixture. These bulbs work in conjunction with the Philips Hue bridge. This bridge connects every bulb together wirelessly and links them to the smart home hub. This way, the user does not have to manually add every light bulb to their Wi-Fi network. The Philips Hue lighting system has several limitations associated with it. The first is that the bridge does not have any built-in AI technology to control the bulbs. It simply connects the bulbs to the main smart home hub which can use its AI to determine when and where to use the bulbs. For example, Philips Hue bulbs that are connected to a Nest protect smoke + CO alarm are able to change to a strobing red light, in order to alert occupants in a particular room that an emergency has been detected. This is the reason the Philips Hue system cannot work without either a smart home hub or the companion app on the user's smartphone. The next major limitation of the Philips Hue lighting system is that, like the Nest suite of products, there is a high initial setup cost, with the cheapest starter kit available for $90 plus an additional $40 per bulb on average.

These products have many implications for business, such as reducing energy consumption by not wasting energy on rooms that are not being occupied. Another implication is that although it is expensive to buy these products upfront individually (for instance, a thermostat ranges from $150- to $250 and the video doorbell is $250), it is an investment in the long run, helping automate a user's home which saves time and money. These products may be used for the most part by a younger demographic. However, these products can also help people with disabilities, who may not be able to perform these tasks unassisted.

The smart home can be divided into two parts: the smart home hub and the smart home system. The two major competitors in the smart home hub are Amazon Alexa and Google Home, both of which use AI systems to help modulate your home. These AI-compatible smart home hubs have numerous capabilities ranging from simple question and answer responses to saving time and money by controlling aspects such as lighting, heating, and security. Alexa Voice Services and Google Assistant are able to mimic real conversations using natural language, machine learning, and deep learning. Moreover, the smart home can be divided into nodes, or devices, that the smart home hub can control. These can range from thermostats to light bulbs, video doorbells, and even security cameras, all of which are controlled and managed by the smart home hub's AI. The future of smart home tech will be one homogeneous system (all Google-based, or Amazon-based), not several different applications to control all devices. This will help regulate the number of smartphone-based applications the user must own to control various functions. A challenge that comes along with AI devices is building trust with them. People naturally tend to fear AI, which will be a major hurdle for companies to overcome, to make people comfortable with AI in the future. Another challenge faced in the smart home is the fact that many smart devices are only compatible with certain smart home hubs. For instance, Google's Nest products are only compatible with Google Home smart hubs. This leaves users with Amazon Alexa unable to control their Nest devices. In addition, some business implications could include improved access control, strengthened security, better energy management, streamlined maintenance, and masses of information acquired from big data, all of which can help businesses gain enhanced consumer insights and improve efficiencies and productivity, all while saving time and money.

Case 19.2: E.ON: Building a New AI-Powered Energy World

One case study we would like to introduce is a German utility company, E.ON (the name of the company comes from the Greek word "aeon," which means age), which has taken the lead of AI application in the energy world and is one of the world's largest electric utility service providers. The company was created in 2000, from VEBA and VIAG. In 2018, E.ON made an announcement about acquiring renewable energy utility Innogy with RWE. Nowadays, it is also one of Europe's largest operators of energy infrastructure with over 33 million customers (On Ag, n.d.).

In the energy field, there are many difficulties, especially for the regulation of renewable energy, such as solar and wind energy, which are unstable. The allocation of resources in time and space is very important. Big data and artificial intelligence can play a very broad role in these aspects. For example, we can get the latest and most reliable information based on big data and then optimize in real time based on this information. This is where data and artificial intelligence come in: they can optimize those complex "Energy Internet" in real time based on the latest and most reliable data and ultimately achieve the goal of saving energy. As Karsten Wildberger, chief operating officer and board member of E.ON, pointed out: "The future energy world will be decarbonised. The question is how fast can it happen and how can this be orchestrated with digitalisation?" In the energy sector, "data is the new oil." It is precisely because of this that the company with the most data and the best algorithm can have the best efficiency in global deployment. Then, those companies that dominate large markets by their scale may not necessarily have a competitive advantage (*How Data Is Transforming the Energy Sector*, 2020). The E.ON company's data team is very good at identifying so-called "big ticket" projects from the development of use cases. Usually these projects have high visibility and significant value potential, such as the automated maintenance of wind turbines. The company's board of directors approved a transformation plan called Data.ON, based on two main pillars: data evangelization and data readiness. In this plan, resuming data-driven culture is a very important part. For the data evangelization, E.ON organized the "Data Visualisation Day" event, which provided opportunities for E.ON staff to learn how to handle data. In addition, their data team also organized events for hands-on demonstrations. More than thousand employees of E.ON participated in the data demo at the end of 2019. For the data readiness, the data team from E.ON formulated a data governance platform to organize protocols and ownership, while the data quality processes were at the core to build trust in data and technology. The data team from E.ON also designed a process for assessing which AI projects to pursue with clear KPIs. To do that, they created AI prototypes with offline data and made a transparent pathway from prototype to product, as they said: "[Business] experts know more than what you captured with the algorithm; also they are not used to using them. This is a micro change management issue. We tried to overcome this by building trust with the user and making sure they were always in control and not the algorithm" (*How Data Is Transforming the Energy Sector*, 2020). E.ON is working hard to realize the so-called "embedded, scaled, and disruptive" artificial intelligence (AI). To achieve this goal, they implemented a financial plan to support this type of artificial intelligence. The funds of the data team have gone from the initial central allocation budget to the current separate digital business part. Because of this, the team using artificial intelligence can rely on its partners (i.e., other E.ON business units) to get more revenue, by proving its business value to achieve development (*How Data Is Transforming the Energy Sector*, 2020).

It is worth noting that E.ON has formed a partnership with Sight Machine to integrate the digital manufacturing expertise from Sight Machine with E.ON's expertise in the energy industry for much more efficient digital solutions and better serve their customers. The AI technology from Sight Machine will be used by

E.ON, so that their customers can visualize their energy flows and identify potential improvements rapidly. According to a new report from consultancy Roland Berger, utilities expect efficiency gains of more than 20% from AI in the next 1–5 years, and E.ON will further improve their efficiency with the help of AI in the future (*A View from the Industry: E.ON, One of the World's Largest Utility Companies*, 2018).

19.4 Conclusion

There is much to be anticipated with the growth of AI in the energy field. The energy data that is being collected and analyzed is literally shaping the future in so many ways. The current AI applications being used are very broad and prove that there is a future in many different directions. The vast ways that sensors and intelligent devices are being deployed mean that there is much to be anticipated. The first benefit of AI is that it increases system stability and reliability. Thanks to big data and advanced machine learning algorithms, it is now possible to explore new capabilities or improve outdated monitoring and detection methods. The second benefit of using AI in energy is that it increases asset utilization and efficiency. Machine learning algorithms have the ability to increase utilization and efficiency and better integrate renewable resources with AI tools. The third benefit is that it provides a better customer experience and satisfaction. AI technologies are in the mass rollout of smart meters in homes which enable easier billing, fraud detection, the forewarning of blackouts, smart real-time pricing schemes, demand response, and efficient energy utilization. These applications mentioned require a high sampling rate by the meters and advanced data analytics, as well as information communication technologies.

There are many positives to be enjoyed in the wake of the data that is coming in. There are benefits for small companies, large organizations, and even some countries that have chosen to make a bigger emphasis on energy. The negatives that came forth presented themselves mostly in the form of expenses and inefficiency in the usage of the energy data. In its never-ending drive towards increased efficiency and profitability, the energy industry is collecting more data, applying unprecedented bandwidth connectivity, faster data processing, and using AI and machine learning in new ways. This requires employees to understand cross-discipline integration in manpower and time-constrained manner. AI technology brings multidisciplinary diversity together to discuss and learn how to adapt, adopt, and move forward with digital transformation in the energy industry.

References

8 ways AI can help save the planet. (n.d.). Retrieved December 28, 2021, from https://www.weforum.org/agenda/2018/01/8-ways-ai-can-help-save-the-planet/

AI Impact on Reliability and Safety Within the Energy Sector. (n.d.). Retrieved December 28, 2021, from https://www.cbre.us/global/real-estate-services/directory/global-workplace-solutions/gws-perspectives/content-articles-folder/ai-impact-on-reliability-and-safety-within-the-energy-sector

A view from the industry: E.ON, one of the world's largest utility companies. (2018, March 27). https://sightmachine.com/blog/view-industry-e-one-worlds-largest-utility-companies/

Bailes, A. (2015, May 20). *Does the nest learning thermostat save energy?* https://www.energyvanguard.com/blog/does-the-nest-learning-thermostat-save-energy/

Chan, L., & Daim, T. (2012). Exploring the impact of technology foresight studies on innovation: Case of BRIC countries. *Futures, 44*(6), 618–630.

Daim, T., Chan, L., & Estep, J. (2018). *Infrastructure and Technology Management*. Springer. ISBN-13: 978-3319689869, ISBN-10: 331968986X.

Helmenstine, A. M. (n.d.). *10 Types of Energy and examples*. Retrieved December 28, 2021, from https://www.thoughtco.com/main-energy-forms-and-examples-609254

Here's how AI fits into the future of energy. (n.d.). Retrieved December 28, 2021, from https://www.weforum.org/agenda/2018/05/how-ai-can-help-meet-global-energy-demand/

History of Computing. (n.d.). Retrieved December 28, 2021, from http://dembinhyen.free.fr/UDS/Ebook/CD1/Kien%20Truc%20May%20Tinh/ThamKhao/200006hc/do200006hc001.htm

History of Smart Meters. (n.d.). Retrieved December 28, 2021, from https://snapenergylatino.com/history-of-smart-meters/

How Data Is Transforming the Energy Sector. (2020, June 29). https://knowledge.insead.edu/strategy/how-data-is-transforming-the-energy-sector-14536

IEEEadmin. (2017, June 1). *Artificial intelligence's role in the energy sector – IEEE transmitter*. https://transmitter.ieee.org/artificial-intelligences-role-energy-sector/

Jha, S. K., Bilalovic, J., Jha, A., Patel, N., & Zhang, H. (2017). Renewable energy: Present research and future scope of Artificial Intelligence. *Renewable and Sustainable Energy Reviews, 77*, 297–317.

Kumar, V. (2018, June 1). *How artificial intelligence can increase energy efficiency*. https://blueandgreentomorrow.com/energy/artificial-intelligence-increase-energy-efficiency/

Lu, J., Sookoor, T., Srinivasan, V., Gao, G., Holben, B., Stankovic, J., Field, E., & Whitehouse, K. (2010). The smart thermostat: Using occupancy sensors to save energy in homes. *Proceedings of the 8th ACM Conference on Embedded Networked Sensor Systems*, 211–224.

Mooney, G. (2018, June 28). *10 ways utilities can use AI and machine learning – Right now*. https://blogs.sap.com/2018/06/28/10-ways-utilities-can-use-ai-and-machine-learning-right-now/

On Ag, E. (n.d.). *E.ON – Power and gas – Info-service – FAQ – About us*. Retrieved December 29, 2021, from https://web.archive.org/web/20120104000930/http://www.eon.com/en/infoservice/32944.jsp

Raj, K. B. (2018). *Smart grid technology for smart homes—Risks and benefits*. https://www.ingentaconnect.com/content/sbit/icrtemm/2018/00002018/00000001/art00119

Self, R., Atashnezhad, A., & Hareland, G. (2016). Reducing drilling cost by finding optimal operational parameters using particle swarm algorithm. In *Day 1 Wed, September 14, 2016*. https://doi.org/10.2118/180280-ms

Smith, J. (n.d.). *Smart Home Technology*. Retrieved December 29, 2021, from https://cs.plu.edu/~caora/SHT/

Tamarkin, T. D. (1992). Automatic meter reading. *Public Power, 50*(5), 934–937.

The History of Smart Homes. (n.d.). Retrieved December 28, 2021, from https://www.iotevolutionworld.com/m2m/articles/376816-history-smart-homes.htm

Yoon, D. (2017). What we need to prepare for the fourth industrial revolution. *Healthcare Informatics Research, 23*(2), 75–76.

AI in Media and Entertainment

20

Abstract

This chapter explores AI for traditional media services (television broadcasting, radio broadcasting, journalism and print media, cinema and films, new media streaming services, social media, web analytics, and music industry). AI applications in television broadcasting like content personalization, targeted ads, video recognition, voice assistance with search and playback, enhanced translation and closed captioning, video compression, and optimization are noted. AI for the music industry examines music research and music psychology. Case studies in the chapter assess Spotify and Netflix.

Keywords

Social media · Video games · Blogs · Podcasts · Video-on-demand · Television broadcasting · Content personalization · Targeted ads · Video recognition · Voice assistance · Video compression · Optimization · Enhanced translation · Closed captioning · Streaming services · Natural language processing · Machine learning · Recommendation systems · Sentiment analysis · Online advertisements · Web analytics · Music research · Quantitative methods · Music analysis software · Music psychology · Deep learning · Personalized playlists · Data-driven content · Targeted marketing

20.1 Introduction

The media and entertainment market is one of the largest and fastest-growing business sectors in the world, generating revenue of nearly $800 billion worldwide in 2021 (PWC, 2021). The term media applies to a broad set of content sources from the traditional forms such as books, journals, television, films, and newspapers to newer forms ushered in by the advent of the Internet and global connectivity. Social

L. Chan et al., *Applied Artificial Intelligence in Business*, Applied Innovation and Technology Management, https://doi.org/10.1007/978-3-031-05740-3_20

media, video games, blogs, podcasts, and streaming video-on-demand (VOD) are an example. The media industry is a globally shared phenomenon that is present in every country around the world and provides a way to connect the interests of many diverse people as well as to open up whole new markets for content producers looking to attract new sources of business profits and to drive business model innovation throughout the industry. These profits and the broadened access to new markets have attracted a large number of competitors to the space. The business challenges that the industry faces are centered around tailoring their content to maintain the interest of very different consumer segments, creating new interesting content to retain their attention and to sell additional adjacent products to increase their share of wallet. The use of AI technologies to solve these problems includes the need to reduce production costs in an increasingly competitive field, to improve understanding of customer preferences, and to generate revenue through the delivery of content through both diverse products and platforms (Lippell, 2014, p. 245).

AI has given those involved in media a new tool they will need to become even more competitive and successful. As stated by Tawny Schlieski and Brian David Johnson (2012), "The era of big data is not coming; it is here… big data was a defining characteristic of the 2000s" (p. 1404). It was at this point that the media services really adopted AI and started to grow their business based on the insights that they could extract using it. Content marketers went from guessing who was buying their products to gaining the ability to know exactly who was buying their product, why they bought it, and how. AI took what used to be a guessing game and transformed it into a competitive game of who can I reach and how well can I reach them. It has transformed the way that businesspeople think and make decisions in the media and entertainment sectors. In this chapter, we will discuss the possibilities of AI in media and entertainment, specifically with regard to social media, streaming services, music, television, radio, and broadcasting.

20.2 AI for Traditional Media Services

In America in the early 1950s, the Nielson ratings were introduced first in radio media and eventually in television in order to gather data to understand the size and composition of audiences (https://en.wikipedia.org/wiki/Nielsen_ratings) and their media listening, viewing, and consumption habits. Although the technology and methods for collecting this data have changed with the advent of the Internet age, the type of data necessary to make more informed content production and budget allocation decisions has not evolved. In the following section, we will touch on the connection between AI and traditional media sectors such as television and radio-broadcasting. We will see how AI has been used to improve the business of such traditional media services.

20.2.1 AI for Television Broadcasting

When thinking about what AI can contribute to television, the biggest idea has been knowing the audiences and their preferences as consumers. This is a practice that the television industry took part in long before the introduction of big data and AI technologies. Although television was created in the late 1920s, it did not become widely used and popular until the 1950s (Hill, 2014, p. 76). In the early years, AI was too computationally expensive to be deployed to analyze television audience viewing habits, but that fact didn't stop businesses from collecting customer data and analyzing it by hand. Rough heuristics were better than precise knowledge in that era. As can be imagined, data was not as easily accessible but that doesn't mean that it was impossible to gather. Businesses actually had employees call people with a cable TV connection and ask them what they were watching at the moment of the call as well as some relevant demographic information (Hill, 2014, p. 77). Hill claims that this method (phone surveys) was the birth of data collection about television audiences. But even with the information they collected, television data was very limited in what they could do with it (MIT Press, 2016).

Just as the way we watch television has evolved over the years, so has the way in which we collect data from television viewers. Data can now be collected from set-top cable boxes, video-on-demand (VOD) services, and even social media platforms that can help to analyze television audiences (Hill, 2014, p. 76). Through Shawndra Hill's 2014 study of predicting television viewership, she found that it is possible to identify trends just by analyzing data from Twitter. Twitter is a social messaging platform where users write short messages to each other or to channels containing groups of people with similar interests. From this information, you can predict television viewership as well as demographic information and show. Knowing who is watching what shows helps to decide the best possible time to air a specific commercial to a receptive group of people with targeted interests (Fig. 20.1). Traditional television with access to only survey data has had to learn to adapt in order to compete with these new media platforms with much more intimate connections to both individuals and their peers with similar interests.

Internet media services such as Netflix, Hulu, and YouTube have quickly surpassed the capabilities of television and have caused major issues for this sector of the media industry (Hill, 2014, 79). This is why television services are starting to reach more into the world of streaming services in order to fight to stay relevant in a world that allows consumers to watch movies and TV shows whenever and wherever they wish to do so. Cable television limits us to only be able to watch where the connection is set up, so specific television networks have been working to offer subscriptions to their channels that allow the user to watch their shows on all of their devices (Hill, 2014, p. 80). Comcast has also developed an app called Xfinity Stream where their consumers can watch live TV from any other mobile device as well as access their video-on-demand services. While this is very convenient, they also have their own limitations. For instance, certain live television programs cannot be viewed if the mobile device used to view the content is not connected to a Wi-Fi base station or the Wi-Fi does not have good enough data bandwidth to make the

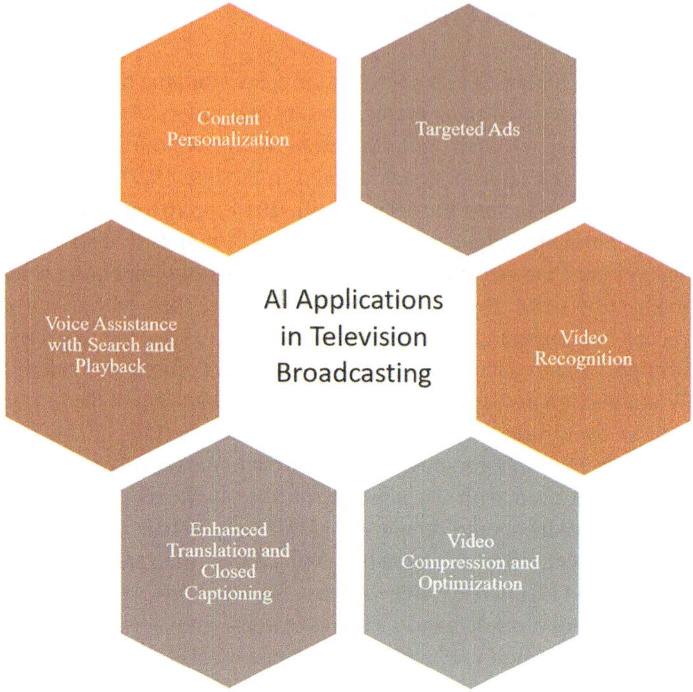

Fig. 20.1 AI applications in TV broadcasting

viewing experience enjoyable. Content licensing agreements can also provide a barrier for streaming content if the show is only licensed on one type of media such as broadcast and not streaming media. From a business standpoint, the cost of cable television services is expensive compared to the small monthly fee of many other video streaming services.

AI in television will provide a competitive advantage to those companies that can deploy it and use it to get to know the preferences of their customers better than other services. Streaming platforms like Amazon Prime have not only a consumer's viewing habits on their VOD service, but they also have access to the consumer buying habits through their web browser storefront. Traditional cable television operators do not have access to this data in real time and thus have an information disadvantage just in terms of the data available to them to draw any conclusions on consumer viewing and purchasing habits. Cable television will need to innovate in order to close this gap and AI will be providing a strong competitive advantage for the streaming media service providers for a long time to come.

An additional benefit to using AI technologies in television and broadcast media has to do with enhancing the content to make it accessible to the hearing impaired. Closed captioning of television content has been a costly endeavor resulting in the technique only being applied to selected programming and not economical to apply to all the content produced by the television broadcasters. Natural language processing (NLP), which is a technique for an algorithm to translate spoken words into text that can be read by a hearing-impaired individual, has reached such a high degree of accuracy in the translation that it can now be used to translate television content during the broadcast and in real time. The reduction in costs in providing this service is beneficial not only to the hearing-impaired customers but also the content producers who do not need to hire other humans to listen to programs and translate them into English or other language forms. News reporters can now translate programming while it is happening in real time and not as an additional post-production step which would cost the organization more money to provide. These benefits are directly attributable to NLP development and promise to reduce the costs of making all content available to those who are disadvantaged with their hearing.

20.2.2 AI for Radiobroadcasting

Media and entertainment are developing in a fast way; sometimes we can't track this kind of development. AI today has a huge impact on the media services, with radiobroadcasting being especially affected. Pre-Internet era, radio used to be one of the major media sources with radio acquiring 33% of the market share of the media along with TV and newspapers. However, when the Internet entered the picture, it disrupted the entire media market. Nowadays, the Internet is by far the most accessible source of media compared to the rest of the market offerings. This is due to the widespread use of smartphones devices and computers among modern consumers.

Before the age of the Internet, a consumer required a radio frequency receiver to listen to radio programs or broadcast music. They could not listen to a radio station that was outside of the range of their radio receiving equipment. Today, such devices have virtually disappeared from homes and are found mostly in motor vehicles. Because of this, radiobroadcasting in vehicles remains the method of choice to reach a wide range of consumers during their vehicle-necessary activities like traveling to work, picking children up from school, or driving to shop at physical retail outlets. Even satellite radio such as that provided by SiriusXM has not garnered a large percentage of in-vehicle media consumption due to cost and reliability issues. According to Susan Ashworth "On a typical weekday, radio's share of in-car listening is 64 percent, followed distantly by other means like satellite radio and personal media libraries" (Ashworth, 2018). Apps on smartphones, tablets, and TVs replaced radio devices and this replacement affected the radio industry positively. By the use of big data, content makers and radio stations along with ad companies can examine listeners' behavior towards a commercial or a station. For example, how many listened to a particular station, how old are the listeners, what type of programs people listen to, or where are they listening from.

Unlike traditional radiobroadcasting with limited direct access to what consumers are actually listening to in their cars, AI now has more reliable and direct data from Internet and satellite radio sources for examining consumer habits. Additionally, they may even have access in some cases to GPS data through the user's phone or vehicle from which to understand the listening habits of their users. Recommendation systems will be a broadly adopted technology to enhance and help consumers in their media consumption experience when listening to the radio in their vehicles. The data available through radio on the Internet and satellite networks will help advertisers to understand people better through their listening and travel habits to make strong recommendations for both targeted commercials and picking better content for people to listen to while traveling in their car.

20.2.3 AI in Journalism and Print Media

AI in journalistic endeavors such as in the generation of news content promises to be both beneficial and potentially harmful. In this section, we discuss the positive benefits to both news content producers and consumers of the content and leave discussion of the possible negative aspects to a later section.

It is now possible through natural language processing (NLP), which is a machine learning and AI technique for understanding written or typed text, for computers to form a basic understanding of the news and articles produced by this sector of the media industry. AI is being used to generate variations of news stories for different segments of readers and generate entirely new articles starting from templated content and filled in by the AI as stories happen. Tools such as GPT-3 and DeepMind are reducing costs through filling some of the more redundant aspects of journalistic writing and print media content generation.

AI in print media can be used for both positive cost-saving purposes and nefarious purposes, such as generating fake news and propaganda. Even with some of these drawbacks, the new techniques being developed in AI and big data promise to have an outsized impact on both the way that we produce news media and consume it.

20.2.4 AI in Cinema and Films

Recent advances in artificial intelligence and content generation for film and television have produced convincing replicas of actors and actresses long after their final films and appearances. Startlingly convincing movements and speech of actors when they were younger but for present-day films illustrate some of the promises of the use of AI content generation in films. From a business perspective, the ability to mimic an actor or actress convincingly in a film can lead to huge reductions in production costs and delays due to the normal issues faced by real human beings in showing up to work and giving consistent performances throughout the year. Not only can they now be in multiple films beyond what an average acting professional would be capable of contracting out in a single year, heirs of the estate of A-list actors could continue to produce new and interesting films long after the actor or actress has ceased being able to work.

Beyond the human actors in a film, massive armies of orcs and goblins are producible with convincing movements for certain types of action or fantasy films. AI can analyze the movements of multiple different types of animals, insects, birds, and fish and allow the creator to customize their on-screen creatures with the behavior patterns suitable to the storyline. This saves thousands of hours of human labor in the production of convincing movements for newly imagined creatures and also saves the production company many millions of dollars in production costs for each new film.

Beyond the impact of AI in the creative process of producing films, the movie industry business can benefit in a similar way as other content creator businesses from the ability of AI to anticipate exactly what kind of movies the audience would like to see next. Recommendation systems, sentiment analysis, and other techniques analyze the preferences of the audience and tailor content to have the highest impact as broadly as possible. This helps to increase the revenue for each individual film and can be used to additionally increase audience engagement and spending on a film by providing better entertainment content than in the past.

20.3 AI for New Media Streaming Services

The continued development of the Internet and improvement in digital speeds has opened up whole new avenues that permanently change the media services. One of the ways that the Internet has changed media services has been with the change in the way we can view movies and TV. With the introduction of streaming services such as Netflix, Hulu, Prime Video, and others came a tidal wave of faster and easier ways to view the shows and movies we love at a much lower price than traditional services. All of these streaming services essentially use AI in the same way, but Netflix has been credited as the streaming service that started it all.

The introduction of AI has allowed for businesses to get a clearer idea of what exactly their consumers wish to spend their free time watching. This is no different for streaming services. We are in a time where consumers are spoiled for choices in their media consumption, especially from their streaming services (Dreier, 2012, p. 24). For streaming services, it is much easier to collect data because the data is produced instantly by their consumers and stored in large data centers for analysis. The factor that makes streaming services much more profitable compared to traditional forms of movies and television is this ability to know roughly what their viewers want and the profiles of their viewers and their peer group. For example, analyzing what users are searching for, whether it is a particular show or movie, can allow streaming services to both offer shows tangentially related to the title they are currently searching if they do not offer the program that was requested or even to add a program that is popular with other viewers in their next monthly update because it was watched by other people with similar interests or a lot of people in general. This capability has allowed for streaming services to move beyond simple search optimization and preference mapping to produce their own original shows and movies that compete head-to-head with traditional forms of video viewing entertainment. Rahul Telang and Michael D. Smith state that, "With the recent explosion of shows produced by Silicon Valley companies like Amazon, Hulu, and Netflix comes a fear that entertainment will increasingly be shaped by analysts crunching numbers rather than creatives following their artistic vision" (2012, p. 1404). There is fear that the use of machine learning algorithms will completely get rid of Hollywood creativity, and while it is a possibility, it is not what streaming services are doing. Yes, they are learning what it is that their consumers want through big data, but they are still using creative teams to write movies and shows. Streaming services have the ability to know when shows are paused, played, rewound, and exited as well. While this data seems to be unimportant, it can actually be very useful. With this information, streaming services can know if a show isn't popular or well liked, which can result in the show later being pulled from the service or even if a movie is too scary. For instance, a scary movie being paused and exited towards the end can signify that the movie was just too scary to finish (Marr, 2018). Data can be drawn from every action a consumer takes while using a streaming service and this data has proven to be the most powerful tool for these services. AI has allowed for streaming services to surpass traditional forms of movie and TV show viewing, allowing for streaming apps to become more powerful than any television service could ever dream.

Online advertisements in media services are becoming more popular and more efficient due to machine learning algorithms. Companies no longer have to search for the right audience because AI does it for them. The only thing that they have to worry about is making their ad stand out from the hundreds or even thousands of other ads that a user sees daily. Every time you search something up on Google or YouTube, an ad will most likely pop up. Millions of businesses use Google ads as a way to advertise their products or services. They can choose from seven campaigns depending on what they want to accomplish with these ads. They offer search, display, video, shopping, app, local, and smart campaigns ("Choose The Right," n.d.). To achieve any of these campaigns they use machine learning algorithms to serve targeted ads to the right audiences. This can benefit both the business and the consumer. The businesses using Google Ads get traffic on their website which can turn into profit and the consumer gets ads that are personalized based on their interest or need. YouTube is also owned and controlled by Google, so they also use the same machine learning algorithm to direct people to other Google services.

TikTok is a newer social media app. It gained popularity over the last couple of years but especially last year during the start of the Covid-19 pandemic and the weeks of imposed quarantine. Today they are probably one of the more addictive social media apps due to their personalized feed. Every user has a different "for you page" and their one-swipe hand gesture-based interface can make it very easy for someone to get trapped watching a mobile device screen for hours. TikTok uses "machine learning to analyze users' interests and preferences through their interactions with the application then display a personalized feed for different users" (Wang, 2020). With machine learning, they are able to recommend video media content based on what the user seems to interact with the most. With this type of algorithm, TikTok is also able to target the right ads at the right users. Different non-media companies also work with famous content creators on the TikTok application to sponsor these creative people for advertisement videos. If the non-media company products or services relate to the style of videos that these content creators usually produce, then the advertiser has a high chance of getting a customer from the content creators millions of followers. Google is a great resource to use, especially for smaller businesses, and the same can be said with TikTok. Posting and being active on TikTok gives a business a higher chance of going viral, producing content that is seen by a large number of people without spending a lot of advertising budget to reach them. If they create good content, then the AI algorithm can push their video to millions or possibly billions of users.

20.4 AI for Social Media and Web Analytics

As a growing field in an advancing technological age where nearly everything is connected, access to the Internet is nearly perpetual, and connectivity is right at the fingertips of consumers, social media analytics can be an exciting topic. Many companies are attempting to get into the digital marketplace and offer their customers products and services they desire in an immediate fashion through their mobile devices. People spend more and more time on their phones and laptops on the Internet every day, and big businesses want to be where the consumers are, attracting their attention and serving their needs to continue to drive profits. As technology improves and media services become more prevalent, companies can gain access to data analytics of consumers on social media. This is a potential gold mine, because people spend countless hours on social media, interacting with news, friends, services, companies, products, ads, family, all kinds of media, etc. Using advanced machine learning algorithms on social media, companies can optimize their own social media sites/profiles to attract customers to their sites, brands, and products. By seeing what people spend their time looking at and how they interact on social media, companies can also optimize their ads to target audiences and give them proper placement, size, and timing, based on consumer behavior.

This deep and complex form of data analytics can be difficult to implement because consumers are always changing and evolving with technology, keeping up with the times. As social media becomes more prevalent, so do trends that flash and fall, seemingly out of nowhere. Pinpointing these consumer trends and behaviors can make big bucks for the companies that catch them, but it is not easy. AI aims to be able to catch these trends so that companies can optimize their interaction with consumers in a way that is most meaningful and profitable, making it a very exciting development in technology for companies and for business as a whole. Many challenges are present, but many positives exist as well, and the future of large companies' online success may very well depend on accurate and meaningful analytics in the near future.

Companies use various types of machine learning algorithms with the intent of gaining valuable insight in order to optimize their websites, boost sales, improve customer service, and display ads. There can be tremendous upside to using conventional analytical tools for companies, but this is not always the case. At times, companies can end up with so much data and seemingly random analyses without direction and they cannot use the data effectively because it has no clear meaning. Relating to this, there are pros and cons to how companies choose to use analytical tools as well. There is the option of using a third-party service and paying a monthly or yearly fee based on the amount of data and analysis being requested. This method can be costly, but ultimately provide clear and customized data and analytics that can be used to meaningfully improve the business. Many third-party data services provide dashboards and solutions based on the data collected, which makes it even easier for companies to benefit from using web analytics. Companies also have the option of developing their own machine learning platform or service using resources and data already available to them. This method can be less costly if the company already has the technology or data available to use it for the purpose of tracking consumer behavior. The downside to this however is that raw data is being collected, which can be difficult to interpret and apply to be able to improve the operations of the company.

20.5 AI for Music Industry

Current and future AI applications for the music industry are varied. Purely within the scope of entertainment, large music firms have been looking toward AI and big data solutions to develop software capable of conducting large-scale music research. Additionally, AI uses for music are also finding their way into the field of music psychology with the advent of biometric measuring devices allowing for advanced research on the effects of music on the human body.

20.5.1 Music Research

In the past, musicologists have often suffered from employing quantitative methods of research on small datasets (Abdallah et al., 2017, p. 1). The proliferation of digital music distribution has naturally increased the size of datasets that musicologists have to work with, necessitating the development of music analysis software. Such software as the Digital Music Lab represents the continuing development of music analysis technology, allowing users to visualize music data from a large library of songs in a way that was not previously possible (2017, pp. 2–3). These high-level analysis programs hold much potential for generating competitive advantage in the music market for firms and artists interested in deploying them. Close analysis and comparison of popular songs to songs in development can allow for greater mass market appeal of a piece of new music. Additionally, these programs can aid in intellectual property protection by preventing the accidental copying of rhythm, beat, and lyrics. AI music analyzing programs represent a strong avenue for generating business intelligence within the music market.

20.5.2 Music Psychology

Research in the field of music psychology has benefited from the growth in available data in recent years as some data can now be unobtrusively collected about individuals that correlates to their mood, physiological metrics, location, activity, and sociability to the song the individual is listening to (Greenberg, 2017, p. 50). While this data has many uses in the field of music therapy, entertainment firms can also look to take advantage of it in several ways. Having this level of detailed information on consumers enables firms to practice targeted marketing by recommending certain albums or songs to individuals depending on their current mood, location, etc. This technology holds particular value for music streaming firms such as Spotify, which can enhance their user experience through integration of music psychology data with their recommendation algorithms.

Case 20.1: Spotify and AI

AI and machine learning are used in many companies today for faster and efficient analysis. Spotify is a media service provider that streams digital music, podcasts, and video. It has been competitive with Apple Music and Pandora. Spotify is known for streaming music and podcasts for free or for a paid premium account. The use of AI helps with the music selection that Spotify provides to its users. Instead of just providing the same playlists to everyone who uses the service, they can create personal playlists for every user to fit their own unique taste in music. This helps Spotify be more competitive within the music streaming industry. Users will be more likely to use a platform that puts them on to new music they like as well as providing them with a customized playlist with all of the music they already like. One of the big things about Spotify is that it personalizes the user experience. By using AI and deep learning, it learns about user listening preferences and provides recommendations to similar music, playlists, and podcasts. It uses collaborative filtering by comparing individual behavioral trends with other users. The AI method that Spotify uses to understand what similar music to recommend is known as collaborative filtering. Unlike other companies that receive user like and dislike feedback using a rating system, Spotify uses implicit feedback such as how many times a certain song is played, what song was in a search, did the user tap on a certain playlist or artists, or what did the user save and add recently. The company uses this information to combine the similarities in these parameters and determine what is similar to something the user would like or prefer. To keep improving, they also use natural language processing (NLP) to scan metadata, blog posts, and online discussions about artists and songs. They look at the reviews and what other people are saying. The NLP system can take certain words or phrases and associate them with what certain users like or prefer.

To keep a constant consumer interest, Spotify uses AI to suggest new songs that the user might want to add to personalized playlists. This prevents their consumers from getting bored of listening to the same songs every day. There are millions of listeners and millions of songs which require AI to track what songs get the most attention and what consumers prefer. Especially in marketing and advertising, it is important to know what consumers want and need when it comes to music streaming. Keeping up on the right trends in the market to catch the attention of consumers is what AI can help with. Machine learning and AI implemented by Spotify helps listeners play any song, anywhere and anytime, instead of waiting to download the song (Budelman & Kizelshteyn, 2019). This is a feature that attracts people to Spotify and provides an easy access for people to the music they want to listen to without taking much time out of their busy schedules. Another feature is called Discovery Weekly, which is a playlist that includes new songs and introduces new music every week (Budelman & Kizelshteyn, 2019). The idea behind this playlist is that when users get bored of the music they've been listening to, they can play this playlist which includes new songs and is less labor-intensive than searching new songs (Budelman & Kizelshteyn, 2019). In the market today, people look for easy and fast service which Spotify does a good job of understanding their target market along with using automation through machine learning to provide better user experience.

Thinking deeply about what a song or artist means to a user is a technique Spotify uses to design their pages on the app. Through this process, they form a relationship with their users by displaying content that connects to them. One of their playlists called Release Radar introduces new songs based on a user's taste (Budelman & Kizelshteyn, 2019). In order to match new songs with their taste, Spotify uses machine learning to gather data and see patterns. They also use natural language processing, which allows them to track multiple activities, such as user discussions about a song or specific musicians and Internet articles about the song or artist, and to detect the kind of language and sentiment from reviews through texts and phrases. By using this data, they are able to categorize songs and terms related to that song (Sen, 2018). This helps Spotify decide if their target market is responding well to a song or not; if not, then they can use this data to filter what genres are successful within a certain age group or geographic location. Doing this would help them understand their users better and the taste they prefer. Artists can also benefit from this because they would know what kind of songs their fans prefer and can create future music based on this.

A related company to Spotify that we can look at is Next Big Sound (NBS). This company has figured out how to use the data from Spotify streams, iTunes sales, SoundCloud plays, Facebook likes, Wikipedia page views, YouTube hits, and Twitter mentions to predict the next big thing in music. The company's analytics provide insight into social media popularity, the impact of TV appearances, and many other nuggets of information that are invaluable to the music industry. Artists can also use the data for their own promotion, thanks to a partnership between NBS and Spotify. Billboard now publishes two charts based exclusively on NBS' data, and they have worked with companies such as Pepsi and American Express to help steer millions of dollars being spent on music-related marketing and sponsorships.

As noted from all the discoveries and usage of AI and machine learning by Spotify or NBS, they aim to provide a better user experience. This is a good marketing technique where they personalize their playlist to make all users feel important and better understand them through the data they collect. With the help of AI and machine learning, they are able to introduce a new variety of songs and eliminate those that are unsuccessful within a certain target market.

Case 20.2: Netflix and AI

Streaming services are one of the major results of the creation and use of big data. One company that is a prime example of how AI has been used successfully is Netflix. Netflix has remained the top streaming media service because of their ability to analyze and utilize AI in an increasingly competitive atmosphere. Netflix got their start in 1997, as an online movie rental service website. In the early days, their service consisted mainly of mailing out DVDs and Blu-Ray disc media to consumers wishing to watch movies at home but not wanting to drive to a physical video store to rent it. After expanding that business to include a monthly subscription service, Netflix moved to utilizing the data created by their consumers by implementing a movie recommendation system that was personalized based on a consumer's ratings of movies. These ratings were used to predict movies that members may like. In 2007, Netflix introduced video-on-demand (VOD) streaming, allowing for their consumers to watch movies and TV instantly over an Internet connection. By 2010, Netflix was available across all electronic computing platforms in the US market and by 2016, worldwide.

Netflix is constantly collecting data from their consumers, which amount to over 158 million paid memberships within over 190 countries. Netflix was able to defeat their primary competitor, Blockbuster video rentals, by allowing consumers a way to rent movies without having to physically go to a store and pick it out. As Netflix collected data on their consumers, Netflix software engineers were able to develop algorithms that were able to," ...steer customers away from high-demand blockbuster movies … and toward its plentiful, lesser-known library titles" (Markman, 2019). Netflix is able to collect data on many things from what the customer is watching to what genre they seem to watch the most. This data is used to customize the user experience and increase the enjoyment and engagement with the consumer facing application. Netflix is using a variety of statistical measurements to help them make decisions about their consumers including what time of day they are viewing, how long it takes them to choose something to watch, and even how many times a show or movie was paused, rewound, and fast-forwarded (The Startup, 2018).

This data collection process does not produce business results immediately. It takes a lot of time and a lot of data to get to where Netflix is today in the technological learning curve. Fortunately, Netflix has been collecting data from the very beginning when they were simply a movie rental business back in 1997. When they ventured into the world of streaming services, they brought in both the experience they had with providing physical movie-watching ability and the data that those customers created. Netflix was able to have a general idea of what programs and movies were most popular and started growing their business from that starting point. One of Netflix's most popular offerings is their Netflix Originals. AI played a large role in the creation of these shows and movies and has helped these shows be recognized for awards that were reserved only for big screen movies and cable television in the past. As discussed earlier, streaming services have grown and improved as a result of big data and AI analytics. Gone are the days of guessing what consumers want. Now, all businesses, especially streaming services like Netflix, are able to thrive thanks to the information they are able to collect directly from their consumers.

Since their start in 1997, Netflix has changed the way they collect data from their consumers, and the reason behind that is to get a deeper understanding of consumer usage. Netflix thrived in the industry of on-demand streaming by collecting data from their 151 million subscribers from all around the world. These data include viewing habits, buying patterns, and customer behavior towards the watched content. This data gives Netflix the ability to customize their website based on what type of movies or TV shows customers most watched and gave a high rating to. Furthermore, data generated from users really gave Netflix the upper hand among its rivals, which are Amazon, Hulu, Disney+, and Apple TV+, as well as accomplished the success that they have today. Netflix collects data through an algorithm they have designed called "The Recommendation Algorithm." This recommendation algorithm suggests contents to users based on viewing history and how users have rated previously watched contents (Bulygo, 2019). The contents were also suggested based on how many times users have watched certain movies, or how many times a movie has been paused, are users continue watching after pausing the movie, where are the users watching from, and when (Bulygo, 2019). This kind of data are inputs that Netflix has to process in their algorithm. Furthermore, Netflix used to have the 5-star rating system, but in 2017, Netflix has changed it to a new one, called the thumbs-up/down rating system (Bulygo, 2019). The thumbs-up informs Netflix that users liked this kind of content and would like suggestions based on their preference. Similarly, the thumbs-down informs Netflix that users did not like the content, and they are not interested in any suggestions related to that content. This system has generated a tremendous amount of data from users than the former system.

The reason why Netflix collects data on their consumers is to better understand their market needs in order to offer consumers the most desirable content when they want it. Being able to stay on top of the increasingly competitive business of data collection and analytics is what allows businesses to continue to stay competitive in an ever-evolving world of business. As one of the first streaming services, it has become increasingly difficult for Netflix to continue to stay on top. Streaming services like Hulu, Prime Video, and Disney+ have made their way into the marketplace, making it difficult for Netflix to remain number one because of a unique technological advantage. These other streaming services continue to add shows and features that set them apart from Netflix. In order to remain competitive, Netflix has introduced Netflix Originals that are based on the data analytic abilities. They also continue to offer and create shows based on the interests of their consumers, updating their selections on a regular cadence. For Netflix, they were able to collect data early on from their consumers, and they were able to use this to their advantage. Netflix started out collecting simple data on their consumers as a way to give them an enjoyable experience. By making suggestions based on consumer input, Netflix was able to decide the interests of Netflix membership holders and suggest movies that fell into those interest categories. But the amount of data collected and what could be done with that data was limited until Netflix ventured into the world of streaming services. Once Netflix became a streaming services, they were able to collect and interpret an enormous amount of data from their 158 million account holders. Now that we know why Netflix collects data, let us dive into how they are able to do it.

Netflix operates in 190 countries across the world and has 151 million subscribers. All of those users generate a tremendous amount of data that needs to be stored somewhere. Netflix turned to Amazon to address that problem. For instance, Amazon offers a cloud computing service "Amazon Web Service" which Netflix relies on as an outsourced storage service, analytic service, and database for the data generated from their 151 million users (Macaulay, 2019). Monitoring and analyzing the AWS network is very critical for Netflix to improve their customers' experience and increase efficiency. In addition, Netflix has implemented a clever way of resolving the issue of streaming latency that would normally occur due to their high volume of users. To address this issue, they rely on their own technology called "content delivery network." CDN consists of hard drive devices that are installed within the Internet service providers' networks around the globe. These devices are crammed in a server and each device collects around 20,000 units of content (Binge Watching, 2016). When a user hits play to watch a movie, the request goes to the nearest CDN within the user's ISP. The content will be streamed much faster due to the higher bandwidth of the Internet connection between ISP and clients which reduces the distance Internet traffic needs to travel from server to consumer.

Netflix has pioneered the use of AI in generating competitive advantage in both data-driven content creation and targeted marketing. Data-driven content creation has led Netflix's original content offerings to greater success than its traditional television counterpart. Furthermore, Netflix's novel applications of targeted marketing in conjunction with their original content has also improved the success of their shows while also reducing costs on their marketing budget. By applying big data and AI technologies to these fields, Netflix has managed to expand their service offerings while also improving their service quality.

Expanding on data-driven content creation, Netflix first began this practice in earnest with their 2013 release of their original series *House of Cards*. The creation of this series was the first time Netflix felt it had enough data to properly understand what its audience wanted out of a show. As such, "Executives used big data analytics to inform all of the most important decisions" and formed a highly successful series that would serve as a model for Netflix's original content projects in the future (Markman, 2019). Looking more broadly, while television writers and producers have always followed popular trends, Netflix took this idea a step further. Through their use of big data analytics, Netflix is able to understand better what their audiences want than the audiences themselves can express. This is illustrated by the fact that approximately 80% of Netflix's original series see a second season compared to roughly 30–40% of traditional television (The Startup, 2018). Netflix's use of data-driven content creation has become a major source of their competitive advantage in the streaming market, particularly as the market has become more and more saturated as time has gone on.

Targeted marketing via AI is not something unique to Netflix; however, their approach is novel in the way that it improves their original content. Referring again to *House of Cards*, Netflix applied what they knew of their customer base to advertise the show in such a way as to make it appeal to almost anyone by producing multiple trailers. Netflix produced ten trailers in total for the show, each of which appealed specifically to different consumer tastes. As an example, if Netflix knew that you preferred shows with female characters, then they would specifically advertise to you a trailer for *House of Cards* that prominently featured the female characters (2019). This approach has not only reduced marketing budget costs for Netflix but has also played a part in the success of Netflix's original series.

As a company, Netflix has evolved with the times to grow from a movie rental service into the industry's foremost entertainment streaming service. This growth and evolution are in no small part thanks to Netflix's prodigious use and collection of big data. By collecting a wide range of data on their user's viewing habits, Netflix was able to create technologies such as the "recommendation algorithm" which drastically improved their user experience. Additionally, Netflix's use of data in content creation and marketing has also granted them a strong competitive advantage in the increasingly competitive streaming market. All in all, Netflix's success as a business can be largely attributed to their application of big data and AI technologies.

20.6 Key Takeaways and Outlook

With the widespread availability of social media platforms and applications today, the vast majority of online businesses are utilizing this resource. In fact, it has almost become impossible for businesses to successfully operate websites and e-commerce without the use of some type of social media apps. However, the impact that these applications and platforms have had on these businesses is astonishing. Because of social media, it is now easier than ever for a company to understand their customers, discover issues, solve these issues, and get to know their competitors. However, the main issue with collecting mass amounts of data from your consumers is the issue of privacy. When is it alright for a company to collect information and data about their consumers and when is it inappropriate? In this type of situation, it is best that the company be honest and open with consumers about when it is collecting this data and what they are using it for. If a company is honest with consumers and does not abuse this technology, then collecting data and information about the consumer can result in a positive outcome from both parties. Overall, social media has allowed companies to be more productive and efficient in marketing and customer services.

What does the media analytics relationship with consumers look like? In today's world, social media analytics is a common tool used by companies to find out vital information about consumers by tracking their web traffic patterns. Specifically, where consumers are coming from, what web browsing technology they are using and how consumers are interacting with the website. Because of social media analytics' success in learning important information about the consumers who use a company's website, it is now one of the most vital and extensively used tools for online marketing teams who attain or sell a large portion of their sales leads from their company's website. The data that social media analytics actually gains from their websites is consumer behaviors such as number of unique visitors that go onto your site; number of times a consumer goes to your website; number of page views a specific page gets; amount of time consumers spend on the website; bounce rate, which would be, for example, the percentage of visitors who leave after visiting one page; number of goals reached (e.g., downloads/registrations/orders), and conversion rate (e.g., number of goals reached divided by number of unique visitors). These consumer behaviors are used to increase customer engagement and increase purchasing on a business' website.

The way businesses use the consumer behavioral data gained from social media analytics and leverage that information to lower bounce rates and increase the sales of their websites is by finding out how users access their site online. For example, do consumers use their mobile phones or laptops? With a heavy number of online users accessing sites from their mobile phones, it is highly important for companies to make sure their websites are mobile-friendly to consumers. The second way is by determining where the traffic of users is coming from. This way companies can decide where to put their time and money for marketing. A third way is by finding out where consumers on your website are located so you can improve your targeting; doing this will help determine which locations or areas generate more sales. The fourth way is similar to the last one, but instead of finding out information about a specific region, you use demographics data to help better understand the customers so you can improve targeting. Using demographics will show the company what gender, age, and interests the customer is and then a company can use this information to create a more improved targeting criteria for future marketing strategies. The last way is by paying close attention to the bounce rates to help find out where you are losing customers. Keep a close watch to pages on the website that have higher traffic and a higher bounce rate compared to other pages. The pages with higher bounce rates might mean that there is a problem with the format or information on the page. In addition to how social media analytics are used by businesses to draw in consumers to their company, it is also important to look at how consumers are affected by companies using social media analytics to gain personal information from the consumers in order to bring in more sales for the company and whether this personal information they gain is an intrusion into the customer's privacy. In today's world with most of people's time spent online, it is no wonder that the activity on our computer can give away so much personal information that can be considered as private information. When a consumer browses website contents, any visited web pages or specific keywords that were retrieved through a search engine platform like Google can be used by companies to improve consumer profiles and later help advertisers put forth the ideal marketing strategy to draw in the customer.

With that said, it is the growth of the global Internet user activity that worries both the company owners and consumers or users. It is a fact that profiles online can stay anonymous, but it is also a fact that a lot of businesses try to match personally identifiable information. For example, this could be an address or name that is gained from the consumer profiles that companies have. In addition, there is information that can be gained by social media analytics even though that is seen as being more private by default. This information, for example, could be race, political affiliation, an individual's sexual orientation, and financial or health information. Knowledge extracted from information like this can be seen as intrusive and cause personal harm, as seen by the retailer Target case in 2012. Most consumers do not realize just how much information a company can get out of them through social media analytics, and in 2012, an article from the New York Times came out about Target. The article explained how the retailer Target studies customer shopping patterns through social media analytics and tries to determine which customers are mothers and pregnant. Target's marketing analytics manager figured out how to identify pregnant mothers before those mothers volunteered that information on the baby registry. Having this knowledge gave Target an advantage because they could sell and advertise baby and maternity products well before competing companies. Also, by getting an early start on pregnant mothers, it contributed to making them lifelong customers. So, what Target is doing could be considered as an invasion of privacy. Because typically what retailers and other companies do is predict what you will buy, not whether somebody is pregnant, which is definitely a private concept and sensitive information (Moylan, 2012).

Furthermore on the topic of consumer privacy and determining which information should stay private, there is an article by the New York Times that examined whether consumers should be able to control how companies collect and use their personal data. This article does a good job at articulating exactly what customers' or consumers' feelings are towards the use of social media analytics or more specifically data mining. In the article "Sharing Data but Not Happily," a study from the Annenberg School for Communication at the University of Pennsylvania came to the conclusion that "Many Americans do not think the trade-off of their data for personalized services, giveaways or discounts is a fair deal." Additionally, the article "Sharing Data but Not Happily" took a "randomized telephone survey of 1,506 adult American Internet users, conducted by Princeton Survey Research Associates International and the results" showed that "84 percent strongly or somewhat agreed that they wanted to have control over what marketers could learn about them; at the same time, 65 percent agreed that they had come to accept that they had little control over it." These quotes show that American online users want to have control over what information companies use, and they also do not agree with the fact that companies can gain information and use that information against them without their knowledge. It is also important to note that these quotes explain how consumers feel like they do not have a choice in the matter and that it is out of their control on what companies do with that information and how they collect it. This has created a sense of resignation among consumers online (Singer, 2015). Some customers are not comfortable with the fact that their online behaviors are being tracked or are unsure of how much data these organizations can really collect from consumers. Therefore, there have to be regulations put in place to limit the type of information taken from customers.

20.7 Conclusion

Media analytics is a subject that will not be going away in the near future. As outlined in the chapter it is clear that if used effectively, social media analytics and AI are key to a company's future business success. There are numerous examples of companies benefiting from applying AI in social media analytics like North Face, Puma, Nike, and Amazon, which are just a few very successful and well-known company names that use web analytics. With the amount of information online, it would be nearly impossible to go through, analyze, and store it without the use of AI. This is also the stage where many companies run into issues with social media analytics and big data because it is just an information overload. However, if companies create AI-based analytical strategies and pick and choose what algorithm is useful to their company, then they can leverage the data and use it to make well-informed decisions. AI and big data also have their downside with issues concerning privacy.

References

Abdallah, S., Benetos, E., Gold, N., Hargreaves, S., Weyde, T., & Wolff, D. (2017). The digital music lab: A big data infrastructure for digital musicology. *Journal on Computing and Cultural Heritage, 10*(1), 1–21. https://doi.org/10.1145/2983918

Ashworth, S. (2018, March 20). *What big data means for radio.* Retrieved October 19, 2019, from https://www.radioworld.com/show-news/what-big-data-means-for-radio

Binge Watching. (2016). *How Netflix content is stored and streamed.* Retrieved from https://blog.uptrends.com/technology/binge-watching-how-netflix-content-is-stored-and-streamed/

Budelman, M., & Kizelshteyn, M. (2019). *Three Principles for Designing ML-Powered Products.* Spotify Design. Retrieved from https://spotify.design/article/three-principles-for-designing-ml-powered-products

Bulygo, Z. (2019, February 15). *How Netflix uses analytics to select movies, create content, & make multimillion dollar decisions.* Retrieved December 10, 2019, from https://neilpatel.com/blog/how-netflix-uses-analytics/

Dreier, T. (2012, February). The state of streaming media and entertainment 2012: Consumers want it all. *Streaming Media, 9*(1), 24–29.

Greenberg, D. M., & Rentfrow, P. J. (2017). Music and big data: A new frontier. *Current Opinion in Behavioral Sciences, 18*, 50–56. https://doi.org/10.1016/j.cobeha.2017.07.007

Hill, S. (2014, June 20). *TV audience measurement with big data.* https://www.liebertpub.com/doi/full/10.1089/big.2014.0012

Lippell, H. (2014). Chapter 14: Big data in the media and entertainment sectors. In J. M. Cavanillas & E. C. W. Wahlster (Eds.), *New horizons for a data-driven economy: A roadmap for usage and exploitation of big data in Europe* (pp. 245–259).

Macaulay, T. (2019). *How Netflix moved to the AWS cloud and created its own CDN.* Retrieved 10 December 2019, from https://www.computerworld.com/article/3427839/ten-years-on%2D%2Dhow-netflix-completed-a-historic-cloud-migration-with-aws.html

Markman, J. (2019, February 25). *Netflix harnesses big data to profit from your tastes.* https://www.forbes.com/sites/jonmarkman/2019/02/25/netflix-harnesses-big-data-to-profit-from-your-tastes/#17fc40bd66fd

Marr, B. (2018, April 18). *Netflix used big data to identify the movies that are too scary to finish.* https://www.forbes.com/sites/bernardmarr/2018/04/18/netflix-used-big-data-to-identify-the-movies-that-are-too-scary-to-finish/#379321143990

MIT Press. (2016, September 6). *Big Data and the Future of Entertainment Part 1.* https://mitpress.mit.edu/blog/big-data-and-future-entertainment-part-1
Moylan, M. (2012) *Target's deep customer data mining raises eyebrows.* MPRNews. Retrieved from https://www.mprnews.org/story/2012/03/07/target-data-mining-privacy
PWC. (2021). *Global Entertainment & Media Outlook 2022–2026.* Retrieved from https://www.pwc.com/outlook
The Startup. (2018, January 12). *How netflix uses big data.* Retrieved November 23, 2019, from https://medium.com/swlh/how-netflix-uses-big-data-20b5419c1edf
Sen, I. (2018). *How AI helps Spotify win in the music streaming world.* Outside Insight. https://outsideinsight.com/insights/how-ai-helps-spotifywin-in-the-music-streaming-world/
Singer, N. (2015). *Sharing Data, but Not Happily.* NYTimes. Retrieved from https://www.nytimes.com/2015/06/05/technology/consumers-conflicted-over-data-mining-policies-report-finds.html
Schlieski, T., & Johnson, B. D. (2012, May). Entertainment in the age of big data. *Proceedings of the IEEE, 100*(Special Centennial Issue), 1404–1408.
Wang, C. (2020). *Why TikTok Made Its User So Obsessive? The AI Algorithm That Got You Hooked.* Retrieved from https://towardsdatascience.com/why-tiktok-made-its-user-so-obsessive-the-ai-algorithmthat-got-you-hooked-7895bb1ab423

Artificial Intelligence in Fashion

21

Abstract

This chapter analyses the history of AI in fashion and current AI applications including computerized analytic systems, AI-serviced checkout systems, business-to-consumer information technology, and big data analytics. Implementations of AI in large companies like American Eagle, Van Heusen, Under Armour, ASOS, and Tommy Hilfiger are described. Multiple customized solutions involving heuristics, mathematical modeling, expert systems, fuzzy logic (FL), neural network (NN), genetic algorithm (GA), multiagent system (MAS), artificial immune system (AIS), evolution strategy (ES), and others are presented. A case study on AI at Stitch Fix explores the use of AI algorithms to discover and recommend customer desired style and sizing needs.

Keywords

Artificial intelligence · Big data analytics · Fashion · Clothing manufacturing · Hypermarkets · Computer vision · Virtual store · Virtual shopping experience · Smart mirror · Recommendation · Fit assistance · Augmentative intelligence · Artificial neural networks · Personalization · Customized clothing

21.1 Introduction

Over the past decade, AI usage has increased dramatically in every aspect of fashion, from the manufacturing department to supply chain management and consumer analysis divisions. Small businesses and large corporations in the fashion industry have always kept a close eye on marketing and following consumers' latest needs and desires. AI has revolutionized the industry by giving owners and analysts the ability to acquire and interpret data at unprecedented speeds and accuracy. Companies in the fashion industry are relying very heavily on AI to provide

L. Chan et al., *Applied Artificial Intelligence in Business*, Applied Innovation and Technology Management, https://doi.org/10.1007/978-3-031-05740-3_21

accurate information to their various divisions using computerized analytic systems. Prior to computers, tablets, and smartphones, businesses would track sales and customer reviews by physically taking count and written records. Now, there are automated systems that customers use to leave their feedback for companies to use in their evaluations and planning.

Companies like Amazon, H&M, and Tommy Hilfiger are powerhouses in the fashion industry, which ensure the growth of AI usage in US markets. All of these companies have joined the mobile shopping movement and have established a robust online presence in order to stay afloat in a rapidly changing market. Aside from having a heavy Internet presence, these companies are relying on AI to collect information from customers regarding trends and ideas. The companies are using their social media accounts as full AI-serviced checkout systems for consumers online. Large companies have heavily shifted their focus to making an ecommerce presence given the current market is heavily inclined towards expediting experiences. The ecommerce interface gives companies an advantage when analyzing the popularity of their products, or planning their seasonal lines.

In the future, large-scale companies will find more ways to further revolutionize fashion and open up new options in ways the average consumer could not fathom. AI is being implemented and updated at such a brisk rate that the industry is struggling to balance, implementing new technology while responding to current data being received. In other words, the process of updating to new technology is too slow, which causes a lapse between communication and response with current customers. While these issues have caused some setbacks in implementation, companies have benefited immensely from the data provided by AI regarding consumers' likes and dislikes. Without AI, large companies would not be able to keep up with the amount of customer responses being generated on a daily basis. In the next decade, we predict the shopping experience, along with digital marketing, will exhibit rapid changes in their field. With state-of-the-art technology, companies will be able to identify the most effective way to reach consumers based on recorded interests online.

21.2 Current AI Applications

The largest amount of AI technology usage within the fashion industry is used by corporations selling to mass quantities of consumers. As such, business-to-consumer information technology is best demonstrated by its usage within retail clothing outlets, hypermarkets, and department stores. Hypermarkets are a less grocery-oriented version of supermarkets, offering their customers a one-stop shopping experience.

Emerging technologies enabled the fashion businesses to move online and keep open during the pandemic. With a large economy of scale, vendors such as Walmart and Amazon selling clothes at extremely low-profit margins, smaller-sized stores, and retail outlets that operate predominantly on a "brick and mortar" business model can be highly susceptible to bankruptcy. Similar to the restaurant industry, sale profits for an individual sale can have an exceedingly low contribution margin, making it a necessity to sell products in large quantities. Clothing can also go "out-of-fashion" quite easily, making bulk purchases of a particular style or brand a dangerous gamble. The popular demand can shift before enough of the product is sold to make a net profit, leading to unfortunate loss and waste.

In an age where AI has become a part of society's everyday lives, the breakdown of big data analytics has become a key factor in how fashion companies operate their business in order to succeed. Companies now have the ability to dissect their business models one by one, evaluating anything from sales forecasting to customer trends. Hence, they have a much better understanding of their products, customers, and demands. In the fashion industry, the demand for new fashion products is always high, which calls for constant up-to-date changes in the fashion supply chains. Companies that have invested in AI and big data are able to break down and analyze business decisions in real time, allowing room for much quicker improvements and maximizing their chances for success.

One of the leading companies currently using and upgrading their AI compatibility and involvement is American Eagle. American Eagle is a famous brand in the United States that young adults and teens constantly turn to for the latest fashion trends and styles. Recently, they have had to adapt to the Covid-19 regulations and mandates, which has reduced their foot traffic drastically and negatively impacted sales. Most recently they have launched a virtual shopping experience with Snapchat. This new feature gives the user the ability to look at their phone and toggle their camera in relation to where they are in the store. From there, consumers can click on, say, a jeans rack, select specific styles, and add them to their cart for checkout and payment. During the virtual store tour, there are pop-up offers as well as review options requesting feedback from customers. The goal behind the virtual store is to restore the positive feelings and shopping experience to consumers and subsequently maintain a competitive edge. The AI systems aren't just seen in the retail and sales aspect in the fashion industry; AI and ML are seen in design and logistics marketing.

The second company worth mentioning is Van Heusen, which is a leader in high-end runway fashion, known for elegant top-line clothing and accessories. They have introduced one of the most innovative and industry-evolving systems seen thus far: interactive mirrors in their changing rooms. The interactive mirror scans customers' clothed figures and computes styles and combinations the customer may like. While the customer is scrolling, the recommendations are sent to the checkout while the customer is still shopping to completely expedite the shopping process. The smart mirror is not only able to generate new combinations for customers, but it can generate new colors and sizes to fulfill the customer's exact wants. This is all accomplished while staying within the privacy of the changing room and successfully saving time and energy. Smart mirrors are not restricted to the changing rooms but can be installed on the retail floor as well. Customers will have the ability to see what the clothing looks like by simply scanning the barcode and standing in front of the mirror. AI and ML are becoming more relevant in today's consumer market as everyday companies and small businesses are learning how to implement AI in their daily operations.

Within the category of fashionable fitness, Under Armour uses AI in their health and fitness app called "*Record*." The purpose of the app is to help people lead a healthy lifestyle and create good habits that will help achieve fitness goals. The app tracks standard health metrics such as workout completion, sedentary time, sleep data, and nutrition. It can also import data from other applications partnered with Under Armour, which may be necessary for acquiring long-term data from a customer prior to them downloading *Record*. With that additionally imported data, their AI would be able to make recommendations for the user much more efficiently. Those suggestions may range from caloric intake to training advice to help achieve a user's fitness goals, all at the tips of their fingers. The company strongly benefits from providing this avenue to its users by relaying key health information for a fraction of the cost of a personal trainer and gym membership. Downstream, the expectation is that user satisfaction with the AI fitness app will increase, the brand's name will become more popularized online, and the company flourishes with an even larger user base.

Technological evolution is not limited to physical clothing retailers, as there are plenty of companies making strides in online shopping while only maintaining headquarters for their administrative staff. ASOS is a British fashion and cosmetic retailer that only has corporate offices and headquarters, but has been able to make revenue through their website and app (Turk, 2018). For example, their app has a sizing tool called, "Fit Assistance," where the users provide their measurements and other proportional information for the AI to interpret. The AI then suggests size and recommendations for products according to the information it was given by the user. This tool is made possible with a large database of garment sizing information called "FitAnalytics." As a final selling point, the AI will also give a percent chance that the customer will be satisfied with the product based off of reviewer satisfaction and data from prior purchases. This percentage is meant to build confidence in the consumer and also add an amount of accountability to the producer of their retail products. As the amount of data is accumulated on a product, the more accurate the AI can be at describing the chance of consumer contentment and increasing overall confidence within the company.

While the AI technology presented thus far has been focused on the consumer experience, fashion requires a significant amount of design work prior to hitting the shelves. Tommy Hilfiger is a major brand involved in fashion retail that has been making use of AI software with the partnership of IBM to reduce lead time and increase productivity within the design team. For the design department, IBM's software allows for computer vision and CGI to be used in the process of designing new outfits (Arthur, 2018). Many new outfits in fashion are being made using a collaborative artificial intelligence, which can view, process, and analyze thousands of different photos to produce new and creative designs that can be manually refined in order to create new outfits. The data that is compiled and analyzed gives an opportunity for designers to broaden their horizons through increased exposure to the various trends happening around the world.

A common issue that fashion companies continue to face is keeping up to pace with the trends in fashion and ultimately getting ahead of them for production. In

Fig. 21.1 Summary of the example companies and their implemented AI technology in section

the past, companies had to rely on the previous year's data to evaluate and work on improving their products/sales. With the help of large databases and rapid computer processing power, companies now examine datasets in real time. With that being said, the use of AI in the fashion industry has allowed companies to maximize the tools needed in order to be successful, and there is still much more to come in the future (Fig. 21.1).

21.3 AI Applications for Fashion

As described in the section above, AI has already made significant contributions to the consumer experience and overall business success. For example, improvements have been made in the following subareas through the use of AI: product design, patternmaking and cutting, three-dimensional scanning, wearable technology integration, robotics, and advanced material logistics. The fashion industry took AI as "Augmentative Intelligence" (Intelistyle, n.d.), as it is built on human creativity and builds by utilizing machine learning algorithms. In general, the objective of AI in fashion is to adopt a customized approach that will add value to the business model. Customers are difficult to understand and predict due to their individualistic needs, tastes, and demographics. Therefore, a diverse product mix needs to be produced in the fashion industry for their satisfaction and subsequent revenue in the company (Pfahl & Moxham, 2014).

AI has been providing multiple, focused, and customized solutions through the whole omnichannel to address various aspects of the fashion industry. When exploring AI in textiles, it is important to note contributions of AI in garment manufacturing, particularly in color matching, fabric quality control and detection of defects, and pattern inspections. Nayak and Padhye (2018) explored the history, types of artificial intelligence in apparel, applications, challenges, and future directions. AI provides solutions to problems with the use of heuristics and mathematical modeling, which leads to improved quality, lower cost, and increased productivity (Shamey & Hussain, 2003).

Clothing manufacturing (Fig. 21.2) uses various AI techniques including expert systems, fuzzy logic (FL), neural network (NN), genetic algorithm (GA), multiagent system (MAS), artificial immune system (AIS), and evolution strategy (ES) (Nayak & Padhye, 2018). According to Nayak and Padhye (2018), one of the types of AI – artificial neural networks (ANNs) – has been used in clothing manufacturing, in particular: in the textile fiber identification and grading (color, length, fineness, tenacity, uniformity, spinning performance), applications of AI are important (Chattopadhyay & Guha, 2004). Several applications of AI in yarn manufacturing have been mentioned in the literature, including yarn engineering (Majumdar et al., 2006) and tensile properties (Üreyen & Gürkan, 2008; Majumdar et al., 2004; Nayak & Padhye, 2018).

There have been some applications of AI in fabric production, especially in predicting fabric properties before manufacturing (Fig. 21.3). Some research and model developments have been performed in this area using artificial neural networks (ANNs) for predicting the aesthetic and functional properties of worsted suiting fabrics by Behera and Mishra (2007) and the use of regression analysis and ANN to predict properties of single jersey fabric by Unal et al. (2012). The use of ANN, NN, Taguchi methodologies, BP algorithms, and image processing has been noted in the classification of woven fabric patterns, predicting the strength and behavior of woven fabrics and fabric design (Jeon et al., 2003; Zeydan, 2008; Behera & Karthikeyan, 2006; Hadizadeh et al., 2009; Nayak & Padhye, 2018).

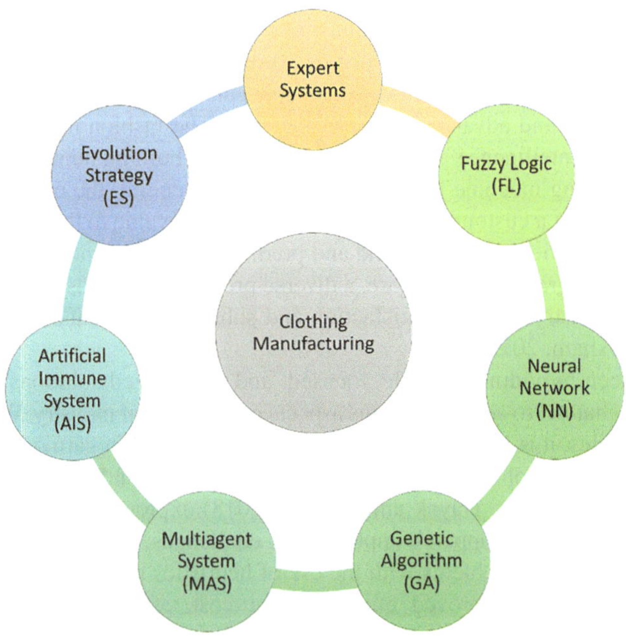

Fig. 21.2 Summary of currently identified AI techniques in clothing manufacturing

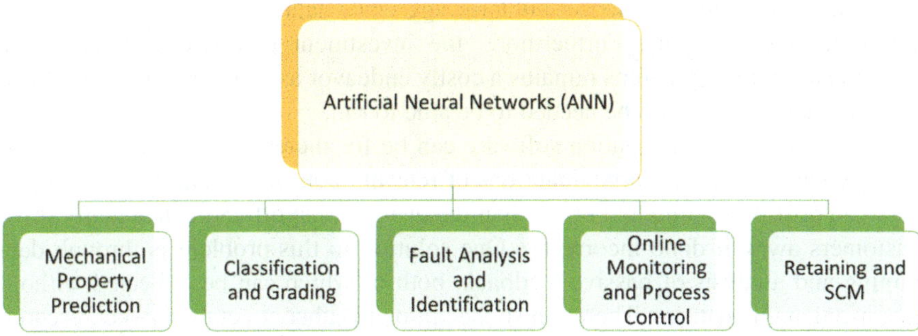

Fig. 21.3 Functions accomplished by artificial neural networks (ANNs) in clothing manufacturing

Since customers' tastes related to fashion and fabrics fall also in the category of fabric feel (sensory comfort), fabric and dress item heat retention and transfer (thermo-physiological comfort), water resistance, and fabric breathability and wicking of sweat, the Kawabata evaluation system (KES) has been used to predict those properties of the fabric (Nayak & Padhye, 2018). There are a number of models for the simulation of heat and moisture exchange with human skin and clothing (Wang et al., 2005).

Case 21.1: AI at Stitch Fix

Stitch Fix is an online clothes retailer that uses personalized tailoring to provide customers with customized clothing that fits perfectly to their individual measurements and lengths. By using both big data from congregated customer clothing and sizing preferences and small individual consumer data, Stitch Fix is able to use AI to analyze customer preferences and offer a wardrobe that gives a customer clothing options that fit their lifestyle and styling needs. This AI feature, along with its subscription nature that sees personalized clothing sent to the user monthly, provides an even more customized shopping experience. While at most clothing stores customers are able to find clothing that fits their style, they have to either spend plenty of time going through the store to find their sizes or have to take a risk with online retailers, whose size specifications may not be standard and could potentially leave customers with ill-fitting products. Stitch Fix eliminates both these by using AI algorithms to discover and recommend customers the desired style and sizing needs. The company sends the user five articles of clothing and also allows them three days to return any unwanted clothing; if all five articles are kept, customers also receive a 25% discount on their total costs. Data from transactions are then used to update a customer's style profile and its recommendations are then reconfigured based on updated stylization preferences. These technologies allow the business to gain customer loyalty and trust because the service provides a highly personalized experience for customers. It also helps the company to engage in a unique value proposition as it is the premier service for personalized clothing retailing. However, with these benefits, the service does require an immense amount of customer data storage and the need for not only warehouses but large aggregate data centers that can be highly costly for the company. Furthermore, the investment required to create these machine learning algorithms remains a costly endeavor as well and a growing/loyal customer base is going to be needed to be able to run.

As useful as personalization software can be for increasing customer base and engagement, it requires large quantities of relevant consumer data. Collecting this data can cost more time and effort than the eventual payoff and can actually drive customers away if done incorrectly. One solution to this problem is through data mining and analysis of passive feedback, both of which can be collected without inconveniencing patrons. There is also the option to subcontract the market research in order to maximize successful data collected for artificial intelligence and machine learning. Unfortunately, the price of such a service can be significantly higher than the perceived value. Despite those limitations, clothing retailers are using these techniques in data collection processes. They have managed to effectively customize their selection of products and the customer experience by analyzing purchases, returns on products, and data from loyalty card users. They have also reportedly been making plans to utilize RFID tracking to allow for further personalization in physical stores (Mixson, 2021).

Other companies like H&M and Walmart are deploying facial recognition software that can analyze customers while they stand in line at the cashier. This data can then be processed using artificial intelligence algorithms in order to determine accurately what the satisfaction levels of their patrons are (Anderson, 2017). More technologically forward examples would include the company like Amazon Go, a chain of retail supermarkets in which artificial intelligence renders checkout unnecessary. Rather than any form of cashier or self-service checkout, there is around-the-clock surveillance, which recognizes patrons as they walk throughout the store and takes note of every product that they take, digitally charging them as they walk out the store. This combination of complex surveillance software and computer algorithms are significantly more expensive than the expense of labor for most stores, which is the main reason why it has not been integrated yet.

21.4 Conclusion

As more AI technology is being introduced during the twenty-first century, it is important to keep in mind that there are positive aspects and potential drawbacks. For a consumer, the changes can create a more user-friendly experience online, where suggested fashion lines and styles are tailored directly to their interests. While striving for efficiency, an unfortunate drawback to pursuing AI is that it could reduce a lot of available labor hours and cut employment numbers down entirely. As is the expectation, computerized machines are built to be much more precise than a person, which means companies would be inclined to avoid flaws in their products. While efficiency and perfection are certainly major goals, denying employment to those who would normally work in the industry can lead to a reduction in disposable income. With that in mind, a delicate balance can be maintained between consumers and retailers in the market while still implementing AI technology.

One major issue with AI being used broadly among companies is that data mining can be a concern to the privacy of online users. Users who access a website to shop for products online may not be consenting to having their search and preference data sold or shared with other companies. As with all new technology, the implementation of stricter regulations typically comes when enough ethical dilemmas have arisen that it becomes a benefit issue. If consumers become uncomfortable with accessing sites that use AI for invasion of privacy, then the companies are negatively impacted. Since establishing a strong base online is of high priority, businesses will become accommodating and compliant to their consumers.

Overall, the public is cautiously optimistic about AI technology and has since been enjoying the perks of using applications and smart technology to enhance their shopping experience. Designers and engineers have been working together on boosting efficiency and pursuing new opportunities in the field. As long as the drawbacks and issues are addressed accordingly, AI can become the cornerstone of the fashion industry as we know it.

References

Anderson, G. (2017, July 27). *Walmart's facial recognition tech would overstep boundaries*. Retrieved from https://www.forbes.com/sites/retailwire/2017/07/27/walmarts-facial-recognition-tech-would-overstep-boundaries/?sh=3492f7e45f82

Arthur, R. (2018). *Artificial intelligence empowers designers in IBM, Tommy Hilfiger and FIT collaboration*. Retrieved from https://www.forbes.com/sites/rachelarthur/2018/01/15/ai-ibm-tommy-hilfiger/?sh=5144573778ac

Behera, B. K., & Karthikeyan, B. (2006). Artificial neural network-embedded expert system for the design of canopy fabrics. *Journal of Industrial Textiles, 36*(2), 111–123.

Behera, B. K., & Mishra, R. (2007). *Comfort properties of non-conventional light weight worsted suiting fabrics*.

Chattopadhyay, R., & Guha, A. (2004). Artificial neural networks: Applications to textiles. *Textile Progress, 35*(1), 1–46.

Hadizadeh, M., Jeddi, A. A., & Tehran, M. A. (2009). The prediction of initial load-extension behavior of woven fabrics using artificial neural network. *Textile Research Journal, 79*(17), 1599–1609.

Intelistyle. (n.d.). *AI in fashion: An extensive guide to all applications for retail*. Retrieved from https://www.intelistyle.com/ai-fashion-retail-applications/

Jeon, B. S., Bae, J. H., & Suh, M. W. (2003). Automatic recognition of woven fabric patterns by an artificial neural network. *Textile Research Journal, 73*(7), 645–650.

Majumdar, A., Majumdar, P. K., & Sarkar, B. (2004). *Prediction of single yarn tenacity of ring-and rotor-spun yarns from HVI results using artificial neural networks*.

Majumdar, A., Majumdar, P. K., & Sarkar, B. (2006). An investigation on yarn engineering using artificial neural networks. *Journal of the Textile Institute, 97*(5), 429–434.

Mixson, E. (2021, August 31). *H&M Restyled: Iside H&M digital transformation*. Retrieved from https://www.intelligentautomation.network/resiliency/articles/hm-restyled-inside-hm-digital-transformation#:~:text=Through%20the%20use%20of%20RFID,precise%20supply%20and%20demand%20predictions

Nayak, R., & Padhye, R. (2018). Artificial intelligence and its application in the apparel industry. In *Automation in garment manufacturing* (pp. 109–138). Woodhead Publishing.

Pfahl, L., & Moxham, C. (2014). Achieving sustained competitive advantage by integrating ECR, RFID and visibility in retail supply chains: A conceptual framework. *Production Planning & Control, 25*(7), 548–571.

Shamey, R., & Hussain, T. (2003). Artificial intelligence in the colour and textile industry. *Review of Progress in Coloration and Related Topics, 33*(1), 33–45.

Turk, R. (2018, November 29). *Asos improves sizing assistance with AI technology.* Retrieved from https://fashionunited.uk/news/fashion/asos-improves-sizing-assistance-with-ai-technology/2018112940243

Unal, P. G., Üreyen, M. E., & Mecit, D. (2012). Predicting properties of single jersey fabrics using regression and artificial neural network models. *Fibers and Polymers, 13*(1), 87–95.

Üreyen, M. E., & Gürkan, P. (2008). Comparison of artificial neural network and linear regression models for prediction of ring spun yarn properties. I. Prediction of yarn tensile properties. *Fibers and Polymers, 9*(1), 87–91.

Wang, Z., Li, Y., & Wong, A. S. W. (2005). Simulation of clothing thermal comfort with fuzzy logic. In *Elsevier ergonomics book series* (Vol. 3, pp. 467–471). Elsevier.

Zeydan, M. (2008). Modelling the woven fabric strength using artificial neural network and Taguchi methodologies. *International Journal of Clothing Science and Technology.*

Artificial Intelligence in Video Games and eSports

22

Abstract

This chapter starts with the introduction and the evolution of AI in gaming and esports. It explores the enabling technologies for AI in gaming (big data, virtual reality, AI chips and GPUs, online gaming, and cloud platforms). AI applications in video games and esports include AI Opponents, AI NPCs, procedural content generation, player experience modeling, antisocial behavior detection, win prediction, player telemetry analytics, intelligent tutoring, and training. Case studies section consists of DeepMind Alpha Go, Alpha Star, and Microsoft HoloLens.

Keywords

Gaming · Esports · Video game industry · Electronic sports · Big data · Virtual reality · Augmented reality · Mixed reality · Metaverse · Graphic processing units · GPU · AI chips · System on a chip · Unreal engine · Online gaming · Video games · Cloud platforms · Emergent behavior · Freemium · Subscription business model · Finite state machines · Artificial neural networks · Convolutional neural networks · Hirelings · Followers · Non-player characters · Recurrent neural networks · Procedural content generation · Intelligent tutoring systems · Simulation

22.1 Introduction

In 2021, the worldwide video game market generated revenue of over $175.8 billion US dollars (NewZoo, 2021), surpassing the total global revenue of the home/mobile and theatrical entertainment market at $80.8 billion US dollars and approaching the $231 billion US dollar cable subscription market (Motion Picture Association, 2020), making it the second most important entertainment industry globally. The video game and eSports market is projected to continue growing at a compounded annual growth rate (CAGR) of 8%–10% by 2025 and beyond making it an

L. Chan et al., *Applied Artificial Intelligence in Business*, Applied Innovation and Technology Management, https://doi.org/10.1007/978-3-031-05740-3_22

important industry with significant traction with consumers that is here to stay and to continue to be an important form of entertainment for future generations. Within the video game industry, the eSports category has been growing even more rapidly surpassing over $1 billion in revenue for 2021 (NewZoo, 2021) with projected revenue nearly doubling to 2021 and continuing beyond.

Artificial intelligence research and development has had a symbiotic relationship with video games since the earliest days of the industry, driving both innovation in the core technologies and dramatic increases in user engagement as the technology has progressed and been deployed broadly in these markets. eSports in particular have opened new vistas of artificial intelligence research in competitive and cooperative arena-style games. In this chapter, we will explore some of the history of artificial intelligence in video gaming and eSports and undergo an analysis of the value that it brings to both the participants and the businesses working in this industry. We will also cover some of the key categories where artificial intelligence is leading the way to deeper user engagement, higher business revenues, and greater value overall.

22.2 Evolution of AI in Video Games and eSports

Gaming and AI have always had a close connection with one another over the course of the past few decades, with AI itself originating and progressing from the use of games. Traditionally, game playing was a form of entertainment that people would engage in as a social activity with each other. Intelligent opponents in physical media, like the venerable board games Monopoly, Chess, Checkers, and Go, were provided by other human beings. The concept of cooperative and competitive play has most likely been with us since the early prehistory of our species and continues to the present day. However, if you were not able to find an opponent among your friends, family, or neighbors, then you could not necessarily engage in very satisfying game play. For single-player video gaming, AI has been used to help fill in the gap between the solitary player experience on their own and the more community-oriented aspect that we inherited from our ancestors. Cooperative game play in the form of eSports has started to fulfill this need and to bring the solitary gaming experience back into its natural more community-oriented form.

The AI applications in gaming can be dated back to several decades ago. The early games started with offering single-player mode and then gradually a player versus player option. Examples include Pong, Space Invaders, Space War, and Gotcha. These computer games were primarily based on discrete logic and strictly based on competition of one-to-many players through direct play or high scores. These games only offered preprogrammed game intelligence which is not considered true AI. Enemy movement for the single-/multiple-player experience was based on stored programmed patterns and with the eventual incorporation of microprocessors would allow for more computation and random elements to be overlaid into these movement patterns.

It was not until the 1990s did video games start to incorporate more advanced intelligent design and more formal artificial intelligence or "game intelligence." Most games to this day still incorporate what critics refer to as "game AI" since the enemy or competition in these games is bounded and restricted from learning in order to avoid an intelligence from becoming too intelligent for the player and ruining the gaming experience. The 1990s era also produced new game genres such as real-time strategy, combat, fighting, and sports. Games like Madden Football, Earl Weaver Baseball, and Tony La Russa Baseball all attempted to base the game's artificial intelligence on the fact that it imitated those coaches and celebrity's managerial or coaching styles.

It was into the mid-2000s that games started to incorporate a different version of intelligence through what is known as "emergent behavior" or use of the "Search Tree" program for interacting with characters in the game. A player's actions or specific dialog choices would all be considered when determining the state and actions of the non-playable characters or artificial intelligence of the game. This was only achievable once the computer processing speeds were to allow constant evaluations of the player's standing and inputs in the game. This offered new and refreshing dynamics to games for the consumer base. Some examples like Bethesda's Skyrim and "The Legend of Zelda: Breath of the Wild" are still seen in the gaming market to this day.

Our definition of electronic sports (eSports) is the platform or service that facilitates a competitive tournament, through a specific game. For example, in the video game Overwatch, their eSports would be the "Overwatch League." Even though AI has been around for a while, AI eSports is a new and flourishing topic. We can date the entry back to the 2010s when we have DeepMind acquired by Google. They began AlphaGO 2014 which was a GO tabletop AI BOT. Soon the BOT was sophisticated enough to beat the current champion at the time. Moving forward, we find Elon Musk's previous AI company OpenAI created a team for a DOTA 2 match against the top pros. Minimizing human error and increasing intelligence range, they were able to apply machine learning and deep learning to polish their team. More recently, we can see the revolution of eSports production teams being overtaken by AI. With the smart camera from Blizzard's Overwatch League, we can witness how AI is utilized to benefit the viewer and create an easier following. AI will not replace the competitions humans chase after, but it will replace, enhance, and evolve the background and applications of AI eSports in the future.

22.3 Enabling Technologies for AI in Gaming

Emerging technologies such as big data, virtual reality (VR), and image processing have helped the boom of AI in the gaming industry. Innovative technologies help influence the research process by streamlining data collection; they also help with improvements in data management, automating quality control, and speeding up communication. New technologies in AI and big data can help predict demand spikes in the gaming industry. This assists companies enhance their data management by improving the storage within their games to make the quality of the games better and more enjoyable.

22.3.1 Big Data in Gaming

Big data is an emerging segment of the gaming industry that is crucial to the industries' success. Big data analytics are used in so many aspects of the gaming industry and keeps it one of the fastest-growing sectors in entertainment. Video games, being an entirely digital medium, provide a wealth of data for video game developers and publishers to take advantage of in attempting to monetize and improve their games. Such advancements are currently being used throughout the video game industry to generate a competitive advantage by developers of all stripes. Advanced data analytics enables companies to improve the gameplay by reexamining the game's storyline, series of quests, or the challenges of the game that are too hard/easy based on the character level, ideally, pushing a higher user rate and larger volume and reducing the number of lost subscribers. Data analysis through the devices used by players also helps developers to create gaming experiences more effectively. For example, an iPhone is different compared with a widescreen such as a projector, so developers need to address screen sizes, navigation, and character interactions more suitable to the player's devices. The amount of user data being collected on a daily basis is massive and when used correctly can help game developers to keep bettering their products. Big data is collected and mined to enhance customer experiences, determine customers' needs, find difficulties within games, improve user engagement, and optimize in-game advertisement. Game developers can use AI and big data to test their games which makes games run smoother and with fewer errors.

An example that demonstrates the benefits of big data in gaming is Zynga. Zynga is the company behind Farmville, Words with Friends, and Zynga Poker. They use big data to determine customers' needs in the game which resulted in massive growth and success. For example, Zynga determined that in their game Farmville, more users enjoyed engaging and purchasing online animals versus always planting and harvesting crops. Therefore, Zynga added more virtual animals to the game and immediately customer engagement and happiness went up. They also used big data to capitalize on "freemium" advertising. Freemium is a type of advertising that is offered on games that are free to download and play. By looking at the data on customer engagement, Zynga determined that customers were growing increasingly frustrated with upgrade or wait times in games. So they decided to offer boosts or exclusive offers that would enhance the gaming experience but for a cheap price of actual money, say $1 or $2. This way they were generating even more revenue on their free games because they knew that customers would pay for play. At their company's peak, as many as 2 million players were playing their games at any point during the day and every second its servers processed 650 hands of Zynga Poker. Zynga is a great example of how gaming companies can use big data to increase revenue and engagement with their games.

22.3.2 Virtual Reality and AI in Gaming

Today, technologies like virtual reality (VR), augmented reality (AR), and mixed reality (MR) focus on giving the customer an immersive experience with devices like video game consoles or training simulators. VR is a simulated experience that can be similar to or completely different from the real world. Applications of VR include entertainment, such as video games, and education, such as medical or military training. Augmented reality or AR is an interactive experience of a real-world environment where objects in the real world are enhanced by computer-generated perceptual information, sometimes across multiple sensory modalities, including visual, auditory, haptic, somatosensory, and olfactory. AR can be defined as a system that fulfills three basic features: a combination of real and virtual worlds, real-time interaction, and accurate 3D registration of virtual and real objects. Finally, mixed reality or MR is the merging of real and virtual worlds to produce new environments and visualizations, where physical and digital objects coexist and interact in real time. Mixed reality does not exclusively take place in either the physical or virtual world but is a hybrid of reality and virtual reality. VR, AR, and MR have allowed consumers to have an immersive experience when it comes to gaming, training exercises, and other experiences.

Artificial intelligence can be naturally connected with virtual reality in gaming and eSports. A common device for 3D gaming is the virtual reality headset and it largely enhances the immersive interactions in the games. The VR headset helps the users with immersive experience and situational awareness. With the support of AI algorithms, this type of simulation could be used to enhance users' capabilities, giving them heat detection, night vision, and the ability to view scenarios and navigation and allowing them to experience a virtual environment that simulates the real world. Facebook has recently announced the metaverse project, which is an integration of various emerging technologies including VR, AR, and AI. The metaverse is a virtual Internet platform supporting online 3D hypothesized environments through various electronic devices such as virtual and augmented reality headsets. To a certain extent, metaverses is not a brand-new technology, but more of a new name coined to describe the integration of available technologies. Some of its features have already been partially implemented in video games like Second Life or social media platforms like VRChat.

22.3.3 Graphics Processing Units and AI Chips

It is widely known among gamers that they need faster hardware for playing games. The gaming computers or consoles need to be equipped with advanced graphics cards that could handle high-speed image processing tasks within games. These high-end graphics cards are usually the most expensive components of gaming computers. The core element of such expansive cards is the graphics processing unit (GPU). Similar to the central processing unit (CPU), GPU is also a sophisticated semiconductor chip, but it is specifically designed to accelerate graphics processing and rendering. Three-dimensional (3D) game characters, landscapes, and VR simulations require heavy workload on GPUs to process image data in real time. Three-dimensional characters are designed, modelled, animated, and rendered using software packages such as MAYA and 3ds Max. There are also professional game development packages like Unreal Engine that create 3D landscapes more conveniently. Traditional CPUs may not be as efficient in processing and rendering huge volumes of image data at high speed. The GPU chips can significantly speed up the computational processes for machine learning. Due to their feature dedicated to image data processing, GPUs are becoming an essential part of a modern AI infrastructure and evolved into AI chips. Nvidia is a California-based company specialized in the development of professional graphics cards. The company produces high-performance GPUs for the gaming and image processing markets, as well as system on a chip units (SoCs) for the mobile computing and automotive market. Their AI chips have been optimized and designed specifically for processing big data and machine learning tasks. Machine learning algorithms provide AI system capability to automatically learn and improve from experience without being programmed. AI chips and GPUs have greatly enhanced the ability of game engines that can handle more data and use it for machine learning.

22.3.4 Online Gaming and Cloud Platforms

When looking at the gaming industry over the past few years, we can see a dramatic shift towards online game usage, gameplay, and how games are purchased and updated. The idea of going to a local store to pick up a physical copy of a game seems like old school. Online gaming platforms usually adopt the subscription business model, in which they charge different amounts of fees to users based on the length of their subscription. With better Internet bandwidth and cloud technologies, there are improvements in real-time communication through online gaming platforms. Advances in telecommunication technology and mobile networks also significantly promoted the development of online gaming platforms and user communities. Most video games today are played online with other players and by improving person-to-person interactions which makes the game more enjoyable. AI and big data collected through cloud platforms can also help companies to improve services and quality of games. With quality control in online games, AI helps find failures in the product early in the creation of these games. This helps the companies to identify the trends of customers' needs, instead of focusing on the long process of manually finding bugs within the games.

22.4 AI Applications in Video Games and eSports

Artificial intelligence has been applied to develop video games since its inception. Although initial video games attempted to replicate the communal board game experience of games like chess, go, checkers, and monopoly, as AI started to be built

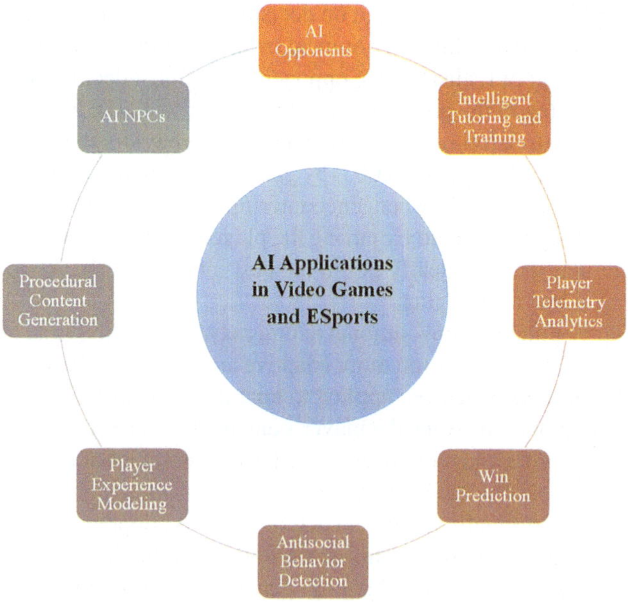

Fig. 22.1 AI applications in video games and eSports

into games, they became a more solitary gaming experience. This increased the need for more sophisticated AI techniques in order to replicate some of the benefits of playing against human players as opposed to dumb machines. Below, we cover some of the broader categories of functionality in video gaming where AI technology has been deployed to achieve this goal after which we will cover how it is being adapted to new uses in the eSports subcategory of video gaming (Fig. 22.1).

22.4.1 AI Opponents

To remain engaged with a video game, a player must have opponents or antagonists that provide them with a challenge or obstacle to overcome. In the early days of gaming, this role was fulfilled by other human opponents much like in the board gaming medium. As video gaming became more of a solitary activity, methods have been developed to simulate intelligent behavior in the opponents that the player faces.

AI approaches of providing simulated intelligence in video games were straightforward, relying on techniques such as finite-state machines (FSMs). In this method, the AI enemies had a fixed number of states that they could be in during the game play. For example, a set of states could be attacking, evading, resting, or dead. A set of transition rules from each of these states to a different state would be written by the programmer beforehand and followed by the AI opponent throughout the game scenario. FSMs came with the limitation that they were very predictable and could get boring once the player figured out the patterns of the rules. A more sophisticated form of the FSM method is one based on decision trees. The idea here is that the AI opponent can react to the game environment by interacting with it and making decisions. This adds a bit of realism to the opponents who must decide what to do based on what is happening in the game as opposed to being in a certain mode of interacting. However, the decision tree method resulted in behaviors that were sometimes termed artificial stupidity (Liden, 2003) by getting stuck in repetitive activities, performing nonsensical actions when encountering scenarios in the game that the developers did not plan for thereby jarring the player out of the game world illusion, or perform actions that are clearly not in the best interests of the AI opponent such as jumping off a ledge and dying.

AI techniques utilizing convolutional neural networks (CNNs) and artificial neural networks (ANNs) lead to even more adaptive artificially intelligent opponents in the games. Algorithms have been applied to tune the difficulty or challenge level of a game in an attempt to fine-tune the player's engagement and to continue to provide more challenges for the player to overcome. This creates a lot of player engagement as they seek out new challenges and patterns to learn in a game. However, sometimes this level of artificially intelligent action by the AI opponent can lead to accusations of cheating from players. This is due to the fact that in order to make the AI opponent more responsive or challenging, game developers sometimes take shortcuts that give the AI access to information that the player would not have in similar situations. For example, the AI opponent in a fighting game could analyze the button presses and timing of a player and know exactly when they release a certain fighting combination. The AI could then provide a countermove that would neutralize any skills the player has built up while playing and practicing the game. A human player would not have access to this information, nor would they have the fast reaction time that the AI opponent has access to leading to frustration on the part of the human player and disengagement with the game.

22.4.2 AI Hirelings, Followers, and Non-Player Characters

In some forms of competitive arena-style combat games, the human players can hire computer-controlled AI characters to aid them through the game. These entities are known as hirelings or followers. In order to follow the player through the complex game terrain map, they need to have sophisticated path-finding abilities and make intelligent decisions about how to best support the player in their game play goals. Hirelings that perform nonsensical actions, get lost, or use up resources that a human player would not choose to do in a similar game situation can be a source of great frustration to modern video game players. Therefore, advanced path-finding techniques such as A* search algorithm, Monte Carlo search, deep neural networks, and other machine learning techniques are being deployed to increase the decision-making capabilities of the hireling non-player characters (NPCs) in modern games.

New techniques such as vision-based NPCs that attempt to play using what they see on the video game screen just like a human player are a new and interesting way to control NPC AI behavior. Essentially, this type of NPC is no different than a human in how it visualizes and interprets the gameplay and reacts to situations evolving with its teammates. Techniques such as recurrent neural networks (RNNs), DNNs, and ANNs play a heavy role in guiding the actions of these nonhuman players during gameplay. Another class of character in video games are third-party NPCs that provide interaction with the player through dialog or specific actions in games. Some of the fun in a video game adventure is having the player interact with the many residents of the virtual world and allow them the freedom to change the course of the game world history by the player's own interaction and choices within the environment. To make this a more realistic experience, the NPCs must behave in the world the way that a somewhat intelligent human would perform and avoid the problems and limitations of the FSM and decision tree-based methods in the previous section.

The success of an eSports competitive team may also depend on how the human players can learn from and defeat generative adaptive network opponents (GANs) during training regimes. Teaching a non-player cooperative agent to adapt to and learn from the strategies of the human team could be used to augment team performance in actual competitive gameplay. This arms race will result in some spectacular entertainment as highly trained AI-augmented human teams compete in arena eSports gaming.

22.4.3 Procedural Content Generation

Procedural content generation is a technique for creating new sets of data programmatically instead of by hand in advance. Machine learning techniques can be used to drive this process and create new game levels and game experiences and add variation to video games to drive user engagement and increase the replayability of a game. In the early days of video gaming, players ran around game environments that were preprogrammed and static. Once these levels were mastered by the player, there was really not much reason to pick up the game again and continue playing and learning from it. By generating the game levels dynamically each time, the replay factor for the game can be increased significantly. However, the dynamic content must be generated in such a way that the game is still challenging, winnable, and engaging to the player. Impossible levels or levels that cannot be generated exactly the same way and replayed by the player will increase frustration and reduce engagement with the game in the future.

AI techniques have been developed for procedural content generation (Summerville et al., 2018). Long short-term memory (LSTM) is an approach for managing in-game events by examining time series data and remembering some sequences but with the ability to forget. This forgetfulness allows it to adapt the game play scenarios over repeated play by remembering some engaging aspects of the scenario and forgetting the less successful or unengaging aspects. Recurrent neural networks (RNNs) can be used for speech recognition and dynamic generation of time series data similarly to LSTM methods. Generative adversarial networks (GANs) can be used to determine whether a procedural generated game play map is playable by a human player. A GAN is essentially an artificially intelligent player that plays against the game itself and attempts to learn how to beat the dynamically generated map environment. It plays against itself and learns from the experience. This allows a sort of validation that the game map is playable by first attempting to beat it through the GAN player.

22.4.4 Player Experience Modeling

Deep learning techniques can be implemented to measure and tailor a game play experience to an individual player's skill level, enjoyment, and mood. The method could be used to detect when a player is getting frustrated with a game play experience and could auto-tune the difficulty to a state where the player is no longer irate but has enough challenge to continue to want to learn and play the game.

Machine learning algorithms can also be used to change elements of the game to appeal to the particular preferences and tastes of the player engaged with it. For example, knowing that the player likes a lot of Gothic fiction books, the game style could be altered to conform to the color overtones and mood of an individual or group of individuals who enjoy the Gothic motifs. By engaging with their own preferences and altering the game play experience to make an individualized experience, deep learning techniques could usher in a new level of engagement value to players. Coupled with procedure generation techniques, player experience modeling through DNNs could lead to truly enjoyable and unique gameplay experiences for players and to even more sophisticated interactive experiences for human beings.

22.4.5 Antisocial Behavior Detection and Governance in Multiplayer Gaming

Artificial intelligence has applications in multiplayer competitive gaming that goes beyond just sophisticated NPC control and learning. In large multiplayer environments, just like in regular human society outside of gaming, there will be those individuals who seek to exploit, misdirect, and aggravate other players. Such antisocial behavior decreases the enjoyment and engagement factor of gameplay, negatively influencing game developer companies' revenue and increasing the cost to police player behavior, and purge the game of bad actors. Just like in the real world, the costs to society are very high when people engage in these types of activities and ruin the fun for many people.

AI has the capability to learn patterns of behavior that people engage in during gameplay and to automatically dial up negative consequences that discourage such behavior. Rather than hiring human analysts or customer support representatives to police online activity in multiplayer games, it will be possible over time to allow AI agents to monitor and respond to this sort of behavior. This will result in a more pleasant gaming experience as players will only be subjected to negative experience briefly and will see that the issue gets dealt with quickly so that they can continue with enjoying their virtual gameplay. Companies will save money on support costs and will have higher player engagement because of reductions in negative player experiences from other bad-acting players. As the market for eSports and online games continues to grow, so do the amount of security requirements that game developers have to meet. Predictive and preventative AI security solutions are developed for online gaming platforms. Behavioral intention is analyzed, and the use of preventative measures is provided through AI algorithms. While enterprise-scale users benefit the most from predictive AI security solutions, everyday customers benefit the most from preventative AI security solutions.

22.4.6 Win Prediction

eSports is a virtual industry made up of numerous players coming from all over the world. They are competing against other players for not only pride but monetary compensation; eSports has become a business career for many professional players and competitors. In most cases, players form teams and compete against each other for prize money. It goes without saying that if players are able to advance their game play, they will take advantage of every avenue available to them. AI and big data are undoubtedly coveted use of game and player analytics to establish a better understanding of the games they are so passionate about. eSports betting has become a multimillion-dollar market due to the competitive and unpredictable nature of eSports competitions (Hodge et al., 2017). Just like in live sports, it is becoming more lucrative to fine-tune bets and increase the win-loss ratio when betting on an eSports team in a globally available competitive market. Artificial intelligence and machine learning techniques have been deployed in order to form a predictive model of how an eSports team will perform in a competition. These techniques have an early advantage over human bettors by their ability to analyze large datasets on eSports team performance as well as potentially millions of factors that lead to a winning pattern over what a human being could reasonably analyze on their own. We can expect win prediction to be a similarly sized revenue business to the existing markets for sports betting in the future.

22.4.7 Intelligent Tutoring and Training

Intelligent tutoring systems (ITS) are slowly being integrated into the gaming industry. This started with the introduction of intelligent computer-aided instruction (ICAI). Studies on things such as knowledge management, knowledge communication, knowledge models, and knowledge misunderstandings helped contribute to the development of ICAI. Intelligent tutoring systems are a step beyond ICAI and are being embedded into gaming simulation environments. This is important because developers want to show that games can be used for learning purposes as well as entertainment purposes. As the gaming society continues to grow, parents are concerned with how much time their children spend playing games. With the addition of intelligent tutoring systems, parents will be more likely to be okay with the amount of time that their children spend playing games because they will know that an education element is being provided along with the entertainment.

Artificial intelligence is used in simulations for training workers in certain areas. These simulation-type games are based on players being able to learn from the ways that the simulation model responds to the decisions that the player makes. The simulations are able to adapt to the decisions that the workers make and allow the workers to learn from the model's responses to those decisions. One example of where this type of training is used is in a simulation game that was developed for worker training in manual assembly lines for main-inserting systems. Another example of where to find this type of simulation is in simulation training for fire escape skills. Simulation developers want to be able to create an enhanced virtual environment, and to do this they combine gaming technology, programming, and fire safety knowledge. It is important to make the virtual environment as realistic and enhanced as possible so that the workers can take their learnings with them into the workplace. When virtual environments can accurately mimic the real world is when people who take part in the simulations are able to take the most meaningful lessons away from the experience.

AI researchers have caught onto the benefits of using video games/virtual realities to teach their projects human behavior and responses, because of the cost effectiveness of repetitive simulation. Instead of training a car to recognize stop signs, researchers may utilize the platform to identify other objects or commands that drivers must be aware of on the road today. Such advancements and modifications to AI technology may be the future to autonomous automobiles. On top of that, focusing on creating a more immersive gaming experience and simulation can keep video game players coming back to buy sequels. The AI used in the games are better to be supportive, but not overbearing. Games that are too easy or too challenging are not enjoyable to play, because there is an imbalance between the human opponent's skill and the AI bot's intelligence. Finding techniques to keep players in the flow channel where the game is not too difficult, nor too easy, will be the key to successful gaming products.

22.4.8 Player Telemetry Sign-Up, Engagement, and Retention Analytics

Within the gaming industry AI has grown both to drive consumer experience and to lead marketing efforts with regards to game monetization. Developers can collect any number of statistics on players and levels within their games, allowing them to identify player bottlenecks within certain sections of the game. This allows the developers to improve the play experience by adjusting difficulty as necessary at these bottlenecks so that they do not overly disrupt the play experience. Additionally, player data allows developers and publishers to target specific marketing at players by advertising in-game purchases relevant to their point of progression in the game

(Rijmenam, 2017). AI currently has many uses in the video game industry for improving both marketing and the consumer experience.

Especially on the marketing and business side, AI can be used to analyze player engagement and increase incentives and decrease costs in order to optimize the player experience as well as to maximize the value that is generated to the business. AI will learn the activities that players are willing to spend on, the ones that result in retention issues, and will provide the game development house with feedback on what players want from their game experience. Machine learning and data analytics will help them to fine-tune their product offerings to maximize the player experience as well as the profits to the business.

Case 22.1: DeepMind AlphaGo and AlphaStar

To create and utilize artificial intelligence, one must understand the different forms that human intelligence can take. DeepMind, a British artificial intelligence subsidiary of Alphabet Inc., was founded in 2010 by Demis Hassabis, Mustafa Suleyman, and Shane Legg. The company is based in London and over the years has expanded to other countries such as Canada, France, and the United States. Then, in 2014, DeepMind was acquired by Google creating a new Google team called the DMG or DeepMind Google. Over the years DeepMind was also able to attract the attention of major capital investors such as Horizon Ventures, Founders Fund, Scott Bannister, Peter Theil, and Elon Musk. The company has an "artificial intelligence ethics board"; however, the members remain a complete mystery to the public leading to much speculation. The company has one overall goal, "to create a general-purpose AI that can be useful and effective for almost everything."

DeepMind began as a small start-up; their first AIs were used to play simple games such as Pong and Space Invaders. Their early experiments came down to introducing an AI to a game with no contextual information. Then, over time the AI will become quite skilled mirroring the process a human would take when faced with a new game. However, DeepMind did not form to train AI to play simple games. They formed to create an AI that can do almost everything and the biggest hurdle to this was a game called Go. Invented over 2500 years ago, Go is a two-player board game that heavily relied on both skill and intuition to win. There are a possible 250 moves that a player can take in a single turn with the overall objective to surround the other player. There are "10 to the power of 170" board configurations which is more than the number of atoms in planet earth (DeepMind, 2021). AI development companies across the world have been trying to create a Go AI that could at least rival professional players. However, none were successful. The best a Go AI could do, at the time, was match the skills of an amateur, and none of them were able to handle the sheer number of possible moves in Go. Then, DeepMind broke the mold with its creation, AlphaGo. Boasting an advanced search tree and deep neural networks that contained "millions of neuron-like connections," AlphaGo learned from amateur games to learn how a human would play and then played against different versions of itself to improve. This process is called deep reinforcement learning. Over time AlphaGo became not only more skilled but better at learning. To test the limits of AlphaGo, DeepMind challenged a professional. In 2015,

AlphaGo faced its first Go professional player, the 2 dan, three-time European Champion, Mr. Fan Hui. It was a five-game match and the ending result made AI history. AlphaGo won 5-0. This marked the first time that a Go AI was able to beat a professional player and not only that but to win with a landslide victory. However, this was not enough. In March of 2016, AlphaGo faced the strongest Go player in the past decade, Mr. Lee Sedol, who was a legendary player and was undoubtedly the strongest in the world in pure skill, intuition, and wisdom, winning 18 world champion titles. The match began with 200 million people watching worldwide. The whole series ended with a score of 4-1 with AlphaGo as the winner. Mr. Lee Sedol would later retire from playing Go, with him stating that he could never be the top player in Go and called AI "an entity that cannot be defeated." AI was able to conquer the world of human intuition and strategy, a feat that many thought to be impossible. However, with AlphaGo, DeepMind was able to create artificial intelligence that not only rivaled some of the greatest strategists in the world but was able to defeat them singlehandedly.

Here we focus on the next version of AI application developed by the same team that brought the AlphaGo AI into existence. AlphaStar is the next generation of AI application that is attracting more attention within the competitive game circuit of StarCraft 2, a real-time, science-fiction-based, strategy war game (RTS). The new AI algorithms are said to have analyzed play styles and strategies of some of the best players of the world, adopting them and improving upon them to the point that it now is said to be impossible to defeat. What sets this AI project apart from its predecessors is that unlike "Go," an RTS game like StarCraft 2 incorporates many more variables that all are important for short-term and long-term strategy for victory.

AlphaStar is a complex AI that learns through a deep neural network fed by raw data from a games interface. The development team started AlphaStar off with some relatively easy games against the standard game AI. Standard game AIs tend to compete at or around the gold skill level with skill levels ranging from bronze to grandmaster. Gold is currently filled with players ranging from 40% to 60% skill levels. After AlphaStar earned a victory percentage of approximately 95%, the developers began to test it on other versions of itself. They replicated AlphaStar into various other agents and pitted them against each other. Over time they began to add replays and play styles of real-world professional players. Another key factor in AlphaStar's training was each agent's individual learning objective. Developers would give specific agents a goal of defeating a certain play style and other agents the goal of defending a broad set of play styles.

The next step in AlphaStar's training was a highly scalable distributed training setup which utilized Google's cloud AI. This system was able to support many thousands of different AlphaStar agents battling against each other. This system ran for 14 days and resulted in over 200 years of real-time StarCraft 2 play. An impossible amount of play for any human to ever realize. It is said to be its own self-contained, learning intelligence, and after the "equivalent of 200 years of practice" (accumulating data and analyzing it), it now mimics strategy that is very humanlike, but also produces actions that have developers questioning its intent. Resulting from all of this training was a highly competitive hard to beat AI that defeated the pro play MaNa 5-0. Interestingly enough, this AI did not win by making simply faster decisions. Actually, MaNa averaged 390 actions per minute while AlphaStar averaged only 277 actions per minute. For comparison, the player named TLO has the ability to average 678 actions per minute. What this means is that AlphaStar is not simply faster than the human players, but it makes better decisions.

AlphaStar's training regimen, progression, and overall ability are sure to rock the gaming world for years to come, but its ability to be applied to other fields is almost just as amazing. AlphaStar could be applied to any real-world problem that consists of many unknown variables and outcomes. StarCraft 2 is just a game, but it is a game based off of warfare. Perhaps, an AI can be developed that once all of the real-world variables are plugged in, it could decide the likely outcomes of wars or ways to avoid them. While AlphaGo and AlphaStar were arguably DeepMind's most popular inventions, video gaming is not the only field in which DeepMind is currently developing AI for. DeepMind has ventured into other areas ranging from healthcare and protein mapping to weather prediction. The virtual sky is seemingly the limit when it comes to artificial intelligence.

Case 22.2: Microsoft HoloLens

Microsoft's HoloLens are mixed reality goggles used in the gaming industry and immerses the user into a simulated environment where physical and digital objects coexist and interact in real time. Gaming often involves players interacting within an AI simulated world. In this case, we will discuss AI gaming technologies that have been applied to simulation using HoloLens.

The first AI software application is called tuServ. Black Marble, a Microsoft Gold Partner, wanted to transform the BedfordShire Police Department by developing a tool officers can use to virtually scan a crime scene and tag evidence. To do so, when an officer steps foot onto a crime scene while wearing HoloLens, tuServ enables officers to map the scene. The AI in tuServ then creates a 3D mesh of it and saves it on the application. That way, personnel with clearance can go back at any time and view the original scene. In addition, officers can use HoloLens to virtually tag evidence in 3D space with the built-in AI. tuServ will save a 3D version with accurate dimensions and sort the evidence accordingly so that it is not just an overwhelmingly large cluster. As a result, the preservation of the original evidence found at the crime scene may minimize the chances of tampered evidence being used in court or other areas of investigation, because an original copy is virtually stored. Inspired by the desire for quicker sharing of crime scene information, the main benefit of tuServ is its ability to transfer all of the evidence on-site officers see in real time back to the senior officers at headquarters. By simply putting the HoloLens goggles on back at base, senior officers are able to view everything at the scene without going to it. Not only does this reduce the number of officers needed at a crime scene, but it also reduces the amount of time on-site officers will spend at any given scene. That means there will be less reliance on taking thousands of photographs to capture every micro-detail of a scene. Going hand in hand with that, the time spent on photographing evidence will decrease as well, because HoloLens will digitally save and sort all of the evidence. Furthermore, officers will not have to be as dependent on crime scene notes when trying to recall what they saw weeks later, because they can put the HoloLens on and see the 3D mesh. Lastly, HoloLens may lead to a lower risk of contaminated evidence being used in the future, because an original copy is stored in 3D space that can be referenced later.

Another AI software application, trace, was designed specifically for using HoloLens in forensic analysis. A group of university students significantly advanced what Black Marble had created with tuServ. Trace still maps a crime scene and saves a 3D mesh of it; however, when logging evidence, officers can add commentary to describe specific details about it and create a holographic artifact of it because trace records its x–y coordinates and dimensions. Similar to tuServ, trace reduces the number of officers needed at a crime scene and the time officers will spend at any given scene and decreases the chances of contaminated evidence being used later on in investigations. However, as mentioned earlier, trace gives crime scene personnel the ability to leave commentary, create holographic artifacts of the evidence, and conduct a blood spatter/bullet hole analysis. These features reap tremendous benefits for forensic analysis. For starters, the commentary and holographic artifact features enable greater collaboration between the different parties analyzing the evidence because authorized personnel can view comments left by others and inspect the same holograph even though the evidence has left the scene. In addition, trace can examine blood spatter patterns and produce an estimated velocity, angle of impact, origin of point, and weapon type. The same analysis can be conducted with bullet holes. Rather than having to conduct an on-site assessment, which can be time-consuming and tedious, or wait for photographs of the blood pattern to get back to the lab for analysis, trace is able to scan a wall where the blood is located and calculate the estimated output in real time. Procedures that used to take days to process can now be estimated on-site.

We foresee more AI software applications being designed and developed for HoloLens. This case is to show how a common gaming tool can be used in different fields outside of the gaming industry. HoloLens has shown success thus far with preserving crime scenes and evidence digitally. With time, the AI technology will mature in these applications and learn more about the evidence database it pulls from. Therefore, the turnover rate from analyzing the crime to solving it could become more efficient, because all the observations and testing that used to take a long time could be instantaneously performed on-site. Overall, the potential for growth of these HoloLens AI software applications is something to look out for in the future.

22.5 Key Takeaways

It is important to note that most of the advancements in AI would not be possible without the improvements in physical hardware associated with computers and computer processing power. AI originates out of gaming itself and overtime the evolution of computers and their capability has led the way to better developments not only in AI, but in gaming itself. In a way you could say they share a symbiotic relationship, advancing each other. Most of the programs, games, and training simulations being utilized today by different industries are the culmination and a direct result of the evolution of computers, computer hardware, and AI.

Up until recent years, a lot of the simulations utilized for training purposes were limited to the preprogrammed responses that were coded into the program. Now with developments in AI, simulations are encompassing a more immersive experience that not only adapts and generates content based on the user's response but collects and tracks the data it receives. This results in better information to be collected and advances the simulations even further, hence creating an even more evolved and better training experience down the road for users. For the gaming industry, this means more immersive game playing experiences for consumers, higher player retention rates, and the potential for higher revenues for game developing companies. For other real-world applications, these games will draw interest into fields not always glamorized. Immersive gameplay experiences in nontraditional games include law enforcement, medical, and even forensics. These games also give an opportunity for companies to collect better and more accurate data on its player base and utilize this information for marketing, statistics, and analysis purposes. New and better games that utilize better artificial intelligence and artificial behavior also provide better games for content creators to showcase to the public.

Game developers and programmers could see their job descriptions change overtime with the advancement of AI in general and in the gaming industry. Developers up to this point always had to find a balance with programming the AI versus the artificial behavior when making a game. Making the game too intelligent can greatly adversely affect the gameplay experience for the player and ruin the game. Much like for managers, advancements in AI have given way to essentially outsource the job of design and production of games and content to the AI itself. This shows great potential for companies to have operations be better streamlined and improve cost effectiveness when it comes to time, money, and labor. Programmers can be more efficiently trained, and manager efforts can be shifted to other processes, allowing them to receive better information and make better decisions. On the other hand, there is concern that with the advancement of AI, there would be a loss for jobs or changing roles in the gaming industry.

Investors and companies would see changes in their fields as well with the progression of AI. Investors would be able to make better, more informed, and sound investing decisions with the data that is collected. How that data is being utilized is the real question at hand now. Concerns for privacy and ethical use of data collected is now a hot topic in the news. The potential for misuse is too great for legislators to not give it any attention or concern. Marketers have already shown the potential by applying the data collected in adapting the business models of mobile games with microtransactions aimed at generating more revenues and mainly targeting kids with it. There has been public outcry for these practices and policy makers are in the progress to push forth legislation that would regulate and control the process of these companies when they utilize essentially a digital format of gambling itself to children.

22.6 Conclusion

eSports started local but then progressed to a global phenomenon. Today, we see major competitions globally attracting sponsors and all sorts of implemented tech. The progression of the sport has transpired to a point where major organizations are now putting their attention and assets into the industry as well, looking at renowned businessman Elon Musk and organizations like Amazon and Google creating, influencing, and supporting the market. With developed AI that can correlate to outside companies, their investment is justified. Even the military who is currently sponsoring a video game named Rocket League is recruiting young adults into their departments for aviation, cyber-related fields, and technological areas. The future of eSports is on path to develop not just the gaming industry, but everything surrounding it as well.

Artificial intelligence will continue to be widely developed, researched, and deployed in the video game industry with particularly rapid growth in the eSports subcategory over the next decade and beyond. The development of these methods in the virtual and safe environments of the gaming metaverse will most likely begin to percolate out into the broader social context of our communities as we learn to cooperate and compete better with AI-enhanced methods. The business value created by the gaming industry and aided by the development of more sophisticated AI will continue to grow apace and with such large resources at stake and be invested. We are sure to see even more rapid progress and adoption of AI and machine learning technologies for video games and eSports long into the future.

References

DeepMind AlphaGo. (2021). Retrieved from https://deepmind.com/research/case-studies/alphago-the-story-so-far

Hodge, V., Devlin, S., Sephton, N., Block, F., Drachen, A., & Cowling, P. (2017). *Win prediction in esports: Mixed-rank match prediction in multi-player online. arxiv.org.*. Retrieved from https://arxiv.org/pdf/1711.06498.pdf

Liden, L. (2003). Artificial stupidity: The art of intentional mistakes. *AI Game Programming Wisdom*, 41–48.

Motion Picture Association. (2020). *THEME report*. Motion Picture Association.

NewZoo. (2021). *Global games market report*. Retrieved from https://newzoo.com/key-numbers/

Rijmenam, M. V. (2017). *The gaming industry turns to big data to improve the gaming experience*. Retrieved from https://datafloq.com/read/gaming-industry-turns-big-data-improve-gaming-expe/137

Summerville, A., Snodgrass, S., Guzdial, M., Holmgard, C., Hoover, A. K., Isaksen, A., Nealen, A., & Togelius, J. (2018). Procedural Content Generation via Machine Learning (PCGML). *IEEE Transactions on Games*, 257–270.

Artificial Intelligence in Sports 23

Abstract

Sports and games are similar in that people do physical and mental activities for leisure or competition. This chapter further explores artificial intelligence technology and its applications for physical sports. Several important topics are covered, including AI for sports management, sports marketing, basketball AI applications, baseball AI applications, and golf AI applications.

Keywords
Artificial intelligence · Sports management · Sports marketing · Machine learning · Semcasting · Dynamic ticket pricing · Optical tracking systems · Expert systems · Data mining system · Golf · Baseball · Basketball

23.1 Introduction

Artificial intelligence is becoming more and more prevalent in many industries, one of these being the sports industry. Now sports typically is not the first industry that comes to mind when one mentions artificial intelligence, but there are many applications of AI in sports. Artificial intelligence is defined as the theory and development of computer systems able to perform tasks that normally require human intelligence, such as visual perception, speech recognition, decision-making, and translation between languages, and this is exactly what we see being introduced into the sports industry. With AI, we are beginning to see jobs in sports being transformed to revolve around emerging technologies. These new advancements are changing the way the sports industry runs in many different sports and various aspects of these sports.

While the involvement of AI in sports was rare 10 years ago, it is here to persist and stay in forms of chatbots – virtual assistants responding to fan inquiries, team

L. Chan et al., *Applied Artificial Intelligence in Business*, Applied Innovation and Technology Management, https://doi.org/10.1007/978-3-031-05740-3_23

stats and live info, or computer vision in auto racing, or automated journalism and wearable technology (Jeffries, 2018) When we think of sports, we think of great athletes, teams, and their incredible performance, striving to achieve the best possible outcomes maximizing the outputs. Artificial intelligence helps achieve those goals in sports management using abundant measured useful data points, obtained by biosensors, smart sensor-assisted apparel, and novel wearables through constant tracking in athletes to tailor solutions for each individual athlete.

Artificial intelligence was even used to create new sports, like Speedgate, which could be described as a mix of rugby, field hockey, and soccer. Other new sports may come forward as a result of neural network algorithms and the needs of the industry. AI is also engaged in sports fan management, providing live statistics on players, engaging fans in a unique way, and getting them closer to the action, their sport teams, or sports idols. Spotting talent and recruitment with AI can dig into hidden metrics of the potential talent that would otherwise not be noticed accurately. Scouts and coaches can analyze larger pools of future young athletes with more precision.

In this chapter, we will explore AI's presence in several aspects of sports management such as organizational operations and sports marketing. We will specifically discuss AI's presence in several popular ball games including golf, baseball, and basketball. We introduce the AI technologies being used and the major applications of AI in each field.

23.2 AI for Sports Management

A key area where AI is used in sports is sports management. When you think of the topic of artificial intelligence in sports, your mind probably goes straight to player development or statistical analysis. Those are the major things that AI has been applied to sports management, but in recent years the sports industry has found some new applications for artificial intelligence. One of these new areas is sports marketing. Sports marketing is applying new AI techniques that not only benefits the sports organization but also the fans of the team. It not only allows the teams to generate more money, but also informs their fans more and brings more fans out to games, which benefits professional sports teams a lot. AIs such as expert systems, machine learning, and data mining systems have dramatically changed ticket sales, fan support and knowledge, and a team's ability to inform its fans.

To completely understand how much AI has affected sports marketing, we first must look at where sports marketing started. Sports have always been popular, with there always being some kind of sports team to follow every day of the year. The great thing that AI has done for it has been to make it more accessible. In the past, fans to acquire a ticket would have to go to the stadium and pay a set price for a ticket no matter who was playing. For people to find out who was playing, or who had won the night before, game fans would need to check the newspaper, which would not have all the information and stats that some fans wanted. Then technology developed and fans were able to look things up on the Internet and buy tickets online. But these technologies do not compare to what AI has been able to do for the industry.

AI today in sports marketing uses data mining, machine learning, and expert systems to inform and sell to its fans. Fans are told stats of their favorite teams by just asking an in-home assistant. AI is also taking in your sports interests, favorite teams, and your other search history to develop a personalized marketing campaign for every person interested in the sports market. Once they compile and analyze all this data, it uses it to sell you merchandise, tickets, and advertisements that it believes that you will click on.

An example of technology that compiles your information that sports teams use is called Semcasting. Semcasting was created in 2014 and its use was to group together certain areas with the same sports and team interests so that sports clubs and organizations could properly advertise to certain areas. This means like in a certain zip code where there are 97 people that follow a specific soccer team and only 3 that follow others, Semcasting is going to give the team that 97 people follow the proper know-how and interests of the people that like their team. This allows for the people to get ads they will actually like and may look further into rather than the team with 3 followers trying to apply to the 97 people that will not buy from them or support them. Sandcasting's goal is to allow companies to invest their time marketing to people that want to buy their products, or tickets, and not waste their time on those that do not. This technology is fairly new to the sports industry and is used by very few organizations, but those who do such as the Dallas Mavericks have found an increase in revenue from finding the people that visit their site, go to a game, look up stats, and look up merchandise. They have done this by giving deals on their information and advertising to those that are interested in their product and just needed a little persuasion to buy.

Another AI tool used today in sports marketing is an expert system called KAI or Kings artificial intelligence. KAI is used by the Sacramento Kings to inform fans of stats, merchandise, ticket prices, game times, scores, and analytics of the Sacramento Kings. KAI is used by people through chatbots or home assistants such as Alexa or Echo. When an assistant is asked a question about the Kings or their history, they are able to have a one-on-one conversation with KAI as it informs them about stats, the stadium, or anything someone would want to know about the Kings. KAI also is constantly evolving and learning from the fans on what they are interested in and their opinions on the team.

Another huge part about sports is a team's ticket sales, and yes AI is being applied to this aspect of sports as well. Mainly used in baseball today, an AI system called dynamic ticket pricing is used (Xu et al., 2015). Dynamic ticket pricing is a machine learning system that changes ticket prices day by day. This is especially important in baseball because a fan's experience is greatly affected by who is playing and who is not, the weather, and other factors. Dynamic ticket pricing looks at all these to create ticket prices that change and adapt up until the moment of the game (Xu et al., 2015). The system sees that a game between two rivals with their best pitchers pitching on a nice sunny day will raise the price of a ticket because there is more demand. But if there is a game that is going to be affected by a thunderstorm, last-minute ticket prices are going to be changed immediately and the new prices can be sent out to fans and get last-minute ticket sales. The AI is able to learn what teams are good, what players are desired to be seen, and what games people want to go to and how to adapt ticket prices to fit the demand. This AI not only brings in more fans but also brings in more money to the teams' organization. This also makes fans think in their head that they paid a reasonable price for their ticket and experience they had at the game. This influences them to come again to feel that they are having a good experience for the money that they paid.

In the future, AI could potentially take over sports management completely. It is already showing that it can do what a human can do and it can do it better. There may no longer be a need for people selling tickets at the stadium or people selling merchandise or marketing to people. AI can do all of that for a sports organization and eliminates some of the people they have to pay. AI has developed so much over the few years that it has been present in the sports marketing area that there seems to be no end in sight of the possibilities of this technology.

23.3 AI Applications for Basketball

In the dawn of basketball, everything regarding scouting, player development, statistics, and so on revolved around the "eye test." Thus, if a player's coach wanted to improve the player's jump shot, for example, the coach would say things like square your feet, land where you jumped from, or arc your shot more, because that was what was said in books and there was no technology to pinpoint what was wrong with that player's shot. Also, because of the sole reliance on the eye test, the only statistics that were recorded were things like points per game, rebounds per game, and assists per game. There was no manipulation of this data; they just kept it as simple as that. The most high-tech technology that was commonly used back then was the jump shot/rebounding machine that one would put under the basket so it could rebound for the shooter and then shoot the ball back out to wherever the shooter set the machine to do so. While not being super sophisticated, this machine is still commonly used today.

Then, the Moneyball revolution came about where statistics and math took a more prominent role in sports management (Jha, 2018). Complex formulas that would produce a player efficiency rating (PER), win shares, effective field goal percentage, and so on, were created by analysts to distinguish the most valuable players by their performance characteristics and their per-minute productivity and find the emerging talented players. AI technologies were not in use for basketball at this time.

It was not until the late 2000s to early 2010s that AI's power began to be realized. One of the first AI technologies that were put to use was the Noah shooting system, which uses machine learning to watch a player shoot a basketball, which then causes the system to deliver a lot of data back to the shooter and whoever else is observing the system. And with this data, the shooter can learn what he or she is doing wrong or right and improve on his or her performance. AI technology today involves the use of cameras with the artificial neural network framework to track and learn player movement at all times. The basketball organizations set up cameras in the arena's rafters to observe everything on the court. There are a lot of companies that sell their data-tracking AI to businesses like the NBA. The NBA's official tracking provider is Second Spectrum. Second Spectrum's cameras track everything in the game 25 times per second. These cameras track the game and record data by recording the time of the game, the quarter, the shot clock, where the ball is and who has it, where every player is and how close they are to each other, the number of the current possession for either team, and an event ID for each player that indicates when a player did something that corresponded to that ID. Every one of those "rows" of data is recorded 25 times per second. Thus, a large amount of data is produced every game that requires complex data management and analysis. While these machines do utilize data mining agents to help coaches obviate the data by calculating parameters like quantified shot quality (qSQ), quantified shooter impact (qSI), and average player speed, a lot of data remains unused ("Second Spectrum Data," 2019).

The need for better data analysis and data mining development is apparent. In the future, optical tracking systems with advanced computer vision and machine learning capabilities could be used not just in professional sports, but also for college- and high school-level training and sports games (Jeffries, 2018).

In the example with the Noah shooting system, mentioned earlier, the coach could use an AI-enabled system for player development. The coach would set the machine up to watch the player shoot. According to the data output provided by the system, the coach could advise the player to change their technique, for example, to turn their feet a little more to better square their shoulders to the basket, or to relax their shoulders more when they shoot to make their shooting motion less stiff and more comfortable. Then, the player would shoot some more with this advice in mind, and the cycle would continue, further developing that player. The AI does not replace the coach; it just assists them.

23.4 AI Applications for Baseball

Baseball, America's pastime, has never been considered to be technologically advanced. All the game requires is a bat, ball, field, and 18 players. For hundreds of years, the culture of baseball has revolved around its complexity and strategy and a large number of statistics, fortifying the belief that the game is far too difficult for a machine to understand and provide valuable feedback on. When artificial intelligence began to surface in the early 2000s, no one believed that it could realistically be applied to baseball. However, the 2002 Oakland Athletics changed this belief entirely.

With the birth and discovery of machine learning and artificial intelligence, few, besides Oakland Athletics' manager Billy Beane, thought of applying it to baseball. Pioneering big data in baseball, Beane discovered often overlooked statistics which could be applied to making a much cheaper and more effective roster than what they had in the past. With less money and very few stars, Beane was able to lead the

Athletics to a playoffs and give the Athletics the winningest season in baseball history. Thanks to Beane and the Athletics organization, artificial intelligence and data management have changed the game and have become staples in the way rosters are created, the play of the game, and the sport's technology.

After the Oakland Athletics had the best season in baseball with one of the cheapest rosters, managers and organizations began to realize that data management and artificial intelligence could help reshape their organizations as well. Technology has now surfaced which processes all statistics of players and helps show organizations who would be the best fit for their specific team. After rosters have been selected, there is also technology which helps with the forming of rosters and batting orders. Some of the statistics include a player's batting average batting home versus away, a pitcher's strength against right-handed batters versus left-handed batters, and how well a player performs under certain weather conditions. Thanks to data tracking and artificial intelligence, managers can now select the best possible lineups based on weather, location, who they are playing, time of the year, and even day of the week.

One of the new data systems that is beginning to shape the game is called HitTrax. HitTrax has begun to revolutionize the game of baseball by helping players see what was previously indiscernible to the human eye. Originally, the only way to improve on one's swing was lots of practice and feedback from coaches. Coaches would stand outside a batting cage or watch from behind home plate or dugouts during games trying to watch their players and provide feedback on their swings. A trained eye could normally detect major irregularities such as a player dipping his shoulder, moving his head, or pulling off of the ball. However, monitoring bat path, swing speed, ball contact, and other minute details which are very important to a swing are very difficult if not impossible to detect with the human eye. Slow motion video cameras began to help with viewing swings and their irregularities, but it was very time-consuming and still difficult to see. With the invention of HitTrax in 2003, coaches' and players' views were completely changed. Coaches and players could now get immediate feedback on their swing and throwing form with statistics and analytics that had never been detected before. HitTrax can monitor statistics such as velocity, ball flight, swing path, ball curve, where the ball connects with the bat, distance, location, timing, and eye level. The software can pinpoint problems in the player's swings by comparing them to professional swings and other ideal swings such as those of Ken Griffey Junior, Barry Bonds, and Mike Trout. Thanks to HitTrax and its technology, the way coaches and players view the game and the way they play have completely changed, creating more effective hitters and pitchers.

A controversial issue of artificial intelligence use in baseball concerns umpires. A typical fastball leaves a pitcher's hand and reaches home plate in the blink of an eye. This amount of speed and the constant change of the strike zone regarding a player's height makes MLB umpire's jobs incredibly difficult. Because of the difficulty regarding their jobs, mistakes are common in the game. To eliminate these mistakes, some analysts, fans, players, and coaches have recommended replacing human umpires with electronic umpires. Electronic umpires would be able to make calls with absolute certainty eliminating any human error in the game. However, this is a very controversial idea as some believe that the human error from umpires is a part of baseball that should be expected and played with.

Baseball is a very complex and strategic sport rooted in old times. However, with the introduction of technology, data management, and artificial technology, the game is being changed. Players are performing better than ever, teams are becoming stronger using less money, and the question of bringing robots into the game is now a strong possibility. If artificial intelligence can take root in a game which was steeped in tradition and nostalgia, one realizes that artificial intelligence truly is becoming an integral part of the world we live in.

23.5 AI Applications for Golf

One of these industries that AI has made its mark is in the world of golf. The sport of golf on the outside may appear very simple at its core; however, it is actually a very complex game where the smallest of millimeters and milliseconds can drastically change the outcome of an action. Golf is a game that deals with lots of angles and symmetry in order to produce the best swing possible. These angles, if thrown off by the slightest of margins, will result in lots of varying results. The key in many people's eyes in golf is consistency. In order to achieve this consistency to succeed, the golf industry now relies on two main forms of AI systems.

Golf is historically a sport where the eye test is used to determine what one needs improving on, or what one does well. By analyzing a swing with a swing instructor, the instructor will merely stand behind or to the side of the player and watch for any problems in the angles and positions he sees the golf club in during the swing. This form of instruction can be traced back to 1457 when the sport of golf was initially introduced to the world. This form of instruction is still in place today, but was revolutionized in 2003 by the invention of an AI system named Trackman (trackmangolf.com). Trackman was invented by Fredrik Tuxen. What his invention did was provide data through the use of an AI machine that can track one's body, club, and ball positions through sensors and a camera. This data given is essentially all the angles, positions, and symmetry that an instructor looks for through the eye test, but it's done entirely by the AI system and with far more precision. This invention was the first of its kind in terms of AI in golf and since then has only continued to be improved in terms of accuracy and knowledge of more data points, which is useful for a player to improve. Today, this device is capable of analyzing one's swing, and along with feeding data points off to the player, it also compares that data to that of a professional or an "ideal swing" to give suggestions on how one can improve. This surely is not the end of the line for such an invention, as there will be far more innovations to improve accuracy and find more important data points to be used. Alongside Trackman today are many more AI systems in the market that have similar features and applications as they all compete towards being the most helpful and efficient AI system.

The technology used in this Trackman device is considered a data mining system. What this means is that the system uses data that it has available, or detects through the system, and is able to detect trends and relationships in the data to bring light to something not necessarily readily apparent. The Trackman AI device is just this. It is a device that is able to create this data by watching one's swing and also be able to track the relationships between these swings to determine the trends that are arising. All of this leads to a solution being generated to help players swing development. The major application of this Trackman AI system is its ability to analyze one's swing and be able to provide suggestions to the player in order for them to perfect their swing. The use of such a device allows for a much more precise way for instructors to teach players and help them improve, as well as allowing players to go off on their own and let the device tell them what they need to improve on its own. The use of such a highly technological system is revolutionizing the way that golf is assessed and taught at each and every skill level.

The game of golf has also evolved from its origins of merely looking at one's score to dictate what happened in their round. Golf has multiple facets such as driving, iron play, chipping, and putting. The simplest way of analyzing one's success in each sector is to use basic statistics such as fairways in regulation (FIR), greens in regulation (GIR), putts, and up and down percentage. Each of these statistics can be calculated very simply; however, it is not the most accurate way of determining where one may exceed or need improvement. In 1999, a system called ShotLink was discovered which took digital images of the holes on the golf course and the system would be able to trace and put exact points where a player hit their ball to and from (Bryant, 2019). This system was implemented onto the PGA Tour so that players and fans could look back and track where each shot went. It was not until 2007 when Professor Mark Broadie of Columbia University used this ShotLink system and added a concept called the "strokes gained model" (PGA, 2016). This model allowed the ShotLink system to not only track each shot's start and end point but also dictate to players where they are gaining strokes and losing strokes throughout their round. The model provides data for strokes gained: off the tee, approach the green, around the green, and putting. These are the four primary aspects of golf and are all displayed here in this model. This technology is sure to evolve further as there are many more smaller aspects of golf that this model does not track, but one day likely will. The technology behind this system and model can be labeled as a data mining system as well. The ShotLink system is able to generate a dataset, and with the addition of the strokes data added into the model, it is capable to analyze the trends of the data and come up with the statistics on strokes gained. This data is analyzed through the ShotLink system in multiple facets of the game which is what makes it a very important AI tool for players.

In this case, the major application of this AI system is to help players, primarily professionals with access to this data, to find out what specifically they need to improve on in their games. As there are many different aspects of golf, knowledge of where one's game fairs in each aspect can be extremely important to the players and their coaches. This knowledge will allow the players to focus on their weakest aspects in order to improve their scores and play. The simple ability to go back and track one's round is extremely important in their ability to improve as a player and that is something this model and system provides them. Throughout all of this, we see how prevalent and important AI is today in the field of golf and the major applications that it is used for to help players improve. The technology and systems today far surpass any form that has ever previously been used. With so much more data readily available to players and instructors, the game of golf itself has completely been revolutionized and can be viewed through a far more analytical lens.

23.6 Conclusion

Throughout all these cases, we are able to see the true importance of AI in sports and the many applications it has in this field. We demonstrated these AI applications through several subfields of sports with baseball, basketball, golf, and sports marketing. Each of these subfields has its own specific and important AI applications specific to the sector, and there will be more in the future.

The future of AI in sports is very bright, since there are so many data points that are precisely gathered and analyzed in the industry. There is a strong potential for AI to be an assistant coach for sports teams, suggesting improvement strategies, analysis of mistakes, and game perfection. Deep learning may uncover important insights that would otherwise go unnoticed. There are some aspirations for the use of smart ticketing technology that could enable fans to position themselves in more engaging spots around the arena, possibly participating with the like-minded, more energetic fan groups. Possible computer vision referees and automatic visual curated game highlights could be future AI applications. We expect AI in sports to continue to develop and grow and support the sports industry, impacting various aspects of this industry as we look towards the next invention or innovation in this wide-ranging industry. This may create more personalized experiences, increased fan loyalty, and closer visual interactions for the involved stakeholders and customers in the industry.

References

Bryant, R. (2019). *Shotlink.com*. www.shotlink.com/about/background

Jeffries, C. T. (2018). *Sports analytics with computer vision*. Open Works. 04 July 2018. 20 March 2019. https://openworks.wooster.edu/independentstudy/8103/

Jha, M. (2018, December 3). Beyond moneyball: How AI is transforming sports. *Analytics Training Blog*. www.analyticstraining.com/beyond-moneyball-how-ai-is-transforming-sports/

PGA. (2016, June 3). Strokes gained: How it works. *PGATour*. PGATOUR.COM. www.pgatour.com/news/2016/05/31/strokes-gained-defined.html

Second Spectrum Data. (2019, March 22). *NBAstuffer*. https://www.nbastuffer.com/analytics101/second-spectrum/

Trackman. TRACKMAN. *TrackMan Golf – Launch monitor – Golf radar – Indoor HD simulator*. www.trackmangolf.com/

Xu, J., Fader, P., & Veeraraghavan, S. K. (2015, February 27). *Evaluating the effectiveness of dynamic pricing strategies on MLB single-game ticket revenue*. In Sports analytics conference. http://www.sloansportsconference.com/wp-content/uploads/2015/02/SSAC15-RP-Finalist-Evaluating-the-effectivness-of-dynamic-pricing2.pdf

Index

L. Chan et al., *Applied Artificial Intelligence in Business*, Applied Innovation and Technology Management, https://doi.org/10.1007/978-3-031-05740-3

Q

R

S

The manufacturer's authorised representative in the EU is Springer Nature Customer Service Centre GmbH, Europaplatz 3, 69115 Heidelberg, Germany. If you have any concerns regarding our products, please contact ProductSafety@springernature.com

Printed and bound by CPI Group (UK) Ltd, Croydon, CR0 4YY
28/09/2026
02224067-0001